CW00703571

The Green Bay Area in History and Legend

Green Bay Press-Gazette articles by Jack Rudolph

Illustrations by Harold Elder

Edited by Betsy Foley

Published by the Brown County Historical Society
Green Bay, Wisconsin
2004

Book Design by Laura Diedrick, Oyster Art & Design
Printed in USA

Library of Congress Control Number: 2004107722

ISBN 0-9641499-9-0

Direct correspondence to:
Brown County Historical Society
P. O. Box 1411
Green Bay, WI 54305-1411
(920) 437-1840

The Brown County Historical Society gratefully acknowledges the support of the following contributors who made this publication possible:

Major donors -
Brown County Historical Society
Byron L. Walter Family Trust
Long Family Foundation
Joseph and Sarah Van Drisse Charitable Trust
Robert T. and Betty Rose Meyer Foundation
Nau Foundation (George Nau Burridge)
The George Kress Foundation, Inc.
Wallace Buerschinger
Vincent Zehren

The project would have faltered without the generosity of the following individuals, families, and businesses -

Bay Towel, John Butz
Mary Bohman
John and Gisela Brogan
George and Eleanor Burridge
Mrs. Robert Cowles Jr.
James and Rosalie Cuene
Dr. Loren and Marian Hart
Mary Jane Herber
James and Joan D. Hogan
Randall Lawton
Leonard Liebmann
Bill Meindl
Meng Foundation
Dr. and Mrs. Kenneth Mickle
Norman Miller Family Foundation
L. P. Mooradian Co.
Dan and Lois Moran
Bernard Olejniczak
Tita and Tom Plouff
Sylvia Pratt
Schauer and Schumacher Funeral Home
Ruth and John Somerville
Jim and Dixie Tubbs
WPS Resources Foundation
Robert and June Zimonick

Revenue from the book's sales will be used to create a fund to support other publications of local history interest.

Acknowledgments

While one person's name appears as editor, this project like others of its kind, reflects the contributions of many people who remain in the background. I am indebted to many people without whose help and support this book would not have seen center stage.

The Brown County Historical Society provided financial and administrative support. I am especially grateful for on-going help from Wendy Barszcz, BCHS executive director; Joan Hogan who chairs the BCHS Publishing Committee; and Loretta Delvaux, BCHS past president. A special nod to the many donors who funded the publication's cost.

Harold Elder was an on-going inspiration. His invaluable cooperation and encouraging optimism helped keep the project alive. Locating and matching the illustrations accompanying each article was a far greater endeavor for Harold and his wife, Margaret, than any of us had anticipated. Let it be noted that Margaret afforded immeasurable assistance and input throughout the process. Harold also designed the book cover and re-worked or re-drew some of the drawings damaged through the years. Would that I have such energy and creativity at 88!

Assistance also came from a number of people who took the time to review the book proposal and generously shared their fundraising expertise. Among these: Arlene Zakhar, formerly of the St. Norbert College Office of Advancement; Nancy Armbrust, director of Community Relations at Schreiber, Inc.; Ken Strmska, Greater Green Bay Community Foundation; Harry Maier, formerly of St. Norbert College; Jim Liethen, formerly with Wisconsin PublicService; Kathryn Hasselblad Pascale, Tom Murphy and others who provided helpful suggestions. For this novice, such input was invaluable.

Credit is due also to Notre Dame Academy students Ryan Kroening and Patrick LaPacz who helped select articles with appeal to a younger audience. The students' thoughtful rationale as well as their opinions on title options, chapter headings, and the book's general outline were all helpful.

Brown County Library personnel, especially Mary Jane Herber and other Local History and reference librarians, helped in the tricky business of sorting out fact from fiction. Assistance from staff at Heritage Hill and Duane Ebert, another local history guru, was helpful as well.

My "no-name" Writers' Group heard about the project over a period of two or three years and was as ready as I was to see it completed. For their patience, support, and title suggestions I owe my thanks.

A tip of the hat also to Carol Hunter, Green Bay Press-Gazette editor, for her on-going interest and encouragement.

Debbie DeGrave, typist par excellence, not only keyed copy onto disk but picked up discrepancies that might otherwise have slipped through unnoticed.

Designer Laura Diedrick's creativity and professionalism shaped the book into its final format.

Special thanks to Bill Kanzenback, Red Barn Antiques, who generously relinquished 18 original Elder sketches found in an Algoma attic. When I happened upon these exhibited in the vendor's booth at the Antiquarians' annual Antique Show in November, Bill voluntarily offered the art back to Harold "where they belonged." Many of these are included in the book.

Hugs to all of you who followed the project's progress with interest and patience and probably wondered, as I sometimes did, whether it would ever see the light of day.

Finally, to whatever Powers enable, inspire, and guide me, I give thanks.

BF

Table of Contents

Jack Rudolph

Mention the name Jack Rudolph and many who know the name will remember him as the area's local history guru. It was but one of many hats he wore during his lifetime. He was also journalist, music and drama critic, football analyst, baseball strategist, military man, traveler, husband and father. As one *Press-Gazette* article stated, "Rudolph's assorted lights would take more than a bushel to hide."

Jack Rudolph was born in Ellsworth, Wisconsin. He moved here with his family as a young boy in 1919. A graduate of St. John grade school (1922) and East Green Bay High School, Class of 1926, Rudolph gained experience in general reporting and sports writing as a summer intern at the *Press-Gazette* while still in high school. After three years at Lawrence University, Rudolph accepted an appointment to West Point Academy. He was sports editor for publications at both schools.

Rudolph graduated from West Point in 1933. During World War II, he was an instructor at Fort Leavenworth, Kansas, spent a brief time in England before serving with Intelligence at the Pentagon, and was regimental commander of the 38th Infantry at Ft. Lewis, Washington. He also served tours of duty in Hawaii, Panama Canal, and Germany.

His introduction to the U.S. Army came early in life by way of his father, Dr. S. F. Rudolph, who served in the Medical Corps during World War I.

Rudolph married Mona Henself of Eau Claire in 1936. She died in 1957. The following year, Rudolph married the late Leora Calkins Quinn, a widow and former classmate at Lawrence.

A twenty-year career man, Rudolph retired from the military with the rank of colonel in late 1953 and joined the *Press-Gazette* staff as a general assignment reporter a few months later. He began digging out local history tidbits shortly after he started at the paper; chronicling little- and well-known facts about the Green Bay area. Four years later the occasional article became a weekly feature and continued for twelve years.

Rudolph usually wrote the history column at home, away from the busy newsroom's many distractions. In those days before computer technology, Rudolph composed drafts and several rewrites in longhand, then keyed the final version on a typewriter. The writer was fond of noting his work had the benefit of a second editor. An assistant professor of English at the University of Wisconsin-Green Bay, Leora Rudolph often critiqued her husband's writing before it went to press.

The on-going series earned Rudolph a citation in 1963 from the American Association of State and Local History. "Perhaps no greater collection of little-known facts about a given geographical area exists than that created for *Press-Gazette* readers by (Rudolph)," the award read.

During his 17-year tenure with the paper - he retired in January 1971 - Rudolph also wrote the daily Twenty and Forty Years Ago Today column and Over the Century for the Sunday edition. Together, these columns fed "the Colonel's" interest in local history. He also covered the "usual" general assignment beats - the courts, fires and accidents, meetings, conventions, and sometimes sports.

Rudolph also established himself as the paper's music and drama critic. Largely self-trained, he learned by reading plays and acquiring an extensive record collection. Over the years, he acquired a collection of record albums said to number about 6,000 which he later donated to the Green Bay Symphony. In 1963, Gov. John Reynolds named Rudolph to the Governor's Council on the Fine Arts.

An avid sport enthusiast and athletics historian, Rudolph owned a collection that included baseball record books starting in 1868. Rudolph the-sports-historian might just have compiled more information on major league no-hit pitchers than any other person in the country. He traveled extensively to research the 186 no-hit games on record and reportedly had information on all but six of them. Rudolph began a book on this bit of major league baseball history but it was never completed. His football records from 1894 included every game played in the Big Ten. His book on Big 10 Football history was never completed either.

Rudolph did write two popular local history books in retirement, however. *Birthplace of a Commonwealth* (1976) chronicled the history of Brown County; he also published *Green Bay: A Pictorial History* in 1983. He also wrote for *The Spirit*, a predecessor of the current Green Bay Diocesan newspaper, the *Compass*. His free lance credits include articles in *American Heritage*; *Sports Illustrated*; *Army*; *Civil War Times*; *American History Illustrated*; and many regional publications. He was a long-time member of the Brown County Historical Society where he also served as president, and a past president and member of the now defunct Green Bay Writers' Club.

Rudolph died of cancer in 1985 at the age of 76.

Harold Elder

Born on Green Bay's east side in 1915, Harold Elder moved across the river with his family at an early age and stayed there until he graduated from West Green Bay High School in 1934. An aptitude in art led Elder to the Layton School of Art (now the Milwaukee Institute for Art and Design - MIAD) where he studied advertising design and illustration, graduating with a degree in 1939.

He worked in the color sketch department at Milprint, Inc., in Milwaukee for a year before he was drawn back to his hometown to work as a commercial artist for Green Bay Drop Forge. At the same time, he maintained an energetic schedule as a free lance artist producing art for many of the area's major businesses and industries, including part-time work for the *Press-Gazette*. He joined the paper full-time as a staff artist about 1957. Elder was deferred from World War II military service because of damage to one eye resulting from scarlet fever suffered as a child.

Besides working with Jack Rudolph on the weekly local history series, Elder engaged in many significant ad campaigns for area businesses during his twenty-plus years with the newspaper. Creation of Barney B. Baer for the Green Bay Plaza earned Elder the coveted W. E. Payne Award for the best advertising piece in the state of Wisconsin in newspaper competition for layouts. The cartoon character was recognized as "the most outstanding locally-prepared display ad of the year." His *Press-Gazette* endeavors also included portraits of national celebrities drawn for the paper's Close Up feature articles.

Elder created Bucky Bear, who plays a prominent role in many of this publication's drawings, in 1945. Bucky began as a cartoon strip in the paper and eventually evolved as the artist's copyrighted signature.

Elder retired from the *Press-Gazette* in 1978 but in the years since has remained actively engaged in art. Until the late 1990s, he taught art classes for the Northeast Wisconsin Technical College. He works in media that includes water color, charcoal, pen and ink, and pastel drawing, painting, or sketching a broad range of subjects. Among them: castle ruins in Ireland, landscapes, still life, nature scenes, cartoon, florals, as well as animal and bird life. His favorite medium? Pen and ink, though he finds himself drawn more to water color in recent years. For a short time after his retirement, Elder also penned a daily comic strip for *The Milwaukee Sentinel.*

Elder's art can be found in homes and museums across the country and he has shown his work in many local and regional exhibits. A one-person exhibit at the Brown County Library in 1984 featured the cartoons from the *Press-Gazette*'s local history series. One of these, the original drawing of Dr. William Beaumont, is displayed at the Medical Museum at Villa Louis State Historical Site in Prairie du Chien.

A *Press-Gazette* article about Elder quotes the artist as saying he "was not particularly fond of history" himself until he got involved in the Rudolph series. Then he found it "fascinated me." According to the same article, "The series provided Elder with the opportunity to work in two distinct styles - a realistic, detailed treatment of portraits for the more serious stories and a lighter cartoonish approach for the more frivolous tales." In researching his subject material Elder frequently referred to historic photographs from The Stiller Company files as well as from the Neville Public Museum.

Elder entered into an important partnership early in his career (1940) when he married the former Margaret Eichwald. The couple have one daughter. The family enjoys an affinity for all forms of art, occasionally traveling to Milwaukee for classical music concerts, ballet, theater, and other programs.

An artist in her own right, Margaret Elder's award-winning hand-made paper art has been included in many area exhibits. She studied with Gisela Moyer and also developed skills in photography and jewelry making under St. Norbert Art Professor Charles Peterson. Like her husband, Margaret also enjoyed a career with the *Press-Gazette* where she worked part-time for three years and fifteen more as a full-time employee. She retired in 1978 as assistant promotions manager under Jack Yuenger.

Together, the couple live in De Pere where they volunteer regularly at the De Pere Christian Outreach thrift store, are active at St. Anne's Episcopal Church, and maintain their on-going interest in art and its expression.

Prologue

For twelve years, from July 5, 1958 until June 26, 1970, Jack Rudolph cranked out a weekly editorial page column for the *Green Bay Press-Gazette* retelling little known facts, as well as more familiar ones, about the area's history. Rudolph's columns chronicled individuals, majors events such as the Peshtigo Fire (his favorite), economic conditions, politics, and the social life of various eras. A collaboration that included cartoon illustrations to accompany the articles, some in the earlier years drawn by William Juhre, but most by Harold Elder, ensured the column's popularity.

One-hundred-fifty of those columns and their accompanying art work are included here. These are arranged chronologically for an overview of the area's history and development from 1634 through 1970. The selections highlight the people and events that shaped the area and present a cross-section of community life.

These writings and their attending art represent a critical piece of history that over time could be lost. Currently the material is, at best, only marginally accessible to the public-at-large. Besides making the work more available, this book will supplement the meager offerings of historical writings about this area and serve as another resource for local history studies. Jack Rudolph's colorfully written columns, coupled with Harold Elder's whimsical art, offer a unique, readable, often entertaining view of the area's history. It is said that teachers often used the widely read columns for their lessons on local history. The BCHS hopes this book will be an equally effective resource for teachers and their students.

A cautionary note

Of his friend Harold T. I. Shannon as well as others featured in the collection Rudolph often said, "He never let the facts get in the way of a good story." Some local historians suggest that Rudolph enjoyed the same art of embellishment. Let the record note, however, that extensive research went into every piece Jack wrote. Nevertheless, it is true that errors occasionally crept in. While efforts were made to correct these in the selections included here, some undoubtedly have slipped through. Still, credit is due the writer for his extensive efforts to bring the area's history to life and light. This book, then, is intended as one more informational tool, not the final word on any given subject. *Changes or corrections made to the original articles are noted in italics within the text.* Otherwise, the articles are re-printed as they appeared originally.

Column started July 5, 1958

The local history feature appeared in thc *Green Bay Press-Gazette* for the first time on July 5, 1958 and was published every Saturday for the next twelve years. The single exception was the year the Fourth of July fell on a Saturday and the paper did not publish. The total collection adds up to more than 600 pieces (415 articles, some of which were reprinted through the years) and roughly 400,000 words.

Whose idea was it? How did it get started?

Rudolph already was writing an occasional article on local history that ran when space allowed, a practice he began when he joined the paper in 1954. The late Jack Yuenger, then the paper's advertising manager, gets credit for making the columns a regular Saturday feature. Yuenger, prodded by his assistant Margaret Elder, came up with the idea of running the pieces regularly on the *Press-Gazette*'s editorial page. That, however, required an okay from the then editor-in-chief Leo Gannon, not an easy sell. It took several weeks for Yuenger and Rudolph to convince their boss of the idea's merit but he eventually bought into it with the strict caveat that, once committed, the column must appear consistently and religiously without fail every Saturday. The rest, as they say, is history.

During the first year or two, Harold Elder shared the art duties with another staff artist, William (Bill) Juhre. Thereafter, Elder handled it on his own. All the cartoons included in this publication are Elder's art. In a *Press-Gazette* article dated July 2, 1966, as the column finished its eighth year Rudolph commended his colleague. "It isn't easy for Harold, who can only go to work after the writing is finished. Sometimes that crowds him unmercifully, since on occasion I barely make the deadline myself.

"Fortunately, Harold's enthusiasm matches mine and he goes to considerable trouble to establish authenticity of background and costume, which means a good deal of digging on his own. Despite an occasional argument over an approach, our collaboration has been exceedingly pleasant and a source of much mutual satisfaction."

The collaboration continued for another four years; the last column and its art appeared June 27, 1970.

Chapter One

Taming the Wilderness

Explorer Carried Thunder and Lightning

Nicolet Began Wisconsin History

June 27, 1970

About 15 miles north of the city, where Highway 57 skirts the edge of the bluff known as Red Banks, a bronze statue of a man in fringed and belted buckskins faces the passing traffic from the middle of a low stone wall. Behind it the ground drops sharply to the bay shore far below.

The figure represents Jean Nicolet. It is located somewhere above the (*legendary*) spot where, on an unknown date in the late summer of 1634, this otherwise undistinguished French adventurer stepped ashore and into history as the first white man to set foot in Wisconsin and the Middle West.

He left no record of what he was thinking when he stepped dramatically out of a birchbark canoe and fired a couple of pistols into the air. It might have occurred to him that he was a long way from home for a mailman's boy.

Jean Nicolet, discoverer of Wisconsin, was the son of a French postman who carried the mails between Paris and Cherbourg, where Jean was born in 1598. He came to America in 1618 as a protege of Samuel de Champlain, governor of New France, who made a habit of enlisting adventurous and promising young Frenchmen and training them as emissaries to the Indians.

Long Apprenticeship

For 16 years Nicolet learned his job, alternating periods as an interpreter with long sojourns among the (*natives*) where he absorbed as much as he could of Indian languages, customs and psychology. He was thoroughly prepared when, in 1634, Champlain sent him west into the unexplored wilderness beyond Lake Huron.

His mission was to establish peaceful relations with whatever natives he encountered, particularly a mysterious tribe called "Puans," who were rumored to live along the shores of a deep bay on a large body of water beyond Huron. Champlain had a fanciful theory that the Puans might actually be Chinese and that in locating them Nicolet would find the Northwest Passage to the Pacific, for which Europeans had been searching ever since the discovery of North America.

At the time Champlain's idea didn't sound so silly. "Puan" in the Huron language meant "men of the stinking water," and the governor reasoned this could mean salt water. On the odd chance he was right, Nicolet took along an ornate Chinese mandarin robe to wear if and when he reached China.

Left in Early Summer

Nicolet left Quebec early in July, 1634. About a month later, with a party of seven Huron Indians, he shoved off from the last French outposts on Georgian Bay and headed into the unknown. Even his companions had no idea of what lay beyond.

Following the north shore of Lake Huron, Nicolet reached the entrance to the Sault rapids but did not penetrate far enough to see the great expanse of Lake Superior beyond. Instead, he turned south to the Straits of Mackinac and into Green bay, where he had heard the Puans could be found.

By this time he knew the Northwest Passage did not lie ahead. The Puans, whatever they might be, were not Chinese.

Pushing down to the mouth of the Menominee River, Nicolet sent two of his Hurons across the bay to the principal town of the Puans to inform them of his arrival and peaceful intentions. A couple of days later, the exact date now unknown (if, indeed Nicolet knew himself), Nicolet made his landfall below the bluff at Red Banks, which was topped by the palisaded fort and village of the Puans, who turned out to be Winnebago Indians. The entire population had come down to greet him.

Got into Costume

Just before his arrival Nicolet put on his fancy Chinese robe. Even if his greeters weren't Chinese, the robe would impress them.

No one knows what color that costume was, beyond the general description of "a robe of China damask, all strewn with flowers and birds of many colors." There are as many different versions as there are artists' conceptions of the historic landing. In the painting most familiar locally — the mural in the Brown County courthouse — the robe is red.

As his canoe swept into the landing Nicolet was an impressive sight, regardless of what the color might have been. He startled the waiting Puans even more when he stepped ashore, raised a pair of pistols and pulled the triggers.

Scared the Women

The flash and report sent the women and children scuttling into the bushes but the men stood their ground. Soon Indians from all over the area were converging on Red Banks to see the stranger who carried thunder and lightning in his hands, until there were an estimated 4,000 to 5,000 gathered there. Nicolet had no difficulties with his peacemaking beyond the strain by repeated feasting on roast beaver.

How long he remained isn't known, but he apparently made a quick trip up the Fox River, possibly as far as Menasha, before turning back. He reached Quebec late in September without having found China but with the knowledge that the continent was a lot bigger than anyone had dreamed.

Almost 25 years passed before anybody else followed the trail he had blazed, and in the interim Nicolet almost lost the credit for his discoveries. He left no written record of the trip, and if it hadn't been for his Jesuit friend, Father Vimont, the exploit might have been forgotten. Vimont included an account of the expedition in one of his reports to Paris, which was published in "Jesuit Relations," in 1642.

Neglected by Historians

Since the "Relations" were not translated into English until 1803, they were neglected as source material by early American historians. In 1853, however, Nicolet's exploit came to light when John Gilbert Shea quoted Vimont in his "Discovery of the Mississippi."

Shea fixed the date as 1639, which was accepted until 1876. Then Benjamin Sulte went back to original sources and came up with 1634. Five years later Sulte's deduction was verified by C. W. Butterfield.

Nicolet never returned to the west. Assigned as an interpreter to the Three Rivers country west of Quebec, he married a ward of Champlain and remained there the rest of his life.

He drowned in the St. Lawrence River on the bitterly cold night of Oct. 27, 1642, when the canoe in which he was traveling from Quebec to Three Rivers capsized. For all his wilderness savvy, Jean Nicolet had flunked one basic skill.

He couldn't swim.

Forgotten Figure

Perrot Held West for France

October 6, 1962

At the opening of the new Neville Public Museum state history section this week one of the outstanding exhibits was a simple silver object set by itself in a striking wall case. Few people attending the opening had any difficulty recognizing the object as the Perrot Ostensorium, famed among American antiquarians throughout the nation as the finest and most valuable relic of the 17th Century French regime in the middle west.

What only a handful could answer, however, was the question — who was Perrot? And this, despite the fact that many of them pass his statue nearly every day.

Nicholas Perrot deserves better from posterity, especially in the region he once dominated so completely. For that matter, he deserved far more than he ever got in his own lifetime.

From 1680 until 1698 Nicholas Perrot, a remarkable combination of fur trader, explorer, diplomat and soldier, was the most influential white man in the vast wilderness of the Great Lakes region. Much of that time he held the region for France practically with his bare hands. Then he was pushed aside to spend 20 years on the shelf vainly trying to get some recognition for his services and sacrifices.

Born in France

Perrot was born in France in 1644 of poor and unknown parentage, neither his birthplace nor date being exactly known. Neither is the date of his arrival in Canada, but he must have come when he was very young. By the time he was 21 he was already an independent fur trader with an exceptional grasp of Indian psychology.

He first came to the Green Bay region on an independent trading junket in 1669 and immediately acquired great influence among the Pottawatamis *(sic)* in the neighborhood. He not only brought them their first iron tools, for which they were always grateful, but his flair for Indian diplomacy also averted what would probably have been a disastrous war with the Menominees.

He even impressed the surly Foxes. In fact, he was the only Frenchman for whom the Foxes ever had any use, and twice in later years they saved him from death at the stake.

Despite his youth Perrot knew his business and quickly broke the Ottawa monopoly on trading expeditions to the settlements. The fur fleet he led back to Montreal in the spring of 1670 was the largest up to that time, including many tribes which had never made the trip before.

Settled Down

With his profits Perrot bought a homestead near Montreal, got married and settled down to raise a large family. First, however, he was called upon to stage an impressive show of French sovereignty on the lakes.

Sent to Sault Ste. Marie in 1671, Perrot persuaded 15 tribes to declare their allegiance to France. To cap his success he arranged a colorful ceremony in which he formally took possession of the region in the name of the King of France.

His wife died about 1681, leaving him a small fortune with which he immediately re-entered the fur trade. He was highly successful, but the long Iroquois War, breaking out in 1680, closed the routes to the east and forced him to store his pelts along the frontier. He had to take the chance but it resulted in financial disaster.

For the next several years, while the French fought with their backs to the wall in the East, Perrot was western commandant with headquarters at LaBaye. As such he shuttled between the Lakes and the settlements, pacifying the jittery western tribes, recruiting and leading war parties against the hated but greatly feared Iroquois.

Explored Wisconsin

In his spare time he pushed up the Fox-Wisconsin River route to the Mississippi, thence north to Lake Pepin, establishing posts at Trempeleau, Pepin and the mouth of the Wisconsin. He also located lead deposits in the vicinity of Dubuque, Iowa, and showed the Indians how to smelt down the ore to reduce its bulk.

It was during a big recruiting powwow at De Pere in 1686 that he presented the Mission of St. Francis Xavier with the famed ostensorium, or monstrance.

The following year, while Perrot was in the east, the Indians burned the mission and with it a valuable stock of furs he had stored there. The loss was a blow from which he never recovered.

Hurrying back to Green Bay in 1688 Perrot found the situation critical as the western tribes, alarmed at French reverses, were on the verge of shifting sides to avoid future reprisals from the Iroquois. At Trempeleau, where a large post had grown up, the Sioux had stolen a large supply of goods and refused to give them back.

Equal to Occasion

Perrot was equal to the occasion. Secretly slipping some brandy into a cup of water, he set fire to it, then threatened to do the same to all the lakes and swamps if the defiant Sioux didn't cough up. The goods were promptly returned.

Twice during those touchy years Perrot's life was in danger when he fell into the hands of Indians whose friendship was wearing thin. On both occasions the Foxes literally pulled him out of the fire.

In spite of the eastern situation and the vacillation of the western tribes, Perrot kept them from kicking over the traces. All his work was undone in 1698, however, when he was recalled to Montreal in consequence of a royal decision to abandon all posts west of Mackinac.

He never returned to the Lakes, in spite of repeated Indian requests that he be sent back. Historians are agreed that had the pleas been heeded the bloody Fox wars of the 18th Century would probably have been avoided.

Harassed by Poverty

Perrot lived on for 20 years, harassed by poverty and unsuccessfully petitioning a government that had never paid him a franc for his great services. He was ignored. The governor of New France did what he could for the aging man but it wasn't much.

When a large expedition was sent against the Foxes in 1716 Perrot, then 72, begged to be sent along, confident that he could patch things up. He was curtly brushed off.

He is believed to have died about 1718 in such obscurity that his death, like his birth, is not recorded. The last reference to him in public documents is in that year.

Bulwark of Control

For two decades, Nicholas Perrot singlehandedly maintained the French position in the Great Lakes country. He made alliances in the face of impending disaster and held the Indians to them through the blackest days, a feat no other Frenchman, except possibly Frontenac himself, could have accomplished.

His integrity was never questioned and the Indians would always listen to him. A superb showman, he understood them thoroughly, had a knack for the right dramatic gesture in a tight spot and was a master of the colorful oratory the Indians loved.

There is no existing description of him but his Pottawatami *(sic)* nickname may be a clue. They called him "Metaminens," which meant "Little Corn."

Perrot has occupied a spot in full view of downtown Green Bay for more than 25 years, but few are aware of it. The white man in fringed buckskins to the left of Sidney Bedore's "Spirit of the Northwest" on the courthouse lawn represents Perrot.

Last of the Early Traders

Lawe Succeeded the Hard Way

November 10, 1962

For a man who came to bat with two strikes against him, John Lawe did all right. Last of the important pre-United States figures to establish himself in Wisconsin, Lawe came as a boy of 15 and remained the rest of his life. He was a prosperous and highly respected figure when he died nearly half a century later.

English, half Jewish and an Episcopalian in a tight little French Catholic community, he made his place the hard way. In an active career of almost 50 years he became one of the most successful men of his day, respected by friends and rivals alike. He never had any real enemies.

John Lawe was born at either Bristol or York, England, in 1782, the son of a British Army officer. He came to Canada as a youngster, his family settling in Quebec.

In 1797 he was sent to LaBaye as an apprentice to his uncle, Joseph Franks. The latter is a little known figure in Wisconsin history but he was probably the first non-French white man to settle west of Lake Michigan.

Bought Out Uncle

Lawe remained with his uncle for several years, acquiring a thorough grasp of the fur trade and an astonishing technique for handling Indians. When Franks decided to return to Canada before the War of 1812 Lawe bought him out, trading extensive lands in Canada for his uncle's Wisconsin holdings. Franks thought he got the better of the deal but Lawe never had reason to regret it.

On the face of things he should have encountered rough going against business rivals entrenched among the Indians through long association and intermarriage. But he knew the game and during his apprenticeship had built a position of trust and confidence among the (*natives*) rivaled only by Augustine (*sic*) Grignon.

His handling of Indians was unique. He always kept just enough distance to impress them with dignity and courtesy, maintained strict and formal accounts and paid them according to a set scale of values.

As a result his redskin customers were loyal, and although he got pretty fed up with them at times, as several of his letters reveal, he never let them know it. He enjoyed a virtual monopoly on the west shore of Green bay as far as Shawano Lake and the Wolf River.

Keen Rivalry

Lawe's rivalry with Jacques Porlier was particularly keen. He and Porlier had trading posts on opposite sides of the river and watched each other's moves like a couple of strange bulldogs.

As Deborah Martin put it, between them the "ethics of the fur trade were always strictly enforced." One of those ethics was to get the best of the other fellow any way you could, short of murder, but Lawe was very good at keeping one eye on the back of his neck.

In spite of competition, he and the courtly Porlier shared a mutual liking and respect. In fact, both looked on the rivalry as a good natured game and strictly a private affair. Let anyone else try to break in and they promptly closed ranks.

The only time Lawe was ever outsmarted was by the American Fur Co. Although he, Porlier and the Grignons were independent operators, they all purchased trade goods from and sold furs to the company. The latter's Northern Department manager, Ramsey Crooks, finally suggested they form a partnership to deal with his firm.

Since Lawe had once worked for both the Hudson's Bay and Astor outfits, he probably should have known better. He swallowed the bait, however, when Crooks promised to help the new combination in every way.

Crooks did, but there was a gimmick in it. The A.F.C. granted liberal credit until the partners were in too deep to get out, then slowly hiked the prices on goods while lowering the price it would pay for furs. To cover the indebtedness the company took mortgages on the partners' great land holdings in and around the Fox River Valley.

For years Crooks let things ride until he had the Green Bay traders on the cuff for about $35,000. Then the company called for immediate payment. Since this was impossible, Crooks and Astor foreclosed the mortgages in 1834. Lawe took a bad beating but being a better businessman than the others he made a quicker recovery.

British Lieutenant

In addition to his fur trading, which he carried on from a large post and landing on a sand spit at the foot of Porlier Street called Lawe's Point, he was active in many phases of community life.

During the War of 1812 he was a lieutenant in the British service. His only active campaigning was against an unsuccessful American thrust at Mackinac but he did a good job of wheedling or squeezing food supplies for English forces out of the little settlement.

After the war he took the oath of allegiance to the United States, was confirmed in the ownership of his land claims and went right on with his business. In 1820 he was named an associate justice of Brown County and succeeded Porlier as probate judge in 1822.

He resigned in 1824 in favor of Nicholas Bean, a protege whom he had more or less pulled out of the gutter. Right up to his death on Feb. 11, 1846, he continued to be an active leader in business and public affairs.

In 1807 Lawe married Therese Rankin, who had previously been the common law wife of Louis Grignon. Bella French delicately explained that she had been the wife of Grignon "according to the custom of the times, and had parted from him." In other words, Therese walked out.

The situation gave rise in later years to the rumor that Lawe and Grignon had traded wives during a drinking bout. It wasn't true. Therese was his first and only wife and she survived him.

They had six daughters and two sons, one of whom never married. The other son, George, attained the distinction of being the oldest white settler in Wisconsin before he died and the "Father of Kaukauna," which he platted in 1850. A daughter, Mary Polly, cut a scandalous swathe in her day and her famous piano is still preserved at Cotton House.

Lawe lived in excellent style and was an extremely generous man. He made it a policy to take care of any old, sick or impoverished Indian who appealed to him and for all his astuteness was a patsy for a good sob story. Almost anyone could work him for a liberal handout, most of which were never repaid.

In one respect, though, he was a typical Englishman. He liked his privacy, and when he built a fine house above his trading post he surrounded the five-acre grounds with a nine-foot fence of sharpened cedar poles. Inside he cultivated a flower garden of which he was very proud, and an invitation to see it became quite a distinction.

Nearly Lost Home

Lawe almost lost his home in the foreclosure debacle. It was only saved by the action of Judge James Duane Doty in deeding the lot to Mrs. Lawe when he platted the village of Astor.

Lawe had always been a faithful friend to the aggressive judge and was the first to come forward to settle with his creditors. To give Doty what little credit is due him in the miserable business, he braved the wrath of John Jacob Astor to help his old friend.

As a young man Lawe was very slender but gained weight as he grew older and in middle age weighed over 300 pounds. In spite of his bulk, however, he possessed great physical strength and endurance.

John Lawe is buried in Woodlawn Cemetery, just a short distance inside the Webster Avenue gates. His grave, marked by a tall marble shaft, is the only one of Green Bay's earliest settlers whose location is known today.

Death of an Army Post

Ft. Howard, Frontier Guardian

December 7, 1968

The frontier military post of Ft. Howard looms large in the history of Green Bay, perhaps larger than the military facts of life warrant. Its strategic importance had begun to wane almost before it was completed, and for nearly half its existence there wasn't a GI on the premises.

It has been only a memory, albeit a vivid one, now for more than a century. When, on Nov. 10, 1864, the Stars and Stripes were lowered for the last time no military honors were rendered. The post had served its purpose long before, and there had been no garrison within its walls for the better part of 20 years. *(Deborah Martin cites 1861 as the year the fort closed; another source reports the Chicago and Northwestern Railroad owned some of the land in 1862 with the rest sold in November 1864.)*

Nevertheless, no responsible historian of Wisconsin can ignore Ft. Howard (named for an undistinguishable general officer of the War of 1812). It exerted an influence upon the development of the city which eventually engulfed it far beyond its strategic or tactical importance.

No shot was ever fired in anger from its wooden walls, its cannon never spoke except in salute. Just the fact that it was there, though, insured the peaceful settlement of Northeastern Wisconsin and opened the door to the west.

The flags of three nations had flown over the site in the century and a half of its spotty existence. By the time the Americans came in 1816, however, no troops had occupied it for more than 40 years and its rude log palisade was a crumbling ruin.

Because the initial force sent by the United States to take formal possession after the War of 1812 was larger than required, the original mission of the fort — to establish American sovereignty, to overawe the pro-British French Canadian traders and Indians and to divert the profits of the fur trade into American pockets — was easily accomplished.

Thereafter, as the frontier line quickly jumped to the Mississippi, the military value of Ft. Howard diminished, although it continued to be useful as a supply base and headquarters for regiments whose companies were scattered in outposts farther west.

Arrival in Strength

On Aug. 7, 1816, a flotilla of small sailing vessels carrying six companies of the 3rd U.S. Infantry and a detachment of artillery under command of Col. James Miller, hero of the battle of Lundy's Lane, dropped anchor in the Fox River opposite the present site of the Northwest Engineering Co. plant. *(Located then at 201 West Walnut, the plant closed in 1990.)* While the guns of the little fleet covered the large Menominee Indian village, the troops landed smartly and Col. Miller took possession of Wisconsin for the United States in an impressive ceremony.

An Army engineer, Maj. Charles Gratiot, accompanying the expedition, selected the site for the proposed fort. He picked the same spot as his French and British predecessors, traces of whose work could still be seen. Shortly after, with part of the force, he returned to Mackinac, leaving Lt. Col. Talbot Chambers to dig in.

Many Changes

There is no accurate description of Ft. Howard in its earliest shape, although there is a distorted pen and ink sketch dated 1818. There are several descriptions of the post in the 1820s as well as a set of War Department blueprints now in the possession of the Ft. Howard Hospital Museum Commission.

The latter are undated, but references to the occupying troops make it possible to place them with some accuracy. They show that over the years the interior of the stockade underwent many changes according to the immediate needs of the garrison and the whims of commanding officers.

The initial plan, cooked up by some armchair Vauban in far off Washington, was an elaborate pipe dream on the scale of a formal European fortress. As soon as Maj. Gratiot was out of sight, Col. Chambers junked it and threw up a typical frontier stockade.

It was a lop-sided diamond, located between what are now Kellogg and Elmore Streets, with the southeast corner almost touching the riverbank. The palisade, originally 30 feet high but subsequently reduced to 15, was made of timbers cut at a sawmill built by Dominique Brunette in the Sullivan's Flats area adjacent to what is now the Oneida Golf & Riding Club.

In Railroad Yard

The stockade, standing in the middle of today's North Western Railway yards a short distance north and east of the station *(now Titletown Brewing Company)*, was 350 feet long on two sides and 375 feet on the others. It enclosed about three acres.

A firing platform ran around the interior of the walls, which were pierced with loopholes. Gun ports for cannon were cut at the corners and a gate was placed in the middle of each wall.

Close to the walls on the inside were built barracks, administration building, mess halls, kitchens and officers' quarters, a few two stories high but most only one. These faced a central parade ground, in the center of which was a tall flag pole.

Mural View Accurate

The familiar mural on the courthouse wall is an accurate view of the fort in its last year of occupation. It was copied from a daguerreotype made in 1852.

The garrison was withdrawn in 1841 and the post placed under a caretaker. Shortly thereafter, that portion of the reservation south of Division Street (so named because it became the boundary of the reserve and the town of Fort Howard) was sold.

Troops returned briefly in 1849 but pulled out in 1852, and the old post was never garrisoned again. It came to life briefly as a recruiting and processing station during the Civil War but was sold before the war was over.

Land Sold Quickly

The large tract of hitherto unavailable land went quickly when put on the market. Sales up to $19,000 in two days represented more than half the appraised value, although less than half the land was immediately disposed of at prices ranging from $1.25 to $75 an acre.

The fort enclosure and buildings, valued at $3,000, brought $6,400. The walls were knocked down and the buildings either razed or removed. By 1869 nearly every trace of the once neatly whitewashed station had disappeared.

Some of the sturdy old buildings, moved to other locations, are still in use. Best known is ... the Ft. Howard Hospital *(at Heritage Hill)*, although a few others are scattered on both sides of the river. All that marks the *(fort's)* site today is a stone monument on Dousman Street, a short distance south of the actual location of the fort. *(The Ft. Howard Hospital was moved by barge to Heritage Hill in the late 1970s.)*

Wilderness Colossus

The American Fur Company

January 28, 1967

In less than four and a half centuries the United States has grown from a trackless wilderness to the greatest industrial power the world has ever known. The foundation of that power was laid by a simple but deadly gadget-a metal trap to catch small, fur-bearing animals.

The trap was the basic tool of the fabled American fur trade. For nearly 300 years the principal and often the only business transacted on the wilderness frontier, the fur trade is beloved of historians and fiction writers, whose villain is its most famous institution, the American Fur Company.

Almost unanimously damned as a ruthless monopoly, the company has not enjoyed a friendly historical press. Some of its unsavory reputation was fully earned but much has also been exaggerated.

No Worse Than Rivals

The American Fur Co. was merciless in its war against competition but its methods were no worse than those of any other business of its time. It never was a monopoly although in its relatively brief existence (less than 40 years) it dominated the field, in which, as fast as one competitor was eliminated, another popped up to take on the giant.

To destroy them the company fought fire with fire. Since it could apply more heat than anybody else, its besetting sin was being too efficient and too successful. Success was rooted in two overwhelming advantages, the unrivaled financial resources and business genius of John Jacob Astor.

For a generation Astor was the American Fur Co. He owned it outright, made the big decisions and ran it brilliantly, ruthlessly and successfully.

Formed in 1808

The American Fur Co. was incorporated by charter from the state of New York on April 6, 1808. It continued under Astor's personal direction until his retirement in 1834, at which time it was divided into two separate organizations, one of which lasted until 1844, the other well into the Civil War.

The new corporation got off to a poor start. Its first big effort, the ill-fated Astoria expedition to the Pacific Coast in 1810, was a failure, while its operations in the Great Lakes region were sharply curtailed by the War of 1812. Not until the return of peace, when Astor began to re-assemble the pieces, did the enterprise start to roll.

Just before the war he had established a dominant position in the Great Lakes trade by organizing a loose federation called the Southwest Co., partly through purchase of the older Mackinaw Co. and partly by arrangement with the British Northwest Co. After the war he combined these interests into a single organization, personally owned and controlled, which he established at Mackinac Island in 1817 under the management of Ramsay Crooks and Robert Stuart.

Resisted Bitterly

His simultaneous attempt to muscle into the trans-Mississippi and Missouri River trade was bitterly resisted by the traders based in St. Louis. In 1822, however, he got a foothold at St. Louis, at which time the company was reorganized into two great departments.

The Great Lakes operation with headquarters at Mackinac, was called the Northern Department, while St. Louis became the base for the trans-Mississippi area as the Western Department. A few years later, in 1829, the Missouri River trade above what is now Sioux City, Iowa, became a subdivision of the Western Department, known as the Upper Missouri Outfit.

With the creation of the two departments, Crooks was brought to New York as general manager, Stuart succeeding him at Mackinac, while Pierre Chouteau Jr., grandson of one of the founders of St. Louis, took charge of the Western Department. Overlord of the far-flung Upper Missouri Outfit until he got caught off base in 1833 was Kenneth McKenzie, one of the great figures of the Far West fur trade.

Crushed Competition

Under the guidance of these brilliant, hard-bitten characters, the American Fur Co. crunched relentlessly over all competition. Using brute force where necessary, fighting ruinous price wars and buying out rivals when it had to, the company became the most powerful, most feared and hated institution in the west. Beyond reach of the law it made its own law, had no friends and acted accordingly.

Technically at least the company operated meticulously within the law. It was accused of all sorts of skullduggery, not excluding murder, but nothing was ever proved against it. There are good grounds for suspicion, though, that the A.M.F. (*A.F.C.*) presented two faces to the world.

Crooks might — and did — issue righteous strictures against all forms of illegality but his agents in the field blandly ignored them. Both they and Crooks worked on the principle that what he didn't know wouldn't hurt the company.

The company was always conservative and cautious. It moved slowly but planned shrewdly, being content to let others do the pioneering, then moving in. It made full use of political influence, did its share of lobbying and dispensing favors and always gave full backing to scientific explorations in the wilderness.

Trading Company

It was basically a trading company, equipping and supplying expeditions into the fur company and taking the latter's collected furs in return. Mostly, its arrangements were grossly one-sided, placing all the risk on the men who did the work, forcing them to stand the losses while coolly and relentlessly raking in the profits.

The home office in New York purchased all the trade goods, which were forwarded to the frontier through St. Louis and Mackinac. Shipments for the latter went through the Great Lakes while St. Louis-destined goods went up the Mississippi from New Orleans.

At each trans-shipment point fixed charges were added to costs, first in New York, secondly in St. Louis and Mackinac and again when forward distributing points were reached, such as Green Bay. Thereafter it was up to the traders to barter at a profit over their own costs. If they failed they took the rap.

Retired in 1834

In 1834 Astor retired. He was 71 years old and the fur company, while a highly sentimental operation with him, was only a minor part of his vast holdings.

The Northern Department and company name were sold to a group headed by Crooks and Stuart. The latter soon got out and Crooks continued to run the Great Lakes establishment until it was no longer profitable. In 1844 he liquidated the business.

Chouteau bought the Western Department and changed its name. As the tide of settlement destroyed the sources of furs the trade dwindled in the west, too. Chouteau eventually sold out and moved to New York where he became a powerful figure in railroad financing. Under a series of other names, the company remained in existence until 1864.

'Father of Wisconsin'

DeLanglade Was Colorful Pioneer

October 20, 1962

Displayed in one of the new cases recently completed at the Neville Public Museum is an old red military coat of a British Army officer. By a strange quirk of fate, it was given by the British government to a man whom, only a few years before, had been infamous all over the French-English frontier as a renegade "butcher" reveling in the scalps of murdered English women and children.

The Indians called him "Aukewingeketauso," which meant either "military conqueror" or "bravest of the brave." As this state's first permanent white settler he is also called the "father of Wisconsin." His real name was Charles Michel DeLanglade.

He earned his bloody reputation during the long struggle between France and England for possession of North America. He had practically cut his teeth on a tomahawk and was almost constantly on the warpath for 20 years. Known, respected and dreaded from Pittsburgh to Quebec, his fame and influence among the Indians were enormous.

Loved Battle

DeLanglade had courage — nobody ever denied that — and he could be vicious. He loved battle and fought well although he usually wound up on the losing side through no fault of his own. And, as is usually the case, he was not as bad as he was painted.

He was no rose, either.

Although he is called the first permanent "white" settler of Wisconsin, DeLanglade was at least half Indian and maybe even more — it all depends on whether or not his father had any Indian ancestry, a point still not clear.

Charles DeLanglade was born at Michilimackinac in May, 1729, the son of Augustin DeLanglade and an Ottawa Indian princess whose brother was the head war chief of his people. DeLanglade was not his family name. Augustin was the first to use it.

Mother's Influence

As a boy his mother's influence overshadowed his French background, although he received some formal education. When he was ten he was taken on an Indian raid by an uncle and the expedition was so successful he went along regularly thereafter, first as a good luck mascot and later as a leader of war parties in his own right.

DeLanglade rocketed to fame in 1752 with a surprise swoop on the Miami (Ohio) River outpost of Pickawillany, an action that triggered the final phase of the Hundred Years War in America. From then until 1761 he ranged the frontier from Virginia to Quebec, spreading death, destruction and terror among the British settlements.

In 1755 he achieved his greatest military success as architect of Braddock's defeat. Having persuaded the discouraged French commander of Ft. Duquaine (*sic*) (Pittsburgh) to stand and fight an overwhelmingly superior British army, DeLanglade planned and organized the victorious ambush and fought brilliantly in it.

Two years later, however, his reputation was tarnished by the massacre at Ft. William Henry. He was not responsible for the outrage but failure to control his Indians gave him a black eye in the opinion of both the French and English.

Publicly reprimanded by the French, he was later given the post of second in command at Mackinac. He was present and fought bravely at the fall of Quebec, then returned to the straits post, which he formally surrendered in 1761. Upon taking the oath of allegiance to the British crown he was permitted to remain.

DeLanglade warned the British commandant of Pontiac's impending uprising but was ignored. He was present when the Indians surprised and over-ran Mackinac in June, 1763, although he didn't know the attack was imminent.

He was powerless to stop it but later saved the prisoners from death at the stake. Subsequently, he was cleared of any complicity in the disaster.

Later that year he received permission to move his family to LaBaye. (The pass is still preserved in the DeLanglade papers.)

Controversy on Date

At this point there is some controversy over when DeLanglade actually settled permanently at Green Bay. Tradition long put the date as 1745 but historians now doubt it was that early. He and his father probably visited LaBaye on trading expeditions as early as 1745 but it is highly unlikely that he had any permanent establishment here.

In the first place, he was too good a family man to leave his dependants in such an exposed place while he went war-whooping all over the frontier. In the second, if his home was here, he hardly needed permission to go home after the French and Indian War. Most likely, his family never saw Green Bay until the war ended.

On arrival at LaBaye, DeLanglade built a large trading post and home at what is now the river end of Doty Street and settled to the routine life of a fur trader. He also functioned as British Indian agent and captain of local militia, which accounts for the red coat.

So great was his prestige among the Indians that his mere presence served to keep them in line, and settlement proceeded slowly and peacefully. In fact, only a few months before his death a rumor that he was coming down the Mississippi at the head of a war party threw the Spaniards at New Orleans into a panic.

When the American Revolution began DeLanglade, now crowding 50, unsheathed his war hatchet and offered his services to England. He appeared with a large Indian force at the headquarters of General Burgoyne just before the latter took off on the campaign that ended in surrender at Saratoga. Gentleman Johnny politely turned down his *(deLanglade's)* proffer of service, and he returned to Green Bay after a few minor raids.

It was his last fling. He had taken part in 99 battles and skirmishes and in his old age used to growl goodnaturedly that he'd like to get in just one more to make it an even 100.

DeLanglade's wife was a strikingly beautiful woman named Charlotte Bourassa, whom he married at Mackinac in 1754. Fifteen years his junior, she outlived him by 18 years.

Their daughter Domitelle married Pierre Grignon, a union that founded the Grignon dynasty in Wisconsin. DeLanglade also had a son, Charles Jr., by a previous marriage who served with distinction in the British Army during the War of 1812.

Stocky Six-Footer

A powerful, stocky man, DeLanglade stood slightly under six feet, with very broad shoulders and a round, expressive face. Piercing black eyes peered from beneath bushy eyebrows. He became partly bald in middle age and what remained of his once jet black hair turned white in his old age. Dressed in his scarlet British uniform, he was an impressive figure.

He is described as a mild and patient man, who could not, however, brook an insult. An outstanding leader, he inspired respect and confidence in white men as well as Indians. Every record testified to his rigid honesty.

Early in March — some say January — 1800 he contracted a severe cold, one of the few illnesses in his long and arduous life. Within two weeks he was dead at the age of 71.

Charles DeLanglade was buried in the old LaBaye cemetery, now covered by the busy Washington-Adams-Mason Street intersection, but all trace of his grave was eventually lost. It is likely, although there is no certainty, that his unidentified bones were eventually transferred to Allouez Cemetery and dumped into a common trench. *(A marker remains at the point where Washington and Adams meet just north of the Tilleman/Mason Street Bridge overpass.)*

The 'Jackknife Judge'

Dispensed Laughs With Justice

April 4, 1959

In the drab, uncomfortable and monotonous existence of a frontier settlement laughter is a precious commodity. People will put up with a lot just for laughs, and the community lucky enough to have a "morale boy" whose antics keep everybody chuckling hangs onto him.

That, apparently, was how LaBaye felt about Charles Reaume.

A preposterous little guy, Reaume (pronounced Rayome) was known affectionately as the "jackknife judge" who dispensed an off-beat brand of justice and a lot of laughs in the shadowy period of Green Bay's history between the Revolution and the coming of the Americans. For over 20 years he was all the law there was west of Lake Michigan.

Looked like Clown

Pompous, vain and lazy, this self-appointed charlatan not only played but looked the part of the town clown. His short, roly-poly body and bald head fitted perfectly the role he maintained with a subtle blending of venality, dignity and cheerful good nature.

How much was a carefully calculated act and how much was sincere there is no way of knowing today. Charles Reaume was clever and he knew just how far he could go without damaging his prestige and authority.

And yet, Reaume was more than the clown that history has painted him. He may have been an imposter but he wasn't a scoundrel, and he filled a need in the struggling settlement. Legitimate or not, he made a lasting contribution to the establishment of law and order in the wilderness, without which Judge James Duane Doty might have found his task much more difficult than it turned out to be.

Native of Canada, Belief

Charles Reaume first turned up at LaBaye sometime between 1790 and 1792. Nobody knew much about him, although it is now generally accepted that he was a native of Canada, where he was born near Montreal around 1752.

As a young man he deserted his wife after failing in business and skipped to the British settlement at Detroit. He was next heard from during the American Revolution as a captain of British militia in Indiana where he was captured by George Rogers Clark, paroled and presumably returned to Detroit.

Thereafter he dropped out of sight until he appeared at Green Bay with a long red coat, a bone-handled jackknife, a dog named "Robash" and very little else. The knife and coat, the latter apparently part of his old British uniform with silk facings and an elaborate array of brass buttons, became the symbols of his subsequent career. The garment, faded and threadbare, is now on exhibition in the Wisconsin Historical Museum at Madison.

Set up as Trader

For a couple of years Reaume worked for Jacques Porlier, then went to Mackinac where he promoted a stock of trade goods on credit. Returning to LaBaye he set himself up as an independent fur trader in a small cabin on Dutchman's Creek in what is now Ashwaubenon.

As a trader he was a complete bust and in no time was broke again. So far as is known he never paid for the supplies he squandered but he managed to hold on to his little farm. He didn't work very hard thereafter at being a farmer, either.

Instead he came up with a claim that he was a justice of the peace with a commission straight from King George III of England. Such a document, if he actually had one, wasn't worth the paper it was written on in territory claimed by the United States, but he made it stick.

Authority Unquestioned

He also claimed, after 1803, to have a similar commission from Gov. William Henry Harrison of the Northwest Territory, but apparently no one ever saw that either. Whatever his authority, it wasn't seriously questioned. The coterie of French traders, including Porlier, Pierre Grignon and John Lawe, who dominated the region, probably found him useful for keeping their excitable engages *(men hired by the fur traders)* in line and backed his play.

Reaume had one bulge on most of the settlers. He could read and write. He also had a battered copy of Blackstone's Commentaries which he flourished as a legal prop, although there is no evidence he ever read it or that his legal decisions were affected by it.

Knife was Summons

Most of them were based on local customs, a shrewd knowledge of events and personalities involved, his own whims and whoever got to him last. A small bribe or a little flattery carried more weight than the most logical argument.

His nickname of "jackknife judge" came from a habit of using his famous knife as a summons. When he wanted someone to appear in court he simply sent his knife and the defendant came running.

Reaume always presided over his court in bleary dignity, decked out in his red coat. His decisions were rendered in halting English, heavily larded with French, and no matter how irregular the procedure or judgment there was virtually no appeal.

A loser could appeal if he wanted to, but the appeal had to be made at Vincennes, Ind., 500 miles away. Reaume was too cagey ever to decide against anyone who could afford the expense.

He was the original "Marryin' Sam," performing marriages, baptisms and even funeral orations for a price. He made a neat and profitable little racket out of the first.

Remarried for Fee

Reaume kept a careful record of all marriages performed for illiterate voyageurs and their Indian wives. Every few years he would summon such couples, inform them their period of marriage had expired and remarry them for another fee.

He wasn't above using his court for his own benefit in other ways. Once, after declaring both parties to a dispute wrong, he ordered one to bring him a load of hay and the other to furnish a load of wood. They paid up promptly.

For all his occasional outlandish judgments and open venality, Reaume never went too far. Most of his decisions were fair and nobody ever got hurt.

Had he been at all tyrannical he wouldn't have lasted. But being essentially a kindly man who enjoyed the moment and lived well by his wits, he made everybody like him even while laughing. Even the very proper Porlier thought well of him.

Having maintained his fictional position for so many years, Reaume finally earned it legally. When Brown County was created in 1818, Gov. Lewis Cass of Michigan Territory appointed him a real justice of the peace.

Maybe the odor of such sanctity was too much for the old rascal — at any rate, he left Green Bay shortly thereafter. A few years later, in 1822, he was found dead in his lonely cabin at Little Rapids.

Curiosity in Wilderness

Porlier, Frontier Aristocrat

November 3, 1962

Jacques Porlier was something of a curiosity on the old Northwest Frontier — he was a gentleman. He must have seemed out of place at times in the crudity of the Wisconsin Wilderness, but he came because he liked it and he stayed for almost 50 years.

Born, raised and educated in the most exclusive and cultured circles of old Montreal, the suave and polished Porlier turned his back on a secure social and financial career when he was 26 and elected to spend the rest of his long life on the frontier. He had little reason for his choice except personal preference, but he never regretted it. In the long run he added more than his share to the development of the struggling settlement at LaBaye.

Jacques Porlier was born in 1765 apparently a descendent of minor French nobility. Originally intended for the priesthood, he was educated in the best Montreal schools but changed his mind and entered his family's large fur trading business instead.

In 1783 he visited the western country, fell in love with its immensity and raw beauty and in 1791 made his move. He abandoned a budding career in Montreal society to do it, having only a short time before being commissioned captain-lieutenant of militia, a post open only to the socially elect.

Grignon Clerk

Porlier came to Green Bay as a clerk for Pierre Grignon and tutor to the Grignon children, a job that probably ranks him as the first school teacher in Wisconsin. Two years later he struck out for himself as an independent fur trader. He remained in the business until shortly before his death, even while deeply involved in public affairs.

He was a business rival of John Lawe and his old employers, with whom he always remained on the most intimate terms outside business hours. He established his base of operations on the west bank of the Fox River opposite Lawe's Point *(at the west end of what is now Porlier Street)*. In 1805 he purchased the nearby house built by Joseph Roi in 1776, now famous as the Roi-Porlier-Tank Cottage, *(one of the)* oldest building*(s)* in Wisconsin.

In 1793 Porlier married Marguerite Griesie, whom he found living with her Indian mother in a Menominee village on the St. Croix River. Marguerite's father had been his predecessor as Grignon's clerk and had abandoned his family.

Porlier's marriage was different from the usual run of Indian-white common law alliances. The couple remained together for nearly half a century, Marguerite surviving him by five years. They had several children, three of whom were still living in the 1880s.

British J.P.

In 1812 Porlier was appointed British justice of the peace, a commission renewed in 1815, just before the end of the War of 1812, when he was also commissioned captain of militia at Green Bay. Nearly 50 at the time, he was too old for active service, and the appointment was probably intended to utilize his prestige in the region.

After the war Porlier took the oath of allegiance to the United States, one of the first French residents of LaBaye to do so, and became an American citizen in 1821. Meanwhile, he had been appointed to a series of important positions by territorial governors. He became an ensign of militia in 1819 and a lieutenant in 1822, although he was then 57 years old.

In September, 1820, he was appointed chief justice of Brown County, a dignity he held until the organization of Wisconsin as a territory in 1836. At the same time he functioned as justice of the peace and county commissioner.

He was also judge of probate, which office he resigned in 1822. Because he was the best educated man in the settlement, all public and business documents were drawn up by him, a service he habitually performed free of charge.

Wouldn't Speak English

Although he could read English he could not or would not speak it. A quirk that afforded later American settlers considerable amusement was his habit, when performing a marriage ceremony, of reading the service first in English and then in French. He was well aware it wasn't necessary but he just felt better doing it that way.

Another example of conscientious devotion to exactness was revealed when the old French laws were replaced by the laws of Michigan Territory in 1822. Porlier carefully and laboriously translated the entire code from English into French for his own reference and use. The handwritten manuscript is now one of the treasures of the State Historical Society.

As a fur trader Porlier was typical of the pre-American breed, open-handed and careless about costs and accounts. In partnership with Lawe and the Grignons he fell into heavy debt to the American Fur Co., to which he mortgaged his extensive land holdings in the Fox River Valley.

Lost Everything

When the company called his notes in 1834 he was unable to pay and lost everything except his cherished home. A stroke shortly after the disaster, which left his left side completely paralyzed, was believed to have been brought on by the foreclosure.

Suave, courtly and gallant, Porlier was held in considerable awe by most of his associates, who deferred to him in every way, particularly in his later years. Fully conscious of his position and titles, he was very proper and probably a little arrogant.

At least Augustin Grignon recalled years later that at every social affair — and none was complete without him — the old gentleman knew how and when to make an entrance. "On his entrance," Grignon declared to Dr. Lyman Draper, "all mirth and impertinence subsided and the company deferred to and awarded him the post of honor."

He was a man of culture and fastidious tastes, none of which ever rubbed off on the crude bark of Wisconsin's wilderness, and remarkable for the purity and elegance of his French speech. The exclusive and formal garden he personally groomed around his home was his pride and joy.

Porlier was a slight, wiry man about five feet ten inches tall, with light complexion and sandy hair. In middle age he became partly bald and his remaining hair finally turned grey. Despite the paralysis of his last three years he carried himself with great dignity to the very end.

He died after an illness of only two or three days on July 12, 1839, at the age of 74. He was probably buried in Allouez Cemetery in a section whose grave markings disintegrated years ago. Because of the complete lack of early records, the location of his grave has been lost.

**The cottage is now at Heritage Hill.*

Green Bay's Forgotten Man

Robert Stuart a Colorful Figure

January 21, 1967

A real estate scheme has been an important factor in the beginnings of virtually every American city between the Alleghenies and the Rocky Mountains and Green Bay is no exception.

Daniel Whitney is correctly regarded as the founder of Green Bay but four other men also had a lot to do with the way the city originally developed. They were John Jacob Astor, James Duane Doty, Ramsay Crooks and Robert Stuart.

Of the quartet the least remembered today is Stuart. And this is somewhat surprising, since Stuart was much better known here in his time than either Crooks or Astor. During his long term as manager of the Northern Department of the American Fur Co., with headquarters at Mackinac, Stuart was in and out of the little settlement regularly and personally knew every one of the local leaders.

Like his great friend Ramsay Crooks and so many other key figures of the American fur trade, Robert Stuart was a Scot, born in Perthshire, Scotland, Feb. 19, 1785. Except for the fact that he received what for his time was the equivalent of a good high school education, nothing is known of his early years.

Came to Montreal

At the age of 22 Stuart turned up in Montreal in 1807 to join an uncle, David Stuart, a well known and influential agent of the flourishing Northwest Fur Co. He went to work for the outfit soon after his arrival and quickly established himself as a valuable man.

In 1810 Astor, maturing his plans for a monopoly of the United States fur trade, sent William Price Hunt to Montreal to recruit Nor'Westers for the project. Both David and Robert Stuart fell in with the scheme, becoming partners in the Pacific Fur Co., which Astor organized to run the Pacific end of the business from the Columbia River valley.

Robert went on to New York to join the expedition fitting out to go to Puget Sound by sea. He took lodgings in a Brooklyn rooming house where he met an Irish girl named Elizabeth Emma Sullivan. Three years later, after his return from the West Coast, he married her.

Astoria Expedition

Meanwhile, he was destined to establish himself as a wilderness leader with the ill-fated Astoria expedition. The party left New York in September, 1810, aboard the ship Tonquin, which Astor sent around the Horn while another expedition (of which Crooks was a member) went overland along the route pioneered a few years before by Lewis and Clark.

The seven-month voyage was plagued by constant friction between the Astor party and the Tonquin's captain, a hard-nosed U.S. Navy lieutenant on leave. Stuart and Jonathan Thorn rubbed each other the wrong way, their hostility culminating in a confrontation in the Falkland Islands when the fiery Stuart pulled a gun on Thorn and threatened to shoot him if he carried out a decision to leave some of the party behind.

From then on Stuart was a key member of the party, which reached its destination in the spring of 1811. A year later, when the expedition was demonstrably a failure, Stuart was sent back overland with dispatches for Astor in New York. He was placed in charge of the party, although Crooks, who accompanied him, had already made the cross-country trip and presumably knew the country better.

Back to New York

After an extremely perilous journey, much of it through rugged country never before traversed by white men, Stuart arrived in St. Louis at the end of April, 1813. He and Crooks went on to New York, delivered the news to Astor and Robert got married.

Astor was impressed by both young men and promptly hired them. After working in the east for a couple of years, Stuart and Crooks were sent to Mackinac where Crooks headed the Northern Department of the American Fur Co. with Stuart as his assistant.

Crooks returned to New York in 1821 to become general manager of the entire operation. Stuart succeeded him at Mackinac, where he remained for 14 years.

In 1834 Astor retired, selling the Northern Department and company name to a group headed by Crooks and Stuart. It was then, in order to pay off the old man, that the two new owners foreclosed mortgages on Green Bay lands owned by traders here, stripped them of their holdings and turned them over to Astor.

Retired in 1835

Stuart did not remain long in the fur trade after that. In 1835 he sold out to Crooks and moved to Detroit. Taking a cue from Astor, he invested heavily in real estate and became active in civic, educational and church affairs.

Among his activities while an influential resident of Detroit was a short term as secretary of state for Michigan and four years as superintendent of Indian affairs for the state. Meanwhile, he became interested in a canal from Lake Michigan to the Illinois River and in the fall of 1845 he went to Chicago.

For the next few years he apparently commuted between Detroit and Chicago. He was on a visit to the latter when he took sick and died suddenly on Oct. 29, 1848. His body was returned to Detroit for burial.

Slender, Distinguished Man

There is no existing physical description of Stuart, although a portrait shows him to have been a slender, distinguished looking man. He was a tough customer, described as "stern in all things," including family discipline and religious observance.

As a young man he had been hot-headed with a low flash point but after he got religion he learned to curb his temper. Energetic, shrewd and highly efficient, he could be ruthless, although his letters to Crooks also reveal a warm-hearted, friendly side to his nature as well as a playful sense of humor.

Robert Stuart's long association with Green Bay is remembered only by two of the city's oldest streets, named for him and his wife by James Doty when the latter platted the village of Astor. Doty apparently used a family nickname of Mrs. Stuart's, though, when he called one of the streets Eliza instead of Elizabeth.

Lacked Human Touch

Daniel Whitney Austere Figure

August 25, 1962

Had Daniel Whitney possessed the human touch he might be better remembered in the city he founded. He had nearly everything else.

A canny New Englander, Whitney could command but he couldn't lead. Men admired — and envied — his success, respected his courage and trusted his rigid honesty but they were afraid of him, too. If he had gone into politics, where his possibilities of success would have been questionable, men might have accepted his generosity (in his cold way he was an extremely generous man) but they would probably have voted for someone else.

But as a businessman of ordinary and hard-eyed vision, willing to take a calculated risk and ruthless enough to see it through, Whitney had no peer in pioneer Wisconsin. In an active career of nearly 25 years he was a fur trader, store keeper, lumberman, explorer, real estate operator and transportation tycoon and a success at all of them. Even John Jacob Astor couldn't lick him.

Had he been less shrewd he wouldn't have made it. Often "land poor," he was frequently overextended and pressed for cash but always managed to land on his feet. He fully deserves Miss Alice Smith's rating as a "giant" of early Wisconsin. Miss Smith, chief researcher for the State Historical Society, is author of the most authoritative sketch of his career.

To Wisconsin in 1819

Born in Gilsum, N.H., Sept. 5, 1795, Daniel Whitney arrived in the struggling settlement of LaBaye as a young Yankee trader with a small stock of goods in 1819. He built the first American store in Wisconsin and used it as a base from which to build his far-flung business.

Alert to every opportunity, Whitney didn't stay put, thrusting into the wilderness in search of additional places to trade. He traced the Fox River to its source, explored most of the Wisconsin River area and established small outposts as far away as the Mississippi and Sault Ste. Marie.

In addition to grabbing the profitable post as sutler *(one who supplies food and drink to military posts)* to Forts Howard and Snelling he built the first sawmill on the Wisconsin River, from which he shipped lumber down the Mississippi to St. Louis, and sent his boats up and down virtually all of Wisconsin's main waterways. He not only used them for his own goods but added a tidy profit carrying cargo for others.

As the fur trade diminished Whitney turned to other phases of river shipping, gradually diverting much of the ore from the southwestern Wisconsin lead mines from the Mississippi to the Great Lakes route. He built a shot tower at Helena, which is now a historical monument, to melt lead into more convenient shapes for handling and in one season sent 12,000 pounds of metal through Green Bay to Detroit.

Ran Cranberry Bog

He was storekeeper and business agent for the Stockbridge Indians for years and also operated a profitable cranberry bog. The berries, harvested by Indians, were sold in St. Louis.

As he spread out Whitney began picking up land titles. He acquired most of the land along the portage between the Fox and Wisconsin Rivers and in 1834 headed a company to build a canal there. The canal was years going through but meanwhile Whitney made a cleanup in real estate sales.

He could operate on such a scale because he commanded capital, although nobody is sure where it came from. He was also a colonizer as well as a trader. From the beginning of his Wisconsin career he imported large gangs of Canadians to work for him, built them houses and ruled them with a tight rein.

This proprietary attitude backfired once. In 1833 a number of his boatmen precipitated what Miss Smith calls the first strike in Wisconsin by refusing to work. Whitney had the whole lot arrested, tried and convicted as "stubborn servants." Since there was no jail they were sold to the highest bidder to work without pay for two months.

Lasting Achievement

Although he promoted Wisconsin's first real estate development at Shantytown in Allouez, Whitney's lasting achievement was the platting of the village of Navarino in 1829 at the junction of the Fox and East rivers. Everybody thought he was crazy, but he partially drained the swampland, laid out streets and built a dock, warehouse and hotel. He even gave lots to his workmen to encourage settlement.

Despite earlier skepticism, Shantytown's residents gradually drifted into Navarino. In 1836 *(1835)* James Doty acknowledged the success of the venture by laying out the rival village of Astor directly south of the new settlement, but Whitney refused to be lured into a real estate war. Three years later the two hamlets consolidated peacefully into the village of Green Bay *(1838)*.

About 1850 Whitney abandoned his competitive operations and went into semi-retirement, content to watch his town grow and manage his statewide real estate holdings. That year he inventoried his Green Bay properties alone at $150,000.

For the rest of his life he played the part of village squire, aloof from Green Bay's growing pains and looking down his nose at its rising attorney-politicians. Not that he had no use for lawyers — he kept Morgan L. Martin busy for years suing everybody from the commanding officer of Ft. Howard to his recalcitrant Canucks.

Lived in Style

Whitney lived in style but not as impressively as he wished. An elaborate four-story mansion *(some accounts describe it as three stories)*, later dubbed "Whitney's Folly," foundered on his wife's refusal to live in it and was never completed. Instead, he maintained a dignified establishment in a rambling cottage on a large private estate on Main Street across from Whitney Park. *(More recent research shows the residence at 118 Main St., the southwest corner of what was then Main and Madison Streets.)* The cottage was a city landmark until it was torn down in 1897.

The Whitneys had seven children, three of whom died in infancy. Only one of his three sons, Joshua Whitney, remained in Green Bay. Daniel H. moved to Menasha and William B. to Philadelphia.

"Josh" was the grandfather of George Whitney Calhoun *(see 'Oldest Packer' Passes On, Chapter 8, page 268)* and Daniel the grandfather of Mrs. Eldridge C. (Harriet Bell) Jacobi. Calhoun and Mrs. Jacobi are the only direct descendants of the city's founder still living in Green Bay — in fact, the last time the original Whitney cottage was used was for the wedding reception of Mrs. Jacobi's parents, shortly before its destruction in 1897.

Daniel Whitney died Nov. 4, 1862, and was buried with considerable fanfare in the old cemetery where Baird Place is now maintained, his body eventually being moved to Woodlawn. His wife, a kindly, charitable woman who not only belied the haughty nickname of "Queen of Navarino" but also seems to have been unimpressed by her husband's reputation, survived him until 1890.

Pioneer Boat Builder

John Arndt, Man of Many Talents

March 28, 1959

John Penn Arndt was a big, phlegmatic German whose mild manner, serene, calm and gentle friendliness fooled a lot of people. Behind this benign front he was tough, aggressive and blessed with a gambler's imagination. In a Green Bay career of nearly four decades these qualities repaid him with wealth, influence and affection from the frontier community he helped to build into a growing, prosperous city.

He had courage, too. It took courage to sever roots that had grown deep for nearly a century, especially for a man crowding middle age and burdened with heavy family responsibilities.

Arndt was 44 years old when he arrived in Green Bay in 1824. By the time he died in 1861 he had achieved a remarkable number of successful "firsts" in a wide variety of enterprises. John P. Arndt deserves more from state and local history than either has ever accorded his memory.

List of Firsts

Among his firsts were the distinctions of being the first licensed tavern-keeper in Wisconsin, the first ferry operator on the Fox River, builder of the first flatboat, first decked scow and first sailing vessel in the state, as well as the first sawmill and brickyard near Green Bay. He almost got the honor of launching the first steam boat but abandoned that after nearly blowing himself up.

He was born Nov. 20, 1780, at Easton, Pa., where his German ancestors had settled almost 100 years earlier. As a young man he ran an inn and built flatboats at Wilkes-Barre, Pa., so successfully that he might never have migrated to Wisconsin had he not been wiped out financially in the depression following the War of 1812.

Nearly 40 years of age, broke and with a wife and five kids, he decided to cut his losses and try his luck in the west. In 1819 he loaded his family and household goods into three covered wagons and headed for the Great Lakes.

Came Here in 1824

He stopped first at Buffalo, N.Y., where he engaged in the fish and fur trade until he had enough of a stake to shift again, first to Mackinac Island in 1822, then to Green Bay two years later. By this time he was well enough fixed to buy the historic DeLanglade-Grignon trading post on the site of the *(former)* Wisconsin Public Service bus barns *(on Washington Street)*, which he converted into a tavern.

He was issued the first license to a tavern keeper in Wisconsin in 1825. Later that year he also was licensed to run a ferry service across the Fox River.

The latter operation quickly brought him into conflict with military authorities at Fort Howard. The commanding officer, attempting to regulate river traffic, first refused him permission to land near the fort, then ordered all traffic to check in at the post for clearance. Arndt refused.

The irate commander hauled him off the river at bayonet point and tossed him temporarily into the post guardhouse, an indignity for which Arndt promptly brought suit. The case, decided in his favor, was important in establishing the supremacy of civil law over arbitrary military regulation. Of more satisfaction to Arndt was the award of $50 damages.

Builds Durham Boat

Having made flatboats back East, Arndt built one of a type called the Durham boat, the first seen west of the Lakes. This craft could operate in shallow rivers with half the crew and twice the capacity of the bateaux then in common use at a sustained speed of three miles an hour. The Durham boats, which also inaugurated a profitable boat building business for Arndt, revolutionized river traffic in Wisconsin.

In 1827 he posted another first when he set up a sawmill on the west bayshore several miles north of Fort Howard, paying the Menominees $15 a year to log their forests. The mill was a veritable gold mine, and in 1834 it produced the first load of finished lumber ever sent from Green Bay to Chicago. Meanwhile, he also built a brickyard near Pensaukee.

Converted to Scow

His attempt to build a steamboat in 1829 almost ended disastrously, so he converted it into a decked scow, the first in Wisconsin. In 1836 he sent the state's first homemade sailing vessel, the 140-ton schooner "Wisconsin," down the waterways.

Transportation was always one of his principal interests. As a flatboat man he was early concerned with river improvements and was an original stockholder in the Portage Canal Co., chartered in 1834. He was also involved in the Fox and Wisconsin River Improvement Co. that completed the first trans-Wisconsin waterway, and fulfilled several lucrative contracts for it. He was too cagey, however, to be caught in the financial trap that ruined Morgan L. Martin.

All his life he was mixed up in canal, plank road and railroad schemes. There wasn't a company launched for such purposes in which he wasn't a key figure, especially railroads, although he died a year before the Iron Horse reached Green Bay.

Obtained Bridge Approval

He was a leader in the first attempt to bridge the Fox River at Green Bay and actually obtained state approval for a bridge here. Refusal of the Legislature to pick up the tab for it delayed construction until after his death.

As a leader among the French fur traders, with whom he was closely associated in everything except the loose business methods that eventually ruined them, his fur trading establishment was once second in size only to

Daniel Whitney's. When the American Fur Co. moved in, however, he bowed out.

When he wasn't coming up with something new, Arndt was deep in territorial and local politics.

He served on the first Wisconsin territorial council and then in the first legislatures. He was twice county probate judge, a member and twice chairman of the county board and four times a city alderman.

Among First Aldermen

He was one of the South Ward's first aldermen when the city got its charter in 1854 and served additional terms in 1856-57 and 1859. He was chairman of the county board in 1854 and again in 1859.

When his son Charles C. P. Arndt was shot and killed on the floor of the Legislature in 1842, the father — who was a witness to the tragedy — was appointed to fill the son's unexpired term as probate judge and was subsequently appointed for another term in 1848-49.

The fatal shooting of young Arndt was one of two filial tragedies to hit the aging man. Another son, Alexander Hamilton Arndt, died in Texas while serving as a volunteer in the Mexican war.

In his last years Arndt was an institution around Green Bay, a gentle, popular old man whose great influence was tempered by a cheerful friendliness that endeared him to everyone. The Green Bay Advocate had no compunctions about giving him a good natured ribbing on occasion.

John P. Arndt died at the age of 81 on June 10, 1861. Throughout the city flags flew at half mast in his honor.

Spectacular Failure?

Doty's Puzzling Career

June 11, 1960

James Duane Doty — judge, territorial governor and land speculator in the grand tradition — was a great figure in early Wisconsin history. A colorful, charming and commanding personality, he was one of the state's most astute political leaders of the early 19th Century. He was also a failure. Why a man with his gifts should have failed after such a spectacular start is one of the fascinating puzzles of Midwestern history.

He was born in Salem, N.Y., Nov. 5, 1799, but grew up in the frontier York State town of Martinsburgh where his father was a leading political figure and hotel keeper and his mother a sister of the town's founder. Doty and Morgan L. Martin, another great figure of early Wisconsin, were first cousins and very close as young men, although they later became bitter political enemies.

Not much is known of Doty's boyhood and youth prior to his arrival in Detroit in 1818. A handsome, strapping six-footer with great personal charm, he quickly became well known in the future motor metropolis, then a hamlet of less than 800 population.

Held Civic Posts

Admitted to the bar shortly after his 19th birthday, he occupied a number of minor civic positions and attracted the attention of Michigan's territorial governor, Lewis Cass, later Andrew Jackson's Secretary of War. For the rest of Cass' life Doty had an ardent and powerful backer.

It was largely due to Cass' influence that young Doty got the appointment as federal judge for that part of Michigan Territory west of the Lake. That was in 1823 when he was only 24 years old.

Judge Doty arrived at the little frontier community near the military post of Fort Howard in the fall of 1824. He remained a resident of the Fox River Valley for nearly 40 years, carving for himself one of the most controversial careers in the valley's long history.

Wed Childhood Friend

Before coming to Wisconsin, however, he returned to New York and married Sarah Collins, a childhood friend. Sarah Doty is a shadowy figure in her husband's checkered career. Not much is remembered about her but she was always beside him, quiet, gracious and very capable.

Doty found his district a forest wilderness dominated by the military and a group of independently minded fur traders accustomed to running their own show. Through a combination of personality, charm and arbitrary command the youthful judge changed all that. Some of his methods were unnecessarily officious and gained him implacable enemies, but he established the supremacy of civil law in a region that had previously recognized only force.

Enemies Succeeded

He remained on the bench until 1832 when those enemies, particularly among the Army officers he had antagonized, engineered his removal. By then he was a figure of consequence in the territory. He was also deep in land speculation, a game in which his exceptional knowledge of the future state was invaluable.

In 1835 he made more enemies when, acting for John Jacob Astor and Ramsey Crooks, he foreclosed mortgages on the Green Bay fur traders, took away their extensive lands and platted the Village of Astor in competition to Daniel Whitney's Navarino. The Panic of 1837 spoiled the makings of a lively land war and two years later the rival towns combined to form the nucleus of Green Bay. *(The consolidation occurred in 1838.)*

Involved Everywhere

Astor wasn't his only real estate operation. He was involved all over the state and owned choice parcels everywhere. The panic caught him overextended, his enemies closed in and he was eventually forced to give up most of his holdings to escape utter failure and disgrace. Today those one-time holdings are worth millions.

In 1834 Doty was elected to the Michigan legislature where he was a leader in drafting the petition that made Wisconsin a separate territory. He was out of office when the first Badger legislature met at Belmont in 1836, but as a private lobbyist he performed one of the greatest coups of his life when he engineered the choice of Madison as the capital. How he did it is a story in itself.

Rival of Gov. Dodge

By this time he was a formidable rival to the supremacy of Gov. Henry Dodge. Wisconsin's 12-year period as a territory was largely a struggle between them, the balance swinging first one way and then the other.

Elected delegate to Congress in 1837 and again in 1839, Doty used his position to unseat Dodge as governor, a post to which he himself was appointed by President Tyler in 1841. Dodge then went to Washington where he repeated the maneuver and Doty was out in 1844.

His three years as governor were stormy. He was on the sidelines when his cherished dream of statehood became a reality but he was promptly elected to Congress from the Green Bay district and served three terms.

Defeated for the Senate in 1851 and again in 1855, Doty's political career in Wisconsin was finished. He retired to his home on Doty Island, now part of Menasha, where he lived until 1861. Little is known of his activities in those years, but he was apparently dealing successfully in real estate and growing old gracefully.

Took Utah Post

In 1861 President Lincoln appointed him superintendent of Indian affairs in Utah. Again he was called on to exercise all his charm, personality and political savvy in dealing with the powerful and suspicious Mormon oligarchy.

He succeeded so well that he was named governor of Utah Territory in 1863. A completely new career was apparently opening when he died suddenly on June 13, 1865 — 95 years ago — at Salt Lake City and was buried in the army cemetery at Fort Douglas, Utah.

For all his ability, James Doty is one of the most difficult of early Wisconsin leaders to analyze. He had exceptional gifts and vision but his character, motives and actions are a mass of contradictions.

He never explained his motives, some of his actions — so far as anyone has ever been able to unravel them — were downright crooked, and his enemies had the last word. Since someone — one wonders if his widow had a hand in it — destroyed all his private papers, his stature will probably never be assessed.

Even his biographer, Miss Alice E. Smith of the State Historical Society, couldn't quite make up her mind. Perhaps the best estimate was that of a Madison editor who wrote at Doty's death that his greatest gifts were also his biggest handicaps.

No Whitewashing

Charming Rogue Left Own Story

April 11, 1959

History has an annoying and unwarranted enthusiasm for wielding a whitewash brush. Any pioneer who attains material success is liable to be so smeared as to be unrecognizable to his best friends — to say nothing of his own embarrassment.

Fortunately, every so often a hardy soul appears who refuses to hold still for the treatment. No matter how hard they try, misguided descendants can't make such a charming rogue respectable, and the history of a community is the richer for the failure.

Ebenezer Childs was like that. An individualist if ever there was one, he combined most of the virtues with many of the vices of a frontiersman. Childs was a lusty, colorful personality, and when the time came he took care of history by getting in the first licks himself. As an old man he wrote his own story, and a delightful one it is, too.

Lived by his Wits

One of the earliest American settlers in Green Bay, Childs would be better known today if he had stayed around. But he left after 25 years for more open pastures, possibly because the place was getting too crowded and stuffy for his taste.

If Ebenezer Childs didn't qualify as a pillar of propriety, it was understandable. Orphaned at an early age, he lived thereafter by his wits, and he did all right.

Childs was born in Worcester County, Mass., April 3, 1797. His parents died before he was 10 and he was on his own. He managed so well that by the time he was 19 he was drawing down the then princely wage of 50 cents a day.

Left to Avoid Tax

He might never have left his home town if an overzealous tax collector hadn't tried to hit him up for a minister tax. Ebenezer couldn't see it, stalled as long as he dared, then took off.

Evading taxes in early New England was serious enough, but young Childs compounded the offense by running away on Sunday when he was supposed to be in church. He successfully eluded the hue and cry, however, and made his way to New York.

For the next few years he was apparently on the bum, working westward through New York and Ohio. Early in 1820 he turned up in Detroit where he was hired by a merchant named Brown to take a stock of groceries and trade goods to LaBaye and open a store. Childs arrived in Shantytown in May, 1820, and went into business. He had just turned 23.

Sly Whisky Smuggler

A shrewd youngster who had come up the hard way, Childs was a good trader. He quickly got in bad with the military authorities at Ft. Howard because his most lucrative traffic was selling liquor to the soldiers of the garrison. He had a trick of smuggling whisky into the post that worked for months, and although the post commander knew he was doing it he never could catch him.

He was always in hot water with the military. A stubborn, hot-headed young man who had been around, he didn't scare easily and when, as he liked to put it, he "got his Ebenezer up" was hard to handle. More than once the defiant youngster invited the army brass to go fly a kite and got away with it.

Childs' ace in the hole was that he stood in well with the other traders, who also had their troubles with the military. Within a year he was working for Daniel Whitney, for whom he built a store-somewhere along the way he had become a competent carpenter — and who thought well enough of him to send him on business missions as far as St. Louis.

Constructed Sawmill

Being fiercely independent, Childs never stayed too long with any one employer. At one time or another he worked for Whitney, John P. Arndt, James Doty and William Dickinson, although he described his association with the latter as a partnership. In 1825 he built the first frame house in Wisconsin for Judge Doty, and in 1827 supervised the construction of Arndt's sawmill on the west bay shore.

That same year he helped Dickinson raise a company of Indian scouts for the Winnebago War and two years later entered some sort of a business arrangement with him. Whether it was a partnership is uncertain, but he followed Dickinson to what is now De Pere and apparently prospered there.

Won First Case

Meanwhile, he had become active in local affairs and soon entered politics. He was plaintiff in the first jury trial ever held at Green Bay and won his case, although years later he couldn't remember what the fuss was about. He was on the jury that acquitted Chief Oshkosh of murder* and in 1824 was a juryman and witness in Doty's drive against common law marriages.

Before that campaign was over Childs wound up before the grand jury himself on the same charges, but his friends didn't try very hard to convict him. He got off, but there seems to have been some fire under the smoke.

Childs was an active man in those years. He traveled all over Wisconsin, was commissioner of a road building project on the east side of the Fox River to Kaukauna, and he took Arndt's first Durham boat on its maiden trip up the river, across the portage and down the Wisconsin and Mississippi to St. Louis. On the way back he brought the first cargo of lead from the mines at Galena, Ill., to Green Bay. Meanwhile he found time to marry a daughter of Augustin Grignon.

Named Postmaster

He was living at Kaukauna in 1829 when he was appointed postmaster there as well as sheriff of Brown County. He only held the postmastership one year but served as sheriff until 1836 when he was elected to the first territorial Legislature.

Childs remained in the Legislature until 1840, but his only significant contribution to its deliberations seems to have been his carpentry skill. This came in handy during the first session at Madison where the unfinished capitol was so drafty the legislators had to recess while he plugged up some of the cracks.

In his recollections he delighted in telling how he used to shut off debate when it got too long-winded. He would, according to his story, stir up a herd of pigs in the cellar with a long pole until their squeals drowned out the speaker.

Childs left Green Bay about 1845, moved about the Lake Superior region for a couple of years, lived in Milwaukee briefly and finally settled at La Crosse in 1852. Apparently he became a figure of some consequence there too, being a member of the county board in 1853.

Thereafter he dropped out of community activity. Except for his charming reminiscences, written for Dr. Lyman Draper in 1858, there is no further mention of him in state historical records. Even the date of his death is not recorded.

** In fact, Judge Doty overturned the jury's guilty verdict and, on his own advisement, acquitted Chief Oshkosh.*

'Father of the Wisconsin Bar'

Success Story of Henry S. Baird

August 12, 1967

Henry S. Baird didn't build a spectacular fortune and he didn't go into politics, although he might easily have been successful at both, but none of his pioneer contemporaries in Green Bay exceeded the respect in which he was held and none came close to being as generally well liked.

The first practicing attorney in Wisconsin, Baird has been called the "father of the Wisconsin Bar." His entire career was bound up in the development of Green Bay, which he lived to see transformed from a rough wilderness community to a prosperous city during his half century of residence.

Baird made it the hard way. Born in Dublin, Ireland, May 16, 1800, he was a poor boy whose financial difficulties forced him early to look out for himself. He was brought to America at the age of five and only managed to become a lawyer (somewhat against his will) after long and sporadic study.

He had to quit school at the age of 15 and never went back. After the family moved to Pittsburgh in 1818 he began to read law but the necessity of earning a living delayed completion of his studies for five years.

Taught School

In 1822 he went to Mackinac where he taught school and continued his legal reading in his spare time. The following year he was admitted to the bar by James Duane Doty, newly appointed judge of Michigan Territory, and in 1824 he accompanied Doty to Shantytown (Green Bay) where he attended the first court term held in Wisconsin.

The young lawyer hung out his shingle in Shantytown later that year after marrying Elizabeth Fisher. The marriage was accomplished in the face of some parental opposition, since he had little to recommend him except personality and future hopes. Besides, his sweetheart was only 14.

The marriage proved a long and happy one, however. The child bride, who had lived all her life on the frontier, adapted herself easily to the crude surroundings of Shantytown and quickly established herself as a charming hostess.

Prospered at Law

Once started on his legal career, Baird prospered. Unlike many of his friends he did not succumb to the fever of land speculation, being content with the considerable and certain fees that went with handling the involved legal procedures. Besides, he had learned the value of a dollar and never had enough to gamble with.

By 1840 he had succeeded Doty as local agent for John Jacob Astor. He continued to represent the Astor interests in Green Bay for the rest of his active life.

In 1835 he moved from Shantytown to Navarino, although he had previously incurred the wrath of founder Daniel Whitney by calling the place a mud hole. The Bairds settled initially on the site of the Minahan-McCormick Building but shortly moved to the corner of Monroe and Main Street where the Edlo Arcade *(once stood)*.

Built Home

Here, in 1836, he built his home and the small law office that is now his memorial on the Cotton House grounds *(Heritage Hill)* in Allouez. The area, then surrounded by swampland, eventually became the finest residential section in the growing city.

Baird quickly became a leader in the little community although he never engaged directly in politics. After the creation of Wisconsin Territory in 1836 he was appointed the first attorney general and was president of the first legislative council, held at Belmont that same year.

He shortly resigned the attorney generalship rather than investigate the affairs of Green Bay's first bank, the Bank of Wisconsin. In 1836, also, he was secretary to Gov. Henry Dodge at a treaty meeting with the Menominees and during the Black Hawk War he served as quartermaster general of territorial militia, although there is no record that he actually took the field.

Mayor in 1861-62

He remained active in local affairs, being president of the village board in 1853 and mayor of Green Bay in 1861-62. The latter office was one of the few for which he ever ran and only then because he was virtually drafted. While mayor, Baird was forced to take action against the draft rioters of 1862, during which disgruntled Belgian immigrants ran Sen. Tim Howe out of town.

Baird retired from law practice in 1860, for the last several years of his career being president of the State Bar Association, which he took the lead in forming. During his long legal career he had appeared on one side or the other in most of the important cases of the day, including the famous murder trial of Chief Oshkosh.

Retirement did not end his civic activity, however, since his term as mayor followed. Despite his age he was chairman of the relief campaign following the Peshtigo Fire in 1871.

Brought Rufus Kellogg

One of his last acts was to persuade Rufus Kellogg to come to Green Bay in 1874 and establish a bank, for which he served as a director and legal advisor. He was an enthusiastic Mason, a charter member of the first Wisconsin lodge, its high priest in 1855 and grand master in 1857.

A charming and sociable Irishman with an earthy sense of humor, Baird was a congenial man with a flair for entertaining. In this field he was ably abetted by his wife, and for years the Baird home was a center of society.

Some time in the late 1830s or early 1840s he started the practice of open house on New Year's Day, a delightful local tradition that flourished for nearly half a century. He was also in demand as a toastmaster at public banquets and as a speaker on Wisconsin history.

Last Public Appearance

An example of the respect and affection in which he was held occurred in the spring elections of 1875. When, a very sick man with only a few weeks to live, he was driven to the polls to vote, the ballot box was carried out to his carriage so he wouldn't have to dismount.

Baird dropped his ballot in the box to the applause of a quickly gathered crowd, grinned feebly at them and was driven home. It was the last time he ever appeared in public.

His death on April 28, 1875, was expected, but the entire city felt a sense of personal loss and genuine grief.

*Heritage Hill.

Lawyer, Politician, Soldier

Rise and Fall of Morgan Martin

December 19, 1959

Five men stand out in the early development of Green Bay from a wilderness trading post to a civilized, prosperous community. They are Daniel Whitney, James Duane Doty, Henry S. Baird, John Penn Arndt and Morgan L. Martin.

The last-named was the youngest, the next to last to arrive, and he outlived the others by many years. A lawyer, land speculator, politician and eventually a judge, he attained early and spectacular success, only to be financially ruined while successfully carrying out the most enduring project of his career. It left him a discouraged and beaten man.

Morgan Lewis Martin was born in Martinsburgh, N.Y., March 31, 1805, of a wealthy and distinguished family. His grandfather had founded the town, which was named for him. Morgan Martin graduated from Hamilton College in 1824, studied law for a couple of years, then spit the silver spoon out of his mouth and headed for Detroit, where he was admitted to the bar in 1826.

Cousin of Doty

In May 1827 at the suggestion of his cousin, Judge James Doty, he came to Wisconsin where he opened a law office in Shantytown and became legal advisor to the little community. He was soon deeply involved in the popular frontier pastimes of land speculation and politics.

Two years later Martin accompanied Doty on a cross-country trip to Prairie du Chien, probably the first overland journey by white men across central Wisconsin. In 1833 he visited the future site of Milwaukee where he met Solomon Juneau.

The two formed a partnership as owners of a fat slice of the land now occupied by Wisconsin's largest city and two years later platted the Village of Milwaukee. Martin apparently didn't have too much faith in its future and got out of the arrangement in 1836. He made a substantial profit on the transaction but it was only a fraction of what he would have collected had he held on.

Active Politically

Meanwhile he was increasingly active in politics. In 1829 he was secretary of the first public meeting ever held in Green Bay, and when the rival villages of Astor and Navarino consolidated to form Green Bay he became the first village president.

From 1831 to 1835 he was a member of the Michigan territorial council, serving as its president the last two years. When Wisconsin became a separate territory he served in its territorial council from 1838 until 1844, twice acting as presiding officer. He drew up the resolutions expelling James Vineyard from the territorial legislature after the fatal shooting of Charles C. P. Arndt.

Martin declined reelection to the council in 1844 but the next year was elected Delegate to Congress where he introduced the enabling act that brought statehood to Wisconsin as well as nursing through another bill giving the territory land grants which, upon admission as a state, would permit financing the long sought Fox and Wisconsin Rivers improvement project.

Despite the fact that his prestige was never higher, particularly in Northeastern Wisconsin, downstate opposition blocked his renomination in 1846. Back home again he presided over the 1847 constitutional convention that produced the state constitution, most of the preliminary work having been done at his home in Green Bay. *(While Martin might have done some preliminary work at home, there is no known documentation one way or the other.)* The table on which the document *(supposedly)* was drafted is now in the Fort Howard Hospital Museum. *(The table is at Hazelwood Museum, 1008 South Monroe.)*

That accomplished, he turned his attention to the big ambition of his life — opening the water route across the state to the Mississippi via the Fox and Wisconsin Rivers. As early as 1829 he had been pushing the scheme and as a member of the Michigan territorial government was actively working for it. It could almost be said that his whole career was bound up in the waterway.

Employed 500 Men

After the state had tried and failed to complete the project, Martin stepped forward in 1851 with an offer to finish the job himself, the state to pay him for the work through land sales. The proposition was accepted and Martin plunged into the task, putting 500 men to work between Green Bay and Lake Winnebago.

A change of administration in 1852 completely altered the picture, and from then on the work was beset on all sides by obstacles as the state tried to get out from under its contract. Martin persevered, however, pouring his entire personal fortune into the task.

The job was completed in 1856 but the state welshed on its word and Martin was financially ruined. He never really recovered and never really seemed to care after that. In a series of attempts to get what was coming to him he returned to the state Assembly in 1855 and went to the Senate in 1858, but got nowhere.

Served in Army

When the Civil War began he entered the Army and served for four years as a paymaster. He came out a major but was ranked by his son Leonard, a West Point graduate and career officer, who wore colonel's eagles. In 1863 he was again elected to the Assembly.

In the congressional election of 1866 Martin ran for the House as a Democrat. The campaign stirred up a bitter newspaper war locally since C. D. Robinson, editor of the staunchly Democratic Advocate, had no use for him and wound up backing Republican

Philetus Sawyer while the equally Republican Gazette supported Martin. Sawyer, representative of the rising lumbering interests, won handily.

Martin then accepted an appointment as Indian agent, a big comedown from his former position, but he needed the salary. He held the job until Grant came into office. He then returned to his long neglected law practice but couldn't resist one last crack at politics. In 1873 he was again elected to the Assembly for one term.

Criticized for Running

In 1875 he ran for county judge. His last minute entry into the race after he had previously endorsed the other candidate brought him considerable criticism and probably cost him the Green Bay vote but he was strong enough in the rest of the county to squeak through in front.

Thereafter he was never seriously challenged, presiding with great dignity until his death on Dec. 10, 1887, at the age of 82.

As the last of the original American pioneers Martin became almost an institution in his lifetime — perhaps that's why he is so difficult to assess as a personality. Contemporary biographical sketches are so laudatory they swamp him in whitewash.

Daughter Said Little

Although he figured so prominently in early Wisconsin history, nowhere is there found a candid description of him or a straightforward estimate of his character. It may or may not be significant, but his daughter Deborah's "History of Brown County," while mentioning him frequently is pointedly silent about what sort of man he really was.

Martin is described in one eulogy as a man of "generous impulses," keen wit, intelligence, great culture and a pillar of integrity — in short, too good to be true. He was apparently a good lawyer, a sharp speculator, generally respected and honest, but not a popular leader. The suspicion won't down that he was, at least in his later years, something of a stuffed shirt.

Senator and Cabinet Member

T. O. Howe Long Forgotten

April 16, 1960

Although the Green Bay region is the oldest settled area in Wisconsin and much of the state's early history was made here, the neighborhood has been weak in the production of state and national leaders. Except for territorial governor James Duane Doty, no state executive has come from Green Bay *(until John W. Reynolds who served from 1963-65),* the city has sent few representatives to Congress and only a handful of the national figures Wisconsin has produced have been home grown.

It is surprising, therefore, that Green Bay's most outstanding national political figure, its only United States senator and sole resident to become a cabinet member, has been almost completely forgotten. On the record, Postmaster General Timothy Otis Howe deserves a better place in the city's history than the almost forgotten distinction of having an elementary school named after him.

The record is pretty impressive. Tim Howe was not only a senator for 18 years, he was a key figure in President Chester A. Arthur's cabinet — or would have been had he lived- and a prominent lawyer in his early career. He could have been ambassador to Great Britain and Chief Justice of the United States but he declined both honors.

Like so many early state leaders, Howe was a New Englander. He was born in Livermore, Maine, Feb. 24, 1816, the son of a forthright Yankee doctor who was kicked out of his church for contrary religious convictions. All his life the son showed the same stubbornness about things he believed in.

Timothy received an "academic" education, was admitted to the bar in 1837 and before he was 30 had achieved success as a lawyer and budding politician. In fact, by moving to Wisconsin Howe may have turned his back on a brilliant career in his home state, having just been elected to the Maine Legislature. He did all right in any event.

To Green Bay in 1845

Howe was 29, married and the father of two children when he decided to come west in 1845. He chose Green Bay because his brother-in-law lived here. The fact that so many of the city's pioneer lawyers were devoting more and more time to politics may also have convinced him that the growing town was a good spot for an up and coming legal eagle to hang his shingle.

He quickly established himself as an able lawyer and was soon accepted in the best social circles. He had already had a taste of politics, however, and was soon back in the game up to his ears.

In 1850 he was elected a state circuit judge, a post that also gave him a seat on the supreme bench. He lost that position when the supreme court was reconstituted as a separate body in 1852 but remained on the circuit until 1855 when he resigned to devote most of his time to the growing Republican Party.

Originally a Whig, Howe threw himself wholeheartedly into the new political alignment and made stump speeches all over Wisconsin. A forceful but not brilliant speaker, he acquired a reputation and a considerable following.

Elected to Senate

It is said he could have been elected to the Senate in 1857 but for his uncompromising views on states' rights. Wisconsin was sharply divided on the issue but Howe was unflinching in his opposition to any compromise under the threat of southern secession.

In 1861, however, he was chosen by the Legislature as a Union Republican senator and took his seat as the country was drifting into civil war. He immediately stood out as a vigorous backer of the government's right to fight for preservation of the Union and was soon tangling with prominent Southern senators whose states had not yet seceded.

Throughout the war Howe was an aggressive advocate of fighting to a finish. It made him unpopular in some quarters, particularly among new immigrants who objected to being drafted and who held him responsible for the national and state conscription acts.

In 1862, while home on a visit, Howe was the center of a local draft riot that almost resulted in serious violence. Several hundred armed Belgian immigrants from the Towns of Green Bay and Scott marched on the city prepared to mob him.

Shaken but determined to face them down, Howe tried to address them from his front porch on Main Street, but the ugly crowd couldn't understand English. The situation became increasingly dangerous before he was persuaded to duck for cover. He was spirited out the back door while someone harangued the crowd out front in Belgian long enough for him to make a getaway.

The war over, Howe was reelected in 1867 and again in 1873. He was one of the most influential men in the Senate and seriously considered for a post in Grant's cabinet.

Offered Ambassadorship

Grant did offer him the ambassadorship to London – then as now the plum of the diplomatic service – but Howe turned it down. He was not a wealthy man and didn't feel he could maintain the position in the style it demanded.

He was later offered the Chief Justiceship but declined that too. Wisconsin had just gone Democratic and he knew a Democrat would be named to his Senate seat. Although it was a great personal sacrifice, he felt he could do more for his party in the Senate than on the Supreme Court.

He didn't run for reelection in 1879, returning to Green Bay where he reopened his long neglected law practice. He even bought a farm and made noises about working it seriously, but it wasn't long before he was on his way again.

In April, 1881, President Garfield appointed him a delegate to an international monetary conference in Paris. He was called home from France in July by the fatal illness of his wife, who died in Washington on Aug. 1.

His children having married and settled in the East, Howe returned alone to Green Bay, but again he didn't stay long. The assassination of Garfield, who died in September, brought Chester A. Arthur to the White House. When Arthur asked him to be postmaster general Howe accepted and returned to Washington.

Died of Pneumonia

Two years later, while visiting a nephew in Kenosha, he contracted pneumonia and died there unexpectedly on March 24, 1883. His body was returned to Green Bay, where he was buried in Woodlawn Cemetery after an impressive public funeral, next to his old friend John Cotton.

In spite of his long and distinguished career there isn't much information on Timothy O. Howe in Green Bay archives beyond the standard eulogies always accorded an influential citizen. His personality, as a result, is difficult to pin down.

He seems to have been a man of courage and integrity, a conscientious statesman as well as a politician. Politically he was a rock-hewn, conservative Republican who put party loyalty and regularity above everything else. None of the scandals of the Grant Administration ever touched him.

Howe was a tall, spare and dignified man with striking, handsome features, witty and sociable, although his wit doesn't shine through the texts of his prepared speeches. He was kindly but could freeze when he wanted to, and he frequently adopted a dead pan, poker expression that baffled opponents. In some circles he was dubbed "Marble Face."

About all that remains to remind Green Bay of his career is a slender unpretentious tombstone in Woodlawn, its epitaph facing away from the narrow road that passes within arm's length; an unimportant street named for him, and Howe School. The long defunct T. O. Howe Post of the Grand Army of the Republic was also named in his honor, but it is doubtful that more than a handful of graduates of Howe Elementary School have the foggiest idea of the man for whom it was named.

Nils Otto Tank

Aristocrat in Frontier Green Bay

December 5, 1959

Green Bay used to do a lot of bragging about the fact that it once numbered among its prominent early characters a man who, if he was what many believed him to be, should have been King of France. But Fort Howard, in the days of its bitter municipal rivalry with Green Bay, liked to counter with a resident who likewise almost wore a crown.

Actually, Nils *(also spelled Niels)* Otto Tank probably came closer to ascending a European throne than did Eleazer Williams.

Tank is only vaguely remembered today as one of the owners of historic Roi-Porlier-Tank Cottage and as a Moravian missionary who attempted unsuccessfully to establish a religious-communal settlement here over a century ago. Yet had the ambitions of his father been realized he would have become monarch of his native Norway.

Leader Against King

The elder Tank was in a position to swing it, too. A member of an old and powerful Norwegian family — his son was the last male of the line — he was prime minister of Norway and Denmark during the era of Napoleon. He was a leader in the deposition of his king and of the split between the two countries.

It is said that he had high hopes his son, a brilliant, well educated and personable young courtier, would be chosen to rule an independent Norway. But the subsequent union with Sweden ruined the scheme and Napoleon's Marshal Bernadotte was elected king instead. *(Later research suggests there is little or no basis for Tank's supposed royal background.)*

Otto Tank became a missionary and ultimately an American business man.

Born in Luxury

Tank was born in almost regal luxury in 1800. Carefully trained for a high, if not the highest, position in Norway, he traveled extensively about the courts of Europe in his youth until he was painfully injured in an accident in the hills of Saxony.

He was nursed back to health in the home of a Moravian minister. During his convalescence he fell in love with the minister's daughter and married her.

Legend had it that he renounced his regal aspirations for love and that his disgusted father threw him out. A good story, but not true. By that time the plot to make him king, if it ever got far enough to be called a plot, had already collapsed.

At any rate, he studied for several years and became a Moravian minister. In the early 1830s he took his wife to the Dutch Guiana colony of Surinam to be a missionary among the Negro slaves.

He wasn't very successful although he tried hard. The planters were suspicious of his work and resented his aristocratic attitude. After his wife died of tropical fever he returned to Europe in 1847 with a four-year old daughter and settled briefly in Holland.

Here he renewed acquaintance with a friend of his court days. Caroline Van der Meulen was also the daughter of a clergyman but her mother had once been first lady-in-waiting to the Queen of Holland. They were married in 1849 and were planning to return to South America when Tank was invited to the United States to do missionary work in Wisconsin.

Brought Fortune Along

The Tanks arrived in Milwaukee the same year, bringing with them, so it was later rumored, a personal fortune of $1½ million in gold. The figure was undoubtedly exaggerated but they were well heeled.

Having conceived the idea of founding a communistic Moravian settlement in Wisconsin, Tank came to Green Bay in 1850 and purchased nearly 1,000 acres of excellent land along the west bank of the Fox River. He laid out a village and invited a struggling congregation of co-religionists to come and occupy it.

About 25 families accepted and the colony eventually grew to about 300 people. For a time, with Tank the absolute boss and footing all the bills, everything went smoothly.

Clashed with Pastor

Eventually, however, he clashed with the group's regular pastor who had agitated the colonists to demand title to the lands Tank had allotted them. When Tank refused peremptorily the settlement blew up. Led by its pastor, the congregation departed for Door County where it founded the Village of Ephraim in 1853.

Tank had given that name to his projected Utopia, but Green Bayites had promptly dubbed it Tanktown. Disgusted and disillusioned but too proud to return to Europe, he resigned his mission and elected to remain on his considerable American estate, which included the Roi-Porlier cottage.

He and his wife had enlarged it by the addition of two wings and furnished it with art treasures from Madame Tank's home in Holland. To recoup his losses from the ill-fated colony, Tank opened his village to the sale of lots and was very successful. The area eventually became the Eighth Ward of Green Bay.

Involved in Ventures

Tank also became deeply involved in a number of business ventures, including the Fox-Wisconsin improvement project in association with Morgan L. Martin, various railroad promotions and in lumbering and foundry operation. His machine shop, foundry and lumber mill in Fort Howard was the largest and most modern of its kind in the area prior to the Civil War.

When he died unexpectedly in 1864, Tank was one of the wealthiest and most influential, if not very popular, men in the Green Bay area. For all his considerable business ability, few associates really liked him. He was too austere — if not downright snooty — toward most of his neighbors.

Being of aristocratic backgrounds the Tanks evidently considered themselves socially a cut above the residents of Fort Howard, mixed very little and were held in considerable awe. This attitude, plus the fact that his widow later destroyed all his personal papers, makes it difficult to assess his true character and personality.

Could Not Unbend

An impressive man, well over six feet tall, well proportioned and with a dignified carriage, Tank always attracted attention. Had he been more friendly he might have become an outstanding community leader.

He never could bring himself to unbend in the free and easy atmosphere of a frontier society. Consequently, few people had much confidence in him, although he was, by all accounts, a sincere, well meaning and rigidly honest man.

Mrs. Tank survived him and his daughter by many years. She had become a formidable personality in the community in her own right by the time she died in 1891.

At her death she left an estate well in excess of $100,000 and a houseful of antiques and art objects the likes of which Green Bay didn't realize were in the city. This disposal at public auction in 1893 drew art connoisseurs from all over the United States and still causes those who remember it to become a little wide-eyed.

*Tank Cottage is located now at Heritage Hill.

Chapter Two

The Growing Community

Menomineeville Struck Out

Ghost Town on the Frontier

February 13, 1965

When Chief Oshkosh was tried for murder in 1830 his trial was held in the U. S. District Court in the Village of Menomineeville, Michigan Territory. You won't find the place on any map today — nor would you have found it a century and a quarter ago — but Menomineeville has its place in the history of Green Bay as one of four pioneer settlements and a frontier military post in which the city had its roots.

Menomineeville scarcely got off the paper on which it was platted and has come down in local history under the unflattering title of Shantytown. The other early settlements involved were Astor, Navarino, the village and town of Fort Howard and the Army post of the same name.

Navarino and Astor were swallowed by the growing town that first used the name Green Bay. The two Fort Howards became a city in their own right before combining with their cross-river rival to create the modern city.

Struggling Line

The American military expedition to the mouth of the Fox River in 1816 found a straggling band of crude cabins and fur trading posts scattered along the east bank from the junction with East river almost to the rapids at De Pere. The settlement was mostly French with a handful of English, many with Indian or half-breed wives. It had no organization and was lumped under the general designation of "La Baye."

Across the river was Indian country, and a large Menominee village occupied the present site of the Northwest Engineering plant. *(Formerly at 201 West Walnut Street, the plant closed in 1990.)* It was this Indian town that was later to be the site of the knifing that hauled Oshkosh and his two accomplices into court.

Not far away were the ruins of the long occupied log stockade, called Fort St. Francis by its French builders and Fort Edward Augustus by its later English occupants. A few Frenchmen had farms south of the Indian town but generally whites and redskins were content to keep the river between them.

Took over Site

The American troops took over the old fort site as the location for a permanent post which eventually became Fort Howard. An early commander, however, violated instructions and shifted base to the ridge where Cotton House now stands and planned to erect the fort there.

His scheme lasted only until the War Department got wind of it, whereupon the garrison was ordered back across the river, but the incident lasted long enough to trigger a frontier real estate boom. A number of young Yankee traders had followed the flag to Green Bay and erected a string of log stores near the east shore cantonment to cater to the needs — principally liquid — of the garrison.

Because of their generally disreputable appearance and atmosphere, these stores were called shanties by the troops. The latter, with their flair for apt nicknames that has always characterized the American G.I., dubbed the place Shantytown.

Not Dignified

In 1824 Judge James Duane Doty arrived and picked Shantytown as the site for his courthouse. Doty didn't think the name dignified enough for the seat of justice, and when the county seat was officially established there he had it changed to Menomineeville. Perversely, the inhabitants clung to the old name.

With the county seat, a nearby military post, an increasing population of young professional and business men plus the best land in the vicinity, Menomineeville's future appeared bright. John Lawe, who owned much of the land, laid out an ambitious village in 1824, although he didn't get around to registering the plat until 1829. By that time Menomineeville had missed the boat.

Among the early American settlers was young Daniel Whitney, who established himself in Shantytown but gradually picked up land at the junction of the two rivers across from the fort. In 1829 he platted the village of Navarino between the rivers north of what is now Doty Street. A year later he moved his store and home to the new development.

Gaudy Swamp Name

Everybody thought he was crazy. Navarino was just a gaudy name for a swamp choked with trees, underbrush and mosquitoes but Whitney pushed enthusiastically ahead.

He put up a dock and warehouse, cleared the trace of what is now Main Street and built the first hotel in Wisconsin where the Beaumont Hotel stood for a century and where the new Beaumont Inn is now taking shape *(and has since become Day's Inn).* Gradually the American settlers abandoned Shantytown for the doubtful charms of Navarino.

The struggling hamlet stuck a feather in its coonskin cap when John V. Suydam began publication of the state's first newspaper "The Intelligencer." Fortunately, the town had more staying power than the paper, which enjoyed only a short and sporadic existence.

Honored Naval Victory

Whitney stripped his imaginative gears in naming the town. In the 1820s everybody was cheering the Greek fight for independence, a struggle that was virtually decided by the naval victory of a British-French-Russian fleet over a Turkish-Egyptian squadron in the Greek bay of Navarino in 1827. Whitney, who liked to buck the odds himself, named his village in honor of the victory.

In 1834 the American Fur Co. foreclosed mortgages on the land of Green Bay's French fur traders just south of Navarino. John Jacob Astor, who had found Whitney one of the few nuts he couldn't crack in the fur trade, was persuaded to make a fool out of him in a real estate war.

The persuader was Doty, who became Astor's agent. He platted a rival village on the foreclosed lands in 1835, which he named for his boss, and opened a campaign to wean business and residents away from Whitney.

Three-Year Rivalry

A merry little rivalry raged for three years, but the Depression of 1837 cooled off both sides. Two years later, in 1839, the two communities combined to form the Borough of Green Bay. *(The year was 1838.)*

They got together too late to save the county seat. Had they combined earlier they could have taken it from fading Menomineeville. Instead, they split their votes and De Pere, founded meanwhile at the rapids by William Dickinson, sneaked off with the prize. Green Bay didn't get it until 1854.

The west bank of the Fox didn't enjoy the same opportunities for early development. Much of it was included in the military reservation of Fort Howard and closed to settlement. Furthermore, the post commanders discouraged homesteading too close to the stockade. They had enough trouble with the boys across the river.

Gradually, however, pioneers began to trickle into the lands the military couldn't control. At the same time the importance of the fort dwindled and the huge reservation was whittled away. The post was evacuated in 1852 and during the next decade the reserved lands were released for sale.

Organized in 1836

The Town of Howard was organized in 1836 and 20 years later formed into the Borough of Fort Howard. In spite of a late start, Fort Howard quickly became an important manufacturing center, a process accelerated by the rise of Wisconsin's lumber industry.

By the time Fort Howard became a city in 1873 its real rival as a manufacturing point was not Green Bay but West De Pere. For a time, according to the Census of 1870, Fort Howard's population actually exceeded that of Green Bay.

From the outset there was no love lost between the cross-river rivals, yet there were forward-looking men in both who believed more could be accomplished together than as rivals. It took a long time for the idea to sink in, but in 1895 the two cities voluntarily consolidated.

Meanwhile, Menomineeville simply disappeared except for a crumbling plat map in county archives. For nearly a century its memory existed only as a footnote to area history, then it emerged again as the modern suburb of Allouez.

Charming, Leisurely

De Pere's Early Promise Faded

June 8, 1963

De Pere has never been a pushy, aggressive place; perhaps that is why it didn't quite fulfill its early promise. A charming little city of lovely, tree-lined residential areas and a leisurely pace, it is not a sleepy town; but neither can it be described as bustling.

There was a time, though, when De Pere was the industrial core of the Fox River Valley with fair prospects of outdistancing Green Bay. The latter's more advantageous position as a transportation center tipped the scales.

Historically, too, De Pere can hold its own with the larger neighbor, although it has never tried very hard to make a point of the fact. After all, Jean Nicolet saw the "rapids of the fathers" almost as soon as he saw the mouth of the Fox River, and there was a white man's settlement of sorts there long before Green Bay ever amounted to anything.

De Pere can trace its origin and name to the Jesuit Father Claude Allouez, who established his historic Mission of St. Francis Xavier at the foot of the rapids only 36 years after Nicolet passed over them. For almost 20 years, from 1670 until 1687, the mission was a religious outpost and fur trading way station.

Didn't Take Root

The efforts of Allouez and his Jesuit successors didn't take very deep root, however. In 1687 the mission was burned by the Indians and never reestablished. From then on the spectacular stretch of foaming water was known as "les rapides des peres," a title subsequently shortened to De Pere.

For almost a century and a half after the Mission of St. Francis went up in flames the sylvan beauty of De Pere — and by every account it was spectacularly beautiful — remained undisturbed. The Indians continued to set their ingenious fishing weirs above the rapids, but the white man didn't intrude again until 1829.

According to Deborah Martin's "History of Brown County" there was an attempt at settlement as early as 1804, but she gave no details. Apparently it didn't amount to much.

The beginnings of modern De Pere date from 1829 when William Dickinson, Ebenezer Childs and Robert Irwin Jr. shifted to the rapids from Shantytown in preference to Daniel Whitney's swampy Navarino. Dickinson, long neglected founder of De Pere, was a man of vision who foresaw the site's water power potential and lived to see his judgment vindicated.

First Use of Name

He organized the De Pere Manufacturing Co. in 1830, although it never manufactured anything except the future name of his settlement. Dickinson, so far as is known, was the first to use the present title.

Five years later, Dickinson, John P. Arndt and Charles P. Tullar formed the De Pere Hydraulic Co. This corporation, its name shortly changed to Fox River Hydraulic Co., platted the nucleus of De Pere and obtained a charter to build a dam across the rapids.

Randall Wilcox, a successful eastern dam builder, was brought in to do the job in 1836, liked what he saw and remained the rest of his life. His wooden dam went out in 1847 but was rebuilt in 1848-49 as part of the Fox River Improvement project.

From the outset the dam gave De Pere tremendous industrial importance because of its water power. During the 1840s the growing settlement was viewed as commercially more significant than Green Bay although it never became as large. Until well into the 1880s De Pere and its rival, West De Pere, constituted the industrial heart of the Valley.

Quickly Attained

How quickly it attained that position is best illustrated by an effusive and complicated sentence in the Hydraulic company's annual report for 1838.

"Eighteen months ago, where stood a solitary dwelling is now the seat of justice in Brown County, with a splendid courthouse, jail, a three-story public house, a schoolhouse, post office, warehouse and dock, one store, one grocery, one blacksmith shop, one cabinet shop and 28 dwelling houses, some of which are the most splendid and best buildings in the territory."

The little settlement even had a bank for a short time until the enterprise collapsed in the Panic of 1837. The memory of its brief existence still lives on in the picturesque "White Pillars," built as its headquarters in 1836, the same year Randall Wilcox erected his fine house on North Broadway.

In 1837 De Pere romped off with the county seat, sneaking in the back door when feuding Astor and Navarino canceled each other. Not until 1854, by which time Green Bay had become a city while De Pere was still unincorporated, did the former manage to pry it loose.

Village in 1857

De Pere did become a village in 1857, at the same time West De Pere was platted by Dr. Louis Carabin, a land speculating physician of Green Bay. From then until 1890 the story of De Pere vs. West De Pere was a smaller-scale version of the Green Bay-Fort Howard rivalry.

Although the dam provided power for a flour mill and a couple of sawmills, De Pere derived its first commercial prosperity from its fisheries. Millions of pounds of sturgeon, walleyes, herring and whitefish were taken during the 1850s from the racks built along the rapids, on much the same principle as the old Indian weirs.

Initially the catch was salted and shipped in barrels all over the east. After the railroad came fish were piled into gondola cars, covered with ice and forwarded to Chicago. The massive catches also created a malodorous problem as thousands of dead fish rotted along the river banks halfway to Green Bay.

Cheap water power came into its own with the beginning of Wisconsin's first great lumber boom of the 1850s. Not only sawmills but numerous woodenware factories sprang up. In the 1870s De Pere, boasting an extensive steam forge and iron works, also built railroad freight cars.

Colorful Industry

A brief but colorful industry in the 1870s was iron smelting. The National and Fox River Iron Furnaces went into production in 1869 and, fueled by the stumps of Brown County's stripped forests, cast a lurid glow across the night sky for about 15 years.

The furnaces didn't last very long but they did contribute vitally to Brown County's agricultural future. By providing an incentive for farmers to grub out stumps and clear the land they were in a large measure responsible for the area's modern dairy industry.

West De Pere was a success from the start. Platted in 1857, it was incorporated as a village in 1870, by which time it was the leading manufacturing center of Northeastern Wisconsin.

Separate Cities

In 1883 both villages were chartered as the separate cities of De Pere and Nicollet. The latter name never caught on, however, and in 1887 was changed back to West De Pere.

As is usually the case the two towns didn't get along any better than their neighbors down the river. However, when it became apparent that the bitter rivalry was hurting them both in what had become a losing struggle for industrial supremacy with Fort Howard, they saw the light.

In 1889 they voted to consolidate, a step taken the following year. Enough antagonism remained however, to require some compromises that still remain. De Pere is one of the few cities of its size in the nation that maintains two post offices and separate school systems, operating under completely different sets of regulations. *(The post offices have since unified; school districts remain separate.)*

'Mud Puddle' Became a City

March 16, 1963

Daniel Whitney was a close-fisted character but few were more willing to take a calculated risk. He took plenty of them in his life, not all of which paid off, and none appeared less attractive than his platting of the Village of Navarino, the mudhole in which the City of Green Bay took root. None was so productive over the long run, either.

In 1830 Whitney abandoned the then thriving community of Shantytown *(later called Menomineeville in what is now Allouez)* and moved, lock, stock and barrel, to the new village he had dreamed up and christened Navarino at the junction of the Fox and Devil Rivers. Everybody thought he had slipped off his rocker. Even the fact that he had picked up the area for little or nothing seemed no excuse to sink himself in it.

A low, soupy swampland covered with pine, tamarack and tangled underbrush, Navarino was as unlikely a place to plant a city as anyone could wish. That part of it not awash between the rivers was practically an island, bounded on three sides by the two rivers and partly on the other by a creek, long known as the Adams Street Slough, that wandered west through what is now Jackson Square, draining a cedar swamp beyond Monroe Avenue into the Fox River.

But Whitney, although lacking in formal education, had read his history attentively. He had undoubtedly noted that communities built near military installations at the meeting of rivers usually paid off. Navarino fulfilled these conditions, in addition to which it was only a hop, step and jump from the mouth of the larger Fox.

Not So Bottomless

What he didn't know but which turned out to be even more decisive was that his land wasn't as bottomless as it appeared. Once cleared it dried up rapidly and firmly.

The canny Yankee platted his village south of the Devil (now East) River but didn't extend it all the way through the swampy forest to the east. Instead, he chopped it off along what later became Baird Street. The southern limit lay between Walnut and Doty Streets, through the alley between the WBAY Building and the *(former)* public library.

He methodically laid out 12 streets each way, the north-south ones being named after presidents of the United States. Since the presidential roster didn't go beyond seven at the time he tagged those after Jackson with plain numbers (Eighth through 12th), probably intending to change them with future administrations.

His east-west streets were named for trees, beginning with Walnut and continuing north through Elm. The only exception was what he intended to be his principal business thoroughfare, which he labeled Main Street.

Little in Common

Anyway, that's how they looked on the neatly drawn plat now preserved in Brown County records. Actually, the plan and the reality long had little in common.

Clearing the land was a slow process, and populating it even slower. Not for many years was the area east of Monroe Avenue even touched, and it was a long time before anyone showed much interest in anything beyond Jefferson Street.

There is no detailed description of Navarino in its early, unlovely childhood. What exists is fragmentary and generally unfavorable. One that was short and too close to the truth for Whitney's comfort was the statement of brash young Henry S. Baird, who got in bad with the stony-faced proprietor by flatly calling Navarino a mud puddle.

Baird eventually moved to Navarino, however, and remained for 40 years. In 1835 he established his first home in lonely grandeur where the Minahan-McCormick Building now stands. *(The building was located at the northeast corner of Washington and Walnut Streets and has since been razed.)*

To Baum's Corner

When he shifted to Baum's Corner *(at Monroe and Main)* a year later he was practically isolated at the end of Main Street, which was so crudely cleared that it was only with much difficulty he brought building materials over its stumps and potholes for the home and tiny law office now preserved on the Cotton House grounds *(Heritage Hill)*.

According to Deborah Martin's "History of Brown County," the only building within the town limits in 1829 was a crude log cabin on the present site of the Kellogg-Citizens National *(now Associated)* Bank. This ramshackle affair, ownership not specified, was a "grocery" store. Considering that the only close source of trade was the fort across the river, the suspicion is strong that its inventory was even more liquid than the land on which it stood.

A tough man with his own buck, Whitney didn't believe in government handouts unless he was on the receiving end. Consequently, the only area set aside for public use was the square now called Whitney Park. Across Main Street from this he reserved a large estate for himself, running north to East River.

When Whitney skidded his store and cabin down the frozen Fox from Shantytown in the winter of 1829-30 he set up temporarily on the Beaumont Hotel corner *(Washington and Main)* until he had finished building a rambling, low bungalow on his estate. He later erected an elaborate three-story mansion nearby.

Didn't Take

The mansion idea didn't take with Mrs. Whitney, who firmly announced she wouldn't live in it under any circumstances. It was never finished, although Whitney wouldn't admit defeat, and it wasn't until after his death that "Whitney's Folly" was torn down. The bungalow remained until 1897.

One of the first commercial projects was a hotel where the now deserted Beaumont stands *(replaced by Day's Inn at Main and Washington)*, which he called the Washington House. He shortly sold the hotel property to Dr. William Beaumont, whose son Israel later built the century-old Beaumont there after the Washington House burned.

For the first few years Navarino's virtues existed only on paper. Gradually, however, the boat landing Whitney constructed at the foot of Main Street began to pay off, and many of Shantytown's young business and professional men moved north. By 1835 such future leaders as Baird, Morgan L. Martin, and Whitney himself had settled there.

By that time a fantastic wave of real estate speculation was sweeping the west, and Navarino was a ready-made base for speculators. A land office was established in 1835 at which sales of $75,000 were recorded in less than four days.

At this point competition cropped up. James Duane Doty, acting as agent for John Jacob Astor, Ramsey Crooks and Robert Stuart, platted a new village of Astor on adjacent land south of Navarino. At once a lively little cold war flared up that lasted for *(several)* years.

Bucked Astor Successfully

Although Whitney appeared overmatched against the Astor fortune, he had bucked it successfully before. He also enjoyed some solid advantages. He was on the ground, his own boss and able to make and carry out decisions promptly, a luxury denied Doty.

Also, nobody trusted the American Fur Co. and there was much local resentment over the way it had crushed such old and respected citizens as John Lawe, the Grignons and Jacques Porlier. Finally, Navarino was a going concern and Astor wasn't.

The fever of speculation soon collapsed. President Jackson's Specie Circular of 1836 swept the foundation from under the land boom, and the Panic of 1837 was on.

Development of both Navarino and Astor came to a dead stop for almost ten years. Meanwhile, in 1839 *(some sources show 1838)*, the two little towns, all the fight knocked out of them by the struggle to stay alive, buried the hatchet and consolidated into the Borough of Green Bay.

*Associated Bank on Adams.

Battled to a Draw

Astor Gave Navarino A Fight

January 27, 1968

Scarcely had Daniel Whitney's Village of Navarino begun to confound its critics and amount to something than it faced another hurdle in competition on its southern boundary. In 1835 a rival Village of Astor sprang up, triggering a lively real estate war until the Panic of 1837 sandbagged the two little communities into a consolidation that became the nucleus of the present City of Green Bay.

There's some question of credit for the Village of Astor. Dr. Alice E. Smith, biographer of James Duane Doty, credits Ramsey Crooks and Robert Stuart, who brought Doty into the picture to sell the project to John Jacob Astor and then promote it.

The project grew out of the acquisition by the American Fur Co. of the lands just south of Navarino through foreclosure of mortgages held against the resident fur traders of La Baye in 1834. Crooks, Stuart and associates had bought the company from Astor and foreclosed to pay him off.

Payment for Purchase

As partial payment for the company, early in 1835 a tract consisting of 75 percent of the foreclosed land was assigned to Astor and the rest split between Crooks and Stuart. Doty was appointed their agent and given an option to buy a 25 percent interest out of his share of land sales.

Doty laid out and registered the plat of a village south of and contiguous to Navarino. The original boundaries included everything between the Fox and East Rivers from the Navarino town line (running east and west through the present courthouse block between Walnut and Doty Streets) to the present city limits south of Grignon Street.

Doty calmly appropriated Whitney's north-south street names for his extensions of them. He named his east-west streets for local and territorial figures beginning with himself and continuing through Grignon. Chicago Street got in because it was to be extended as a projected military road to Chicago, while Emilie and Eliza were named for the wives of Crooks and Stuart, respectively.

Plenty of Parks

In contrast to Whitney's Navarino, Doty set aside plenty of squares for public use — five, all told, all of which are now incorporated into the city's park system. Those squares are now St. John's, St. James', Jackson, Astor and Baird Parks.

Jackson Square was the only one named at the time. Astor wasn't intended as a park but was reserved as the site of a "manual training school" that never materialized, while Baird Park was to be a public cemetery — which it was until the opening of Woodlawn after the Civil War.

Also like Navarino, there was a wide gulf between the fact and fancy of developing the plat. Initially only a quarter of the plat, the portion bounded by the Fox River, Doty, Monroe and Mason Streets was surveyed, and it wasn't until 1866 that the swamp east of Monroe was cleared and put on the market. The only street extending beyond Monroe was Mason, which was opened as far as the cemetery.

There is another interesting difference between Doty's plan and the eventual development. His plat called for two diagonal streets running northeast and southeast from the eastern corners of St. James Park. When the area was opened up later these thoroughfares were ignored and the present grid system substituted.

Doty centered the business section around the junction of Washington, Adams and Mason Streets, facing the pie-shaped wedge where No. One Fire Station now stands. In this vicinity he erected the fabulous Astor House and, in 1838, a large warehouse and dock on the river end of Mason.

He built a block-long office building on the north side of Chicago Street between Washington and Adams. Because its first tenant was the short-lived Bank of Wisconsin, it was known as the "Bank Building" until destroyed by fire in 1880. The large stone vault remained on the site until the turn of the century.

Only Four Buildings

When Astor was platted there were only four buildings within its limits. John P. Arndt owned the old DeLanglade property astride Washington Street where the Public Service bus garage *(once stood)*. Joseph Jourdain had a cabin and blacksmith shop on the river bank south of Mason, and there was a long log building on the site of the old water works.

John Lawe's fine home stood at the foot of Porlier Street. Lawe had lost it in the foreclosure of 1835 but Doty, an old friend, deeded the house and lot to Mrs. Lawe, all he could persuade Astor to part with.

To pull residents from Navarino, Doty persuaded Astor to donate lots for church sites to congregations then being organized. Whitney beat him to the punch with the Episcopalians but Doty got the Methodists and Presbyterians. All still occupy the properties except the latter, whose original site now contains the Elks Club *(300 Crooks Street)*.

Began Well

The development began well. Even before the plat was registered Doty had sold about $13,000 worth of lots, always on condition that buyers build on and occupy them. Sincerely interested in creating a real town, he did not encourage speculators.

Thereafter, however, the Panic of 1837 and general distrust of the ownership slowed down Astor's progress. By March, 1839, only 169 lots had been sold or given away, of which 90 were wholly and 40 partly paid for.

Despite Doty's blandishments, few Navarino residents deserted Whitney for the new town. One was Morgan L. Martin, who bought a large parcel on Monroe Avenue, including the present St. Joseph's Academy grounds *(now Aldo Leopold School)*, on which he built his famous home Hazelwood, now a museum *(and headquarters for the Brown County Historical Society)*. For many years, however, Hazelwood stood alone on the hill, virtually a country estate.

Lost County Seat

Doty also tried to close the Menomineeville and Navarino post offices and get one for Astor. He didn't succeed but he did pry the county seat loose from Menomineeville *(also called Shantytown in what is now Allouez)*.

His scheme to move it to Astor backfired, however. After he had engineered an 1836 referendum to relocate the seat, the rivalry between Astor and Navarino resulted in a split vote, and De Pere walked off with the prize. Green Bay didn't get it back until after it had become a full-fledged city.

Although Astor failed to destroy or swallow Navarino, with which it was combined in *(1838)* as the Borough of Green Bay, and the hopes of John Jacob Astor for a quick return weren't fulfilled, the old man wouldn't part with his holdings. It wasn't until 1911 that the last of the Astor-owned lots in the city were finally sold by his estate.

West Side Has Rich History

Fort Howard's Colorful Past

February 10, 1968

Preoccupation with the colorful aspects of the fur trade and the rowdy virility of lumbering in the building of the city of Green Bay can very easily obscure the fact that the West Side has a story of its own as vivid and interesting as that of Navarino and Astor. Nearly 75 years have passed since Green Bay and Fort Howard consolidated in 1895, however, and the distinct history of the latter is fading.

A major reason is lack of reliable source material upon which to reconstruct the West Side Story. Too many of the records, particularly the old Fort Howard newspaper files, have been lost.

Yet there was a time when the City of Fort Howard had high hopes of eclipsing Green Bay in size and importance. They were well founded hopes, too, and it is still something of a mystery why they didn't pan out.

Platted in 1842

The Town of Howard, which became successively the borough and then the city of Fort Howard, was originally platted in 1842, less than 15 years after the founding of Navarino and only four years after the consolidation of Navarino and Astor as Green Bay. The borough of Fort Howard was established in 1856, just two years after Green Bay became a city.*

Ordinarily, the immediate vicinity of a frontier military post would have been the center of the earliest development but a number of factors worked against this trend at Fort Howard. In the first place, a settlement of sorts had already grown up on the east bank of the Fox River.

Also, the West Side was largely unavailable. The military post of Fort Howard included a large military reservation closed to settlement and post commanders discouraged a civilian enclave squarely between the fort and the nearby Menominee Indian town on the present site of the Northwest Engineering plant. *(Located then at 201 West Walnut Street, the plant closed in 1990.)*

Not Accessible

What good land was left was owned by the original French settlers who were not interested in selling. Not until the Indians moved out, the French land owners were cleaned out by the American Fur Company and the military post virtually abandoned did the west side of the river become easily accessible.

These developments occurred largely between 1835 and 1845, and at once the West Side began to stir. First move was the formation of the Town of Howard at a meeting in the home of Daniel Hubbard in 1842, but it wasn't until 1850 that much came of it.

The Village of Howard was platted in 1849* and a year later a part of the military reservation was released to private individuals. There followed a bewildering series of real estate transactions that occurred so fast and often that even today abstractors shudder every time a piece of property in that area changes hands.

Ownership Consolidated

Eventually, most of it wound up in the hands of Joel S. Fisk, John Wallace Arndt and Frank Desnoyers. In 1850 Arndt and Fisk pooled their interests to expand the village.

The original town lay between what are now Hubbard and Howard Streets and was bisected by a thoroughfare called Main Street — now West Walnut.

Shortly thereafter Fisk and Desnoyers got together on an addition farther west. Some poor surveying and a fight complicated the deal, out of which came the familiar jog between Walnut Street and Shawano Avenue.

When Otto Tank's Ephraim settlement to the south failed, he platted the village, popularly called Tanktown, as Tank's Addition in 1851. His remaining holdings were platted by his widow as C. L. A. Tank's subdivision in 1863.

Steady Development

Development was steady thereafter. Francis Blesch erected the first brewery in Brown County in 1851, Oscar Gray opened the first store in 1852 and in 1854 the village got a post office. Gray was the first postmaster and habitually carried the mail in his tall plug hat from Green Bay to his store where it was passed out.

The village promoters were far ahead of their time in one respect. With a fine enthusiasm that vastly amused the Bayites across the river (who eventually learned to their sorrow that cities, like kids, outgrow their baby clothes) they flung their town limits far beyond the built-up area. It took nearly a century but the foresight eventually paid off.

In 1862 Fort Howard got a big jump on its cross-river rival when the Northwestern Railroad came into that town instead of into Green Bay. Immediately the latter began to agitate for bridges across the Fox but Fort Howard would have little part of the scheme.

Uneasy Feeling

There was an uneasy feeling that a bridge or bridges would do Fort Howard more harm than good. The first bridge was built by Green Bay alone in 1863 and the West Side fears began to acquire substance.

In 1873 the borough was incorporated as a city, putting it on a social and political level with Green Bay. With lumber mills booming on all sides, prosperity on every hand and the railroad on the West Side, Fort Howard residents could be pardoned for thinking their future was bright indeed.

Almost at once, however, business began to slacken and Green Bay forged slowly but steadily ahead. Long before 1895 it was obvious to all but the most stubborn that consolidation was the only answer, in which case Fort Howard would lose its identity in the larger community.

Professions Lagged

In one respect Fort Howard had always lagged behind. Since it was a manufacturing and shipping center while Green Bay was primarily a city of services, the West Side never managed to build up a system of professional services of its own. Nearly all the lawyers and doctors lived and practiced in Green Bay.

A small group of diehards held out against consolidation to the bitter end. When it finally came, they did manage to put one provision into the consolidation charter that still exists — one of the few portions of the document that has never been changed.

Few people think of it, but there are no taverns in the city west of Broadway in what was once Fort Howard and there have been none for almost three quarters of a century. The charter contained a clause prohibiting taverns west of Broadway and it is still in force.

* *Rudolph's dates are confusing at best. More recent research shows the west side "Howard" became an independent entity in 1835; J.B.W. Arndt and Joel Fisk platted the Town of Fort Howard in 1850; and the city of Fort Howard established in 1873.*

Proper Spot for Kermis

How the First Belgians Came

August 31, 1963

When the Federated Belgian-American Societies of the Middlewest decided to hold their first annual kermis in Green Bay they picked the right spot — or close to it. Actually, the most appropriate place would have been Champion, lying as it does in the middle of the largest rural concentration of people of Belgian ancestry outside Belgium itself.

The community of nearly 40,000 Belgian-Americans has been here, growing steadily, for 110 years, but surprisingly little is known about the history of the group. Including a 100-page book written 30 years ago by the late H. R. Holand and a more recent study published in Belgium by a Belgian historian, its entire printed story doesn't fill 200 pages.

Maybe it's because the Belgians are simply taken for granted. Northeastern Wisconsin's oldest residents can't remember when the area wasn't celebrating kermises and telling Belgian dialect jokes, or a time when they didn't know somebody named Petiniot, Destache, Delwiche, Evrard, Geniesse or Bodart, to list only a few. The Petiniots, Delwiches, Evrards, et al were here first.

These and many others have been familiar names in Brown, Door and Kewaunee Counties for over a century. Some were among the first Belgians to arrive in 1853 and the rest came in the next five years. The story of the Belgian immigration to the Door Peninsula is as much a part of the history of Northeastern Wisconsin as the era of lumber and of more enduring consequence, although the two are closely interwoven.

Bachelor Started It

Although Belgians are notable family people, it was all started by a bachelor. Sparkplug of the original emigration to the region was a young, unmarried farmer from the commune of Grez Doiceau named Francois Petiniot.

Early in 1853 young Petiniot visited Antwerp. There, in a tavern, he picked up a pamphlet on America. Reading of the vast tracts of land available almost for the asking, the young fellow decided that was for him.

Things were in a mess at home, politically and economically. There was too much religious bickering for his taste; and possibly, too, he could feel his draft board breathing down his neck.

Talked It Up

Back in Grez he began to talk it up. He must have been quite a persuader because he soon talked nine other small farmers, all married and with family responsibilities, into throwing in with him. The nine hardy gamblers were Martin Paque, Etienne and Jean Detienne, Adrien Masy, Philippe Hannon, Joseph Moreau, Lambert Bodart, Joseph Jossart and Jean Baptiste Martin.

In May, 1853, the party sailed for the United States from Antwerp. The exact number in the group isn't known — even Belgian records are vague — but there were between 40 and 50 men, women and children.

They had no specific American destination, but aboard ship they fell in with a party of Hollanders bound for a place with the outlandish name of Sheboygan in a state called Wisconsin — wherever that was. They talked it over and decided to tag along.

Temporary Split

Arriving in New York after a 48-day passage, the party split temporarily. Most of them headed directly for Sheboygan, but the Paques and Martins went to Philadelphia where they stayed for several months, a side trip destined to be of considerable significance for the future of the Wisconsin Belgians.

Martin had a 19-year-old son named Xavier, an intelligent, aggressive youth who had already shown a flair for leadership. When the families rejoined their friends in Wisconsin, Xavier remained behind to go to school and learn English. He would do much for his countrymen in later years.

The original party reached Sheboygan in July but was disappointed. Most of the good land was already occupied and none of the settlers there could speak Belgian.

Shifted Base

Shortly, however, they met a Frenchman from Green Bay, who told them of the possibilities here, adding that the population was largely French-speaking. They shifted base and arrived in Green Bay in August.

The men left their baggage and families at Green Bay and went to the government land office at Menasha. After prospecting in the latter neighborhood they selected and were allotted land in the vicinity of Kaukauna. Well satisfied with their choice they returned to Green Bay, only to find that death had taken a hand in their affairs.

The child of Philippe Hannon had died in their absence and they had to delay their departure for the funeral. On the day of the services the officiating priest had a visitor, another young Belgian whose accidental presence changed the whole course of settlement in Wisconsin.

Enter Father Daems

The visitor was also a priest, the Rev. F. Edward Daems, recently appointed pastor of the wilderness parish of Bay Settlement. Father Daems easily persuaded them to abandon their Kaukauna venture and accompany him to Bay Settlement, where he told of land they could get for 50 cents an acre, less than half of what they would have paid up the valley.

The group followed Father Daems to his parish and staked out claims in the heavily wooded area along the boundary of Brown and Kewaunee Counties. The center of their settlement eventually became Robinsonville (now Champion), although for many years it was known as "Les Premiers Belges."

Initial prospects must have seemed

pretty grim. They had more land than any of them had ever dreamed of owning but it was in the heart of a dense pine and hardwood forest, miles from the nearest settlement and completely innocent of any kind of roads. It was good land; being peasant farmers, they could see that, even if it was choked with trees.

Built Rude Cabins

With autumn advancing the pioneers hurriedly threw up rude log cabins for the winter. They weren't used to northern Wisconsin winters and their shelters weren't very substantial, but fortunately that first winter was mild. By spring they had cleared enough of their new acres to plant their first crops.

By this time they were writing enthusiastic letters back home. Their friends considered and decided to follow. Only a few came in 1854 but the number increased the following year and reached a flood in 1856-57. By the time the tide ebbed in 1858 an estimated 7,500 Belgians had poured into Wisconsin and spread north through Kewaunee and Door Counties. *(Another account puts the number closer to 12,000.)*

The first years were tough. Lacking livestock and even plows, they planted their early crops by scratching furrows between the stumps with sticks and laid seed by hand. The rise of the lumber industry helped by converting their forest into a cash crop of lumber and shingles and gave them added incentive to clear the land.

It was hard, grinding labor, but they were a hard-working, frugal people. It wasn't long before they had carved the beginnings of a prosperous farming area out of the wilderness.

Gratitude for Pioneer

Albert Weise Led Germans to City

July 5, 1958

Green Bay owes much to its German pioneers, most of whom came here between 1840 and 1880. Albert Weise was one of the first, and to him the city can be especially grateful. It was largely through his persuasiveness that so many more followed — solid German immigrants named Straubel, Hagemeister, Barkhausen, Schuette, Rothe and Klaus, to list a few.

Weise came to Green Bay as a stripling of 20 with little more than a set of carpenter's tools and a willingness to work. When he died 55 years later he was wealthy, respected and one of the largest property owners in town. Green Bay did well by him, but Weise repaid it with loyalty and enthusiasm.

Albert Weise — his full name was John Henry William Albert — was born in Blankenburg, Germany, in 1820. His father, a cooper, died when *(Albert)* was only two, and his mother married a miller named Christoph Frederick Straubel, destined 20 years later to plant the name of Straubel deep in the soil of Green Bay.

Sought Steady Work

After some early schooling, training as a wagon builder and the inevitable military hitch, young Weise left Germany in 1841. He turned up here a year later, lured by promises of steady work.

The promises didn't pan out, but John P. Arndt took a fancy to him and helped him get established at his trade. He barely managed financially and got married on a shoestring, but was gaining a good reputation when, in 1845, an unexpected $300 inheritance from Germany put him over the hump.

With it he bought a lot on Cherry Street, between Washington and Adams, and set up a small wagon shop. He soon had to expand and built a factory that is now the Manger Casket Co. on Harvey Street. *(E. C. Manger & Son Co. is now located on Day Street.)* In a short time his Green Bay Carriage Co. was booming. In 1846 he persuaded his mother and stepfather to follow him to Green Bay.

Married in 1844

Meanwhile, in 1844, he married Maria Holzknecht, whom he met while she was visiting here. Maria was the daughter of a descendant of Andreas Hofer, Tyrolese patriot of the Napoleonic wars, and a Prussian noblewoman who had been disinherited for marrying a commoner — even though his relative was an Austrian national hero.

His wife's noble lineage apparently bothered the cooper's son and he fussed about it in the early days. He probably made more out of it than she did, and in any event she never had to. Albert did all right.

It was pretty tough, though, until he got that windfall. For the first year of their marriage Mrs. Weise had to take in boarders.

Although his carriage factory prospered, real estate was the backbone of his fortune. Either he or his wife had a nice eye for property values, and they soon started to buy. As soon as one piece was paid for they picked up another, then skimped to pay for that.

Choice Holdings

Eventually they had choice holdings all over town. Among them were the present Stiefel Store,* the YWCA building *(then at 202 North Adams St., now the site of Associated Bank)*, which Weise built and on which his name can still be seen; the entire Town and Country Club tract *(on Riverside Drive, since sold and developed as residential and business properties)* from river to river; the telephone company site on Adams Street *(then located just north of Walnut Street)* and most of the land now occupied by the WBAY building on Jefferson.

On the latter site he erected an imposing brick mansion with 10 bedrooms (with nine kids he needed them all) and the first coal furnace in town. For years the home was a social and cultural center.

When, in 1921, the Woman's Club was looking for a clubhouse, the choice narrowed down to the Weise residence and the old Morrow home. One faction, led by Mrs. Francis T. Blesch, wanted the Weise place; the other, headed by Mrs. W. P. Wagner, held out for Morrow's *(at 345 S. Adams)*.

Mrs. Wagner out-talked Mrs. Blesch and the Morrow home won. A few years later the old mansion was razed to make way for the Columbus Community Club *(now the WBAY Building)*.

Into Crockery Business

In 1870 Weise branched out into the crockery and chinaware business, founding Weise & Hollman in partnership with his son-in-law, Fred Hollman. Six years later he turned over his carriage factory to a son to concentrate on the crockery firm, located in the building now occupied by Stiefel's.*

As he prospered, so did his enthusiasm for Green Bay. Weise was a fervent city booster, game for anything that might help it grow. Sometimes he took a financial shellacking, but he kept bouncing back for more.

His range of interests was fantastic. He invested in Michigan mines, early Pennsylvania oil fields, was president of a bank and director of several large companies here. From his earliest affluence he was a ringleader in railroad projects, one of which eventually jelled into what is now the Green Bay and Western.

An early Republican, he was active in politics, although the only office he ever held was a seat on the city council. He was repeatedly elected to the council, often against his will, and he served as its president for years.

After the death of his wife in 1887, Weise gradually eased into retirement, turning his interests over to his sons. He died at the age of 75 on Nov. 19, 1895.

** A men's and boys' clothing store, Stiefel's was located at 304-306 North Washington, now part of Washington Commons, formerly known as Port Plaza Mall.*

Surpassed P-G Record

Old Advocate Lasted 60 Years

August 21, 1965

The Press-Gazette has been making a Big Thing this year out of its 50th anniversary. However, if its earliest rival were still alive, the P-G would be keeping a respectful tongue in its head as befits a youngster in the presence of his elders. Had the old Green Bay Advocate survived it would be 120 years old next August.

The Advocate was not the oldest newspaper in Green Bay's history, being 13 years behind the original Intelligencer, but it was more successful and lasted for 60 years. When the Press-Gazette's first ancestor was born right after the Civil War the Advocate was already 20 years old.

The brainchild of a couple of ambitious young brothers from New York, the Advocate was founded in 1846 by Charles D. and Albert C. Robinson. They launched the project on guts and credit when the entire white population of Brown County was just a little over 2,000, not all of whom could read.

Typical Weekly

A typical four-page weekly of its day, the Advocate was published for the first time on Aug. 13, 1846, and rarely missed an issue until it folded 60 years later. Editor Charley Robinson never forgot that date and as long as he lived he wrote an anniversary editorial, many of which contained details of early life in the little settlement found nowhere else.

Like most of his readers, Robinson was a Jeffersonian Democrat. He remained one all the time he held down the editor's desk, and his outlook mirrored the views of his subscribers. The first issue carried a quote from Thomas Jefferson in its masthead that remained there for years.

From the outset the little paper satisfied a deep hunger. Settlers filtering into Wisconsin wanted news from home and a vehicle for crystalizing frontier opinion, and the Advocate supplied both. Not the last of its attractions was the popularity of its politics.

Burned Out

Even so, the infant enterprise was almost choked off at birth. A few weeks after its first issue a fire destroyed a large part of Green Bay's business district, including the little shop. Things looked black for the brothers until their mother, a remarkable woman who became a local personality in her own right before she died in 1872, took ship for Buffalo.

She raised another press on her own credit and managed to get it shipped to Green Bay before the navigation season closed, and after a few weeks the boys were back in business. Fortunately, the one item of equipment salvaged from the blaze was a small safe containing the paper's subscription list.

By 1860 the Advocate was one of the most influential papers in Wisconsin. Robinson backed Stephen A. Douglas against Lincoln for the Presidency but when the Civil War broke out he became a loyal "Union Democrat" and supported the administration. He even closed his desk and joined the Union army.

Tilton Filled In

During his absence the editorship was brilliantly assumed by his assistant, Frank Tilton, one of the great pioneer newsmen of Wisconsin. One of Tilton's first moves was to inaugurate what was in effect the first daily news service in this part of the state.

He accomplished it in spite of the fact that the telegraph line ended at Oshkosh and it took another full day for wire news to reach Green Bay by river boat.

Tilton beat the clock by loading forms, type and a crew of printers on the first upriver boat each morning. When they met the northbound vessel at Appleton they shifted to it, went to work on wire dispatches and exchanges and had important items set in type by the time they docked at Green Bay in early afternoon.

The locked forms were rushed to the Advocate office where one-sheet bulletins were run off in time for afternoon circulation locally as well as for shipment on outgoing lake vessels.

Dropped in 1862

The elaborate arrangement was no longer necessary after the telegraph line reached Green Bay in 1862 and was discontinued. So far as is known, the only specimens to survive are a partial set in the archives of the State Historical Society.

The coup gave the Advocate great prestige, which came in handy after the war — especially when young Dwight I. Follett, who had learned the printer's trade from Tilton and who had handled the Daily Bulletin project, established the Green Bay Gazette as a Republican organ in 1866.

For the next 20 years the two papers waged a spirited war of their own, in which the older Advocate held a distinct advantage as long as Robinson was in the saddle. In the late 1870s his health began to fail. For the last three years of his life he was mentally incompetent and the paper had to be run by his wife and Tilton.

Fight for Control

Before his death a fight for control broke out between Abbie Robinson and A. C. Robinson, who had remained in the background all through the years as business manager. The controversy was settled in Mrs. Robinson's favor in 1885, after which she bought out Albert's share.

Charles Robinson died in 1886 and the family control lasted only three years more. Tilton left the paper about the same time and from then on the Advocate began to slip.

In 1889 Abbie was finally convinced she couldn't do the job alone. Having no children to carry on the work she reluctantly sold the paper.

Thereafter the Advocate faded steadily. A succession of editors and publishers failed to re-establish its prestige, and a local shift in political sentiment during the Free Silver campaign of 1896 completed the debacle. Meanwhile the Gazette, under skilled direction of Rosamond (*sic*) Follett, forged ahead.

Last Publisher

The old paper changed hands several times prior to 1902 when Frank Singleton took charge. Singleton was an aggressive publisher but he apparently didn't know how to cope with local sentiment.

Although he converted the old sheet, first to a semi-weekly, then to a tri-weekly and eventually to a daily, he couldn't buck the Gazette, which had also passed to more progressive management.

On Dec. 15, 1906, virtually without warning, Singleton gave up. In a stinging editorial that severely castigated the public and local merchants for failing to support the Advocate he suspended publication.

The Gazette took on the subscription list, bought what it wanted of the physical plant and locked the door on a long and colorful existence.

Immigrants Had Their Say

Foreign Settlers Named Towns

April 30, 1960

The first American settlers in the Green Bay area came from New England and the Atlantic seaboard states, notably New York and Pennsylvania, and their influence was shown in the naming of such early towns as Pittsfield and Lawrence. In the 1840s, however, the tide of foreign immigrants began rolling in with Germans, Dutch, Irish, Belgians and Scandinavians arriving to make marked contributions to the culture of Wisconsin. There presence also began to be felt in the naming of Brown County towns in the mid-1850s.

First to show it was the Town of Holland in 1854. Here a group of Dutch families had settled in 1846, coming to Wisconsin under the sponsorship of the Dutch priest, Father Vanden Broek, and establishing a settlement which they called Franciscus Bosch. Being proud of their new home as well as the old, they compromised on an anglicized title for their community by eventually naming it Holland.

Another was New Denmark, where a number of Danish families came in the 1840s. They first called their village Cooperstown, which acquired a post office in 1848. When the town was lopped off De Pere in 1855 the present name was selected for obvious reasons.

Irish pioneers settled what eventually became Morrison, the first settler in the community being Alphonse Morrison, who established his family there in 1851. When it became a separate town in 1854 Morrison's position as first settler was honored by giving it his name.

Bellevue, settled originally by Germans in 1842 but subsequently acquiring a predominantly Belgian population, was formed in 1856. The county board suggested the name of Manitou, as the East River was then sometimes called, but the idea didn't click.

The job of selecting an appropriate name was then passed on to Henry Eastman and David Agry, who came up with Belleview, apparently for no other reason than the pretty scenery. This was adopted and later changed to the present spelling.

That same year Glenmore was set off from De Pere. Here the settlers were mostly Irish, Samuel Harrison having been the first in 1846. The title is said to have been selected from a spot in Ireland of the same name.

Rockland was established in 1857, also being cut off from De Pere. The population was mostly Irish and German, the pioneer settlers being James Hobbins in 1850 and Stephen Joyce, who came in 1855. The town's name presumably is derived from the limestone ledge that runs through it, although there is no real evidence to that effect.

Up to this time the town christeners had studiously avoided Indian names, but in 1858 the settlers of Suamico recognized the importance of the river in their prosperity by adopting a corruption of its Indian name for their new town. The Indian title was "Ousuamingong," meaning "the beaver's tail."

Considerable uncertainty exists over the background of the four towns established in 1859, only Eaton's title origin being positively known. This was named for another original settler, Austin Eaton, who came to the area from Connecticut.

Named for "Admiral?"

Residents of Preble have always believed, although without any official proof, that their town was named for "Admiral" Preble. The "admiral" referred to is probably Commodore Edward Preble, ranking officer and builder of the U. S. Navy in the years before the War of 1812. The rank of admiral was not instituted in the American naval service until the Civil War.

In the case of the Town of Scott there is even more confusion. When it was created in November of 1859 the name of Liberty was suggested but nobody seemed to like that.

Then John P. Arndt pulled "Pochequette" out of his tall beaver hat, an idea that aroused even less enthusiasm. Finally, so the story goes, one of the Scotch settlers named Robert Gibson proposed Scott in honor of Sir Walter Scott and it was adopted.

As for Humboldt, nobody knows the answer, and it doesn't seem to make much sense. Heavily populated by Belgians at the time of its organization, the German name appears out of place.

One suggestion is that it was actually named by Anton Klaus, an influential citizen. At the time, however, Klaus was just a young man, only four years out of Germany and not a resident of the area. He was trying to make a living running a small hotel in Green Bay.

No Proof

Whoever tacked the title on was probably thinking of the famed and widely traveled writer Baron Alexander von Humboldt, then very much in the public eye. There is no proof, however, that it happened that way.

After the upsurge of the 1850s things were quiet until 1872 when Ashwaubenon was created and named for the Menominee chief Ashwaubemie, who had given much of the town land to his descendants. The following year Allouez was set off, the honor going to Father Claude Allouez, the Jesuit missionary whose name figures so prominently in early Wisconsin history.

In 1906 the last town in the county was formed on land once part of the Oneida reservation. It was named for Bishop John H. Hobart, Methodist Espiscopal bishop of New York, who sent Eleazer Williams with the Oneidas when they moved to Wisconsin.

Why, while they were at it, the town fathers didn't honor Williams himself — he had become quite a celebrity by that time — isn't known, but Eleazer got his licks in anyway.

Hardly anyone remembers Bishop Hobart, but nearly every time someone buys land in the adjacent Town of Lawrence Williams' name pops up in the transfer records.

First of Two Articles

Street Names Part of History

April 8, 1961

Ever wonder how the street you live on got its name?

In Green Bay, as in every other city some street names are obvious; others have their roots deep in the origins of the city and carry undertones of old rivalries, conflicts or friendships. In some cases, nobody remembers where they came from.

People take street names pretty much for granted, especially if they are old, often not realizing that they memorialize long forgotten economic, social and political rivalries that once bristled from every mudhole. Wives, sisters and daughters of local figures long dead are also honored, and in these cases the origins are not so easy to recognize.

Within recent years, the building up of the city's western outskirts has brought and continues to bring new street names into existence — the total number in Green Bay is now around 300. Many of the new ones have no historical significance, or any other significance, for that matter, beyond the fact that someone thought they were pretty or might mean what they say some day.

In older sections of the city, however, it's different. On the East Side, particularly, street names go back to the rival villages of Astor and Navarino, more than 130 years ago.

Plat of Navarino

When Daniel Whitney platted the Village of Navarino, nucleus of the present city, in *(1829)* he laid out a grid of 12 streets each way, a few of them north of what is now the East but what was then called Devil River. The southern boundary of his settlement, incidentally, was south of Walnut Street, running east and west through the present courthouse and between the *(former)* Kellogg Public Library *(at 125 South Jefferson Street)* and the WBAY Building.

He labeled his north-south streets, beginning with Washington, after presidents of the United States. Since there had been only seven presidents up to that time, however, those east of Jackson were simply numbered Eighth through 12th streets.

His east-west streets were named after trees, beginning with Walnut on the south and continuing north through Elm.

When he came to what he planned as the principal business and residential thoroughfare, Whitney stripped his imaginative gears and could produce nothing better than Main Street.

In 1835 James Doty, Ramsey Crooks, Robert Stuart and John Jacob Astor, having failed to drive Whitney out of the fur trade, decided to take a fall out of him in real estate and at the same time cash in on the property once owned by Green Bay's French fur traders, which the American Fur Co. had obtained by mortgage foreclosures. The Village of Astor was platted immediately south of Navarino, and a neat little real estate war was in prospect.

Provoked a Fight

Doty laid out the new village with deliberate intention of provoking Whitney into a fight. He started hooking onto and extending Navarino's presidential series, adding Van Buren who was a cinch to succeed Jackson as president in 1836.

He further stoked up the dour Whitney's blood pressure by naming the first street south of the boundary for himself. Next he honored his employers, Stuart and Crooks, as well as his political allies, Stephen Mason, Michigan territorial governor, and Secretary of War Lewis Cass.

Chicago Street was so named because it was to be part of a military road Doty was planning from Green Bay to Chicago. Emilie and Eliza were named for the wives of Crooks and Stuart, respectively. He then made a gesture toward the dispossessed traders with Lawe, Porlier and Grignon Streets.

Astor didn't rate a street because the village itself was named after him. He did, however, get the pie-shaped wedge called Astor Place, planned by Doty as the business center of the new town, and later Astor Park.

Reserved for Parks

While Whitney had reserved only what is now Whitney Park as a public square, Doty set aside five such blocks, now known as Jackson Square, Astor, Baird, St. James and St. John's Parks. The only one named at the time was Jackson, an honor Old Hickory might not have appreciated had he known the present attractive little park was then covered by a slough. Baird Park was reserved for a public cemetery.

For nearly 30 years thereafter much of the ambitious plan remained on paper. The area east of Monroe Avenue was covered by a dense swamp and was not opened up until 1866, the only east-west streets to be cut through being Main and Mason. Main Street was opened all the way to the East River, while Mason was extended to what is now Baird Park, the Town cemetery.

After the two villages consolidated into Green Bay in *(1838)* and Van Buren's name was added to the presidential roster local followers of Daniel Webster and Henry Clay demanded streets for their heroes. Since both seemed good bets for the presidency the council went along, but when they didn't make it the continuity was broken and never restored.

The 1895 consolidation with Fort Howard required renaming of 11th and 12th Streets to avoid duplication. The first was eventually named in honor of Theodore Roosevelt and the latter for an early local resident, Robert Irwin. Later other streets were added and named for Henry S. Baird, Nathan Goodell and John V. Suydam.

Businessmen Get In

When the area north of the East River was opened for development, some of the north-south streets were extended and east-west street names went to men financially interested in the project. Thus, Reber Street was named for Henry Reber, Eastman Avenue for Harry Eastman, Day Street for Louis J. Day and Berner for Charles Berner. Smith Street went to Perry H. Smith, Chicagoan interested in the scheme who probably never saw Green Bay.

The plat of the Bay Beach section follows the original plan adopted by John Lawe for his projected village of Menomineeville in Allouez. Streets running south from the bay shore are named for various Indian tribes, as in the Lawe plan.

Diener Drive is named for the late Mayor John V. Diener, while Radisson, Perrot and Doblon memorialize early French explorers who helped open the Great Lakes region to white settlement.

In 1876 Monroe and Webster were changed from streets to avenues. At that time there was some mild agitation to rename Main Street for Whitney, an idea that still has a lot to recommend it.

Last of Two Articles

Confusion in West Side Streets

April 15, 1961

Tracing the origins of East Side street names is relatively easy; the West Side is something else. Finding any rhyme or reason in them is like trying to follow the Communist Party line, although a lot more fun.

Unlike the East Side streets, whose names have continued more or less on the basis of Green Bay's original plats, Fort Howard had no coordinated plan. The problem has been further complicated by numerous name changes through the years, particularly at the time of the 1895 consolidation.

Also, unlike the East Side after the fusion of the rival settlements of Navarino and Astor, the West Side's development continued for a long time as a series of rivalries. Real estate developments were planned and carried out by competing groups of individuals who fought rather than cooperated with each other, each addition taking on aspects of separate villages.

Because rival operators tried to block each other, streets are often not continuous, there are numerous gaps which have no apparent reason, and little streets wander all over the place. Even the familiar jog in the continuation of West Walnut and Shawano Avenue was the result of a fight.

Not all the confusion was pure cussedness, however. The West Side was once split by two large sloughs, long just memories but in their day difficult hurdles in trying to lay out any continuous street system even if anyone had been interested.

Original Plat in 1850

The original plat of Fort Howard was made in 1850 by Joel S. Fisk, John Wallace Arndt and Francis B. Desnoyer (*Desnoyers*). The village ran from a line just south of Howard Street to just south of Hubbard and was divided by a cross thoroughfare called Main Street. North-south streets were named Water, Pearl, Broadway, Chestnut, Cherry, Cedar and Willow.

There appears to have been no significance to the titles other than that someone thought *(tree)* names were pretty and Green Bay already had some, and nobody remembers how Pearl Street got its name. Hubbard was named for the Hubbard family, among the earliest residents.

When the cities of Fort Howard and Green Bay consolidated many of these early names had to be changed to avoid duplications. Thus Main Street became West Walnut, Chestnut became an avenue, Cherry was renamed Ashland and Willow became Oakland Avenue.

Later Fisk and Desnoyers projected an additional west to Oakland on both sides of Shawano Avenue, then known simply as the Wolf River road. As planned the road was to be a continuation of Main Street (Fort Howard style), but either through faulty surveying or because of confusion over the lines of some of the old French claims — which still plague abstractors — the line was off center. The promoters got into a wrangle, neither would give in, and the existing jog was the only way the two streets could be joined.

Tank's Addition

Fort Howard's next big expansion was Tank's Addition, made by Caroline Tank in 1863. Not being an imaginative sort and not on friendly terms with the townfolk, Madame Tank went her own way and adopted a completely independent system, numbering all her streets and calling those running east and west streets and the north-south thoroughfares avenues.

Later some were renamed Clinton, Clark, Elm and Oneida. Clark Street, named for an early resident, Thomas Clark, was again changed to West Mason in 1895. The original numbered avenues eventually became extensions of Broadway, Chestnut, Maple, Ashland and Oakland.

At first Fort Howard was blocked off from expansion northward by the Ft. Howard Military Reservation. The street just south of the boundary was therefore called Division Street.

When the reservation was opened for settlement Andrew Elmore got hold of a big share of it and platted an addition in his own way, honoring members of his family and close friends, many of whom never saw Green Bay. Dousman Street was named for his partner John Dousman, while Bond and Mather honored old friends rather than local figures.

Named for Family

Elmore, of course, was named for his own family; James, Phoebe, Augusta and Mary for his children. Phoebe Street, originally, was spelled Phebe and not as it is today. Kellogg was named for Horace Kellogg, then superintendent of the Dousman and Elmore grain elevator, who later moved to Alabama; Alexander and McDonald Streets remember Alexander and Hugh McDonald, proprietors of a mill and cooperage at their intersection near the river.

Streets in the Oak Circle subdivision are named for former Green Bay mayors except Wilson, which was named for William Wilson, proprietor of a dairy farm on the property that became Oak Circle shortly before World War I. Among mayors so honored are W. C. E. Thomas, L. S. M. Marshall, John and Arthur C. Neville, Winford Abrams, Frank Desnoyers (both of them) and R. E. Minahan.

Such streets as Christiana, Carolina, Cora, Camm Place, Reed, Gray and Allard honor once prominent citizens and their families. Howard (originally Baird) commemorates the Army officer for whom Fort Howard was named; Christiana was the wife of Sylvester Hartman; Caroline the wife of Sebastian Landwehr; and Cora the daughter of C. W. Lomas.

Thomas Camm Honored

Camm Place was named for Thomas Camm, first American white child born on the old military reservation. William Reed was a former city engineer, Oscar Gray was Fort

Howard's first postmaster, and the Allards were an old and prominent West Side family.

School Place apparently got its present name because it passed the old high school, having been originally Shawano until that title was given to the Wolf River Road. Norwood Avenue (who was Norwood, by the way?) was originally George Street and Arndt was John. All these changes were made in 1895.

Motor Street was so named because it was designed to give access to the old Oneida Truck Co. plant and Liberty Lane commemorates victory in World War I. The presidential series abandoned on the West Side has been haphazardly restored to honor Benjamin Harrison, Grover Cleveland, James Garfield, Abraham Lincoln and James Buchanan.

Of course, streets don't have to be named for persons or even events of local history. In the ever expanding areas of the far West Side imagination and possibly future hopes have been employed to come up with Shadow Lane, Syringa, Rockdale, Locust, Thrush and Thorndale. Still, every once in a while an old timer is remembered, and we get such titles as Platten, Gross, Biemeret, Shannon and Katers.

Long, Proud History

Firefighters' Oldest Facility

February 15, 1964

Do kids still get that old urge to grow up to be firemen when they see the big red wagons wheeling around the corner? Maybe not. Firefighting is a highly technical, professional skill now (although still dangerous, as the men who fought the Northern Paper Mills chip bin blaze recently can say) and some of the glamour may have disappeared with the prancing three-horse teams and smoke-belching steam pumpers of years ago.

It has been more than 40 years since a horse-drawn fire engine raced through the streets of Green Bay. But 40 years isn't much in the history of the local department, which moves into the second decade of its second century this spring.

Oldest public facility in the city and as old as the city itself, the Green Bay Fire Dept. is 110 years old this year. It dates from 1854 when a group of young German immigrants banded together to form the original Germania Fire Company. The present department stretches back in an unbroken line to that volunteer unit.

Typical of Time

Only a well-drilled bucket brigade at first, Germania Company was typical of its time-half serious, half social. Members were hand-picked, they elected their own officers and they took their duties seriously.

The unit never had any trouble recruiting members, either. It was an honor to be invited to join, and the company usually had an eager waiting list.

Many of Germania's charter members eventually became leaders of the community, but as long as they were physically able to race on foot to a fire they clung proudly to their membership. Since the majority were Germans, they kept all their records in German, right up to the day the unit went out of existence nearly 40 years later.

Filled a Need

Germania Company filled a serious need in the small frontier city, whose lack of organized fire protection had been highlighted by a disastrous conflagration in 1853 that left most of the business district in ashes. In fact, the work of the company was so obviously effective that in 1856 a second unit, called Guardian Company, was formed.

Initially both were bucket brigades, but in 1858 the city purchased its first fire engine, paying $250 for a mothballed hand pump machine that had been in storage at the Army post of Ft. Howard since the troops pulled out. The engine was issued to Germania Company, in whose hands it ultimately became locally famous as "Old Crocodile."

Shortly thereafter, exact date unknown, another hand engine was acquired for Guardian Company. One of the two machines is now on display in the Neville Public Museum, where it poses an interesting problem of identity.

Again Expanded

In the early years of the Civil War — again the exact date is uncertain — the fire department was again expanded, this time by the addition of a hook and ladder company. Over the next 20 years the department organization fluctuated as hook and ladder outfits went in and out of fashion.

The tiny hand pumpers, which also had to be dragged to the scene of a fire by hand, were basic equipment until 1868 when the city got its first steam pumper, a "second class" Amoskeag engine whose pump worked by steam generated in a wood-burning firebox and boiler. At that time "Old Crocodile" was apparently handed down to the hook and ladder boys, who became Astor Co. No. 3.

That Amoskeag complicated the research of future historians. In those days fire engines, like railroad locomotives, had names. Germania's pride and joy was called the "Enterprise."

Mistakenly Labeled

Since the company adopted the practice of wearing its engine name on caps and belt buckles, the unit later came to be called Enterprise Company. Actually, as members periodically were at pains to point out, the unit was still officially Germania No. One.

Five years later, in 1873 a second steamer was purchased, a "third class" Clapp & Jones model, and issued to Guardian Company. At the same time a fourth volunteer unit was formed which inherited Guardian's hand engine and adopted the name of Franklin Co. No. 4.

Meanwhile, across the river in Fort Howard, a volunteer unit had been organized as early as 1858. Exactly what its original equipment was isn't known, but in 1873 it also got a horse-drawn steamer, a Button & Sons machine.

No Connection

This was strictly a Fort Howard outfit, having no official connection with the Green Bay department. In practice, however, all the units worked closely together when the need arose, as all too often it did.

By 1875 the Green Bay "independent fire department" consisted of four engine companies, two equipped with horse-drawn steamers and two with hand engines, while Fort Howard had a single steamer company. Germania had 25 members (it was getting old and a bit exclusive), Guardian had 30 and Astor and Franklin 35 apiece. Fort Howard's unit was much larger, mustering 60 men.

Although the steamer units used different model machines, they were otherwise similarly equipped. Each had a pair of high-wheeled horse carts; one horse, the other hand pulled.

Got More Hose

The Green Bay department had 1,350 feet of hose and later that year got an additional 1,000 feet. Hose was divided between the companies and stored in individual engine houses, which were also elaborately fitted up with club rooms. These houses, it might be pointed out, were the private property of the companies and did not belong to the city.

The city did own the equipment and thus had some control but otherwise had little to say about the fire department's operation. The companies were extremely jealous of their "independent" status and proud of their records. Every effort to change the system was promptly shouted down.

The department could get away with it because most members of the city council were also volunteer firemen, with fierce loyalties to their units. The companies made full use of the tactic of splitting the council when they wanted to stall action on changes.

The volunteers elected their own company officers as well as the fire chief, whose nomination was subject to city council approval. This was usually automatic, although a deadlock ensued on one occasion when the council wouldn't go along and the firemen refused to budge.

Worked up to Job

Theoretically, anyone could be elected fire chief but in practice he worked up to the post. Nominees always started as company foremen and took a turn as assistant fire chief before stepping into the top slot.

In spite of the loose control, the system actually worked well. The companies were choosy about their membership, being a fireman carried prestige, and the volunteers were well aware of their responsibilities. They trained hard and conscientiously.

Keen rivalry existed between the companies but it never got out of hand and was encouraged as a good thing. Annual inspections and drills kept them on their toes, and there were enough real fires to prevent them from getting rusty.

Cooperative social activities also helped maintain a friendly atmosphere. The "Firemen's Ball" became a city fixture almost as soon as Germania Company learned to swing its original leather buckets by the numbers.

Things Different in 1856

City Primitive Century Ago

August 12, 1961

A few years ago a former Bayite, returning to his old home town for the first time in 60 years, got lost smack in front of the site of his boyhood home on Adams Street. It seemed funny at the time, but it could have been worse.

Had he come back after a century instead of only 60 years his predicament might have been even greater. The Green Bay of 1961 is a far cry from the raw little town of 1856, whose only real dignity was the new one of being rated a "city."

In what is now the main business district getting around might not be too tough for a pioneer who remembered his streets but beyond that he would be navigating strictly by the seat of his pants. In 1856 the area bounded by the Fox and East Rivers, Monroe Avenue — it wasn't an avenue then — and Mason Street was laid out as it is today, but there all resemblance ceases.

Most of the community of 1,644 people was concentrated in that quadrangle, whose outer fringes were thinly settled. There were a few homes dotting the foot of "The Hill," then known by its formal name of Astor Heights, but they almost qualified as farms. East of Monroe there was only heavily wooded swampland, drained by a creek running through Jackson Square and along Stuart Street.

City a Trading Center

Green Bay, being principally a trading center, had no factories and almost no business establishments east of Adams Street — itself largely residential. Everything was concentrated along Washington Street and the river front, trickling east for about half a block along the side streets between Main and Walnut.

A few warehouses, docks and wholesale houses — and a couple of saloons — were located along Main Street and the East River, but east of Jefferson the "best people" lived on Main, where Daniel Whitney had his home and had built his elaborate "Folly."

River frontages were lined with warehouses and docks piled high with lumber where sailing vessels and steamers tied up in ever increasing numbers during the navigation season. There were no bridges across the Fox River and only one across the East River at Main Street and that was out of whack.

The only contact with Fort Howard was by personal rowboat, skiff or canoe and by Carlton Wheelock's ferry, which operated in season from the foot of Cherry Street to a landing below the gate of the recently abandoned Army post on the west bank.

Bridge Not Important

The condition of the East River bridge wasn't too important because it was used largely by farmers whose visits to town were most frequent in winter when they could cross on the ice. The present industrialized and thickly populated North Side was a flat, unoccupied prairie stretching to the bay shore, covered with tall grass that burned over a couple of times a year.

Those grass fires were spectacular shows, sometimes lasting for days and easily watched from the roof of the Astor House at Mason and Adams Streets. The purchase of 485 acres of this wasteland by John Day and Harry Eastman from Whitney for a rumored price of $10,500 created quite a stir.

For a time in 1856 it looked as though a bridge might be thrown across the Fox. The State Legislature authorized one and preliminary surveys were made at John Arndt's landing on the approximate site of the WPS bus barns *(on South Washington Street until recently).*

The authorization made no provision for financing, however, and when it developed that Green Bay and Fort Howard would have to foot the bill, the project collapsed. Fort Howard balked, Green Bay refused to go it alone and the river remained unspanned until the first bridge was built at Walnut Street during the Civil War.

Attitude Understandable

Fort Howard's attitude was understandable.

As a community it was only half a dozen years old and less than half the size of Green Bay. Like all bustling and ambitious little towns struggling for a foothold in the shadow of an older and bigger settlement, it was fiercely jealous of its position.

Confident it would one day surpass its rival — a hope that wasn't as unreasonable as it sounds — Fort Howard was not about to get sucked into any scheme that figured to hurt more than help. Its fears were well grounded, too, as the eventual construction of a bridge in 1862-63 demonstrated.

The little village, population about 750, but already showing signs of manufacturing development, became a borough in 1856. Corporate limits extended west from the river to a line along Oak and Columbia Streets and south from James Street to Lake.

Northward expansion was blocked by the Fort Howard Military Reservation which was shortly opened up for sale and quickly grabbed by Morgan L. Martin, Whitney and a few others. Two wide sloughs to the south, one of them swinging wide to the north through what is now Seymour Park almost to Velp Avenue, hampered development to the south and west until filled in many years later.

As in Green Bay, business activity was spread along the waterfront and west to Pearl Street, then the principal business street. Broadway was the best residential section. Beyond that there was very little settlement, even within the town's meager boundaries.

Looked Much Alike

Except for the difference in size both towns probably looked much alike with unpaved, unlighted streets and buildings mostly of wood. In both, however, there was increasing use of brick and stone construction.

Outside the "downtown" areas there were no sidewalks. Such walks as existed were wooden, duckboard affairs, raised several inches above the roadways to afford some protection from the mud and to permit water to run off beneath them. These walks easily became dilapidated and were slick with mud in wet weather. It was a finable offense not to make some effort to keep them clean.

The principal business thoroughfares, dust choked in summer and ankle deep in mud in the spring and after heavy rains, were a major source of annoyance. Washington Street almost got out of the mud in 1856 but a wrangle over paying for it scuttled an effort to plank the street, which remained a mess for another decade.

In winter, when the ruts were filled up and the snow hard packed, travel about town was pretty easy. Advocate editor Charles Robinson, a sleighing enthusiast, was always remarking about the "delightful sleighing," but he took a dim view of another civic habit.

Most people and businesses disposed of ashes by spreading them in the streets. Not only did this make it difficult for teams to get to the stores, but it also spoiled Robinson's fun.

Stayed in the Mud

Hassle Broke Up Paving Project

May 14, 1966

When was the last time you bogged down in the mud of Washington Street?

The question is purely rhetorical, since the city's main drag has enjoyed paving of one sort or another for just 100 years now. It might have been longer if the first serious attempt to pave the street hadn't blown up ten years earlier, in 1856, when property owners along the street raised a stink about paying for the badly needed improvement.

Today it is almost impossible to imagine the primitive condition of Green Bay's main business streets a century and more ago. Having been built on reclaimed swamp land, the downtown area was pretty soft and heavy rains or spring thaws annually transformed otherwise dry, dusty thoroughfares like Washington Street into oozy morasses.

Heavy horse and wagon traffic churned the mud into an ankle-deep gumbo that frequently bogged bulky vehicles to their axles. It was an adventure for a pedestrian just to cross a street under such conditions and impossible to do it without being covered with goo to the boot tops.

Messy Aftermath

The aftermath of a spring thaw or rain was a twisting mass of deep ruts that had to be broken down by continued use. Thereafter, in dry weather a heavy pall of dust hung over everything.

Charles Robinson of the Advocate had been yelling for years about fixing up Washington Street. His drum fire apparently bore fruit late in June of 1856 when the city council received a petition from 26 citizens to plank the main business thoroughfare.

In July, much to the delight of the Advocate, the council voted to go ahead with the job. After the usual bids, the firm of Tyler & Arndt was awarded the contract to plank Washington Street from Main to Doty, a distance of 100 rods, at $50 a rod. Work was to be completed by Oct. 30.

Uproar Began

Then the uproar began. The authorizing ordinance, instead of spreading the cost over the entire city tax base, specified that it would be born by assessment against owners of property fronting the improvement.

A howl immediately went up, some of the loudest squawks coming from signers of the original paving petition. After threats of legal action if the city tried to collect any such assessment, the council called the whole thing off.

The city fathers may have been only slightly impressed by the hue and cry. Of possibly greater significance in their thinking was an unforeseen development.

Closer study had revealed that the east side of the street was several inches higher than the west side. An expensive grading job, not initially counted on, would have to precede the planking.

Held the Bag

Meanwhile, Tyler & Arndt — the latter was old J.P.'s son, John Wallace — had purchased, cut and stacked the necessary planking. When the contract was cancelled the firm was left holding the bag.

The company promptly yelled about being out of pocket because the now unnecessary lumber could only be disposed of at a loss (the purchaser was the city of Oshkosh, which used it to plank its own main street). A damage claim for $500 was subsequently settled for half that amount.

Green Bay didn't know it, but a decade was to pass before the street finally got out of the mud. The depression of 1857 and the Civil War put a stop to most expansion and improvement plans.

There was no further effort to do anything about the street until after the Civil War. In 1866 the project was revived, almost foundered again in a wrangle over the kind of pavement to be installed, but finally went through.

Done in 1866

Just a century ago Anton Klaus laid the first Washington Street pavement from Main to Doty. The type chosen was a cedar block process known as Nicholson pavement, and the price was much stiffer than $50 a rod.

The badly needed paving job was about the only construction project that didn't come off in 1856, though. It was a year of great business boom, led by lumber, which triggered a riot of speculation that led directly to the financial panic of the following year.

One reason for some of the heated feeling over the paving project could well have been the weather. The year 1856 provided just about everything calculated to inspire extremes of optimism and frustration.

The winter of 1855-56 didn't produce as much snow as the record fall of the previous year but was bitterly cold. The first 20 days of January averaged 12.5 degrees below zero, the minimum being 25 below on the tenth.

Green Bay Flies

By July the city was sweltering in oppressive heat and slapping at unusually heavy incursions of mosquitoes and Green Bay flies, the latter an annual phenomenon here until they disappeared about 30 years ago. On July 10 one of the worst hail storms in years pelted the region with hail stones an inch in diameter that caused a lot of damage.

The summer was exceptionally dry, and the surrounding woods were afire until the end of October. At times the forest fires were so bad vessels were smoke bound on the bay and river.

The town lived, as most did in those days, in constant fear of forest fires but was never seriously threatened. Fort Howard wasn't as lucky, a good part of the business section being burned out in August.

Careless Indians

In that case, however, the origin was laid to the carelessness of a party of *(local)* Indians. Only the timely arrival of Green Bay's Germania Fire Co. via Wheelock's ferry prevented a real disaster.

The winter of 1856-57 surpassed in depth of snowfall the record of 1854-55. So frequent and heavy were the blizzards that from three to five feet of snow in the open was average, with even greater depths in the thick woods.

Such snows practically ruined the season's logging. Many companies pulled their crews out of the woods weeks ahead of time after cutting only a fraction of the anticipated harvest.

1856 Political Pot Bubbled

September 9, 1961

Green Bay has been a municipality for more than 100 years now, and during that century has witnessed a lot of political battles. But just in case any of the modern generation thinks it has it on the old timers when it comes to political consciousness and activity, it can be said right here and now the idea is wrong. If anything, politicking a century ago was hotter than today.

There wasn't much else to do outside business hours in 1856. The result was that politics were not only important to the opening of the forest wilderness that covered most of Wisconsin but as a diversion took the combined places of TV, radio, movies, football and automobiles, none of which had even been dreamed of then.

The year 1856 saw almost continuous turmoil, opening with a wrangle over the governorship and closing with a heated presidential campaign. The new Republican party, born in Ripon only two years before, was moving into the national as well as the state arena and its sectional activity was making inroads on the domination of the Democrats.

This was particularly true in Green Bay where Timothy O. Howe was embarking on the career that would send him to the U.S. Senate for 18 years and culminate in the postmaster generalship.

One-Sided Record

Unfortunately, much of the locally printed record has a one-sided cast. Although the Republicans tried to establish a party organ here they couldn't quite make it, so the staunchly Democratic Green Bay Advocate had the field to itself. Republican efforts, as a result, were pretty well ignored while Democratic principles hogged most of the editorial ink.

The year began with a bitter fight in Madison over the governorship between Democratic incumbent William A. Barstow and Republican Coles Bashford. The 1855 election had been tighter than a Yankee banker, and with communications primitive and claims and counterclaims flying in all directions nobody knew exactly who had won.

Barstow, whose previous administration had been notorious, claimed re-election by 157 votes and duly had himself inaugurated under the rifles of armed supporters. Bashford was also sworn in and demanded the office, which Barstow refused to vacate.

While both sides oiled their shooting irons the squabble went to the State Supreme Court, where a brilliant array of legal talent — including Tim Howe — squared off. The court found for Bashford, who was eventually seated after Barstow's last minute maneuver to give the office to Lt. Gov. Arthur MacArthur (Gen. Douglas MacArthur's grandfather) failed.

Followed Tense Situation

Green Bay followed the tense situation avidly all through its three-month course, expecting to hear at any moment that the shooting had started. The Advocate seems to have sensed something fishy, however, and steered a cautious editorial course.

Scarcely had the state's political pot ceased to boil when city elections rolled around. Held April 1, they resulted in a clean sweep, only Porter Parish being returned to office as an alderman of the South Ward. Issues, however, revolved around purely local problems and personalities rather than party affiliations, and the election itself was unusually quiet.

Frank Desnoyers did not run for re-election as mayor, and Harry E. Eastman beat Henry S. Baird, 198 votes to 131. Neither city treasurer Anton Klaus nor school superintendent James H. Howe stood for a second term, their respective replacements being H. H. Albright and Dr. Charles E. Crane.

Albright's margin over Henry C. Reber was 160-146 while Crane won a minority decision from attorney Myron P. Lindsley and hardware merchant Alonzo Kimball. Crane's vote was 133 to 104 for Lindsley and 87 for Kimball.

Aldermen named for the North Ward were County Judge David Agry — also elected county supervisor — H.M. Cady, Louis J. Day and S. H. Marshall. They replaced Dan W. King, Washington Parish, Nelson Langton and C. J. Bender.

Arndt into Office

In the South Ward old John P. Arndt was elected alderman-supervisor, together with Thomas Green, Porter Parish and Albert C. Robinson. Parish was the lone holdover, others stepping out being Louis Hoeffel, Alfred Pelton and Albert Scheller.

The new City Council first met on April 5, a Saturday afternoon. The vote was canvassed with great punctilio and Eastman declared elected mayor. After choosing Arndt to be council president, C. H. Kies, city clerk, and George Langton, city marshal, Kies was directed to wait upon the new mayor and inform him of his election. The council then adjourned until Monday evening, April 7.

At that time the new aldermen were seated with due formality and Eastman was escorted into the chamber by a committee of two. After being sworn in by Arndt, Eastman announced his appointments to standing committees and delivered his inaugural address. The appointments didn't take very long as there were only five committees, those on Accounts, Poor, Streets and Bridges, Plant Roads and Printing.

Specific points in the inaugural address, printed in full in the next issue of the Advocate, were calls for a new East River bridge to replace a worn-out span unusable for two years; a new jail (the old pokey had already been sold); and widening of the principal business streets. Eastman also plunked for a railroad and had some caustic things to say about the previous council's action in issuing city bonds to the Green Bay & De Pere Plank Road Co., during which his opponent Baird came in for heavy criticism.

Fall Campaign Spirited

That fall's presidential campaign was spirited, although the national issue of slavery didn't cut much ice locally. The young and eager Republicans put up such a good fight that the Advocate breathed a sigh of relief when James Buchanan took two-thirds of the 1,500 county vote from John C. Fremont.

The Democrats also won the congressional seat, Harrison C. Hobart of Outagamie County beating Charles Billinghurst by about the same margin. Morgan L. Martin did not run for reelection to the Assembly, and his place went to Edgar Conklin, who defeated James Howe. Perry H. Smith's Senate seat was not up for grabs.

County offices were likewise dominated by the Democrats. F. Edward White won a three-cornered battle for the post of sheriff from Daniel M. Whitney and James Porlier. Albert Robinson beat William C. E. Thomas for register of deeds and James B. A. Masse was elected clerk of court over John P. Dousman.

Henry Reber became county treasurer, John V. Suydam, surveyor, and Lucien B. Wright clerk of the county board. John McCarty Sr. was victor over Daniel Hubbard for the office of coroner.

Hot Off the Wires

1856 News Coverage Excellent

September 23, 1961

Residents of Green Bay and Fort Howard a century ago may have put up with living conditions that seem fantastic and even appalling in this day of push button housekeeping, fancy plumbing and jet age transportation, but they were remarkably well informed on what was going on in the world. Although the community enjoyed no railroad, telegraph or telephones and had only one weekly newspaper, a check of the four-page Green Bay Advocate of 1856 reveals a surprising wealth of local, regional, national and international news.

Despite the lack of rail and wire facilities, news of distant places reached here with surprising speed, especially in the summer when lake transportation was open. Items published in New York City were known in Green Bay within 96 hours, thanks to excellent steamer service from Buffalo, N. Y., and Collingwood, Michigan.

In winter, when everything had to come overland it took a little longer. Even then, however, news from Washington was received in less than two weeks via Chicago, Milwaukee and Fond du Lac by rail and stage coach.

European news usually required about a fortnight to reach New York by steam packet from London and the continent. On arrival quick telegraphic summaries were wired to Buffalo and Chicago and then sent to Green Bay from one point or the other, depending upon the season.

Late European News

The Advocate published on Thursday. Latest European dispatches were condensed into a single column headlined "Arrival of the Steamship Adriatic!" — or Pacific, Baltic, Artic, whatever vessel it might be. If time permitted details were culled from the New York papers arriving at the same time. Otherwise they were left until the next issue.

Since many settlers in the area were recent immigrants they were hungry for news from home. Consequently, continental dispatches were given important play.

The doings of royalty were closely followed, particularly the activities of Napoleon II who appeared about to revive the glories of the great Bonaparte. On the other end of the scale the commodity markets of London and Paris were reported with equal care.

In 1856 the Crimean War was dragging to a close and had ceased to draw the attention given it in the previous two years. News of the signing of the peace treaty in Paris on March 30 reached New York on April 17 and appeared in the Advocate as a routine story on the 24th. More space was currently being accorded William Walker's filibustering expedition to Nicaragua which was shortly to leave New York.

Gold Rush Past Peak

The California Gold Rush had passed its peak but the drama of riches for the taking still gripped the imagination of the area, to which several disillusioned 49ers had already returned. Transmission of stories of violence, great fortunes and the Vigilantes from the gold fields was astonishingly rapid.

News from San Francisco took only nine days to reach New York via the Isthmus of Panama, one dispatch datelined Jan. 20 in California being published in New York on the 29th and in Green Bay on Feb. 7. The ship that brought it from Panama was the "Star of the West," destined to find her way into the history books a few years later because of her unsuccessful attempt to reinforce Fort Sumter on the eve of the Civil War.

Dispatches from Oregon, where another Indian war was raging, were a little later. A letter written there on Nov. 8, 1855, reached Green Bay on Jan. 31, 1856, while a later news story dated Jan. 26 was published on March 6.

Interested in War

Green Bay was keenly interested in the progress of the Oregon campaign since some of the troops involved had only recently left Ft. Howard. This was particularly true of the Haller Expedition, Major Haller being well known here.

Other prominently played national news included the trouble in Kansas — two weeks from Leavenworth — renewal of the Seminole War in Florida, and politics, especially the annual message of President Franklin Pierce and the election of 1856 that put James Buchanan in the White House. Political parties on the national and local stage that year were the Whigs, Democrats, "Know Nothings" and the new Republicans.

The assault on Sen. Charles Sumner of Massachusetts in the Senate chamber by Preston Brooks of South Carolina was one of the news sensations of the year. A spate of ghastly wrecks on eastern railroads also got a big play.

In addition, a mass of miscellaneous information was lifted from exchange newspapers and printed with customary credit. Some of the latter appear to have been selected more for space filling qualities than for any burning interest on the part of local readers.

State News Excellent

State and regional happenings were fully reported, many of them by clipping exchanges. A top story early in 1856 was the battle for the state governorship between Coles Bashford and William Barstow, in which Tim Howe of Green Bay was involved.

Proceedings of the state legislature got a lot of ink, apparently being covered principally through letters to editor Robinson from county representatives. Railroad legislation, attacks on the Fox River Improvement Co. and the chartering of several plank roads centered in Green Bay were closely followed.

Important regional developments

outside the state capital included the arrival of the steamer Aquila, signaling completion of the Fox and Wisconsin waterway; construction of the North Western Railroad to Fond du Lac and plans for its extension to Appleton; and the death of Solomon Juneau. The founder of Milwaukee had once lived here briefly, had married a Green Bay woman and was well known locally. His death on Nov. 14 and his elaborate funeral were extensively covered by clippings from the Milwaukee Sentinel.

The booming lumber industry and iron mining in Upper Michigan were of great concern to local business and were covered accordingly. The assassination of "King James" Strang and the crushing of his fantastic Mormon "kingdom" on Beaver Island was one of the year's highlights.

Population Swelling

With settlers pouring into Wisconsin on a constantly rising tide, population figures were popular even though admittedly obsolete as fast as compiled. A state census of 1855, published early the following year, showed a population of 552,109, up a quarter of a million from 1850. Brown County's total of 6,699 wasn't much above that of five years before, but everyone was at pains to point out that the 1850 figures applied to an area since carved into seven counties whose combined population was 19,653.

Although traffic on the Great Lakes had reached tremendous volume it was highly dangerous, as a compilation of lake disasters of 1855 demonstrated. It showed that $2,821,591 in property and 119 lives had been lost in 603 shipwrecks and fires.

Hazards of lake travel were brought close to home on Oct. 1, 1856, when the steamer Niagara, en route to Green Bay from Collingwood, was destroyed by fire about 25 miles up the bay. Early estimates of over 100 fatalities were subsequently scaled down, but it was still a real catastrophe. Two or three Green Bay men aboard were saved.

Project Isn't New

Waterway to the Mississippi

July 30, 1966

The project of the Brown County Harbor Commission to build a river waterway from the Mississippi to Green Bay via the Wisconsin and Fox Rivers is not, as recently indicated, a dream of nearly 100 years standing. As a dream it is much older than that, and a century ago the waterway was an accomplished fact, thanks to a number of Green Bay pioneers whose timing was not as precise as their vision.

As long ago as 1856 a shallow draft, paddle-wheel steamer passed over such a waterway to mark completion of the project. It went through a system of locks and dams, moreover, that is almost exactly what is envisioned as another possibility today.

Completion of a Fox and Wisconsin River waterway to the Mississippi was fulfillment of a hope as old as the white settlement of the Northwest. Ever since the early French explorers had discovered that a small boat could proceed from Quebec to New Orleans with only a short haul across the hump between the rivers at Portage, men had talked of linking the two and, by taming the rapids on the lower Fox, provide a cheap and uninterrupted means of transportation.

Began in 1825

Real action began in 1825 when a few Green Bay men, led by John P. Arndt, began to study its chances realistically. In 1829, Morgan L. Martin, then a member of the Michigan territorial legislature, introduced a bill to charter a construction company to cut a canal, build docks, warehouses and wharves along the route and a turnpike parallel to it.

The bill was duly passed and a corporation formed. Arndt, Martin, John Lawe, Lewis Rouse, Henry Baird and Joseph Watson were named commissioners to sell stock in it.

Although the Michigan Legislature was willing, it could not provide funds to do the job. For several years pressure was exerted in Congress to provide customary land grants.

Nursed through Congress

In 1845 Martin, by then Wisconsin's territorial delegate, nursed a bill through Congress authorizing grants for two separate jobs, a canal at Portage to connect the two rivers and improvement of navigation on the lower Fox. The act, signed by President James K. Polk in 1846, was to become effective upon Wisconsin's imminent admission to the union.

One of the first acts of Wisconsin's new state Legislature was to start the project, but since the constitution forbade going into debt for internal improvements the job had to be a pay-as-you-go affair, financed by land sales. After a promising start, however, sales lagged. Although the Portage canal was dug, work slowed so badly the state decided to call the whole thing off.

Governor Opposed

Not so Martin, who offered to finish the job himself, the state to reimburse him through toll charges on the waterway and further land sales. A contract was approved by the Legislature in 1851 and Martin put a crew of 500 men to work, starting near Kaukauna and working both ways.

A change of administration in 1852 put Gov. Leonard J. Farwell in the statehouse. Farwell questioned the constitutionality of the contract, refused to pay Martin state script owed him and vetoed a bill which would have by-passed his objections.

The bill was passed over his veto, but the following year Farwell proposed another to get the state out of the business entirely and put it in private hands. The Fox & Wisconsin Improvement Co. was duly organized with Martin, Otto Tank, Joseph G. Lawton of De Pere and Uriah H. Peak among the key officers, and the job transferred to it.

By 1855 the series of locks and dams was well enough along to permit use by shallow draft boats. In June, 1856, the steamer Aquila, out of Pittsburgh by way of the Ohio, Mississippi and Wisconsin Rivers, made the first official passage of the system to Green Bay.

Triumph Short-Lived

Martin's triumph was short-lived. Before the year was out the state forced the rebuilding of a portion of the work, resolved a dispute over land grants in its own favor and put the whole thing, together with all remaining unsold lands assigned to the company, into the hands of a hand-picked board of trustees.

Faced with unexpected reconstruction costs and deprived of its major source of revenue, the company was forced to seek assistance from New York financiers. The latter soon outplayed the local men and maneuvered the company into such a shaky position the trustees were prevailed upon to sell out. The buyers? The New York crowd.

The easterners promptly formed a new corporation called the Green Bay & Mississippi Canal Co., then unloaded on the federal government, retaining, however, waterpower rights which it still holds. Today the company is only a paper corporation, but every time an electric turbine generates a kilowatt of electricity along the Fox River the company collects a royalty.

Off the Hook

By selling, the state got off the hook but the original builders were left holding the bag. Principal victim was Martin, who had poured most of his considerable personal fortune into the project and who was financially ruined by the state's repudiation of its contracts with him.

In any event, the completion of the waterway came too late. By the time it was finished railroads were putting skids under internal canal systems, and the expectations of the builders of the Fox-Wisconsin link were never realized.

The lower Fox portion of the system has proved valuable, however, but not as its builders had figured. For many years there was considerable barge traffic between Green Bay and Lake Winnebago, but of greater significance was the harnessing of the tremendous power potential of the river.

Today the numerous manufacturing plants and paper mills that line the banks of the Fox from Oshkosh to Green Bay derive their power from the system envisioned and pushed to completion by Morgan Martin over a century ago.

Frustrated Editor

How Green Bay Heard of Sumter

April 22, 1961

One hundred years ago last week news of the firing on Ft. Sumter reached Green Bay. The word came a few days after the event and was greeted, as everywhere in the North, with patriotic indignation. To no one was the news more frustrating than to C. D. Robinson.

Not that he wanted war any more than anyone else. But as editor of the weekly Green Bay Advocate Charley would have appreciated more regard for his deadline than the Confederates displayed at far off Charlestòn.

April 12 was the Advocate's publication date and the presses had already been closed when the South opened fire that morning. Very likely the paper had already been delivered by the time the first reports reached here; consequently, Robinson had to wait another week to print the news, and by then everybody knew all about it. His only consolation must have been that the rival Bay City Press, which came out on the 13th, didn't have the story either.

Actually, the town didn't know all about the event even a week later. The Advocate's April 19th issue gave the story a big play but the news was still fragmentary and confusing. Robinson's editor friend on the Oshkosh Northwestern had sent him the telegraphic reports as fast as they came in and he printed them all, but the account still wasn't very coherent.

Lines Still Open

Telegraph lines between Charleston and Washington were still open and the Charleston operator was conscientious. He sent a series of flashes all through the bombardment but he was excited, rumors were flying all over the southern city and his dispatches reflected the confusion. Even the personal account given to the press by Maj. Robert Anderson on his arrival in New York, which the Advocate printed intact, was fragmentary.

The whole affair must have had an air of unreality about it here. Cut off in its annual winter isolation, Green Bay hadn't really sensed the mounting crisis that followed the series of secessions in the winter of 1860-61. A few residents had gone east and returned with accounts of events there, but by and large the little community had been preoccupied with its own affairs.

What direct news it got was always several days late and so badly garbled it was difficult to separate facts from rumor. In fact, Robinson had complained in print several times about the sensational play given the winter's events in other state papers, which he accused of being more interested in stirring up emotions than in keeping readers calmly and accurately informed.

Word that the shooting had begun wasn't exactly a surprise although, in communities like Green Bay where Democratic sympathies were predominant, there had been hopes things wouldn't go that far. Robinson, a staunch Douglas Democrat and no admirer of anything Republican — including Abraham Lincoln — had since the first secessions been printing and editorializing on every scrap of information he could get about the various attempts to prevent open hostilities.

Hopes Seem Naive

Today his hopes seem naive, but thousands then were not convinced of either the necessity or the inevitability of war. Even without being isolated between the election of 1860 and the bombardment of Sumter, most of the people of Green Bay would probably have felt the same way.

The closest railroad connection ended at Fond du Lac, although the North Western reached Appleton in March, and Oshkosh was the end of the telegraph line. The river and lakes were frozen and the only outside contact was by stage to Oshkosh and Fond du Lac. By mid-April the roads through the Valley were quagmires, and it took a full day or more to make the uncomfortable journey.

As soon as word of the surrender of Sumter came through, however, any doubts about the area's attitude were quickly swept away. During the following week a big mass meeting at Klaus Hall volleyed fire and patriotism and the official attitude of the town was similar to that following Pearl Harbor. At the same time there were strong feelings that fighting wouldn't last long — Robinson, to his credit, felt differently — and beyond starting a patriotic welfare fund the town settled back to see what would happen next.

There wasn't much else to do. Green Bay was a small place, the entire population of the city, Fort Howard and De Pere combined being less than 3,500. In fact, the 1860 Census gave a population of only 11,800 for all of Brown County, although that was almost double the figure of 1850 when the county also included Outagamie, Door, Oconto, Kewaunee and Shawano counties. Green Bay's population was 2,265, the Borough of Fort Howard had 696 and the Village of De Pere another 505.

Description of City

The city's residents were clustered in an area between Monroe Avenue and the Fox River and north from Mason Street to the East River, with still plenty of open spaces on the outskirts. Everything east of Monroe was still a tangled swamp, the area north of East River a grass-choked marsh and there were only a few homes like Morgan L. Martin's Hazlewood south of Mason.

The rest of the county was covered with forests just beginning to feel the renewed attack of the lumbermen and dotted with prosperous farm clearings as well as a few small villages. Roads were poor and people used them only when they had to.

Except for incoming farmers, many of whom couldn't speak English, the townspeople had no contact with these areas, whose economic importance was only beginning to be realized. If the farmers wanted anything they had to come in and get it.

One reason the city was more interested in its own affairs than in either the surrounding wilderness or the distant east was because it was just beginning to feel a revival of prosperity after the depression of 1857. A war that threatened such a revival was not welcome.

A key indication of conditions in the county had cropped up early in 1861 when an unprecedented stream of farm wagons began rolling into town with excess produce stored in barns over the winter. For the first time in its short history an area that had always imported food found it was not only producing all it needed but had an impressive quantity left over for export.

Observance Sunday

Diocese Hits Century Mark

September 28, 1968

Wednesday morning in St. Francis Xavier Cathedral, in the presence of Archbishop William Cousins of Milwaukee and the other Roman Catholic bishops of Wisconsin, Bishop Aloysius Wycislo will concelebrate a Mass honoring the centennial of the Catholic Diocese of Green Bay. It will mark the only major observance of the centennial, although the following Sunday, Oct. 6, more informal rites will celebrate it in the parishes of the diocese.

Actually, Wednesday's celebration is late. The Green Bay diocese could mark its existence from two different dates a century ago.

The first might be March 3, on which date Pope Pius IX actually created the diocese in 1868. The other could be July 22, the day on which its first bishop, Joseph Melcher, was installed in old St. Mary's Church 100 years ago.

The March 3 date was passed this year because of the lack of a bishop following the death of Bishop Stanislaus V. Bona. By July 22 his successor, Bishop Wycislo, had not been here long enough to be thoroughly familiar with his new see.

Dates from 1669

Catholicism in Green Bay goes much farther back than a century, however. Properly, it dates from 1669 when the Jesuit Claude Allouez arrived and celebrated the first Mass in the area at what is now Oconto on Dec. 3. In 1871 Father Allouez established the Mission of St. Francis Xavier, at De Pere.

A famous installation in the history of Wisconsin, the De Pere mission was burned by the Indians in 1687 and never rebuilt. Although there were sporadic visits by missionaries thereafter, it was not until 1825 that a successor, a chapel to St. Francis, was constructed at the corner of Adams and Mason Streets.

Throughout the pioneer years Green Bay was part of a number of dioceses but usually far out on the limb, a wilderness outpost too far away for its bishops to visit regularly. In fact, it wasn't until 1821 that Bishop Fenwick of Cincinnatti got his first look at the place, later sending the Rev. Samuel Mazzuchelli to Wisconsin to further the cause of Catholicism.

St. John's First

Green Bay's first permanent parish was that of St. John the Evangelist, whose first church was constructed in 1831. Five years later a second parish, St. John Little Chute, was established. Such well remembered pioneer priests as Fathers Mazzuchelli, Theodore Van den Broek and Florimund Bonduel roamed the area, moving from one community to the next on their missionary rounds.

The initial step toward creating a Catholic diocese was apparently taken at the Council of Baltimore in 1856 but nothing came of it. The idea was renewed at another council in 1866, and two years later Pope Pius IX took the necessary action.

The Rev. Joseph Melcher, vicar-general of the archdiocese of St. Louis, was named for the see, consecrated at St. Louis on July 12, 1868, and installed at Green Bay ten days later. He took over a wilderness area of 15,378 square miles, largely populated by Indians and pine trees but containing 26 churches, 37 stations, 12 parish schools and 40,000 Catholics.

Number Uncertain

The number of priests is uncertain. Earlier histories said there were only 16, but a centennial book just published under the editorship of Fathers Gordon Gilsdorf and William Zimmer puts the figure at 26.

Since the turn of the century, as new dioceses were created in Wisconsin, the size of the Green Bay diocese has been reduced. Today it encompasses 10,851 square miles, within which are 317,500 Catholics served by 354 priests.

Bishop Melcher was a hard working man but he only had five years in which to work. When he died in 1873 the diocese had 56 priests, 93 churches and a Catholic population of 60,000.

Cathedral Builder

The present seat of the bishop of Green Bay, St. Francis Xavier Cathedral, was the work of his successor, Bishop Francis Krautbauer. Bishop Krautbauer personally drew the plans for the cathedral rectory, an impressive French mansard style building on Madison Street, which was originally the bishop's residence. *(Whether Krautbauer designed the rectory is debatable though he did design the Cathedral based on a European model.)*

Detailing the growth of such a vast establishment as the Green Bay Diocese over a period of 100 years requires more space than can be given here. Suffice to say that the figures involved, in terms of people, buildings and money, staggers the imagination.

Other than the normal activities of the diocese through four generations the story of the Green Bay Diocese has one unusual highlight. In the 1870s and 1880s peaceful progress was upset by a fascinating character, one Rene Vilatte, who called himself the "Archbishop of the Old Catholic Church."

Although his right to the title was clouded, Vilatte posed a problem to Bishop Sebastian G. Messmer, who was never quite sure that, whatever Vilatte's activities, his consecration as a bishop was not valid. Consequently, Bishop Messmer treated him with kid gloves.

Norbertines Came

At the height of Vilatte's influence, Bishop Messmer called for help, which was forthcoming in the person of Rev. Bernard Pennings, a little Norbertine from Holland. From the arrival of Father Pennings dates the establishment of the Norbertine Order in America, its only Western Hemisphere abbey *(at the time of this writing)* at De Pere, and St. Norbert College.

In 100 years the Green Bay diocese has had eight bishops, including the recently installed incumbent, Bishop Wycislo. Two of them, Bishops Paul P. Rhode and Bona, headed the diocese for 52 of those 100 years.

Education has kept pace with the growth of the diocese, too. From no schools in 1868 and a school enrollment of 10,785 in 1892, the Green Bay Diocese today operates 120 parochial elementary schools with 40,500 pupils, 14 high schools with 6,365 students and two colleges whose enrollment last year totaled 2,274.

Chapter Three

The Economy Takes Hold

No Arid Desert

City Once Brewed Plenty of Suds

December 6, 1969

Caroline Stewart's *(former Press-Gazette writer)* recent pitch to change Green Bay's nickname from "Titletown" to "Tippletown" is rooted (perhaps "floats" would be a better word) in some pretty impressive statistics. In one vital respect, though, she was, literally as well as figuratively, "all wet."

While it may be true now that Green Bay has no local suds to help maintain its newly acquired reputation as the beer-drinkingest town in the nation, things weren't always in such arid surroundings. It was only three years ago that the city's last brewery closed the tap.

If cities, like people, establish habits early, Green Bay comes honestly by its suds-quaffing proclivities. Over a period of more than a century this city has had five breweries — in fact, at one time the vats of all five were bubbling merrily away at the same time.

Like so many other items in the history of Wisconsin, Green Bay had something of a first in brewing, too. The first brewery in Northeastern Wisconsin was established here in 1850.

Founded in 1850

The founder was Francis Blesch, who settled in Fort Howard that year and promptly went into the trade for which he had been trained. Born in Germany 1834, Blesch learned what were then the combined skills of cooper and brewer before he struck out for America in 1849.

Sensing his place in the vanguard of the influx of German immigrants into an area where beer was not easily available, Blesch set up a small brewery on Broadway in Fort Howard, about where the Larsen Company *(more recently Agrilink Foods)* is now. Since he had a monopoly to begin with, his suds factory prospered so well that about 1856 he built a new and larger plant, the first two-story stone structure in the city.

While the Blesch name was long remembered in Green Bay, most of the credit goes to old Francis' son. Francis T. Blesch wasn't interested in beer brewing, though. He went into merchandizing, was a co-founder of the Jorgenson-Blesch store *(now Prange's, and more recently, Younkers).* Sometime before the father's death in 1879 — the exact date has been forgotten — the Blesch brewery went out of business.

Too Much Competition?

Maybe it was the competition. By that time Green Bay had four suds mills of its own to keep pace with the demands of its 90-odd saloons.

Blesch's first competition came from another pair of young German immigrants — August Hochgreve and Henry Rahr — who arrived in Green Bay in 1858 and 1857, respectively. Like Blesch, Gus Hochgreve was a trained brewer and cooper, as his father had been before him, although Rahr was not. His only experience had been gained working for a few years in an uncle's place in Manitowoc before coming here.

Hochgreve, born in 1832, came to the United States in 1852 and to Green Bay in 1858. He shortly got together with Rahr and they set up in Allouez, where the Reimer Cold Storage plant now stands. *(The site on Riverside Drive, with some modification to the original building, now houses Schenck Business Solutions.)* Their business grew so rapidly that they built a second plant in Green Bay.

Partnership Split

The partnership split up in 1866, Hochgreve retaining the Allouez business and Rahr taking over the Green Bay brewery, which he promptly rebuilt. Hochgreve died in 1877 but by that time his son Chris had taken over.

Rahr, two years younger than Hochgreve, had come to America at the age of 19 and worked in his uncle's Manitowoc brewery before moving to Green Bay. His establishment on Main Street, originally called the East River Brewery, outlived all the others and by the time Henry died in 1891 was flourishing under the management of his sons.

Meanwhile, two other breweries got going in the late 1860s. Fourth man in the suds ring was Franz Hagemeister, who came to this country in the early part of the decade and opened a prosperous meat market in Green Bay.

No Brewing Background

There is no record that Hagemeister had any brewing background in Prussia, where he was born in 1826, but he had capital, and in 1866 formed a brewing company with four partners whom he later bought out. Actually, the business was built by his son Henry (born 1855), who went into the brewery at 17 and took over when he was only 24.

A huge man, a colorful character and a business and political leader until his death in 1915, Henry Hagemeister made his brewery the largest in northern Wisconsin. He reorganized the company in 1886, incorporated the Hagemeister Brewing Co. in 1890, and eventually added a branch at Sturgeon Bay.

He came up with a pretty good advertising slogan, too. For years Hagemeister lager was known statewide as "The Beer That Made Milwaukee Jealous." The main plant stood on the present site of the Schreiber Cheese Co. *(at 1607 Main Street. Schreiber's corporate offices have since moved and are located now at 425 Pine Street.)*

Hollander in the Act

In 1868 Louis Van Dycke got into the act. A Hollander, Van Dycke was born in 1829, came to the United States in 1855 and settled in what was then Red River and later became Dyckesville in his honor. Van Dycke made his pile as a shingle operator there and moved to Green Bay in 1868 where he invested in several enterprises, including a brewery.

Located at the corner of Jackson and Chicago Streets, the O. Van Dycke brewery was always small. After Louis' death the business was managed by his widow Octavia and later by their son Julius until it went out of business about 1908.

The various breweries carried on a spirited rivalry right up until Prohibition, with ownership of saloons and the large German population keeping all solvent. It was then a common practice for breweries to own their own bar outlets where only their product was sold.

Felled by Prohibition

With the advent of Prohibition, all four closed down. Hochgreve simply buttoned up, rode out the "Noble Experiment" and was the first back in business in 1933. Rahr's went through a series of ownership changes and reorganizations but was also ready to resume brewing shortly after Hochgreve, whose shop folded in 1949.

Hagemeister converted into a manufacturer of candy, soft drinks and ice cream as the Bellevue Products Co. The venture was not successful, however, and the company liquidated in 1926.

Plenty of Opportunity

If Green Bay shows a reluctance to mix two different kinds of suds, it's not for lack of opportunity. There was a soap company here shortly after the Civil War, and the Green Bay Soap Co. has been part of the local scene ever since it was organized by Nic Meyer in 1881.

Located first on East River near Joannes Park and since 1937 on its present west side premises *(on Shawano Avenue)*, the company's "White Queen," "Big Boy" and "World's Best" brands of laundry soap were widely used locally before World War II. There is no evidence that the firm ever made toilet soap.

With the growing demand for tallow during World War II, the company gradually converted to rendering and made its last soap in 1959. Somebody must have been using the stuff, though. The company has outlived all the breweries.

Shawano Was By-Passed

How Green Bay Got Its Railroad

June 6, 1959

Attendance by the president of the Chicago and North Western Railway at last Saturday's dedication of the National Railroad Museum was not only appropriate to the occasion but of greater significance than anyone appears to have mentioned. If it hadn't been for the North Western, Green Bay probably wouldn't be the site of the museum today.

It was 97 years ago this fall, in November 1862, that the C&NW completed the track of the first railroad into Green Bay. Some other road would have tapped Northeastern Wisconsin eventually if the North Western hadn't, but it might not have come through Green Bay, in which case the city's history would have taken quite a different turn.

In fact, it very nearly happened.

Route through Shawano

Although the North Western's plans at the time called for an extension into the lumber and mining regions of Upper Michigan, the contemplated route was through Shawano and the road's land grants had already been awarded on that premise. It took a bit of doing to change them.

A railroad had been a Green Bay dream almost from the minute the first locomotive had snorted down an American track. As early as 1846 a company had been formed by local promoters, including Otto Tank, Morgan L. Martin and John P. Arndt, to build a road to the Mississippi. Although it obtained a charter and maintained a formal organization for a number of years, the project never got off the ground.

Meanwhile, the Chicago and North Western, organized in 1836, had pushed slowly but steadily northward into Wisconsin. After reaching Fond du Lac in 1856, further progress was halted by the Panic of 1857. The road went through a bankruptcy reorganization, however, and built to Oshkosh in 1860. A year later it reached Appleton.

Authority from Legislature

From there the line had land grants along a right of way to the Michigan border through Shawano. This route had future possibilities but the North Western's financial condition was still too shaky to wait. The only prospect for immediate success was by way of Green Bay or Fort Howard and everybody knew it.

Accordingly, in April 1861 the State Legislature authorized the road to extend its line to the Menominee River through one or the other in preference to Shawano. Neither was specified but geography was on the side of Fort Howard. Green Bay wasn't happy with the prospect but was willing to go along for the sake of the connection even though it meant a big leg up for the bitter rival across the river.

Two obstacles remained: Getting a land grant amendment through a Congress overwhelmed by the outbreak of the Civil War and winning the approval and financial support of the rest of Brown County. To obtain either, the united pressure of both cities was a must.

Officials Came Here

In June 1861, a party of North Western officials that included President William B. Ogden of Chicago visited Green Bay, coming downriver by boat from the Appleton railhead. They held a conference with local officials which inaugurated a long series of negotiations. At the same time mass meetings were held in both Green Bay and Fort Howard to whip up enthusiasm for raising necessary funds.

Six months later the North Western presented a definite proposition. It would build to Fort Howard instead of Shawano provided its land grants were protected and Brown County would buy $49,500 worth of stock. Construction would begin by May 1, 1862 and would be completed by Dec. 1.

Such a commitment required a county bond issue and therefore a referendum, which was held on Jan. 30. Although there had been some apprehension over the outcome, the referendum was a smashing vote of approval. The Fort Howard City Council thereupon hopped aboard the cowcatcher by voting to buy $15,000 worth of the county's stock.

Opposed by Appleton

Congressional approval was obtained in April in spite of determined opposition from Milwaukee and Appleton. The amendment not only permitted the railroad to keep its original grants but added 80 acres of the Fort Howard Military Reservation, including the long unused stockade.

Construction began on schedule on May 1 with grading from both Appleton and West De Pere. Surveys had apparently been completed during the negotiating period.

Throughout the summer and early fall the rival communities divided their attention between the campaigns of the Civil War, in which Wisconsin troops were heavily engaged, and the progress of the road building. The work moved along so rapidly and smoothly that early in October it was apparent the project would be completed on time.

Special Train Came

By mid-October bridges were being thrown across the Fort Howard sloughs and on Nov. 1 construction trains reached Ashwaubenon Creek, a third of the distance between West De Pere and Fort Howard. A week later the scream of the Iron Horse was heard for the first time at the mouth of the Fox River.

On Nov. 13, 1862, completion of the long awaited rail link was formally celebrated by the arrival of a special train from Chicago. The eight-car special brought about 150 people from Chicago and other cities along the route.

The celebration was hurried and not as elaborate as everyone had hoped. The decision to have one wasn't made until the last minute; it was late in the year, and the visitors could stay only a few hours.

The train arrived at noon after an overnight stay in Oshkosh, to be greeted by an overcoated crowd consisting of nearly everyone in the two proud cities who could reach the end of the track in what is now the middle of the North Western yards. Guests alighted amid a wave of cheering, the blaring of a brass band that had come along and a round of handshakes and waving handkerchiefs.

Parade Was Formed

After an unnecessary and uncomfortable boat ride on the wind-tossed bay, the party, augmented by a large reception committee, docked on the Green Bay side of the river at 1 o'clock. A parade was formed and marched to Klaus Hall where Theodore Noehle, the town's leading caterer, had laid an elaborate banquet for between 300 and 400 guests.

It took them more than two hours to plow through a menu that would founder modern diners, after which everybody loosened their gussets and sat back for the speeches and toasts. Since the party had to break up within an hour the oratory was short and snappy, but nobody ignored the champagne. Nine flowery toasts were tossed off before the clock caught up with proceedings.

At 4 o'clock the visitors returned to Fort Howard and boarded their special for the long return trip to Chicago. They didn't arrive until the following afternoon, the trip again being interrupted at Fond du Lac where there was an elaborate ball in their honor the night of the 13th.

'Green Bay Legal Tender'

Shingle Capital of the World

February 27, 1965

A century ago a booming little city at the mouth of the Fox River intently watched the long agony of the Civil War drag to its fiery conclusion. Although Green Bay was prosperous beyond anything it had previously known, the area was on the verge of a colorful era of prosperity beyond even the wildest dreams of visionary pioneer promoters.

The key to the coming era was lumber, and virtually everybody in Green Bay was in some manner up to his ears in lumber. The city's real stake in the industry, however, was shingles.

For nine years, ever since the shaved shingle industry had been launched in Brown County by recently arrived Belgian immigrants about 1856, the business had been growing. By 1865 it was only beginning to hit stride. It would continue to grow until by 1875 Green Bay was the largest shingle market in the world and the lowly shingle widely referred to as "Green Bay Legal Tender."

Staggering Volume

The volume of that trade was staggering. An Advocate survey in December, 1866, was to reveal that more than 25 billion — repeat, billion — shingles had poured through the city in the preceding 11 months. A decade later the figure had tripled.

By the end of 1866 there were at least 20 shingle mills in and immediately adjacent to Green Bay, plus dozens more running as auxiliaries to sawmills along the bay shore, most of whose output cleared through this port. In addition, millions were made by hand throughout the surrounding farm area.

Initially, all shingles had been shaved by hand, from split blocks or bolts, shaved or "reaved" into shape by twin handled draw knives. Shaving shingles was a common winter occupation of most farmers, whose isolated homes had rooms exclusively devoted to the job.

Whole families, from children to grandparents, took part in the operation, some members staying the entire day on benches in these rooms, laboriously whittling bolts into finished shingles. It was not uncommon for them to start work at 4 a.m. and to keep at it until midnight.

Hard Job

Even for a home operation, shaving shingles was a hard job. Older members of the group cut the bolts in the woods and hauled them to the house. Here the bolts had to be split, then shaved into the proper size, after which they were packed in bundles of 1,000, stacked in sleighs and eventually taken to market.

Long before 1861 Green Bay shaved shingles had achieved a high reputation for quality and were in great demand. Since the hand manufacturing method couldn't keep up with it, small shingle mills inevitably sprang up in competition.

The mill process wasn't very dependable at first and there was a great deal of waste. By the end of the Civil War, however, machines had been perfected to chop out shingles that closely matched the shaved article.

100,000 a Day

Some of these mills could produce up to 100,000 a day, although that volume was rarely achieved. T. R. Willard's mill on the East River had one machine that in 1866 turned out 353,250 shingles in a week. Such volume eventually crowded the hand shaved shingles out of the market.

Shingles finished by hand were packed into standard bundles and stacked on a wagon or sleigh. When a full load had been accumulated and weather and road conditions permitted, the farmer took off for town.

Since everybody else had the same idea, the loads converged on the city in long "shingle trains" that frequently stretched the full length of Main Street and far out into the country as far as the eye could see. Sometimes there were as many as 100 ox or cow-drawn vehicles in the street at once with more coming.

The Green Bay shingle market was an informal open air exchange at the corner of Main and Washington. Here the buyers — local men working on commission from Chicago and eastern brokers — met the teams and bid against each other for every load.

Had Its System

The resultant uproar was bedlam to the uninitiated but it had its own system, just as a tobacco auction today. As sales were made the loads proceeded to specified unloading areas.

Since the round trip for the farmer often covered 20 miles, most of it over wretched roads, he usually made a two-day affair of it, staying overnight, loading up with needed supplies in the morning and then heading home.

Cargoes were usually held here for summer shipment by water, and at the height of the industry it often took half the summer to clear the docks of accumulated shingle piles. Some went out by rail, the North Western on occasion loading as many as 750,000 shingles into box cars in a single day. Meanwhile, the accumulated stockpiles represented a tremendous fire hazard.

With the assault on standing pine, it wasn't long before the supply of timber was exhausted. Green Bay's short reign as shingle capital ended when the tide of the lumber industry moved west, shingle mills were dismantled and moved or simply burned down. By 1880 the glory days were over.

Renewed Demand

In 1889, however, there was a renewed demand for shaved shingles, and this time the Belgian farmers on the Door Peninsula had the market to themselves. In 1889 the number of shingles hauled into Green Bay and sold totaled 5.5 million, only a trickle by former standards but enough to make it profitable even at prices half what they once had been.

Many farmers actually found it more profitable to make shingles of their remaining timber stands than to cultivate their fields, even though it meant going as far as ten miles for bolts. Even stumpage that had not been cleared was uprooted for more shingle stock.

Initially, the shingles were made of pine but as that dwindled it was discovered that cedar was just as good if not better. The later boom was in cedar "shakes."

No Puny Wafer

The old 1865-1890 shingle differed greatly from the puny wooden wafer of today. It was a wedge-shaped slab of 16 to 18 inches long, six inches wide and as much as four inches thick at the butt end.

Old barns still covered with these "shakes" are as weatherproof on top today as they were when built years ago. There aren't many left, though. People are now buying entire buildings just to get the shingles.

Among the prominent local buyers in the 1860s, '70s and early '80s were Anton Klaus, Lewis Day, Earle and Case, Lambert Nau, Sherwood and Holmes, Marshall & Bros., Strong and Clark, F. Hurlbut and George Schauer. Day was the leading dealer in 1865 with a total of 36 million forwarded, but Klaus passed him in '66 en route to a brief but spectacular career as the biggest shingle operator in the United States.

Klaus built a dock at Bay Settlement to which farmers who couldn't make the long trip into Green Bay brought their loads. During the winter he sent them into town over the ice, one remarkable load thus transported in the winter of 1865-66 totaling 40,000 shingles on two extra-large sleighs pulled by a single team.

Load Size Varied

An average load was between 5,000 and 6,000 shingles. On occasion, however, loads might run up to 15,000.

Louis Van Dycke, founder of Dyckesville about 1856, wasn't strictly a Green Bay operator but he had a good thing going out there. In addition to running a profitable general store, tavern and grist mill, he built a dock, sawmill and a shingle mill.

He also bought shaved shingles from as far away as Casco. Between the opening of 1866 navigation and July, Van Dycke forwarded 5,100,000 shingles, of which 1,300,000 were hand made.

In the late 1860s prices on the Chicago market hovered between $4.50 and $5 a thousand. At $4.50 in Chicago, the going price at Washington and Walnut Streets was $3.75.

Santa's Iron Horse

Rails to New London Laid in 1871

August 20, 1960

Green Bay has known many exceptional years in its long history as a fur trading post, lumber headquarters, lake port and papermaking center. Few, however, were more colorful than 1871.

That was an unusual year for both Green Bay and its cross river rival, Fort Howard. The lumber industry was booming as never before, trade was prosperous and the air was electric with optimism. It was also full of smoke as the two communities sat out the summer in the midst of a drought-parched, burning forest area that finally exploded in the holocaust of Peshtigo.

But the most significant trend of the year was the fever of railroad building that saw the rival towns transformed from the northern terminal of a shingle road into a hub of railways stretching north, west and south. Most concrete evidence of the change was the construction of Green Bay's "own" railroad, the Green Bay & Lake Pepin — now the Green Bay & Western — to New London in December.

A railroad to the west, tapping the rich potential of central Wisconsin and linking up with the traffic of the Mississippi River, had been a local dream of many years. As early as 1846 the Green Bay & Minnesota Railroad had been organized with John P. Arndt, Morgan L. Martin and Henry Baird among the principal promoters, but nothing came of it.

Incorporated in 1866

Twenty years later, in 1866, the Green Bay & Lake Pepin was incorporated, its leading officials including Henry Ketchum, subsequently elected president; Dr. A. H. Van Nostrand, one of the city's most enthusiastic post-Civil War promoters; Oscar Grey and Daniel M. Kelly. Financing, maneuvering for land grants and other activities typical of 19th Century railroad building proceeded slowly, however, and it wasn't until 1871 that the show actually hit the road.

Meanwhile, Kelly had resigned as an official and stockholder to take on the lucrative job of its construction. He was awarded the general contract, and the work of surveying and grading a right of way began. The firm of Call and Farnsworth was engaged to lay the rails, but before this final and most colorful phase could get under way a series of unexpected delays cropped up.

The great forest fires of 1871 delayed grading and bridge building as well as destroying stockpiles of ties along the route. There were injunctions and court fights as farmers strove to prevent the road from cutting through their lands and unexpected difficulties were encountered in obtaining rails from the east.

Rails Almost Lost

One important load was almost lost when the vessel carrying it ran aground on the "Whale's Back" reef. Early ice in the bay interfered with other deliveries.

On Nov. 3, 1871, however, the first spikes were driven at Green Bay amid enthusiastic fanfare. Immediate goal was New London, 40 miles away, where a $75,000 bonus awaited the road if it could be in operation by the beginning of 1872. Once started, construction proceeded at a rate of nearly a mile a day, and the whole area avidly watched the iron ribbon stretching westward.

The halfway mark was reached on Nov. 28 and the Wolf River crossed on Dec. 11, remarkable progress during a Wisconsin winter. Spanning the Wolf virtually assured victory in the race against time, and from there to New London was a breeze.

The latter community was in a dither, too, and in spite of the season and hour most of the town's 1,700 people were on hand to greet the first locomotive when it puffed and clanged into the little city at 1 a.m. on the morning of Dec. 19. The 40-mile stretch had been completed in 46 days.

Invitations Issued

Almost immediately traffic was inaugurated with a daily combination passenger-freight each way and several log trains a week carrying logs from lumber camps along the route to the sawmills of Green Bay. The enthusiastic New Londoners wanted a formal celebration, however, and invitations were issued for a gala event there on Christmas Day.

At 8 a.m. that morning a special pulled out of Green Bay for New London with 50 prominent merchants of Green Bay and Fort Howard aboard. It didn't arrive in New London until 11 o'clock, but the Daily State Gazette was careful to point out that the trip was deliberately leisurely and running time could have been cut in half.

A well bundled and cheering crowd greeted the arrival. After a salute by the New London Fire Dept. the guests were tucked into sleighs and escorted to the New London House where a short and enthusiastic reception was held.

Shortly before noon a procession formed outside and everybody marched to a nearby public hall where a "splendid repast" was laid. The banquet service was provided by the "fair ladies" of New London to whom the Gazette was properly gallant next day.

Impressive Hostesses

According to this account the hostesses made "a decided impression upon some of the youthful and impressionable members of the party." This was probably a gentle ribbing by Editor George Hoskinson of his young partner, Dwight I. Follett, who was still a bachelor.

The banquet was followed by a series of congratulatory speeches by the mayor of New London, railroad officials and visiting dignitaries. Among them were Kelly, Morgan L. Martin, Grey, Van Nostrand and Ketchum.

After the speechmaking and appropriate toasts the diners returned to the New London House, climbed into waiting sleighs and were taken for a ride around the proud little city, now a full-fledged rail terminal. They were finally deposited at the rail siding — the account isn't clear about whether a station had actually been constructed yet — for a round of final thank yous and goodbyes.

The return journey began about 3:30 and ended at Green Bay at 7 o'clock. There was still time for the gentlemen to have their Christmas dinners at home — something few of them probably wanted but which they didn't dare refuse.

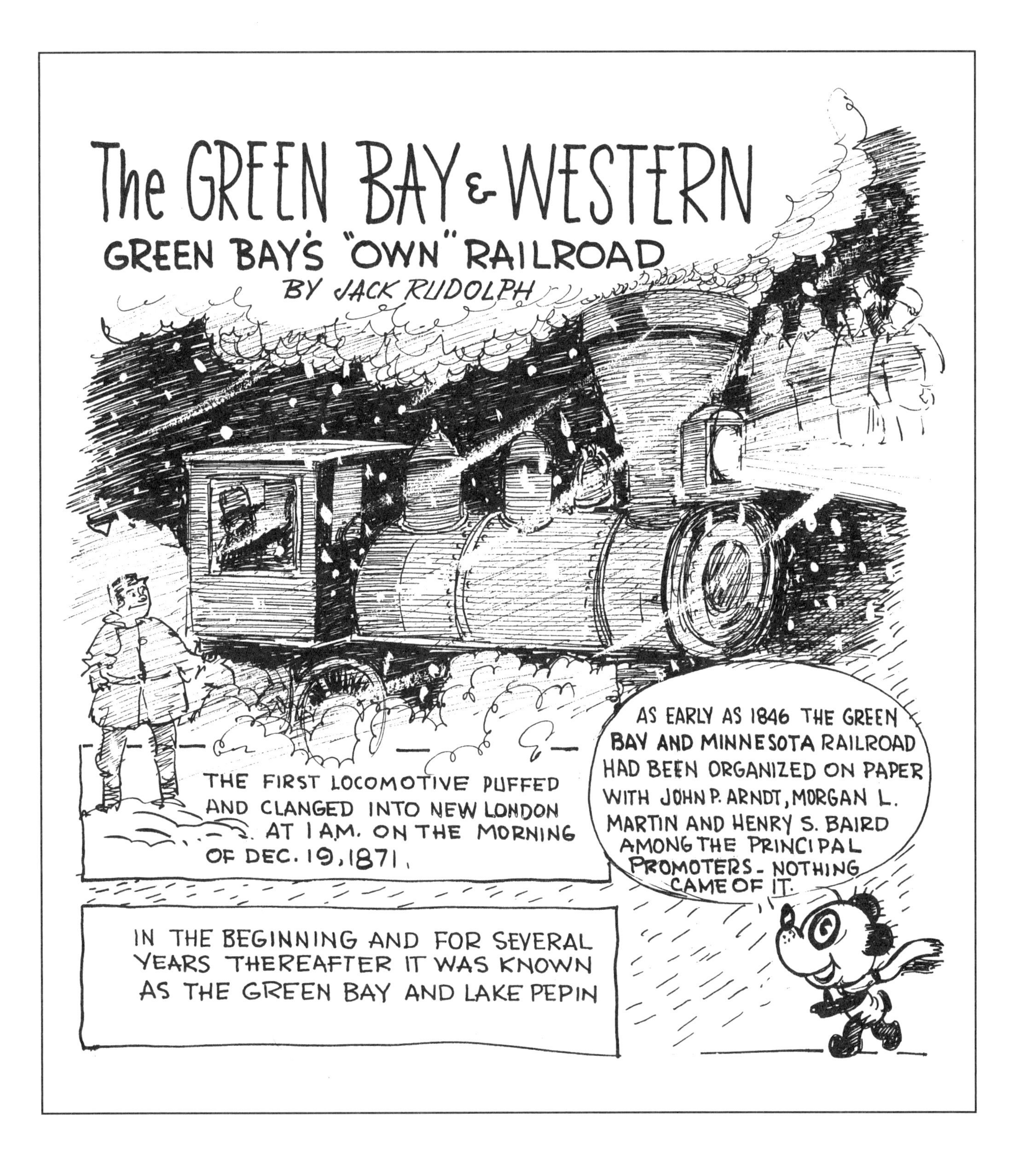

Enlivened Election

City Prohibited Cows' Roaming

July 12, 1958

A fascinating aspect of local government is the heat often generated over purely community issues. The smaller the city and the better everyone knows everybody else, the more bitter the fight. Green Bay has proved the point repeatedly in the last 100 years; never more emphatically than in the boisterous "Cow Ordinance" election of 1882.

The issue was whether cows would continue to roam freely about the city as they always had; or whether a recent ordinance prohibiting such circulation would stick. The fight broke out unexpectedly, touched off a lot of name-calling and wise cracks, and resulted in a standoff. In the end the only real losers were the eloquently defended and equally cussed out cows.

In Green Bay, as in every frontier community lacking a "commons" or public pasture area, cows had been permitted to wander about unhindered from the arrival of the first animals. As population — human and bovine — increased, however, the custom became a jealously guarded nuisance and eventually as much of a problem as parking on Washington Street.

Subject was Touchy

Lots of people, including the most prominent, kept cows in those days, and all took advantage of the right to turn them loose to forage every morning and round them up for milking in the evening. Getting rid of an accepted institution of lacteal freeloading was a touchy subject.

By 1880, although prohibited in the business section, a swarm of between 400 and 500 Bossies was a real problem in the residential districts. Not only did they mess up the streets and hamper traffic; they broke up the wooden sidewalks, invaded private yards and tore up flower beds and shrubs while grazing unconcernedly off the grass. Even fences didn't keep them out.

Could be Dangerous

Strange cows on the prod could be dangerous, too. It was the goring of one little girl and an attack on another by a couple of infuriated animals that triggered the City Council into outlawing the ancient custom in the fall of 1881. Henceforth, cows were to be kept at home.

The action caused a lot of griping, principally due to the enthusiasm of city poundmaster Greg Biemeret for enforcing it. Biemeret pounced on every unescorted cow, dragged her off to the pound and kept her there until the owner bailed her out. Such fees belonged to Greg.

Most people were satisfied, however, and disgruntled cow owners seemed resigned to the situation as the city came up to what figured as a routine municipal election on April 4, 1882. Then the pot boiled over.

Handbills Call Meeting

On March 24 a flood of handbills, printed in English and German, hit the streets. They called for a meeting to discuss "whether your cow and mine may enjoy a little fresh air and feed on earth's green grass without being gobbled up by the miscreant or highwayman employed by the (tyrannical) city council." Nobody knew who was behind them.

The following evening a large crowd, half impelled by curiosity, was on hand. The leaders turned out to be Elisha Morrow and W. C. Bailey. Morrow, an independent, hardheaded character, was an early settler, well-to-do, and lived in a fine home on Adams Street, now the headquarters of the Green Bay Woman's Club.

Candidates Named

After some organizational confusion and an eloquent oration by Morrow on the rapacity of the poundmaster and the tyranny of the council, a committee was appointed to select a full slate of city officials and aldermen to turn the rascals out and restore to Bossy her traditional freedom. Another meeting was called for the 29th.

In the interim heat built up, with all three local papers ridiculing the whole thing. Morrow was a prime target, particularly after word leaked out that he wouldn't go along with the recommendations of the committee, of which he was chairman. The State Gazette ran a series of windy facetious letters to the editor.

On the 29th what the Gazette scathingly called the "Cow Convention" nominated its "crumpled horn ticket." It was led by Atty. J. H. M. Wigman for mayor and included a complete slate of elective officials as well as three aldermanic candidates for each of the city's three wards.

Tale of Poor Widow

A highlight of the meeting was the defiant appearance of Greg Biemeret. When one John Halder told a tear-jerker about a poor widow with 11 children who had to sell her only pillow "from beneath her head" to rescue her cow from his ruthless clutches, Greg took quite a booing but refused to be intimidated. He later got in his licks on Morrow with a letter to the Gazette describing the sorry condition of Elisha's cows, regular boarders at the pound.

By this time the other side was uneasy. On March 30 a "citizens" meeting pooh-poohed cows as an election issue and put up its own ticket, headed by incumbent Mayor W. J. Abrams.

City Gets Business

The controversy was now rating plenty of ink. Delighted editors all over the state were giving Green Bay the business, and it made Dwight Follett of the Gazette unhappy. Intercity rivalries were intense and vocal in the 1880s, and civic pride very thin-skinned.

After all the uproar, the actual election was so quiet as to be an anticlimax. There was no excitement and the vote so light that Wigman managed to nose out Abrams, although "Cow Convention" candidates for all other offices but the council were badly trounced. Council results were a narrow victory for the repealers.

In due time the council reversed the action of its predecessor. Then came an unexpected switch.

Wigman, ostensibly the cows' best friend, vetoed the repeal on legal grounds. H. J. Huntington, reelected city attorney on the anti-cow ticket, took issue, and the city was treated to the spectacle of two top officials sniping at each other, each from the position on which the other had been elected.

The mayor's veto, however, doomed the cows. The restrictive ordinance remained in effect.

An Old Story

River Bridge-Busting Not New

October 30, 1965

The traffic snarl created this week when a visiting freighter knocked the Mason Street bridge out of whack wasn't the first time in city history that damage to one of the three Fox River spans caused a local crisis. Just 90 years ago the same thing happened to the Walnut Street bridge, only then the trouble wasn't too much traffic but not enough.

In the late summer of 1875 during a severe wind storm a schooner attempting to negotiate the draw was caught by the wind, slammed into the structure and knocked it completely out of kilter. It stayed that way for nearly two years while the cross river rivals of Green Bay and Fort Howard argued about who would pay for the repairs.

When, shortly after the accident, Green Bay suggested the two communities get together on the repairs, Fort Howard bluntly declared she wasn't interested.

Green Bay's Baby

Green Bay had built the thing, Green Bay could darned well fix it. In fact, Fort Howard couldn't have cared less if the bridge never was restored.

Green Bay promptly got its own back up and refused to go along. For almost two years the structure stood open and unused until a compromise was worked out and the bridge put back into commission.

The principal reason both sides could be stubborn was because they already had two other connecting spans, then as now at Main and Mason Streets. Both had been completed and opened that very year, only a few months before the original Walnut Street bridge was damaged.

Solid Legal Ground

Legally, Fort Howard was on solid ground. The Walnut Street bridge, built in 1863, belonged exclusively to Green Bay and the west bank town neither had nor wanted any part of it.

Reasons were largely commercial. Green Bay was the larger of the two communities with bigger and better stores. For many years before the bridge was built Fort Howard merchants had bucked the project on the grounds that Fort Howard shoppers would desert them for greener pastures across the river.

Their fears turned out to be well founded; consequently, they weren't at all unhappy when the span went out of commission. Although the other two bridges were available, shoppers were no different then than now. They simply wouldn't go the couple of blocks out of their accustomed way, and as long as the Walnut Street bridge was useless the Fort Howard merchants recovered a good percentage of their lost customers.

Near Miss in 1856

As far back as territorial days there had been periodic agitation to put a bridge across the Fox here but nothing came of it until the arrival of the North Western Railroad at Fort Howard. Green Bay almost got a bridge in 1856 when the state Legislature authorized construction but the scheme collapsed when Fort Howard refused to help pay for it.

Then came the railroad. This time there was no question about the fact that Green Bay had to have a bridge to get access to the line. Its necessity was so obvious that the city swallowed the unpalatable truth that if it wanted one it would have to go it alone.

In January, 1863, the ball started rolling and by March all the necessary preliminaries had been cleared to authorize a $25,000 bond issue after a referendum. No public improvement in Green Bay history was ever approved so overwhelmingly.

The vote was 137 to 1. The lone dissenter came from the South Ward, where the total was an even 100 to 1.

Unexpected Delays

Construction began about June 1, with a completion date of Aug. 1. There were unexpected delays — not exactly an unheard of situation today — and it wasn't until Sept. 22, 1863, that the structure was officially opened. Significantly, Fort Howard took no formal part in the ceremonies.

Almost at once, too, the brand new bridge was subjected to a prophetic test. The very next day a sailing vessel beating up river in a stiff breeze smacked into it head-on, but damage was minor.

The original wooden structure, over 1,200 feet long with a two-lane vehicular roadway and sidewalks on each side was the pride and joy of Green Bay. Its turntable draw, at first designed for a 60-foot opening, actually swung 75 feet.

Engineering Feat

A considerable engineering feat for its time, the bridge was so solidly constructed it lasted for nearly half a century. Repaired so often that there probably wasn't an original timber left in it, the old span was replaced in 1909 by the present Erector set monstrosity, widely hailed in its day as the largest single lift buscule bridge in the world. *(That bridge closed in January 1985, replaced by the present bridge which opened late the next year.)*

For a dozen years after it was built, the Walnut Street bridge was the only Fox River crossing north of De Pere. In 1874, however, the two towns finally got together on the construction of two more, one at Mason and the other at Main Street, sites selected to give Green Bay easier access to the two railroads then serving the community.

Both bridges were also built largely of wood, and they gradually deteriorated. The Mason Street structure was finally replaced shortly before World War I *(the current Don A. Tilleman bridge opened 12/21/1973)*, but the Main Street span remained in use until 1923, even though it was notorious for many years as a rickety and unsafe structure.

As early as 1885 Henry Hagemeister tore his pants when he

broke through the floor while sprinting to catch a train. Since the affable brewer wasn't hurt, the town got quite a chuckle out of his mishap.

Too Important

One of the reasons for the delay in rebuilding the Main Street bridge was its importance in the scheme of cross-river traffic. From 1896 on it carried, in addition to all the freight traffic to the North Western station, the only street car connection between the east and west sides.

Although it was an open secret that the bridge was in an extremely dangerous condition, the city tried to get by on piecemeal repairs until another and much more serious break-through precipitated its closing in 1923. That year a Wisconsin Public Service sprinkler car, an exceptionally heavy vehicle, went completely through into the river, almost drowning two men aboard.

The bridge was then condemned for vehicular traffic and street car tracks were quickly laid across the Walnut Street bridge. Construction on the present Main Street bridge began late in 1923 and it was completed early in 1925. *(It was replaced in 1998.)*

The Crash of Strong's Bank

October 28, 1967

Green Bay has had its share of financial disasters and bank failures over the years. None ever hit the city with more stunning force, though, than the failure of Strong's Bank in 1884. The town couldn't have been more shocked if 79-year-old Morgan L. Martin had run off with Henry Baird's widow.

Not that the failure itself was so surprising. There had been a rash of bank closings that spring, including the Bank of De Pere; the country's financial health was queasy and a number of local businessmen had their doubts about the stability of the institution anyway. But that Henry Strong would bug out after looting his bank of a quarter of a million dollars was unthinkable.

For nearly 25 years Strong had been a business and social pillar of Green Bay. The son of a prominent New York financier, he had virtually cut his teeth on a bank ledger. Thoroughly trained in finance, he had come west to Oshkosh in 1854 and established a successful bank there.

Came Here in 1859

Five years later he settled in Green Bay as founder-president of the Bank of Green Bay. Holder of more than four-fifths of its capital stock, he remained at its head through a number of reorganizations, from the last of which Strong's Bank emerged in 1877.

Neither his integrity nor his social position had ever been challenged. As early as 1874 there had been rumbles about the strength of his bank which had resulted in the establishment of Kellogg's Bank *(now Associated)* but everybody trusted him personally.

On a late May Saturday in 1884 Strong and his family left on a well advertised trip to the east. Since such journeys weren't unusual, nobody gave the departure a thought, but it was a different matter on Monday morning when Strong's Bank didn't open its doors.

News Swept City

News of the suspension swept through the city like the great fire of four years before. After the initial shock, though, people were inclined to be sympathetic and take his word that the bank's affairs were in good order.

His assurance was contained in a letter to the Daily State Gazette, mailed just before train time Saturday. His explanation was that "malicious withdrawals" had weakened the bank's ability to pay on demand and that he had closed to protect depositors.

Aside from some criticism of his failure to stay and face the consequences, people believed him. His dropping out of sight was forgotten in the initial excitement and there were no runs on the remaining banks, which spent a jittery day or two.

James H. Elmore was appointed receiver and went to work on the books. Pending his report the town went about its business confident that everybody would be taken care of.

Bombshell Report

Elmore's report, released a couple of weeks later, was a bombshell. Instead of assets of nearly $350,000, Strong's Bank had been looted. Its securities portfolio of a quarter of a million dollars was worthless and Strong had absconded with all the ready cash.

Most of the "securities" were speculative stock certificates not worth the fancy paper they were printed on. Some of the companies represented had failed at least a decade earlier.

Scarcely had that news been digested when a letter from Strong to Elmore explained what had happened. It also revealed that he was safe in Canada where he couldn't be touched.

Took Full Blame

To give him what little credit he deserved, Strong took all the blame, exonerating his associates who, he insisted, were unaware of his activities. Over a period of several years he had used bank funds to speculate in the market and had lost his shirt.

As local businessmen had suspected, Strong's Bank had been skating on very thin ice since 1874. Actually, Strong had surrendered his national charter that year and reorganized to avoid being forced to close at that time.

Early troubles weren't his doing but the fault of the Panic of 1873. When his situation showed little improvement, however, Strong took the desperate gamble of playing the market for a quick killing which would put his business back on its feet.

Didn't Work

It didn't work. His personal fortune went first, then he began dipping into the till. Each time he bet and lost he plunged deeper.

Strong had covered up for years by boldly placing the worthless stock certificates in the bank's portfolio and reporting them to the directors at par value. Because he was the largest stockholder and trusted implicitly his associates took his word for it.

When Elmore finally got the mess straightened out, he found that depositors would be lucky to recover 20 cents on the dollar. Actually, by meticulous handling over a period of two or three years, he managed to squeeze a little more out of the wreckage.

Business wasn't badly hurt. Because of reservations, most firms had quietly withdrawn their funds long before, leaving only enough cash on deposit for day-to-day requirements. By not pulling out entirely they had enabled Strong to save face.

Small Depositors Hit

Unknown to all the business community, Strong's Bank had become little more than an individual account savings institution. The real sufferers were the individual depositors who had trusted him with their life's savings.

Although Strong made gestures about coming back to take his medicine, he never did. He stayed in Toronto where he eventually set up a small real estate agency and prospered.

The big winner was Elmore. Largely because of his brilliant salvage job he was elected mayor of Green Bay a few years later and went on to earn the distinction of being the only man to serve as mayor of Fort Howard, Green Bay and the combined cities after the consolidation of 1895.

Early Vote Still Stands

1885 Election Curbed Saloons

May 21, 1966

Most Green Bay residents have probably never given the subject much thought — if, indeed, it ever occurred to them — but there are no taverns within the city limits west of Broadway. What's more, there haven't been any for almost 80 years, an astonishing record in a town whose enthusiasm for prohibition has never been among its more notable features.

To find the reason, the historian has to dig deeply, as far back as 1885 when a referendum in the city had results whose effects are still felt even though the details have been long forgotten.

In the old lumbering days both Green Bay and Fort Howard were rowdy, wide open towns catering to the appetites and thirst of hordes of lumberjacks pouring in and out of the woods. Exactly how many saloons flourished in Fort Howard isn't known although one old resident, now dead, once said that when Fort Howard became a city there were 2,500 people and 60 grog shops. In 1875 Green Bay had over 90.

As the forests receded things began to quiet down. By 1884, according to the city directory, the number of saloons in Green Bay had dropped to 63, with only 23 open in Fort Howard.

Upsurge of Temperance

Meanwhile, there was an upsurge in the cause of temperance. Temples of honor flourished, even little kids were encouraged to pin on the white ribbon, and temperance lecturers enjoyed wide popularity.

Under the pressure of the moral crusade the prohibition movement began to make headway in Wisconsin. Early in 1885 the Drys pushed through a state law setting up a new procedure for licensing saloons. Essentially, it was designed to put the brakes on tippling by shutting off the taps.

The act permitted communities over 500 population to set local license fees higher than the state-prescribed $200. Referendums could be held every three years to set the amount, which could be either $200, $350 or a $500 jolt. The first such referendum was set for Sept. 13, 1885.

Real Money

The $500 tab was real money, a fee which would automatically kill off a lot of unsavory, marginal groggeries. That was the purpose of the bill and everybody knew it.

The $350 figure didn't mean much. The contest was between the Drys, who were shooting for the top amount, and the Wets, intent on keeping the tax as low as possible. Both had an eye on the future.

In Green Bay, where four breweries supplied the suds, the brewers and saloonkeepers went to work early. While the temperance people were congratulating themselves on having passed the original bill and doing little else, the Wets were whipping up opposition.

Screaming Placards

All over town, on back bars and especially around the polling places on election day, there were screaming placards calling the faithful to stand up for their sudsy rights. Everywhere signs proclaimed such revolting possibilities as "$500 License Means Prohibition" and "$500 Leads to $5,000."

It was just the reverse in Fort Howard. There the Wets suffered from overconfidence while the Drys were on the ball. Much the same sort of campaign was conducted but it was run by the temperance people and wasn't so flamboyant.

In Green Bay on election day beer and whiskey flowed freely — and free — lubricating a lot of noisy electioneering along the polished bars. As soon as patrons were properly fired up they were loaded into waiting vehicles and driven to the polls.

Spun Their Wheels

On the West Side, however, the Drys saw that the "right people" turned out. The Wets got some help from Green Bay but mostly they just spun their wheels.

Both efforts paid off. In Green Bay, although the result was in doubt most of the day, the election was a resounding victory for organization and uproar. The $200 fee was retained by a vote of 768 to 482 for the $500 license, only 16 being cast for the $350 compromise.

The vote in Fort Howard, after what was described as one of the liveliest elections in history, wound up 317 for the $500 license, 296 for $200 and nine for $350. Temperance had squeaked through by a tight margin of nine votes. *(Assuming the numbers are correct, the difference should be 21 votes.)*

Fears Soon Realized

The fears of the beer barons were quickly justified in Fort Howard. There the total of saloons dripped to 12 within a year.

Three years later the Fort Howard Drys hit 'em again, hiking the fee to $1,000. As a result, the saloons in operation were reduced to six, all on or east of Broadway, then the dividing line between business and residential districts.

Oldest in Town?

All were elaborate and well managed places whose proprietors were highly respected in the community. One was John Gross, R. M. Wilson was another, and the others were John Early, Con McGinnis, John Shaughnessy and Fred Gross.

John Gross' place was a combination bar and hotel on the corner of Pearl and West Walnut Streets that may, incidentally, boast the distinction of being the oldest continuous saloon in town. So far as is known, it has never been anything else.

When consolidation of Fort Howard and Green Bay came to a head in 1895 the West Side saloon tax was much greater than that prevailing in Green Bay. Knowing that in another citywide referendum the East Siders would win hands down, the West Siders insisted on a compromise in the new city charter.

They agreed to accept the lower Green Bay saloon license fee but in return got a clause in the consolidation charter banning saloons west of Broadway. The clause is still in the city charter, can't be changed without a West Side referendum and has never been seriously challenged.

Depression Hangover

Business In Doldrums in 1885

November 19, 1960

There is a time in the course of every hangover when the victim is afraid he's going to live. Something like that seems to have been the mood of Green Bay business in 1885. The Depression of '73 was over but so was the roaring prosperity of the great lumber boom as the pine forests receded to the north and west and other cities usurped Green Bay's former position as a trading center for the industry.

Lacking manufacturers to take up the slack, business was in the dumps. A revival was shortly to set in but nobody believed it and the prevailing spirit was one of pessimism for the future and a reluctance to take any more chances.

Not that everyone was on the bread line. People still made a good living and some businesses were prosperous, but the bumptious optimism of the lumbering era was dead.

Sawmills Moved On

The sawmills that had ringed the city 10 years before had moved on, the shingle flood that made Green Bay the world's primary market in 1875 had receded to a trickle and the prosperous trade of supplying the lumber camps and mills was finished too. Of the number of wholesale houses engaged in it a decade earlier only four were left, of which Joannes Bros. was the only one of consequence.

Even here emphasis had shifted to the servicing of lake vessels and the increasing number of farmers crowding into the cleared area. There were 34 retail grocery houses, seven hardware firms and 12 dry goods and general stores competing for the once neglected farm trade.

Leading Merchants

Leading dry goods merchants were T. L. Best and Co., George W. Lamb, George Sommers and Chris Woelz. The principal hardware firms were Alonzo Kimball; J. J. St. Louis; Cook, Case and Sorenson; Charles Hartung; and the Findeisen brothers. Nau Bros. were still in general wholesaling but were shortly to close out and concentrate on their tug line.

Among the "services" establishments were eight meat markets, of which the two run by Joseph Kalb were the most elaborate; three restaurants, six jewelers, the same number of livery stables and seven blacksmiths. J. P. Schumacher and the Lefebvres had the two furniture stores as well as the largest of the town's four undertaking parlors, while Carl Manthey operated his monument works on Walnut Street, next to the bridge.

Five Harness Shops

There were five harness shops. Gus Kuestermann and his brother ran the largest of the two music stores and Fred Hurlbut was the leader among five coal and fuel merchants. Albert Weise and Fred Hollman owned a top-notch crockery and glass shop about where Stiefel's now stands *(a men's and boys' clothing store at 304-306 North Washington Street, in the area now occupied by Washington Commons)*, although Hollman was outnumbered by a whole platoon of Weises.

One factor that may have handicapped commercial activity was the paucity of banking facilities. Following the collapse of Strong's Bank in 1884 the only one left was the Kellogg National *(now Associated)*. Strong's Bank was still very much in the news, however, as James Elmore struggled to bring some order out of chaos and salvage what he could.

Professions Still Tops

Among the professions the law and medicine still held top place with a dozen law firms and 11 doctors practicing. There were also three architects, three dentists, two veterinarians and seven druggists.

Prominent law firms included Ellis, Greene and Merrill; Hudd and Wigman; J. C. and A. C. Neville; Vroman and Sale; Van Buren Bromley, John J. Tracy and Willard C. Bailey, the latter also postmaster. Thomas R. Hudd was state senator and shortly to become Green Bay's first congressman. The Ellis, Greene and Merrill partnership consisted of E. H. Ellis, George G. Greene and Carlton Merrill.

One Woman Physician

Medical names still remembered were those of W. H. Bartran, B. C. Brett, Charles E. Crane, A. F. Olmsted and W. B. Coffeen. Another was Dr. Louis Carabin, whose father had platted West De Pere.

The city also had something of a curiosity in a woman doctor. Mrs. Camm lived in Fort Howard but maintained offices in both communities.

The pioneer dentist, A. H. Ellsworth, was still practicing. Dan King had retired but his drug store, the oldest in Wisconsin, continued under his son who was trying to get rid of it. Aside from the King establishment the leading drug store was Robinson and Phipps.

Of the 17 hotels, Cook's was the best, the other leading hostelries being the Bay City and American Houses on the present sites of the Bellin and Minihan buildings. Henry Bertram owned the Cook and the Hagerty brothers the American House, although with all five of them living there they couldn't have had much room for guests.

Beaumont Closed

The Beaumont was closed, having passed from the ownership of Bud Beaumont through foreclosure of a mortgage by the Charter Oak Insurance Co. Philip Klaus, company agent, was trying to find a buyer and threatened to remodel it into an office building if he couldn't peddle it. Fortunately, Bertram stepped in before any such drastic step was taken.

The number of saloons had been cut in half but there were still 41. Of these the best known were Fred Gehr's White Bear, Joe Lonzo's Casino, Mitchell Resch's New York Saloon and

Charles Pfotenhauer's. All were on Washington Street except the latter, which was on Cherry. Pfotenhauer, only 26, was also fire chief and a leader among the young businessmen.

Five Breweries Prosper

The only manufacturing plant of any stature was the Britton Cooperage at the foot of Monroe Avenue. There was also a branch of the National Iron Furnace Co. on East River but it was shut down all through 1885. Five breweries were prospering, including Hagemeister's, Van Dycke's, the East River brewery owned by Henry Rahr and his sons and Chris Hochgreve's in Allouez. The old Blesch Brewery was still running in Fort Howard.

Virtually unnoticed, however, until the Gazette called attention to it late in the year was a new industry destined to have an important impact on Green Bay's future — the manufacture and distribution of cheese. The business was only a couple of years old but had already made significant progress.

The Gazette story related how, two years before, only low grade cheese was available and a drug on the market. Then a few creameries were established in Brown County and farmers found they could get better prices for their milk by processing it into good cheese. By the end of 1885 this quality had attracted a steady and constantly expanding market. Cheese from Brown County already ranked with the best.

Outgrowing Rowdy Youth

City Growing More Sedate in 1885

November 12, 1960

The 1885 files of the Daily State Gazette provide abundant proof that 75 years ago the city was outgrowing the rawness of the rowdy 1870s. Although Bayites apparently liked to read about violence they no longer accepted it casually too close to home. There were a number of violent crimes during the year, all of which aroused much public indignation.

The most vicious, and the one causing the loudest uproar, was an acid-throwing assault on John B. Owens, a conductor for the North Western Railroad. Owens was walking home at dusk one September evening when he encountered a loiterer near the corner of Jefferson and Cherry Streets. Suddenly and without warning the stranger threw a cupful of oil of vitriol into his face and fled.

Fortunately, Owens was wearing a wide-brimmed hat and his attacker's aim was poor. The hat saved his eyes but he was badly burned.

Police didn't have much to go on except the metal cup which had held the acid and the fact that Owens had recently been involved in an altercation on his train, during which he put a troublesome passenger off. With the help of railroad detectives they went to work and more than two months later arrested a traveling salesman as Owens' assailant. Had he been apprehended immediately after the attack the city might have forgotten its new manners and lynched him.

Scarcely had the Owens case simmered down than the community was further shocked by the fatal shooting of a man during a drunken brawl in a disreputable shanty on the west bank of the Fox River. A young De Pere man was arrested and charged with murder.

Sympathy for Accused

Despite the sordidness of the case there was considerable sympathy for the accused, who had an exemplary reputation. The trial attracted much attention, and the conviction for second degree murder caused some dissatisfaction. It was feared the verdict might save the woman in the case, a notorious strumpet.

Other shockers included the discovery of the body of a newborn infant in a barn on Main Street, the death of a woman by accidental discharge of a shotgun in the hands of an eight-year-old boy and a suicide attempt by a demented woman who jumped off the Walnut Street bridge. There was also an attempt to wreck a North Western passenger train near Fort Howard, averted only shortly before the train was due by the discovery of a logging chain wound around the rails.

Fires were no longer so common, the city enjoying one stretch of over four months without a single alarm. Even so, there were a number of costly blazes. The most spectacular was the destruction of the Armory Opera House on Pine Street the night of July 3-4. Two adjoining residences were also gutted.

On a bitterly cold January night Jules Parmentier's dry goods store on Washington Street between Pine and Main went up, and in May the Desnoyer Block, a square farther south, was badly damaged. Just a week after the Opera House fire a third Washington Street blaze destroyed the Dequindre Block and the McCormick and Co. store.

Early in the year De Pere's Commercial Hotel *(presumably Commercial House at the foot of George Street)* burned to the ground and in May the Broadway House in Fort Howard, at the corner of Broadway and Hubbard Street, was a total loss. The latter fire got out of hand because the Fort Howard engine was out of commission and the Green Bay department late getting to the scene.

1880 Fire Recalled

An aftermath of the great conflagration of 1880 was very much in the news when the combined damage suits against the Goodrich Transportation Co. were tried again in Oshkosh. After a long and fully reported trial the jury took only an hour to find for the plaintiffs, but the company promptly appealed to the state Supreme Court.

Another indication of Green Bay's breaking bonds with its infancy was the passing of a number of pioneers. Best known were John V. Suydam and Albert G. Ellis, co-founders of Wisconsin's first newspaper, the Green Bay Intelligencer, in 1833.

Both had come here as young men in the early 1820s. Suydam, 75 at the time of his death, had remained but Ellis, 85, had lived for many years in Stevens Point. He was, however, a frequent and popular visitor at the home of his son, Judge E. Holmes Ellis.

Two who predated American settlement were Joseph Ducharme and Capt. William Powell, both born in the vicinity in 1810. Ducharme, sexton of Allouez Cemetery in his last years, was the son of "Colonel" Dominic Ducharme, a colorful character of the French period, Powell a well known Menominee Indian interpreter. Ducharme's wife survived her husband by only a few weeks.

Other old settlers who passed on were Joseph Vieau and Daniel J. Hubbard of Fort Howard. Vieau had come to Green Bay as an employee of the American Fur Co. in 1829, while Hubbard was one of the leaders in the organization of the West Side community.

Chris Straubel Died

Another death was that of Chris F. Straubel. The 84-year-old Straubel was one of the earliest German immigrants, arriving in 1846. The deaths left Morgan L. Martin, now 85, virtually the only surviving pioneer.

Prominent figures dying during 1885 were Fred Glahn, well known cigar manufacturer of the 1870s; Bishop Francis X. Krautbauer, second Catholic bishop of Green Bay; and George Strong, a prosperous businessman before the Civil War.

Strong died destitute in the county poor house, where he had been an invalid and public charge for many years. When he died "friends" among the city's business leaders bestirred themselves to see he got a decent burial, a gesture in marked contrast to their indifference during Strong's declining days.

Everything wasn't violence and tragedy, however. There were lighter moments too.

Probably the one that got the most chuckles was the time 300-pound Henry Hagemeister broke through the planking of the Main Street bridge. Hagemeister sustained only a skinned knee and a torn pair of pants but had to endure a terrific kidding.

That week was rough on the portly brewer-politician. The next day a runaway horse pitched him out of his carriage on a downtown street.

Paper-Making Pioneer

Hoberg Started the Ball Rolling

March 4, 1967

The Press-Gazette's series of "Progress" tabloids ends tomorrow with a review of the city's heavy industry, in which paper making occupies a major spot. In telling the paper industry story the name of John Hoberg crops up periodically.

Which is as it should be. Hoberg was responsible for the birth of the industry here, and he did it by flying in the face of prevailing "expert" opinion. Unfortunately, he didn't live long enough to benefit fully from his gamble or to establish his rightful place in the story of Green Bay's industrial development.

Hoberg died just as his business was getting well under way, literally giving his life for his paper mill. He was killed in a plant accident in 1904 while doing a job he didn't have to do and in which he had little reason to be involved.

When John Hoberg moved his struggling paper mill to Green Bay from Kaukauna in 1895 he was taking a long chance but his decision couldn't have come at a more opportune time for this community. The valley was still in the paralysis of the depression of 1893, the lumber industry upon which Green Bay's economy had been based since before the Civil War was on its last legs, and the city faced an uncertain future.

Pointed the Way

Paper changed all that, and John Hoberg pointed the way.

Another of the German immigrant success stories that cram the pages of Wisconsin history, Hoberg was born in Prussia in 1840 and brought to Detroit by his family when he was only a year old. In 1848 the Hobergs moved to the pioneer hamlet of Sheboygan, where the father opened a brewery and also established a general store.

Before he was 20 young John was deep in the retail business as well as shipping produce all over the lakes. Restless, ambitious and aggressive, he wasn't satisfied with modest success in Sheboygan, and in 1879 moved to Kaukauna.

There he built Kaukauna's first pulp mill, which he operated for a year before returning to the produce shipping business. At the same time he opened a liquor store, and in 1881 shipped the first carload of grain ever sent out of Kaukauna. In 1882 he moved to South Kaukauna where he dabbled in real estate and was moderately successful.

Still Unsatisfied

Still he wasn't satisfied. In 1885 the "mining fever" drew him to Bessemer, Mich., where he was a real estate promoter and general merchandise dealer. He returned to South Kaukauna in 1887, however, and built his first paper mill, the first tissue mill in the area. It was incorporated as the John Hoberg Co. in 1891 for the manufacture of toilet tissue, which was sold as far afield as California.

The depression of '93 hurt Hoberg and when a couple of years went by without improvement he began to look for a new location. He found it in Green Bay where his friend Fred Hollman was president of the Businessmen's (*sic*) Association.

Hoberg agreed to move here if the city would give him some land on which to build. The association offered him a lot on the north bank of the East River, now part of Charmin Paper products, eventual outgrowth of his small enterprise.

Opened in Fall

Ground for the new plant was broken in mid-August, 1895. Two months later production began in the little mill with machinery and part of a crew brought from Kaukauna.

In coming here Hoberg was thumbing his nose at established papermaking techniques which held that water power could not profitably be displaced by steam to run the heavy machines. Hoberg thought otherwise.

Besides, fantastic as it may seem today, the East River was then an ideal source of water. It was then a pure stream, much cleaner than the Fox.

The enterprise didn't get off to a smooth start. There were bugs in the steam power plant and Hoberg needed help in the first years. By 1900, however the gamble was a proven success, to be followed shortly by the founding of the Northern Paper Mills here.

Small but Active

A small but active man, Hoberg stood only about five feet six and weighed only 155 pounds. A congenial sort, he was well liked by his employees in spite of an annoying habit of insisting that nobody could do anything as well as he could himself. In fact, that insistence led to his fatal accident.

On a Saturday afternoon in July, 1904, the mill was installing a new machine. As usual, Hoberg was in the middle of things, and when one of the belts needed adjusting he pitched in to do it himself.

Something went wrong. His arm was caught in the whirling belt and he was thrown violently against the machine, then tossed several feet to the floor.

Although his arm was badly hurt his general condition didn't seem particularly dangerous. He had been injured internally, however, and a week later early in the morning of July 17, he died unexpectedly at his home.

Buried in Sheboygan

In accordance with his wishes, his body was sent to Sheboygan for burial in the family plot after an impressive funeral here. As it passed through Kaukauna, where it had to be transferred from one station to another, the little city accorded him a unique memorial with the incumbent mayor and five previous mayors acting as pallbearers.

In the years after his death the Hoberg Paper Co. continued to prosper and expand. Half a century later, in 1953, the name of the mill was changed to Charmin Paper Products Co. and four years later, in 1957 it became a subsidiary of Proctor & Gamble.

From its small beginnings with a single papermaking machine and a crew of 45 men, the mill has grown to its present size, employing a force of more than 1,300.

First in History

City's First Labor Day in 1893

September 7, 1968

Green Bay celebrated Labor Day last Monday, but it was a far different kind of celebration than it used to be. Everybody who could make it simply took off for a three-day holiday and, except for flag displays here and there, little was evident that this was Organized Labor's big day in the United States.

It wasn't that way 75 years ago this week — on Sept. 4, 1893, to be exact — when Green Bay and Fort Howard staged a joint celebration of the first observance of Labor Day here. In fact, that first celebration set a pattern that lasted for more than half a century.

The idea of Labor Day wasn't new, even then. As early as 1882, Peter J. McGuire, founder of the Brotherhood of Carpenters, had suggested some sort of day be set aside to salute the American laboring man, and the first such celebration was held in New York City's Union Square that fall.

Spread Gradually

Other cities and eventually states took it up. Oregon was the first state to make it a legal holiday in 1887, and in August of 1893 Gov. George Peck proclaimed the first Monday in September that year as Labor Day in Wisconsin, almost a year before President Grover Cleveland signed a bill making it a national legal holiday.

Following Governor Peck's proclamation, Green Bay Mayor James H. Elmore asked for its observance here, requesting that business cooperate by closing down for at least part of the day. With that much assurance, members of the city's five labor unions — Cigar Makers, Clerks, Coopers, Machinists and Bricklayers — went to work.

The names of those who actually planned the first celebration have not been preserved, but they did a good job. The weather was ideal, everybody was enthusiastic about a two-day holiday and nearly all business places in Green Bay and Fort Howard cooperated by closing for the afternoon. The resulting celebration was a great success.

Opened with Parade

Shortly after noon the downtown streets began to fill up as people gathered to watch the scheduled parade. The march began at 1:30 p.m. with members of the five unions in line, from a starting point at Walnut and Adams Streets.

Heading the parade were marshals Adam Spuhler and S. W. Peters on horseback, followed by the Star Trombone Band. Next came the five unions, each with colors and banners as well as big badges for each man, then the speakers of the day in open carriages, with citizens on foot and in carriages bringing up the rear. It made for a respectable turnout several blocks long.

Moving west on Walnut to Washington, the parade route turned north to Main, east on Main to 11th (now Roosevelt) Street, then south to Cherry. Turning east on Cherry, the parade ended in Washington Park, which was also the county fair grounds and largest recreation area.

Refreshment Time Out

Arriving at the park everybody took an hour off to refresh themselves at the numerous refreshment booths set up in anticipation of the Northeastern District Fair, scheduled to open later in the week. An hour later the regular exercises began with a series of selections by the Trombone Band to bring the crowd together before the speakers' platform.

Mayor Elmore gave a brief speech of welcome, after which John F. Dockry spent 20 minutes in which he "said a good many things suitable to the day and occasion," to quote the Daily State Gazette.

The Rev. H. W. Thompson, pastor of the First Methodist Episcopal Church, was the main speaker of the afternoon. One of the finest speakers in the city, the Rev. Thompson surpassed himself.

Fiery Oration

Exactly what he said was not reported but for over half an hour he "held the crowd's earnest attention by his elegant, sensible and logical words, delivered with all the spirit and fire with which his public utterances are characterized."

That splurge and the added remark that his talk "contained much food for thought" might indicate that he didn't really say much. However, the Gazette story also added that it was one of the best addresses heard in the city in a long time.

The Rev. Thompson's oratory ended the formal program, after which the crowd of 3,000 or more scattered through the park to "amuse themselves until the supper hour," at which time presumably, everybody went home. There was plenty to do and see, too.

Exhibits were already arriving for the forthcoming fair, and many people visited the exposition halls and the stables to get a look at the horses already on hand for the racing program. There was a merry-go-round and other games to amuse the children.

Plenty of Beer

There were also "games of chance or skill" to amuse their elders. There were "plenty of refreshment booths and no lack of anything to eat and drink," meaning that the beer was flowing copiously as it always did at public picnic affairs in those days. However, the big crowd was cheerful and orderly and there were no disturbances.

The celebration ended that night with a labor ball at Turner Hall that was described as being as big a success as the afternoon program. The Trombone Orchestra played and more than 250 couples danced until after midnight.

That first Labor Day celebration set a pattern that was followed here for more than 50 years. Every Labor Day thereafter there was a big parade with representatives of all the city's unions in line, followed by a program of speeches and fun in one of the city parks.

As late as 1918 the scene was still Washington Park *(renamed Hagemeister Park)*. When Hagemeister Park was torn up to make way for the present East High School in the 1920s the celebration was transferred to Bay Beach. The parade feature was abandoned about 20 years ago, and ultimately the program yielded to the desire of labor and everybody else to take off for the long weekend.

Green Bay, Fort Howard Combine

Seventy-Five Years of Union

April 4, 1970

Green Bay had an important anniversary this week, which, like so many others in recent years, went by comparatively unnoticed. Seventy-five years ago Thursday, April 2, the bitter and often openly hostile cities of Fort Howard and Green Bay finally buried the hatchet and united into a single community.

Although the two towns had been at each other's throats for more than 40 years prior to 1895 the idea of getting together was not new. Periodically since the 1850s the proposal had been kicked around but each time the thing had collapsed on the dirty word "annexation." Twice, in fact, it had come to a vote, only to be overwhelmingly defeated in Fort Howard, which wasn't about to be swallowed by Green Bay.

In fact, the suspicion persists that the successful 1895 movement was carefully engineered behind the scenes, so quietly and efficiently that the outcome was in the nature of a steamroller. Six months before the event nobody would have bet a Confederate Shinplaster that the question would come to another vote within the foreseeable future.

Subtler Tongues

By the late 1890s subtler tongues were at work and the fighting word "annexation" was shelved in favor of "consolidation."

First intimation that another try was in the wind came in mid-February when the Green Bay Gazette published an interview with Andrew E. Elmore, the "Sage of Mukwonago" and Fort Howard's biggest taxpayer, who came out unequivocally for union. Evidently the interview was a combination plant, trial balloon and carefully timed fuse.

Less than a week later a mass meeting was held in Fort Howard's Music Hall. It was one of the longest, noisiest and most disorderly affairs in the city's history, but shortly before midnight a resolution to do something put the show on the road.

Battle Joined Early

The session opened when Philip Sheridan introduced a committee report favoring consolidation. Somebody made a motion for adoption, the opposition launched a delaying action and the fight was on.

Speaker followed speaker as tension mounted and tempers flared. There were slashing attacks on business interests which were accused of trying to ram the proposal through for their own profit, and both city administrations came in for enthusiastic flayings.

Fort Howard's justice of the peace, Maurice A. Sellers, delivered what proved to be one of the most telling speeches. Sellers favored the idea but was irritated by the tactics.

Caught Public Fancy

His declaration that the night before a wedding was no time for a family fight caught the popular fancy. The simile was effectively used in the weeks before the final vote.

Just before midnight a motion was carried that a committee of leading citizens of both cities be appointed to work with an outside attorney to draw up a consolidation ordinance. Once this committee got down to cases it found the job surprisingly easy.

By March 6 it had hammered out an agreement which was approved by another mass meeting, then sent to both city councils. Three days later the latter adopted it unanimously and the date for the referendum was set for April 2, also the time for regular spring elections.

Fair Division

The ordinance provided for all the necessary pooling of services and set up a political division of eight wards, five on the east side and three on the west. The ward organization was achieved by retaining Green Bay's five existing wards and combining Fort Howard's six into three. Since Green Bay's population was approximately double that of Fort Howard, it was considered fair.

The ensuing month was full of sound and fury but it soon became obvious that consolidation would go through. Still, nobody was taking anything for granted, and regular city elections were held as usual.

It was agreed, however, that the referendum ballots would be counted first and results announced immediately. The Gazette made elaborate arrangements for ward results to be rushed to the paper by the speediest bicycle racers in town.

Crowds Hit Street

By 6 p.m. on April 2 crowds began to clog the street in front of the plant. Shortly after 7 o'clock the first results came in, and within half an hour the decision was known.

The only real surprise was the magnitude of the victory — a 2,559 to 217 landslide. In Green Bay the sweep was 1,631-60 and in Fort Howard the ordinance carried by 928-157.

A few minutes after 7:30 a signal cannon at the foot of Pine Street was fired and at once pandemonium broke loose. Such an uproar had never been heard in the city before and wouldn't be exceeded until the Armistice of Nov. 11, 1918.

Red fire blazed in the business districts, a bonfire of tar barrels went up on a raft in the middle of the river, and every bell and whistle in the two towns cut loose. The noise almost drowned out the periodic thudding of the Pine Street cannon.

Impromptu Parade

An impromptu torchlight parade swarmed through Green Bay's business streets, swept across the river to Broadway where it picked up a west side contingent and came whooping back. By that time nearly everybody who could make it out of doors lined Washington Street to cheer the marchers, some of whom kept up the racket all night.

All city officers except the east side aldermen promptly resigned and a special election was called for April 30. James H. Elmore, first mayor of Fort Howard and incumbent mayor of Green Bay, was elected mayor of the consolidated city without opposition, as was city clerk Xavier Parmentier. In the only contest, H. E. Brehme trounced H. J. Maloney for treasurer. New west side aldermen were also named.

That same evening the new council met in a flower-bedecked city hall, which had been completely refurnished for the event. April 2 was officially declared to be the actual date of consolidation and the administration buckled down to making the new regime work in a fine glow of enthusiasm and mutual congratulations.

Turn of the Century

City Pleasant, Leisurely in 1897

April 21, 1962

Green Bay has traveled a long and colorful road in its century-plus history as an incorporated city. By 1897 it had not yet reached the halfway mark of its first 100 years but was already assuming the appearance and characteristics familiar today in the older districts.

In fact, a modern Bayite set down in the city of 65 years ago (some are still around who were actually there) would have little difficulty making his way through the downtown and adjacent areas. Many of the familiar Washington Street facades were already there, although most of the business houses bore names only memories today.

The Fox River had been wiped out as a boundary line two years before when Fort Howard and Green Bay consolidated, although the once bitter rivalry was still very much alive under a placid surface. Consolidation had raised the city's official population to nearly 20,000 and the bigger Green Bay was beginning to flex its larger muscles.

It was, really, a charming little city with wide, tree-shaded residential streets and still plenty of room to grow. Although the eastern, southern and western city limits were essentially what they are today the areas west of Antoinette and east of Clay Streets were mostly wide open spaces dotted by clusters of houses here and there.

No Clay Street

Clay Street actually wasn't so labeled yet. All the streets east of Webster Avenue, except for the southern end of Suydam, were still numbered, Clay being simply one of two Tenth Streets. Consolidation had raised the problem of renaming to eliminate duplications but it hadn't been done yet.

The far west side was still largely a stretch of farm land cut off from the city proper by the big slough that ran through what is now Seymour park, then north along Antoinette before petering out along Velp Avenue near the city limits. Another and smaller slough still existed farther to the south.

The farmers out that way weren't very happy over the new deal, either. After muttering for two years about higher taxes that weren't doing them a lick of good they got their backs up in 1897 and threatened to pull out if something wasn't done. Since everybody admitted they had a legitimate beef, the City Council rejuggled the tax structure to give them demanded relief and they stayed in.

Washington Street was the principal business street, as it always has been, with Pearl the corresponding west side business thoroughfare. Everything east of Jefferson and west of Broadway was primarily residential.

Some Paved Streets

The only paved streets were in the business areas and they consisted of wooden block pavements. Other streets were still dirt and gravel roadways with shallow ditches for gutters. Since the city had a regular pipe sewage system, the once deep roadway ditches were gone.

Sidewalks were still mainly of wood, although that year saw the beginnings of pavement downtown as a number of merchants took it upon themselves to pave the sidewalks in front of their own shops. Biggest contributor to this trend was John Baum, who paved both sides of his growing department store at Main and Monroe.

Business buildings featured a lot of General Grant Gothic architecture, some of which is still in evidence. Among the buildings now familiar landmarks but brand new then was the Brusky Building, known as Rahr's Block *(now a parking lot on the northwest corner of Washington and Walnut opposite the Bellin Building).*

Except for the dirt roadways, which presented problems of dust and mud during the summer, the residential areas were lovely. Huge trees spread their branches over the streets to create shaded tunnels, and everybody vied to keep nice looking lawns. The high picket fences around each yard, once so familiar, had disappeared with the roaming cows that made them necessary, and the town was proud of its summer appearance.

No Automobiles

There were as yet no automobiles. So far as is known no auto had appeared in the city and very few residents had ever seen one. Most people kept at least one horse and buggy and nearly every home had a barn to house the family rig and dobbin.

The city did have an electric street car system — two, in fact. In the early summer of 1897 a two-year battle over control ended when tracks were laid across the main street bridge and the two systems finally united.

Except for the interurban to De Pere, however, most of the trackage was in the downtown area. The De Pere tracks ran via Mason-Monroe-Porlier and then out Webster, entering De Pere over what is now Ridgeway Boulevard. The line was only a year old and still something of a novelty that people often rode just for the fun of it.

Electricity was not a fairly common utility, although many homes were gas-lit. The downtown streets were well lighted electrically and the system was creeping into residential areas whose streets, when lit at all, were illuminated by gas lamps.

The individual home wells were going out too, as the water and sewage systems expanded. Outhouses were gradually disappearing, except in the poorer districts and on the fringes.

Phone the Status Symbol

Telephones were no longer a novelty. Nearly all business houses used them and many homes, although a residential phone was still the big status symbol.

After a period of depression lasting from 1893 through 1896 business began to improve after the inauguration of President McKinley, but local industry still faced serious problems. Most of it was still geared to lumber, which was phasing out. The Murphy Lumber Co. was the biggest single industrial unit but it had to bring in all its logs for cutting and had already threatened to move.

John Hoberg's little paper mill on the north side had not yet proved itself. The handwriting was on the wall, however, and the triumph of papermaking just a few years around the corner.

Those were pleasant years, just before the turn of the century. Nobody, least of all the modern housewife, would want to turn time back that far, but life was generally cheerful and leisurely and people took their time in most things.

Everybody knew everybody else, the city was a sociable place and with four breweries booming, the citizens — the conservative German element was pretty much in control — could quaff their suds in its 100-odd saloons, argue local politics, get excited about the town baseball team or the new game of football the boys at East High School had recently begun to play.

Chapter Four

Into the Twentieth Century

Prophet of Diversification

George D. Nau, City's Booster

April 28, 1962

As Green Bay moved through 1897 toward the opening of a new century, a young man was just beginning to establish himself as one of the most progressive leaders and businessmen of the growing community. George D. Nau had only recently acquired full control of his family properties and was getting ready to show his faith in the business potential of a city that had been hurting for years because of reliance on a single industry.

If George Nau were alive today he would be 99 years old. It is quite possible, however, that he would highly approve of most, if not all, of the things going on these days. Certainly, he would approve the new home going up for the banking institution he helped create. Above all, he would approve of the diversification of industry that has made the city relatively immune from the business difficulties it was facing 65 years ago.

George D. Nau was a son of Lambert Nau, the shy, crippled German who established the Nau name and enterprises in Green Bay in 1856. He *(George Nau)* was born in Green Bay March 10, 1863, and died here March 27, 1928, after a career of 44 years as one of the city's leading and most respected businessmen as well as one of Green Bay's most ardent boosters.

He was only 17 when his dad died in 1881. Although his brother Lambert Junior was a year his senior and both boys were gay blades about town, with a liking for fast horses and racing yachts, their father apparently sensed that George was inherently the better businessman.

Under Kellogg's Eye

Lambert Senior arranged his affairs to keep them under the eye of banker Rufus B. Kellogg until George attained his majority. Thereafter, the brothers operated as partners, although it was apparently George who made most of the decisions.

Lambert died suddenly in 1896, like his father a victim of tuberculosis, at the early age of 34. George was completely on his own, just as the country was beginning to come out of the depression of 1893.

When George assumed full control of the family enterprises they were based primarily on lake shipping, a ship chandlery and the wholesale meat, fish and poultry trade. George didn't like storekeeping and apparently wasn't very good at it.

Unloaded Store

As fast as he could he unloaded it, at the same time selling off the family sailing fleet and replacing it with a number of tug boats. By the turn of the century the Nau Tug Line was one of the best known on the lakes and continued to prosper until it was discontinued shortly before World War I.

Those tugs weren't ordinary vessels used to push ships around a harbor. They were unusually big and powerful, designed and used for hauling great log rafts down the lakes. They were a familiar sight on Green bay and Lake Michigan as they slowly pulled the huge rafts, some of them a mile long, to the lumber mills at Green Bay.

By 1895 lumbering was beginning to decline but papermaking was coming in. The Nau Line shifted its emphasis to carrying pulp for the new mills, and from there it was only a step for Nau to get into the new industry.

He was an early stockholder in Green Bay's pioneer paper mill, the Hoberg Paper & Fiber Co., the Green Bay Paper & Fiber Co. and the Northern Paper Mills. For many years up to the time of his death, he was treasurer of the Hoberg mills. At one time he was also president of the Green Bay Paper & Fiber Co.

Active in Finance

Paper was not his only activity, however. He had a finger in practically every banking and investment concern in town, being president of the Citizens National Bank until its consolidation with the Kellogg Bank and thereafter a director of the Kellogg-Citizens *(now Associated Bank)*. Nau worked hard on that merger, which he considered one of the biggest deals of his career.

He was president of the Citizens Securities Co., which he helped organize, and a director of Citizens Loan & Investment Co., Peoples Trust and Savings Bank and the Morley-Murphy Co.

For all his interest in paper, Nau was a believer in diversification and always interested in any new possibilities. His standing in the community was both a help and a hindrance. Since anything he backed was sure to be supported, he felt a sense of responsibility not to hurt those who trusted him, although he was perfectly willing to take a gambling flyer on his own.

Generally, he did all right, but once in a while he missed. One of his fumbles was the Lawton *(Lawson)* Aircraft Factory, which might have succeeded at that had World War I lasted a little longer. Another was the Lummi Bay Packing Co. But the one that brings wry smiles to the survivors who were singed with him was the Cluley Multiplier Co., a venture that had hilarious overtones as well as a whopping financial loss.

Married in 1885

In 1885 he married Miss Frances Miner at Mannersville, N.Y. Miss Miner was the daughter of a Great Lakes ship captain who met Nau over the counter of his father's ship chandlery when she accompanied her father on one of his voyages to Green Bay.

The couple had one daughter, Julia Gladys, who became the mother of George Nau Burridge. A beautiful and talented young woman with a fine singing voice, she was tragically burned to death in 1912.

Mrs. Nau was a strong-willed, forceful person whom her grandson affectionately describes as a "pistol." Throughout her long residence in Green Bay she was a community leader with a variety of interests that ranged from welfare activities to painting.

She continued to be a dominant figure in the life of the city right up to her death in 1948 at the age of 82.

Genial, Friendly Man

Unlike his father, who was shy and unapproachable to most people, George Nau was a friendly, genial man whom everybody knew and liked. As a youngster he had been quite a sportsman and he was always active socially.

He made it a point never to say anything unkind about others, at least in public. If he couldn't say something pleasant he kept quiet.

In 1927 Nau contracted the same disease that had finished his father and brother — tuberculosis. For months he was confined to his home but the illness didn't appear to be very dangerous. His sudden death on March 27, 1928 was a surprise to the city, just as those of his father and brother had been.

On the day of his funeral all the city's banks and paper mills shut down as a gesture of respect. The Press-Gazette came out with a laudatory editorial written by John K. Kline, who wasn't in the habit of throwing bouquets to anyone, dead or alive, unless they had them coming.

King-Size Ice Cubes

Ice Harvesting Colorful Business

January 14, 1967

Keeping things cold is simple nowadays. You merely plug in a refrigerator, set a dial and forget it. To cool a drink you simply pop an ice cube out of a metal or plastic tray from the freezer.

If you run out of ice cubes you go to the nearest beer mart, stick a coin in a slot and out comes a neatly packaged bag full. There are probably teenagers in Green Bay who, never having seen a piece of ice bigger than a cube, are unaware it ever came from anything but a home refrigerator or a slot machine.

Their grandparents remember when things were different. Less than 40 years ago electric refrigerators were unknown, food was kept in ice boxes and ice was taken from the frozen bay in dead of winter. From the turn of the century until the early 1930s the annual ice harvests were familiar operations.

For generations cutting ice from the frozen waterways was a flourishing business. Workable chunks weighing hundreds of pounds were lifted from the bay, stored in insulated sheds and delivered to homes during the summer in horse-drawn wagons. The famous Red Grange, in fact, earned his nickname of "Wheaton Ice-man" by working part of his way through the University of Illinois on the back end of an ice wagon.

Beautiful Product

In earlier days — and as late as the 1920s — the Fox River and bay were unpolluted and ice taken from them was beautiful. "Ice" blue and clear as crystal, tons of it were harvested every winter.

It was hard work, often bitterly cold, sometimes dangerous and a relatively small operation until power-driven machinery was developed to speed it up. At the height of the business about four decades ago Miller-Rasmussen Ice Co. took as much as 60,000 tons a year out of the bay.

Harvesting usually began in January when the bay had frozen to the depth of at least a foot. It sometimes froze as deep as 24 inches, but the average and preferred depth was 18 inches.

During the harvest, which lasted from six to eight weeks, as many as 150 men and 80 horses were busy cutting the ice fields, hauling the blocks — technically called bales — to the ice houses and storing them for summer use. Most of the workers were area farmers, who also rented their teams, but a professional crew of about 20 men was the backbone of the operation.

Off West Shore

The principal fields were off the west shore of the bay about two miles from the mouth of the river. There the bay bottom was clear sand, water six to eight feet deep and sparkling clean and the resulting ice was pure and clear.

From its formation by John Miller and Lawrence Rasmussen in 1903 until the 1930s, Miller-Rasmussen was the big harvester. At first it shared the business with Charles Le Clair but after the latter sold out and retired in 1917 Miller-Rasmussen had the field to itself.

About half the annual harvest was sold on contract to the railroads, of whom the North Western was the largest customer. When the railroads, cold storage plants, breweries and other industries were supplied, Miller-Rasmussen filled its own storage bins.

First step in the harvesting operation was to break a road across the open bay and marshlands from the big ice house on North Broadway to the selected ice field. At the same time drag plows, drawn by horses, scraped the snow off the field.

Several Fields

Several such fields, each about 500 by 400 feet, were cleared. They had to be some distance apart and restricted in size, otherwise edges would break off and somebody would get dunked — no joke in freezing weather when the nearest warm shelter was miles away.

Despite the hazards, in nearly 30 years the Miller-Rasmussen company lost only one man and one team of horses. The lone casualty was co-founder Lawrence Rasmussen who died of pneumonia in 1921 after falling into open water while harvesting on Shawano Lake.

Once cleared, the fields were scored in gridiron fashion with a movable circular saw propelled on a sled frame by a powerful gasoline motor. Lines were cut 22 inches apart one way and 44 inches the other, making a bale weighing from 500 to 700 pounds, depending upon thickness.

A narrow channel was opened from one end of the field to a loading point where an engine-operated belt lift raised the bales onto sleighs for transfer to the ice houses. These sleighs were huge flat beds, drawn by big, two-horse teams, extremely strong and heavy enough to hold several tons.

Not Rugged Enough

Originally, farmers furnished the sleighs but they weren't rugged enough to withstand the loads and the long, jolting drive. Miller-Rasmussen built its own, eventually operating a fleet of 40.

Myron Miller, present head of the company and son of the founder, recalls that each sleigh cost about $100 to build. When the harvesting ended farmers didn't want the big, cumbersome vehicles, and the last were sold for $15 apiece.

After a field had been scored, experts with pike poles broke off the bales and guided them into the loading channel. At the lift end a sleigh could be loaded with about five tons in half a minute.

The load would then head for town while another empty sleigh took its place. When the work was in full swing two continuous lines of sleighs, empties going one way and full loads the other, shuttled back and forth from daylight until dark.

Packed in Storage

At the ice house bales were skidded onto another moving belt which carried them up an incline to the top level of the stored ice. Inclines were adjustable and rose with the level of the ice in the building. When a bin was filled to a height of about 20 feet, the ice was covered with a thick layer of sawdust and a roof laid over it.

In the late 1920s mechanical ice-making machinery was perfected and in 1929 Miller-Rasmussen built its own plant. At first there was considerable resistance to "artificial" ice and the company continued to harvest in diminishing quantities.

Meanwhile, harbor dredging dumped spoil onto the bottom of the old ice fields, muddying the water and forcing the harvests farther out on the bay. By 1932 the distances, quality of the ice and declining demand made harvesting unprofitable, and an old and unusual industry quietly died.

'Number, Please'

The Miracle of the Telephone

July 20, 1968

Time was in Green Bay when the status symbol to top all others was a "telly-phone" in the front hall. Today the telephone is such an integral and vital part of life that the ultimate status symbol is to be so important you won't have one around — or, next best, to have an unregistered number known only to the chosen few.

People take the telephone so much for granted they are unaware of how great a change it has made in their lives. Well within living memories it was a real production to put through a long distance call to as far distant a spot as Appleton.

Today, people whose grandparents got a thrill out of talking on the phone to the neighbors across the street think little of picking up an instrument, dialing Hawaii and having the call go through in seconds. Of course, this is expensive but try telling that to some reveler with a yen to converse at great distances when in hiccups, particularly if he's using your phone.

Less than 90 Years

It was less than 90 years ago that the first crude telephones made their appearance in Green Bay, and that was only six years after Alexander Graham Bell had perfected (not invented) the thing. In 1882 a man named Charles Haskins blew into town, set up shop and began to build a system.

According to the records the first Green Bay user of the gadget was Henry Hagemeister, who had a line installed from the Hagemeister Brewery to his home. The Kellogg National Bank also put one in between its Green Bay and De Pere offices. Within a short time Haskins had a list of 35 subscribers going through a switchboard at 110 N. Washington St.

The day of the single operator was short, however. Setting up an elaborate city system was too much for the resources of most individuals and before the year was out Haskins had sold out to the newly organized Wisconsin Telephone Co. The latter sent in Edwin P. Parish as manager and Ed, with the assistance of chief operator Eliza Le Page, ran the show until 1893 when his sideline insurance business got so prosperous he had to resign.

The Early Phones

Very few are left now who remember those first telephones. They were big, box-like affairs fixed to the wall, with a mouthpiece sticking out of the middle, a couple of bells near the top and a black receiver hanging from a rack on the side.

To make a call you lifted the receiver, turned a crank on the other side to raise "central" and when her lilting "Number, please" came through you gave her the number. You had to stand up to make a call, but that had some advantages. For one thing, the phone was up high enough so the kids couldn't reach and play with it.

There were disadvantages, too. Most people were on "party lines," so when one phone rang every other on the line did too. The person wanted was identified by the number or combination of rings but anyone could get into the act, and eavesdropping was a favorite indoor sport for gossips and busybodies. By the same token, if somebody was monopolizing the line you could tell them to get lost.

By 1888 the exchange was bulging with 135 subscribers in Green Bay and Fort Howard, many of them business houses. That year the switchboard was moved to Cherry Street but it was shortly back on Washington, where it remained until 1904 when a new exchange was built at 112 N. Adams Street to take care of 1,450 subscribers.

Further Expansion

Now the telephone company office building, the Adams Street location *(at 112 North Adams which now houses Associated Bank offices)* also contained the exchange until 1949, when the present exchange was opened on South Jefferson. The latter location is still the heart of the system, although a second was added on Ridge Road in 1959 and the company is now looking for a site for a third.

Shortly after the turn of the century telephoning got complicated when a rival company, the Fox Valley Telephone Co., invaded the city. Since the two systems did not connect many people had to have two phones to contact everyone, a situation that continued until the Wisconsin Telephone Co. bought up its rival in 1921.

By 1918 the number of phones in use had increased to 5,776, and in the 1920s it was necessary to add exchange names to numbers. Everybody thought Green Bay was a really big city when they had to prefix numbers with "Cherry" or "Adams," just like in New York.

Tremendous Growth

Up to the 1930s the growth of telephone service was pretty gradual, but by 1940 it had jumped to a total of 17,367 phones in the city. World War II temporarily stopped expansion but by 1964 there were 46,655 phones in use. With additions at the rate of 1,000 a year, according to Green Bay area manager Frank Shekore, the number is now over 50,000.

The average number of calls placed in Green Bay in 1940 was 86,000; today it runs nearly 250,000. Green Bay folks are a chatty lot — this is about 40 percent above the national average, according to Shekore.

Such volume would be virtually impossible without the present dialing system, introduced in 1953. This was a massive changeover, necessitating the replacement of every instrument in the system. Today, if you are too lazy to dial, there are push-button instruments to do it even faster.

Radio Phones Too

You can even have a radio-telephone in your automobile now, as many emergency service vehicles have. They've been available since 1946 when Mayor Dominic Olejniczak placed the first call from his automobile at Dyckesville to his office in City Hall. Telephonic communication with lake vessels within a 50-mile radius has been standard since 1955.

The telephone company is always coming up with new gimmicks, too. Some of the new phones soon to be introduced are tricky enough to make your hair curl.

Things have come a long way since Heinie Hagemeister's dad swanked it up with the only telephone connection in town, and they're a lot better than in 1922. That year a destructive sleet storm blew down all the lines south and east of the city and practically isolated Green Bay for days.

Automobile Changed 1915 City

June 26, 1965

Fifty years ago next Thursday a new newspaper made its bow in Green Bay. The newcomer was the Press-Gazette, a consolidation of the upstart Free Press and the old, familiar Gazette (which just missed by the margin of a few months achieving the half century mark itself).

The paper hit the streets of a prosperous little city on the verge of transition from a conservatively complacent 19th Century town to a modern municipality. Driving force in the changeover, although most people weren't aware of the impact, was the automobile.

Not that autos were a brand new phenomenon. They had been around since the turn of the century but were just beginning to be taken for granted. Compared to today, however, there were only a handful, probably not more than 1,200 in the entire county.

Here to Stay

Still, the fact was plain to see that the automobile was here to stay and that it had successfully challenged the ages old supremacy of the horse as a major means of transportation. In fact, there were almost as many cars in town as there were horses and the gas propelled vehicles were gradually moving into business fields hitherto dominated by the horse and wagon.

City streets reflected the balance, too. Most of the downtown streets were paved and so were some in the nearby residential areas, but the majority were still gravel roadways.

Nearly all existing pavement was brick or cedar block. Only the year before one short city block had been paved with concrete as an experiment, as had a stretch of the Cedar Creek Road, but city and county officials were still waiting to see whether the new-fangled stuff was all that its enthusiasts claimed.

Pavement to De Pere

Part of the doubt was removed in the spring when the Cedar Creek Road came through the winter of 1914-15 in excellent shape. Before the year was over another forward step was taken when the lower De Pere road *(Riverside Drive)* was paved with concrete, although it was completed too late to get much use before automobiles were put up on blocks for the winter.

If the automobile had begun to supplant the horse and buggy for pleasure riding and in a number of commercial activities, the street car was still the backbone of public passenger service. Only a few people could afford to own cars (which ranged in price from $700 to $5,000), the street cars could run in any weather, and everybody — car owners not excepted — regularly rode them.

The principal difficulty with street car transportation was the Fox River. The East Side was pretty well covered with a system of tracks and the West Side slightly less so, but the only river crossing was the Main Street bridge. Several more years were to pass before additional tracks were laid across the Walnut Street span, and by that time the gasoline engine had won the fight.

Train Travel Heavy

Since country roads were still rough on automobiles and often impassable and since the airplane was still a novelty, traveling any distance meant taking the train. Green Bay's three railroads were booming with passenger as well as freight traffic, the city had large railroad shops and passenger trains arrived and departed practically every hour.

Aside from the paper mills, in fact, railroading was Green Bay's major industry. The shops and roundhouses as well as the yards and rolling stock employed even more men than the Northern, Hoberg and Green Bay Paper & Fibre Co. mills. That portion of the West Side then known as the "Irish Patch" was almost solidly occupied by railroad families, many of them in the second and third generation of railroading.

Green Bay was changing in other respects, too. Although the downtown façade had remained substantially the same since the 1890s, the year 1915 saw a renewed burst of building activity.

New Skyscraper

The Bellin-Buchanan Building, which would replace the Minahan Building across the intersection as the town's skyscraper, was going up at Washington and Walnut. Up on Webster Avenue the Deaconess (now Bellin Memorial) Hospital was under construction and on the West Side the new McCartney National Bank was completed.

There was also a good deal of residential construction and many new homes, some of them still in use, were abuilding. The "Hill" section centered around St. James Park still dominated the exclusive East Side residential area with what were mansions of the time, but newer homes were sprouting on the perimeter of the city's social citadel.

With a population of about 27,000, the city had plenty of room to spread out. South of Mason and east of Clay Street there were still large open spaces, and there was nothing but farm land west of West High School (also new).

Open Country

Farther south, west of Broadway, there was plenty of open country across the railroad yards. Allouez, except for the Reformatory, was entirely rural and so was much of Preble* north of the paper mills.

The stretch between the city limits and Bay View Beach *(shortened later to the present Bay Beach)* was still occasionally called Mushrat City and not without reason.

Professional services in the city were adequate with 43 doctors, the same number of lawyers and 17 dentists. Newcomers Alex Enna and

Walter L. Larsen were just getting started in the face of competition from over 40 other music teachers.

All Gone Now

A few of the 1915 law firms are still operating but none of the original practitioners are — the present attorneys are sons of the earlier men. The same is true of the doctors.

The pre-World War I era was still the day of tailor-made clothing and the majority of the city's business and professional men had their clothes made to order by William Engels, David Detienne, Will Hoffman, Arthur Norgaard, Fred Thirion or 17 other needle pushers. If women didn't make their own clothes they had plenty of seamstresses to do it for them.

There were 82 dressmakers and 11 milliners in town, nearly all of them women who worked at home or in the homes of their clients, although a few had downtown shops. Norgaard and Jacob Davidson were the only men in the feminine-dominated field. Ready-to-wear shops were coming in, but they got only a small portion of the apparel business compared to the seamstresses.

Modern Aspect

In one respect, Green Bay was thoroughly modern. It was plentifully supplied with taverns (they called them saloons in those days) with 133 flourishing. Many were either owned outright or subsidized by the city's three large breweries.

As a result a man could get only one brand of suds in most of them. Beer was the alcoholic staple, though, and relatively little hard liquor was consumed — usually neat with a beer chaser.

A few places had "family rooms" with separate entrances but otherwise the saloon was exclusively a male haven. Dad, Uncle Fritz and big brother Joe could belly peacefully up to the bar, nurse their five cent schooners of brew and cheerfully argue about women, politics, women, baseball, women, whether the Jess Willard-Jack Johnson heavyweight title fight was a tank job and women.

** The Town of Preble consolidated with the City of Green Bay in November 1964.*

Changed Business Pattern

Green Bay Business Boomed in 1915

August 7, 1965

Last week's announcement that William Engels' old tailor shop on Cherry Street was being demolished for a parking lot must have jogged the memories of a few veterans who can hark back to the days when a large proportion of men's clothes were handmade to order. Half a century ago Engels was one of the best known of more than a score of Green Bay tailors who dressed the city's business and professional leaders.

Bill Engels, a "schneider" of the old school who did most of his hand sewing while seated cross-legged on a table, was more than a successful tailor, however. He was also typical of Green Bay's business and commercial life in 1915, when virtually all enterprises from paper mills to tailor shops, were locally owned and managed.

In that respect Green Bay was the same as it had been since before the Civil War, but the turn of the century had otherwise witnessed a revolution in its commercial existence. Except for the Diamond Lumber Co. and a sprinkling of planing mills, the saw and shingle mills that had been its arteries for nearly 50 years had disappeared.

Railroad, Paper Town

Green Bay was now a railroad and paper mill town. The three railways maintained large shops here while the Northern, Hoberg and Green Bay Paper & Fibre Co. mills had replaced the once numerous lumbering enterprises. Between them the railroads and paper mills employed the bulk of the city's labor force.

Next to the mills and roundhouses, the city's major industries were its 11 machine shops, themselves closely allied with the paper industry. Among them were the Green Bay Barker Co., Green Bay Machine, Hudson-Sharp, Hartmann-Greiling, Sectional Roll Manufacturing Co., the Cluley Multiplier Co. and the Straubel Machine Co.

Cluley, which had a patent on a computer that could do anything but work, was one of the all time busts in Green Bay's business history. Not so Straubel, which not only made marine gasoline engines but was acquiring know-how through repairing and improving paper finishing machines that eventually moved it into the paper making field.

Dead Heat

With the horse and automobile running a dead heat for supremacy (there were slightly over 1,000 of each in town), businesses tied to one or the other were about evenly divided, too. Compared to ten garages, five auto dealers and a handful of tire and accessory dealers, the city still supported seven blacksmiths, three horse-shoers, five livery stables, seven harness makers and a horseshoe factory.

Bigger than all the other harness makers combined several times over was the McIntyre-Burrall Saddlery Co. Located on the present site of city hall, McIntyre-Burrall was running night and day to fill war contracts for the British and French armies and permeating the air around the Walnut-Jefferson Street corner with the now almost forgotten aroma of freshly worked leather.

Other good sized operations were three carriage and wagon makers, the John Ebeling Milling Co., the Green Bay Drive Calk Co., Willow Grass Rug Co., two wholesale candy manufacturers, two wholesale grocery firms and three breweries. The D. W. Britton Cooperage was also large and prosperous, as were the Hart and Denessen Steamship Lines and the Nau Tug Line.

Three Breweries

The Hagemeister, Rahr and Hochgreve Breweries supplied most of the suds to the city's numerous saloons. Among the favorite watering places, where innumerable barrels of local draft beer were consumed were Allen & Levitas (now part of *the former* Kaap's Restaurant), Ed Barth, the Beaumont Hotel Bar, William Birmingham, Billy McGinnis, George Schwartz and Joe Windhauser on the East Side and John Gross and John Shaughnessy across the river.

To handle the finances of the town there were seven banks. They were the Kellogg and Citizens Banks, still more than a decade from consolidation; McCartney's, the Farmers' Exchange (now Wisconsin State), Bank of Green Bay, the year-old West Side State and the brand new Peoples Savings and Trust Co.

Professional services included 43 attorneys, the same number of doctors, 17 dentists and a strong representation of insurance agencies and realtors. Prescriptions were filled in 15 drug stores. Most prominent of these, all of whom displayed ornate jars filled with brightly colored liquids in their front windows, were Raphael Soquet, Charles LeComte, Will Luckenbach, Popp & Rather, R. L. McDonald (later Brock's) and the Corner Drug.

The latter was run by Joseph B. Holzer and August Neveu. The latter also had a drug store on North Broadway, managed in those days by Ed Schweger.

Enough businessmen preferred made to order clothes to keep 22 tailors busy, including Engels, David Detienne, Will Hoffman, Art Norgaard and Fred Thirion. They competed comfortably with 13 retail clothing establishments of which the leaders were the Continental, Counard & Neville, Herrick's, Homer Maes, Stiefel's, and now C. A. Gross & Co.

Since the same men smoked cigars in preference to cigarettes, there were 17 cigar makers in town as well as six cigar stores, two of which were operated by Bobby Lynch and Joe Bosse. The barbershop, like the saloon, was still a strictly male hangout and there were 26, among them the Beaumont Hotel shop, Charles Radick, Walter Blaney, Phil Janelle, Hy Smith and Billy Van Beek.

Like their men, the womenfolk either had their clothes made or made them themselves with the help of 82 dressmakers and seamstresses. There were only six ready-to-wear shops plus eight department (usually called dry goods) stores. Largest of the latter were Jorgensen-Blesch, Baum's and A. Spuhler, others being Davidson's, M. Allard, A. L. Gray & Son and the White Store, which opened for business that summer.

Home Hair Styling

Women also did most of their own hair styling but there were six hairdressing establishments, all run by women. The term beauty shop hadn't been invented yet.

In those days people bought groceries in a grocery store, meat in a butcher shop and baked goods in a bakery. If there were only eight of the latter (including Henry Willaert, John Rockstroh and J. V. Micksch) it was because housewives did their own baking, but they could shop in 80 grocery stores and 24 meat markets.

There were no supermarkets or grocery chains, the closest to the latter being Cornelius Denessen, who had two stores. Other leaders were Bur's on Washington Street, Ed Stapleford and Henry Platten, while the best known butchers were George Stenger and the Platten Brothers.

Neighborhood Grocery

Out on Webster Avenue was a neighborhood grocery called New Year's because its owner's name was Niejahr, which employed a teen-age clerk. Art Brauel owns and runs it himself now.

People ate out a lot but in the dining rooms of such large hotels (the city had 30) as the Beaumont, Sherwood, and Broadway rather than in supper clubs. George DeLair had the most fashionable restaurant although Schwalbe's also got a good play.

In addition to 19 candy stores, all featuring their own handmade confections, Green Bay had two candy factories in the Brenner and Gazette Candy Companies. One made the Hinky Dink and the other the Beaumont Lunch, two of the most delicious nickel candy bars ever manufactured. The Hinky Dink was the king sized ancestor of the Oh Henry and Baby Ruth.

Paper Research Milestone

Press-Gazette Hits Half a Century

January 2, 1965

The Press-Gazette has arrived at an important milestone in its career with the dawn of 1965. As of this year the newspaper is 50 years old. The actual anniversary date is June 19, the day half a century ago when the first issue of the paper was published in 1915 following the merger of the long established Green Bay Gazette and the youthful but anemic Free Press.

The new enterprise was the outcome of a newspaper war between its predecessors that had driven both close to the wall. Their groggy condition had paved the way for a completely new deal under the direction of two young newcomers to town and a well known local attorney.

The latter was Victor I. Minahan, member of one of the most influential and colorful families in Green Bay's history and brother of Doctors John R. and Robert E. Minahan. A highly successful lawyer, Minahan had founded the Free Press, although he took no part in its actual management, nor did he become active in the Press-Gazette for another 15 years.

Ambitious Young Men

The newcomers were John K. Kline and Andrew B. Turnbull, a pair of ambitious young newspapermen from Saginaw, Mich. Kline was the editor and Turnbull the business manager of the fledgling Press-Gazette.

Minahan had launched the Free Press in May, 1914, invading a field the Gazette had monopolized since the suspension of the venerable Green Bay Advocate in 1906. The only reason he ever gave for getting into the business was that he felt the city was big enough for two daily papers.

He was wrong. The Gazette had become stuffy and self satisfied and needed a jolt, but the plain truth was that Green Bay was not big enough to support competing dailies. The attempt nearly killed both.

Good Publication

The Free Press, which began publication on May 14, 1914, was a good paper, much more aggressive, modern and newsworthy than its stodgy rival. However, after a promising start it failed to live up to Minahan's hopes. He once ruefully declared that the best month it ever had in its 14 months existence cost him $1,100.

Although it never came close to breaking even, the Free Press hurt the Gazette even more. By early 1915 both were virtually on the ropes, although neither realized how close to a knockout the other actually was.

Both Minahan and N. C. Pickard, publisher of the Gazette, were fighters and neither would give in. At this point Kline and Turnbull entered the picture, thanks partly to the persuasiveness of one of Green Bay's most enthusiastic drumbeaters — Capt. John A. Cusick.

Saginaw Newsmen

Kline was then managing editor of the Saginaw News and Turnbull advertising manager of the U.S. Graphite Co. of Saginaw but anxious to get back to the newspaper field where he had previously spent 15 years. They had worked together on the News and had dreamed of running their own paper. Both being young and not too opulent, however, their sights were set somewhat below anything the size of Green Bay.

Early in 1915 Cusick, a Green Bay real estate promoter and developer of Bay View Beach, called on them in Saginaw, apparently at the instigation of Minahan and others who were concerned about the situation here. Neither Kline nor Turnbull actually fell for Cusick's bait but they came to Green Bay, looked the situation over and took an option on the Free Press.

Back in Saginaw — before they made the down payment — they began to cool off. The Free Press, they felt, had possibilities, but they weren't sure of the wisdom of coming into a strange community with a long established rival still in the field. On another trip to Green Bay they informed Minahan the deal was off unless the Gazette could be acquired too.

Turnbull Had Hunch

The latter wasn't convinced Pickard was ready to quit but Turnbull had a hunch he might. Turnbull had heard a rumor the Gazette had once been offered for sale for $125,000 and he suggested Minahan make Pickard the same offer — although neither had any idea where they would find that kind of money.

Minahan caught the Gazette publisher in his office one morning when Pickard was feeling low and the latter accepted the offer. Surprised but determined not to let his competitor off the hook, Minahan hurriedly drew up an informal option on a piece of scrap paper and bound the agreement with every cent he had in his pockets, about $25.

Raising the $125,000 as well as the initial payment on the Free Press plus enough to get the show on the road took considerable scrambling, but the new owners made it. The Press-Gazette made its bow at the end of June and hasn't missed a deadline since.

Touch and Go

Things were touch and go at first. Turnbull used to recall with a grin how he would wait in his darkened office on Saturday nights for his subscription collectors to report in to see if he had enough to meet the next payroll. He didn't dare turn on the light.

The Gazette-Free Press had depressed advertising rates murderously, and the Press-Gazette had to raise them again to survive — a touchy business. The break came when John Baum, owner of Baum's Department Store *(at 531 Main Street, the site of the current Camera Corner-Connecting Point)*, agreed to the increase and talked other merchants into going along, an action for which Turnbull was vehemently grateful the rest of his life.

Because of inherited conditions

the Press-Gazette lost money in its first months. By the end of 1915, however, it had not only made up the lost ground but ended the year modestly in the black.

Used Gazette Plant

The first issues were published in the old Gazette building at Adams and Pine Streets — now the Architects Building *(302-310 Pine St.)* — but shortly after the merger it moved to the Free Press plant in the former Crikelair Opera House on Cherry Street. The site is now part of the new Kellogg-Citizens National Bank *(now Associated Bank)*.

The Press-Gazette published from there until the present building was occupied in 1924. When opened, the new plant was one of the most modern small newspaper spreads in the country, a distinction it still enjoys, although it is no longer small.

To maintain the distinction through 40 years of expansion and mounting circulation, the building has undergone extensive alterations, culminating ten years ago in the addition of a third story. From it today a force of 209 employees issues a daily and Sunday paper with a daily paid circulation (as of November) of 43,643 and a Sunday paid average of 50,849.

Went Sunday

Three years ago last fall the Press-Gazette "Went Sunday," inaugurating an edition that now covers 22 counties in Northern Wisconsin and Upper Michigan. A staff of 630 carrier boys delivers the 50,000-plus papers every Sunday morning throughout the area.

In half a century the paper has had only three editors. Kline occupied the position until his sudden death in 1930, at which time Minahan emerged from the background to take over the desk. He continued as editor until he died in 1954. Leo V. Gannon, who joined the staff as a reporter in 1922, then stepped into the editorship.

Turnbull, last survivor of the original triumvirate, died in 1960. Management of the paper is continued by his heirs. *(The Green Bay Newspaper Co. sold the Press-Gazette to the Gannett Corp. in 1980.)*

First of Two Articles

The 'Tramp Truck' Rolls West

February 11, 1961

Long distance trucking has become one of the great industries of America and the sight of huge semi-trailers rolling over concrete highways such a familiar part of the American scene people forget how new it all is — so new, in fact, that truck drivers still call their union The Teamsters. Yet it has all happened within the span of the average middle-aged individual's lifetime.

It's easy to forget, if, indeed, one even bothers to give it a thought, that just 40 years ago trans-continental trucking was only the dream of a few visionaries. That's why it's not so remarkable that one of the pioneering efforts toward realizing that dream had been completely forgotten, even though it began in Green Bay and one of the participants is still active around town.

When the history of the trucking industry is written, though, the hegira of the Oneida "Tramp Truck" from Green Bay to Seattle will have its due, and Johnny Arens and Harold T. I. Shannon will get credit for their part in it. As a matter of fact, the whole idea was Shannon's in the first place.

One of Green Bay's most prosperous and promising industries in 1920 was the Oneida Motor Truck Co. Formed shortly before World War I, the concern assembled a good vehicle, one which enjoyed a national reputation for ruggedness and performance. Much of that reputation rested on such exploits as Hi Johnston's speed run to New York in 1919 and the Tramp Truck's journey to the West Coast a year later.

Friends Lay Back

Shannon was then Oneida's advertising manager and its most enthusiastic drumbeater, given to making claims people thought extravagant. His friends lay back, confident he would eventually go too far.

They thought they had him over the barrel when he came up with the statement that he not only could take one of the standard Oneidas to the Pacific Coast but could make it pay its way. When called to make good, Harold knew he had a good thing going and grabbed it. Soon he had both the company and the Association of Commerce committed to his scheme.

His proposition was straightforward enough. It was simply that a standard all purpose, 1 3/4-ton Oneida truck could work its way from Green Bay to the coast, paying all operating expenses as well as those of a two-man crew.

The trip would be made in 90 days and — this was the kicker — no hauling job would be repeated. The idea being to demonstrate versatility as well as durability, each assignment would be different.

Didn't Need Tires

As it developed the truck avoided one important expense — that of replacing tires. The Goodyear company had just developed the first heavy-duty, pneumatic truck tire and saw in the proposed scheme a chance to demonstrate the superiority of pneumatics over the then standard solid rubber shoe.

It offered to furnish replacements as needed — an offer, incidentally, that wasn't needed. The truck finished the trip on its original rubber. Shannon and Johnny Arens of De Pere were selected as the crew. Arens, who died a few years later, was a fiery little fellow, afraid of nothing, a wounded and decorated combat veteran and a top mechanic. Harold still marvels at his genius with a bit of wire snipped from some farmer's fence.

A more oddly matched pair would have been hard to find. Shannon was the incurable optimist who didn't know when he was licked; Arens prided himself on being a reasonable man who knew when to quit.

As a result they fought boisterously all the way across country. Several times Johnny told Shannon off and quit, only to come marching defiantly back when he couldn't get an immediate train heading east.

Began Aug. 18

The historic stunt got under way with considerable ceremony on the afternoon of Aug. 18, 1920, when a brand new truck, decorated with a gilded horseshoe and a large sign proclaiming its mission, pulled out with the blessing of the truck company, the Rotary Club and the Association of Commerce. It had one gallon of gas in the tank and neither Shannon nor Arens had a dime in their pockets.

Wallets and even watches had been confiscated to eliminate any temptation to cheat. All the two men carried were kits of toilet articles and the clothes on their backs. Whatever they might need they'd have to earn.

The first job was a commission from John Dousman of De Pere to deliver a copy of the De Pere newspaper to a friend in Seattle. The fee was only 50 cents but it got the show on the road.

At Appleton the truck picked up a job taxiing a bridal party to one of the lakeside roadhouses for a wedding dance. The trip almost ended before it was well started when the vehicle tore down the electric wires leading into the resort, but Arens got them working again. First day's receipts were $12.

Through Illinois

Rolling out of Appleton next morning, the "Tramp Truck" worked its way up the Fox River Valley, to Freeport and Rockford, Ill., then swung west across northern Illinois. It cut back into Wisconsin briefly near the Iowa border, crossed the Mississippi at Dubuque and zig-zagged westward through Iowa, its route depending on the work it picked up.

Spanning Iowa was easy. The fair season was in full swing and the truck found plenty of hauling from one fair to another. Once it carried a loan of grain, again a pair of valuable race horses and a third time a sideshow freak who endeared himself to Arens by insisting upon addressing Shannon as "Fat."

One fair job that caused Arens considerable merriment was a load of prize hogs that Shannon accepted under the impression they were ordinary pigs. They turned out to be monsters that required three trips. Furthermore, they objected loudly and strenuously. Arens later wrote a delighted account of Shannon trying to drag one out from under the truck by its tail.

On another occasion they picked up a quiet but nervous stranger who was willing to pay well for his ride. Shortly after dropping him they discovered the entire countryside was on the alert for an armed bank robber. Shannon is still wondering.

Driving Tricky

If finding work in Iowa was simple, driving wasn't. There was a lot of rain, there were only dirt roads, and Iowa mud was as notorious then as it is now. Just keeping on the slippery, high crowned roads without skidding into the ditch was a real balancing act.

By this time Shannon and Arens had developed a routine. Arriving in a town late in the afternoon, they would park on a busy street and wait for a crowd to gather. Harold would then launch into a regular medicine man's spiel, extolling the virtues of the Oneida and inviting questions.

The spiel and question period usually developed into a serious evening session, often conducted by lantern light inside the truck. Arens would answer mechanical questions and Shannon would explain the manifold uses of the vehicles. The bull sessions often brought in the next day's business.

The safari had been going so well Shannon and Arens thought they had it made. Receipts went almost as fast as they came in. Harold is still vague about his spending but admits they didn't build up much of a reserve. They soon had cause to regret it.

Last of Two Articles

Shannon Comes Down Mountain

February 18, 1961

As Harold Shannon and Johnny Arens tooled their big Oneida truck across Iowa in the first stages of their transcontinental trek in the fall of 1920, they thought they had things under firm control. Jobs were easy to get, the vehicle was paying its way, and the big, wide world seemed to be their special oyster.

The situation changed abruptly after they headed into South Dakota. Towns were farther apart, the fair season was over, roads were poor and jobs scarce. To make matters worse, gasoline prices went higher the farther west they went.

Fortunes hit bottom at Huron, where they arrived late on a chilly October afternoon. They hadn't eaten in 24 hours, the gas tank was about empty and they had 35 cents between them in a town where fuel was 42 cents a gallon.

Worked Old Gag

Arens was ready to call the whole thing off, but not Shannon. It was too cold to sleep in the truck and they looked like a pair of thugs, but Harold worked the old $50 bill gag on a hotel night clerk to get a room. They were at least able to rest comfortably if a bit hollowly.

Next morning, after parting with 30 of their 35 cents for two doughnuts and coffee, they went looking for work. The first prospect whom they found curiously inspecting the parked truck, turned out to be their AWOL angel.

Harold tried putting a brave face on the situation but Arens made no bones about it. Fortunately, the stranger was a Chamber of Commerce type who decided that if the expedition was going to blow up it had better not happen in Huron.

First Square Meal

He took them to the Elks Club where they were offered the job of cleaning an accumulation of several months' trash and garbage out of the basement. It was messy but the boys were in no position to haggle. Besides, they got their first square meal in two days before pitching in.

With Arens loudly bemoaning the low estate to which they had fallen, they turned to with shovels. Three trips to the city dump were required to do the job and they had to scrub themselves and the truck down afterward, but they earned $12 and were back in business.

By this time word had gotten around and offers for other jobs began to come in. Most of them were local hauls that would have kept them in Huron too long, but finally they landed one moving a complete restaurant to another town farther west.

49 Miles Per Hour!

Huron was the low point. Things picked up after that and by squeezing nickels for a few days they managed to keep moving. An indication of their restored good fortune came on the anniversary of the day Hi Johnston set a speed record on his 1919 New York run when they broke it by hitting 49 miles an hour.

Crossing the Missouri at Mobgridge, S.D., the truck moved into Montana. At Butte they picked up a courier mission carrying official notice of his victory to the governor-elect at Missoula, by which time they were pretty sure they were going to make it. Before reaching Missoula, though, they encountered some of the roughest going of the entire trip.

Outside Billings they ran into a Montana norther that immobilized them briefly but resulted in an offbeat job of functioning as a hearse. When the regular, hard-tired hearse was unable to get into an isolated ranch to bring out a body for burial, the Tramp Truck was hired. Thanks to the pneumatic tires, the job presented little difficulty.

On Home Stretch

From Missoula the truck was on the home stretch and rolled merrily along, crossing Idaho in only two days, then sweeping easily through Spokane, Coulee City and Ellensburg, Wash. They cleared the Cascades just ahead of the season's first serious snowstorm, a blizzard that might have ended the trip tantalizingly close to the goal.

In fact, beating that storm was typical of their weather luck all the way. They encountered lots of rain, especially in Iowa, but little snow except for the Montana storm, which didn't last long.

At 9:30 p.m. on Nov. 12 the truck chugged into Seattle, bringing the long run to a successful conclusion in a fanfare of publicity. It had been on the road a few hours over 83 days, beating the deadline by a full week.

Truck, Crew Celebrities

After a short rest and general cleanup the truck moved leisurely down to San Francisco where it was met by Lafayette Markle, president of the truck company, and Goodyear representatives. By this time the battered vehicle and its crew were celebrities.

On the 83-day jaunt they had covered something over 2,000 miles and handled 66 different jobs, cargoes varying from pigs and garbage to caskets and newlyweds. The truck had not only made all expenses but had turned a slight profit, although the crew's salaries apparently weren't included in the expense figures and the vehicle would never be the same.

What was more important, the trip had demonstrated that long distance hauling was practicable, even over the atrocious western roads. At this distance it is impossible to gauge the effect of an isolated incident on future developments, but the immediate impact must have been considerable.

Shannon's Career Founders

The only real casualty of the expedition was Shannon's career as an automobile driver. That foundered on an experience just outside Bozeman, Mont.

As the truck topped the last mountain ridge before dropping down into Bozeman, Shannon was driving. He admits he saw a sign warning motorists to shift into low gear as he cleared the crest but he disregarded the advice.

Soon he had burned out the brakes and the unwieldy vehicle was going too fast to shift. What followed was the most hair-raising ride of Harold's life, one he shudders over even after 40 years.

Ready to Jump

The road was winding and narrow, wide enough only for one car, and sometimes it skirted the shoulder of the mountain with sheer drops — most of which seemed to be on the driver's side — of hundreds of feet. When Arens quietly opened the other door and poised himself to jump if Shannon lost control, Harold knew he was in deep trouble.

Fortunately, they met no traffic. How long that wild career down the mountain lasted Shannon has no idea, but eventually the road leveled off and the truck, still unable to stop, hurtled through the main business district of Bozeman. Harold finally halted it by scraping the wheels along the curb.

When it did stop Shannon found his hands clamped so tightly to the steering wheel he couldn't open them, and Arens had to pry his fingers loose one by one. Once outside the cab Harold became violently sick all over someone's well groomed lawn.

Right then and there Shannon made up his mind that if he finished the trip he would never drive a car again. He never has.

Forgotten Era

When the Trolley Ruled the Streets

August 29, 1964

It may come as a shock, like the discovery that the snappy 1928 automobile in which you learned to drive is now classified as an antique, but there are people who have lived all their lives in Green Bay and are preparing to vote in their third or fourth presidential election yet who never saw a street car come clanging down Washington Street. It has been 27 years since the city's once familiar trolleys made their final runs.

On Nov. 17, 1937, Green Bay's first public transportation system expired when the Wisconsin Public Service Corp. sent its cars out for the last time. Next day they were replaced by motor buses. They had lasted for nearly 45 years, although they had been quietly dying for half that period.

The city's first street car line went into operation on June 9, 1894. Contrary to popular belief, the first cars were not horse-drawn (Green Bay never had horse cars, although it might have had the first schemes for a local system been implemented). The line started and finished with electrically driven trolleys at a time when Chicago was still using the old fashioned method.

Started in 1886

As early as 1886 there was talk of setting up a street railway here and in 1888 a franchise was actually issued for the purpose. Nothing came of it but a lot of talk, however, until 1893 when the Fox River Electric Railway began construction of a line.

The tracks were finally laid and trolley wires installed by the summer of 1894. The entire city was in a dither about the new system, and most of the population turned out to celebrate its inauguration.

At 10:30 p.m. the evening of June 9 (a Saturday night), a small, Toonerville Trolley-vintage car loaded with city dignitaries pulled away from the car barns on the site of the WPSC garage for the first official transit of the line. The trip covered nearly seven miles and lasted about an hour.

Only Four Cars

All along the route the convoy of four cars — all the new line had available at the time — was greeted by cheering crowds on every street corner. The biggest outburst came at Washington and Main Streets, where red fire was burned in the street in front of the Beaumont Hotel and firecrackers popped up and down Washington.

The original trackage ran mostly east and west, along Mason Street to Webster Avenue, on Walnut from Washington to what is now Joannes Park and on Main from Washington to the East River bridge. Connecting north-south lines ran from Main to Mason on Washington and Monroe Avenue.

Following a celebration that lasted well into Sunday morning, the line went into regular operation on Monday. The city had a lot of fun with its new toy and riding the street cars just for the thrill of it became so popular it eventually became fashionable, too.

'Trolley Parties' the Vogue

Nobody remembers what enterprising hostess started it, but by the summer of 1896 "trolley parties" were all the rage. Ladies deserted their card tables for the open air cars that were placed in service, to bounce through the streets playing cards and partaking of refreshments en route.

At night parties piled aboard chartered cars, donned funny hats and bucketed about town blowing on horns and bellowing Green Bay's version of the "Trolley Song" long before Judy Garland was born. Such affairs became so frequent the railway company rigged up a specially lighted car for hire.

Later, as the lines extended between communities, the company made a good thing out of amusement parks and picnic grounds. What is now De Pere's Urbandale residential section was then the end of the line from Green Bay and the wooded area was transformed into a picnic grounds, complete with bandstand and croquet courts. Ridge Point Park *(south of De Pere on the east side of the Fox River)* was originally developed as an excursion center that way, too.

Small Cars

The city's original cars were small, one-man affairs operated by a motorman stationed on an outside front platform where he had little chance to collect fares. A cash box was placed inside and passengers dropped red celluloid chits (six for a quarter) into the box as they got aboard.

At switching points the motorman counted chits and passengers. If the totals didn't match he simply refused to move until somebody coughed up. By 1904 traffic was so heavy that conductors were placed aboard to collect fairs.

Shortly after the Green Bay line went into operation David McCartney built one in Fort Howard. When the two cities consolidated in 1895 there was considerable haggling before the lines were combined, and service over the complete system was not achieved until 1897.

Crossed at Main

From then until 1921 the only river crossing was via the Main Street bridge. The aging structure took quite a beating from the heavy cars — in 1913 one of them broke through the bridge floor and dropped into the river — and had to be rebuilt in 1923-24. At that time the Public Service Company laid tracks over the Walnut Street span.

Meanwhile there was a great expansion of interurban lines, beginning with a track to Duck Creek in 1902, to De Pere via the West Side in 1903 and then on to Kaukauna. It has been said, although never checked out, that at one time a careful traveler could get from Duck Creek to New York City by street car.

Another colorful short line was the

summer route to Bay View Beach, built and operated as an auxiliary to the beach from 1906 to 1923. For years the road to the beach was so bad nearly everybody rode the street cars to get there.

Autos Sneaked In

Not long after the completion of the Kaukauna line the automobile began to cut into traffic. The line continued with dwindling patronage until 1928 when an original investment of $1.5 million was sold for scrap.

A year earlier buses had replaced cars on the Duck Creek line and soon street car service in De Pere and through Allouez was abandoned. Gradually buses were incorporated into outlying city runs.

As automobiles became more numerous the street car tracks through the crowded business district became not only a nuisance but a traffic hazard. It wasn't until 1937, however, that Public Service persuaded the city to agree to replacement of the old cars by buses.

A fleet of 12 "Mainliners" was purchased, brought here by coal boat, and on the night of Nov. 17 street car service ended. The changeover was the occasion for a nostalgic ceremony even more elaborate than the inauguration of the system 43 years before.

Final Parade

There was a parade through the business district with bands, drum corps and a Queen of Transportation and visits and speeches from city dignitaries at key points throughout the town. On that last day people could ride the street cars for nothing.

Finally one of the company's oldest cars was piloted out of the car barns by John Noel, who had been at the controls of the first trolley so long ago. There was a christening of the buses as well as the firing of a funeral volley over the aged trolley by a St. Norbert ROTC squad.

The final touch was a last run of the old car with Noel on the platform. Among those making the trip through crowded streets were former Mayor Frank Desnoyers and Louis Daggett, both of whom had ridden in the 1894 celebration.

Anniversary of 'Noble Experiment'

City Never Bought Prohibition

January 25, 1969

Fifty years ago last week the United States embarked on the "Noble Experiment," a misguided attempt to regulate morals through the prohibition of alcoholic beverages. The Wisconsin Legislature ratified the 18th Amendment to the Constitution in mid-January, 1919, but the action didn't mean much.

Wisconsin was the 39th state to ratify, the amendment had already been adopted with the necessary 36 states, and the action of the Legislature was merely a political leap onto the bandwagon.

Actually, Prohibition never really took in Wisconsin where, between 1920 and its repeal in 1933, it was usually wetter than a spaniel in a thunderstorm. The prohibition era was Green Bay's last big fling as a wide open town, a colorful but now generally forgotten period of speakeasies, "soft drink" parlors and roadhouses.

No Immediate Change

When the Volstead Act, implementing the 18th Amendment, went into effect on Feb. 16, 1920, Green Bay had about 130 saloons, most of them well stocked with now illegal bottled goods. Since it soon became apparent that immediate enforcement wasn't very effective, many of them simply converted to "soft drink" establishments and went right on selling their usual potables.

By 1922, when most holdover stocks had been exhausted, a flourishing series of moonshine stills and wildcat breweries were filling the demand. By that time, too, federal and state enforcement was more stringent but largely helpless in the face of public resistance and a remarkably efficient warning system.

There was good money in bootlegging and no loss of prestige. Anyone caught simply served his time without suffering any loss of standing in the community, and there were plenty of young fellows ready and willing to take a chance. There is a remarkable number of staid, law-abiding senior citizens around town today who, with a little prodding, will regale you with tales of their youth when they picked up easy money running liquor for the local trade.

Raids Ineffective

Alcohol stills in private homes, in barns and hideouts in remote corners of Brown County were occasionally raided without substantially interfering with the flow of "moon." Some were elaborate plants, like the one knocked over near the Fern Dell Dairy Farm that was valued at $100,000 and had a capacity of 800 gallons of alcohol a day.

Raids on dispensaries were largely futile, too. The feds would barely get inside the door when the word was all over town and everybody promptly buttoned up for the night. Sometimes the word was out before the raiders ever left Milwaukee.

Judge Moved Court

The most successful raid ever carried out here was in the fall of 1928 when a small army of agents swooped down one Saturday night and in a series of simultaneous pinches, closed a score or more places. Contrary to usual practice, moreover, the agents were back on Monday, Tuesday and Wednesday.

By the time they were through they had arrested more than 100 individuals and closed a total of 51 spots. The case load was so heavy that Federal Judge F. A. Geiger of Milwaukee simply moved his court to Green Bay until he had cleaned up the local docket.

When Judge Geiger slapped padlocks on 48 of the 51 emporiums the city council got its back up. On the night of Oct. 17, 1928, the council passed a resolution that pretty well reflected the sentiment of the community but also gave the city nationwide publicity.

The resolution, an involved sentence in itself, protested the padlock action on several grounds, among them that it would be detrimental to the city's tax base, would interfere with business, and anyway prohibition was unpopular to begin with. Furthermore, the resolution said, the police knew where all the spots were and could control them, but now everything would go underground.

Having unburdened itself, the council had second thoughts, however. At the next meeting the resolution was expunged from the record.

No Trick

It never was any trick to get a highball or a brew in or around town. Within the city many of the old saloons, especially on Main Street, kept right on going, while numerous speakeasies sprang up in well concealed spots.

A new development was the roadhouse, which proliferated outside the city limits. The Cedar Creek Road and the old Manitowoc Road were popular locations. *(Cedar Creek Road was the continuation of Willow Street, now University Ave.)*

Friday night was a great time downtown as the "soft drink" parlors competed for business with free fish fries. For a 15 cent stein of "needle beer" one could eat fried perch and French fries to his heart's content — heavily salted, of course, to keep the thirst blooming. On other evenings the come-on was chili or boo-yah.

In Local Hands

With local initiative meeting demands, bootlegging was not a serious problem until about 1931. Even then it was largely in the hands of home towners, boys tough enough to drive out invaders from Chicago and elsewhere.

In the early 1930s a highly efficient "alky" ring was set up, in which alcohol made in small home stills was collected, purified and distributed as far west as Montana. According to rumors of the time, the sales center was New London and the ring had a "credit manager" who had learned his trade with the old Purple Gang of Detroit.

Smooth Delivery System

A customer arriving in New London would leave his car at a certain garage with keys in it, then check in at a local hotel. About 4 a.m. he would receive a call that his car was ready and would find it loaded with his order and ready to go.

The profits attracted some mean characters and things got rough for a while. Several shootings, one murder attributed to gang warfare and the 1932 "Battle of Flintville" finally jolted the public and the ring was eventually broken up.

The return of legal 3.2 beer on April 7, 1933, was the occasion for a big celebration, complete with little oomm-pah German bands roaming the streets and bars full of customers anxiously awaiting the arrival of the first truckloads of beer from Milwaukee. The climax was a big parade in which most of the leading citizens of the city took part.

Student Politicians, 1934 Style

March 22, 1969

With college campuses throughout the nation wracked by disorders, student demands and boycotts these days, St. Norbert College is a relatively quiet institution. It was a different matter just 35 years ago this month when the campus erupted in a political campaign, the like of which had never been seen before at the De Pere institution — or since.

In March, 1934, De Pere was coming leisurely up to a municipal election that figured to be a routine run for incumbent mayor Rudolph Rupiper and his administration when the political pot came to a sudden and unexpected boil with the appearance of an "Independent Democrat" slate, complete with candidates for city office, campaign organization and a full platform for municipal reform.

The "Independent Democrats" were all students of St. Norbert College. The organization appeared seemingly out of nowhere and within a few days was whooping it up, to the delight of many political opponents of Rupiper and the dismay of Hizzoner and a number of city councilmen, who took a skittish view of the whole thing.

Student Candidates

Leading the slate was Joseph M. Trainor, a junior from Brookly, N.Y., as candidate for mayor. He was bulwarked by candidates for every other city office, among them two bona fide De Pere residents in Norbert Schumacher, who declared for county supervisor, and Virgil Kohlbeck, seeking the job of street commissioner.

The rest of the ticket consisted of James Lang, Kaukauna, city clerk; Henry J. Platt, Milwaukee, city treasurer; Clarence Baumgartner, assessor; Stanley Ostrem of Green Bay, for Third Ward alderman; Robert Noonan of Oconto, Clarence Mileski of Escanaba, Joseph Schouten of Freedom and Marcel Rademacher of Dundas.

Running the campaign was George Stoecker of Chicago as chairman, others being David A. Yuenger of Marinette; William Marquis, De Pere; Arthur Anderson of Oak Park, Ill.; and Adrian Martin, De Pere. All were either members of the staff of the St. Norbert Times or the varsity football squad.

Started as a Gag

Actually, the whole thing had been hatched in the office of the Times as a gag. When the idea began to catch fire, however, the students and a substantial number of De Pere residents, for reasons of their own, swung in behind the move. Before Mayor Rupiper knew it he had some lively competition on his hands.

Soon rallies were being scheduled all over town, campaign posters were in preparation and news of the move spread far and wide, being picked up by newspapers all over the middle west. Nomination papers were placed in circulation and well before the filing deadline enough signatures had been secured to enable the group to get on the ballot.

Touched All Bases

A major factor in the momentum of the plan was Trainor. A smooth operator, he was an excellent and persuasive speaker. Trainor could view with alarm or point with pride with the best of the politicians and he was pretty good, too, at calling for reforms without being specific about where the money would come to pay for them.

The whole thing was well thought out, and the wily group carefully touched all the bases. Everybody had thoughtfully enrolled to vote and, being college residents and over 21, there appeared to be no legal obstacles to their candidacies.

The only possible question revolved around Ostrem, who was actually a resident of Green Bay and therefore ineligible to run for office in De Pere. In any event, the point was never raised, since the whole thing collapsed after a period of about ten days when Abbot Bernard H. Pennings blew the whistle.

Shortly before the campaign committee was ready to file nomination papers, Mayor Rupiper and Third Ward alderman David Wishart descended on the little abbot with an ultimatum. If the boys persisted in going through with it, Rupiper threatened, he would withdraw rather than run against a group of "young smart alecks."

Abbot's Ultimatum

First intimation the students had that a wrench had been thrown into the machinery was a surprise visit to a planning meeting by the Rev. L. A. V. DeCleene, dean of students, who suggested gently they forget the whole thing and stick to the books. The second was an invitation from the abbot for the ringleaders to report to him.

Ushered into an abbey parlor, the culprits were allowed to sweat it out for a while, after which the abbot marched in. Fixing the group with his light blue eyes, in which the normally friendly twinkle had been replaced by a couple of ice cubes, the little abbot delivered his ultimatum.

"Cut it out."

Having issued his orders, the abbot turned and walked out.

An appeal by some De Pere citizens to the abbot to change his mind having failed, that was the end of it. Nomination papers were not filed and the whole thing blew over quietly.

All but Trainor

For everybody, that is, except Trainor. A rally had been scheduled in West De Pere that night at which he was to speak, so Trainor kept the date.

That did it for him. When the student body reassembled after Easter Vacation a few weeks later, Trainor was missing. He had been informed his presence on campus was no longer desired and he was canned.

One reason there was no looting of the abbot's office, no police confrontations or picket lines was basic in those days. As one of the group explains it, there was a depression on, most of them were lucky to be in college at all and those with scholarships weren't about to compromise what was then considered a privilege and not a right.

Solid Platform

That the move was more than a student prank, however, is revealed in its platform, which called for a new and efficient fire department, supervised play activities in public playgrounds, a water purification system, reassessment of property values, reorganization of the police force, public accounting of expenditures of city funds and reduction in tavern taxes. In the next 20 years every item except the tavern tax reduction was subsequently adopted by the city of De Pere.

One of the "walking wounded" of the affair was the Rev. Anselm Keefe, then college rector. "Padre" Keefe had not encouraged the scheme but he hadn't discouraged it either, and the whole thing had been cooked up in the Times, of which he was founder and advisor.

When the heat began to get uncomfortable, Father Keefe discovered a botany meeting in Denver, Colo., at which his presence was imperative, and he happily took out, not to return until everything had blown over. Shortly after his return he gave an explanation of the affair and the college approach to it before the Green Bay Rotary Club, which reflected general thinking in 1934 but makes pretty weird reading today.

Symbol Isn't Official

'Gateway' Emblem Has No Status

March 17, 1962

Cut in granite alongside the main entrance to City Hall is an impressive emblem showing an ocean vessel with the slogan "Green Bay, Gateway to the Great Waterway." Long familiarity through its use on the city's stationary, promotional brochures and trash trucks has given most people the impression that the design is the official seal of the city.

It isn't, although it would be much more effective than the dull, unimaginative symbol the city has used for more than 100 years. In fact, it has no official status whatever, unless decades of use and its place on the wall impart a quasi-official prestige.

The slogan is the brainchild of a 10-year-old schoolboy who won $100 with it in a prize contest 40 years ago. The original design (the current one has been brought up to date) was made by a long forgotten artist-draftsman who never received any credit for it.

The slogan was submitted by a lad named Lawrence LaFond in a contest sponsored by local merchants and the Press-Gazette in 1921. At the time Larry was a fourth-grader in St. John's School.

The prize was probably a windfall to his widowed mother, who had to work for a living after the boy's father died during the 1918 flu epidemic. But then, she undoubtedly thought of it anyway.

Elaborate Promotion

In the late fall of 1921 the Association of Commerce planned an elaborate Booster Week, to be held early in 1922 to publicize Green Bay's business opportunities. A ringleader in the project was the late John K. Kline, editor of the Press-Gazette and one of the most enthusiastic drumbeaters the city ever had.

Several contests were part of the buildup, including one for a city song. Miss Abbie Robinson's lyrics to the tune of "Columbia the Gem of the Ocean" won that and were promptly forgotten, as was another with original words and music by the leader of the Strand Theater orchestra.

The slogan competition was the big one. It was open to all school children of Brown County under 18 and the prize was $100 "in gold." Judges were V. I. Minahan, E. M. Krippner, W. R. Whittenburg, N. L. Ferslev and Mayor Wenzel Wiesner.

In those days $100 was real green lettuce, even for teenagers, and the contest, which ran from Dec. 1 to Dec. 15, attracted over 2,600 slogans from 2,000 contestants. A great many, like the winner, tied the city's future to the St. Lawrence Seaway.

A major factor in the final selection was the current preoccupation with the projected waterway scheme which, it was generally expected, would get under way shortly. As the Press-Gazette reporter who wrote the story announcing the winner said, in a burst of misguided enthusiasm, "It is generally conceded that (the waterway) will be built soon."

Took 35 Years

Considerably closer to the truth was his estimate that the slogan's "real punch will increase as time goes on." It took 35 years but today it does mean something.

Following selection of the winning slogan the design was drawn and many merchants adopted it for use on their business stationery. Nobody remembers who designed the emblem but it may have been done for the Press-Gazette. In those days the paper did not have an art or engraving department.

It first appeared as an "official cut" in the Press-Gazette in late February, 1922, and was long used by the paper to illustrate news stories of local significance, particularly those dealing with the city's economic status. As hopes for quick construction of the waterway faded, however, it gradually fell into disuse. The P-G's own drawing and engraving went into the discard many years ago.

The symbol got on the official city stationery shortly after its inception, largely at the insistence of Frank Cartier, a member of the three-man city commission government. Cartier was then, as he has always been, an indefatigable plugger for the seaway.

In Use 40 Years

Everybody else finally dropped it and the commission government system was eventually displaced, but it has remained on the city's official letterhead for 40 years. Indeed, it isn't unlikely that even members of the present city council are under the misapprehension that it is the city seal.

The city hall emblem is not an exact duplicate of the original design and neither is that now on the city's stationery. The original, still carried on the city's vehicles, depicts an old fashioned "three stacker" ocean liner with tall smokestacks. The vessel on the cutting has only a single, low, streamlined stack and looks more like a freighter than a passenger ship.

A few years ago when the long used cut for the city letterhead was wearing out Harold Elder of the Press-Gazette staff drew a design that incorporated the modern approach to the emblem on City Hall, and this is the one now in use.

The actual city seal is a prosaic emblem beside the "Gateway" symbol. It consists of two concentric circles with the statement "City of Green Bay, Corporate Seal" in the border between them and a five-pointed star in the middle.

The city just recently got a new stamp to apply the seal. The previous stamp, still in the possession of City Clerk Cliff Centen, wore out after more than 30 years of constant use.

What became of Larry LaFond?

He grew up in Green Bay, graduating from East High School in 1930. A handsome young man, he was active in many early Community Theater productions.

For about a year, around 1935, he

worked as a proofreader for the Press-Gazette and was later a salesman for a clothing store and a tire company.

Sometime between 1937 and 1939 he headed for the West Coast. Periodically he has visited his home town and ultimately he returned to the Middle West. Married and the father of five children, LaFond now lives in Milwaukee.

** Updating of the current seal/logo shown here is in process.*

Chapter Five

Wars, Fires, and Other Disasters

The Shooting of Charles Arndt

Early Territorial Tragedy

June 10, 1967

The halls of government are supposed to be places of great dignity and decorum where statesmen orate, consider the fate of the realm and pass laws to benefit the same. Not always. Men can be hurt — even killed — in legislative assemblies.

A Green Bay representative was killed on the floor of the Wisconsin legislature. It happened a long time ago, of course, and, to the credit of the American legislative process, the victim is the only man in American history to be shot to death by a fellow legislator while serving his constituency in a governmental body.

On Feb. 11, 1842, Charles Coatsworth Pinckney Arndt, Brown County representative on the Wisconsin Territorial Council, was shot and killed on the council chamber floor during a regular session in Madison. Firing the fatal shot was James R. Vineyard of Grant County.

Heat of Debate

In the heat of debate, tempers are apt to flare, threats are hurled and sometimes — but not often — blows are exchanged. Legislators being much like baseball players where actual fighting is concerned, things are usually patched up before they erupt in physical combat.

There wasn't any excuse for the shooting of C. C. P. Arndt, even though he lost his head and kept asking for trouble. It happened so fast that Vineyard himself was never sure of the details.

Charles Arndt was a young and coming man in Wisconsin politics. The son of Green Bay pioneer John Penn Arndt, he was a graduate of Rutgers University, an attorney, probate judge, newspaper editor and apparently headed for a brilliant career. He had been a member of the council since 1840.

He and Vineyard, although on the opposite sides of the political fence, which in those days consisted largely in being for or against Gov. James Duane Doty, had known each other for several years and were apparently the best of friends. Just the night before the tragedy they had been co-managers of a legislative ball in Madison and at its end had parted on excellent terms.

Source of Friction

The following morning the council took up the confirmation of Governor Doty's nominee for sheriff of Grant County, Vineyard's constituency. There was strong opposition, especially from Vineyard, and a motion was made to table the matter.

All fired up, Arndt objected, saying he couldn't understand Vineyard's position since the latter had previously recommended the nominee most highly. Vineyard promptly called Arndt a liar.

In those days there were plenty of names one could safely call a man. When you used the term "liar," however, you had to be prepared to fight or back down with a smile.

Argument Resumed

Arndt swung around in his chair and demanded a retraction. Vineyard refused and there was a vigorous exchange of unpleasantries before the chairman rapped for order and the two men subsided.

A few minutes later, however, during the vote on adjournment for the day, Arndt apparently left his seat, stalked over to Vineyard and resumed the argument. The flare-up quieted at the demand of the chair but as soon as the chamber adjourned, Arndt was at it again.

Once more he demanded a retraction or explanation. Vineyard not only refused but repeated the accusation.

The infuriated Green Bay man thereupon took a poke at Vineyard, who swung back. The session dissolved in noisy confusion as they mixed it up closely and other members rushed to pull them apart.

Suddenly there was a shot. Arndt staggered back and collapsed with a bullet in his chest.

Died Quickly

Within five minutes he died in the arms of his horrified father, who happened to be in Madison and had been given the courtesy of the floor as a spectator. A thoroughly chastened Vineyard promptly surrendered to the Dane County sheriff and, from jail, submitted his resignation from the council.

That shocked and indignant body returned his resignation unopened and unanimously expelled him instead. The resolution, although offered by another member, was actually written by Morgan L. Martin, Brown County's second representative.

Dickens Wrote Indictment

The shooting caused a national sensation. Eastern newspapers played it up vividly and some Washington circles used the incident to bolster their claim that the western territories, especially Wisconsin, were too uncivilized to be trusted with statehood.

Charles Dickens, then visiting the United States and taking a sour view of everything he saw and heard, seized on the tragedy to compose a stinging indictment of the barbarism and lack of social discipline among Americans. His account was taken almost word for word from that written by Arndt's successor as editor of the Green Bay Republican, hardly an unprejudiced source.

The Green Bay district was furious and demanded the right to try Vineyard for murder. Tempers were not soothed when he was tried for manslaughter in Green County and acquitted on a plea of self defense.

There was no question that Arndt had been the aggressor and that Vineyard had been defending himself. At the same time, even the most anti-Doty men conceded he didn't need to pull a gun, much less to be carrying one on the council floor.

The tragedy had an unusual aftermath a few years later in which

Vineyard again played a leading role.

Similar Incident

In 1849 another fight broke out on the floor of the Assembly under almost identical circumstances. Somebody gave Moses Strong the lie.

Although Strong had been present at the shooting of Arndt (in fact, he had been chairman of the fatal session) he lost his head and made for the other fellow. There is no evidence that either man was armed, but before they could come to blows, Vineyard, again a member from Grant County, grabbed Strong by the shoulders and shook him, shouting at the same time.

"Don't do it! Look at me! Look at me!"

The sight of Vineyard's tearstained face brought Strong up short. Apologies were quickly made all around and the incident blew over.

City's Worst Fire

Downtown Gutted in 1853 Blaze

February 27, 1960

Early in the morning of Nov. 1, 1853, a small, unoccupied shack on the bank of the Fox River, behind a closely built row of wooden buildings on land now occupied by Prange's *(Younker's)*, burst into sudden flame. Had it not been for a strong wind blowing from the west the blaze might have burned itself out harmlessly.

Instead the flames jumped the gap. Before the sleeping town (population about 1,500) was aware of the danger one of the most disastrous fires in the history of Green Bay was raging out of control.

When it was over an area of nearly six acres along both sides of Washington Street between Pine and Main — then as now one of the most important business sections of the city — was a stretch of blackened ruins. Thirty commercial buildings, some of them the largest and best in the rising community, had been completely destroyed at a loss of over $100,000.

Too Much for Brigade

Once among the dry frame structures, built so close together that narrow wooden stairways between any two served the upper stories of both, the fire couldn't be halted. It was too much for the capacities of the drowsy bucket brigades and the single hand engine that constituted the city's fire fighting equipment.

First to catch was the building occupied by A. H. Green's drug store a couple of doors north of Pine Street. Although Green was sleeping in the back room the blaze spread so quickly he was lucky to get out with what clothing he could hastily throw on his back.

Barely Escaped

S. M. Marshall's dry goods store next door was quickly engulfed, almost trapping Myron P. Lindsley, Linus Marshall and J. B. Wing, who shared a second floor bachelor apartment behind Lindsley's law office. Like Green, they escaped with only the clothes they were able to grab on the way out.

Leaping Washington Street in a shower of sparks and burning shingles, the flames caught Daniel Butler's dry goods store, Burley Follett's book and stationery store and another dry goods house run by William D. Colburn. Sweeping north, the conflagration took in turn a vacant building owned by Morgan L. Martin and two belonging to Daniel Whitney to reach Main Street.

Documents Lost

The corner building, used by Whitney as an office, contained all his records and accounts, which went up with an estimated loss of $20,000. The offices and press of the Green Bay Advocate, above Follett's shop, were gutted but the newspaper's accounts and subscription lists were saved when the safe containing them was hoisted out of a second story window.

Editor-publisher Charles D. Robinson never knew whom to thank for it. He slept soundly through all the excitement and didn't know what had happened until he arrived at work that morning to find he no longer had a newspaper.

The historic Washington House, predecessor of the Beaumont Hotel, caught fire several times but was saved to halt the further spread of destruction northward. Behind Whitney's office on the southeast corner of Main and Washington the residence of a man named Boughton went up, as did barns and outbuildings all the way to Adams Street.

Indian Records Lost

Further south the wall of flames jumped an open space to ignite a combination home and office of Dr. E. Crosby in the middle of a large lot at Washington and Cherry Streets, where Woolworth's now stands *(then at 200 N. Washington)*. The principal loss here was in the office of John V. Suydam and E. H. Ellis where the records of all government transactions with the Indians back to 1818 were filed.

Meanwhile, on the river side of Washington Street the original fire ate its way both north and south. Northward it swept through three more of Whitney's buildings, including R. P. Harriman's grocery store and a warehouse rented by Joel S. Fisk.

J. McMullen's boot and shoe shop was next, followed by a warehouse in its rear, then two more Whitney-owned buildings. One was the largest structure in town and the other was a warehouse of D. H. Whitney & Co., in which a number of merchants had stored surplus winter inventories.

Moving south from Green's, the blaze got W. Mitchell's grocery and provision store on the corner of Washington and Pine. It jumped Pine Street to the roof of Joel Fisk's store, but a combination of an adverse wind, a crew of thoroughly awakened and determined fire fighters and the town's lone fire engine called a halt after only minor damage.

Docks Destroyed

Docks along the river, piled high with lumber awaiting shipment, were destroyed along with several freight boats. Three hundred thousand shingles owned by J. Ingalls caught fire but were extinguished with the destruction of only 20,000.

The price of the holocaust, while only a fraction of a similar conflagration today, was staggering. Principal victim was Daniel Whitney, who lost seven buildings, all his business records and about $30,000.

Many of the town's leading merchants, their capital tied up in goods stockpiled for the coming winter when the close of navigation would isolate the area until spring, were virtually wiped out. The buildings themselves didn't represent much loss when lumber for replacements stood practically in their back yards.

Whitney could stand such a blow

but it was rough on druggist Green. He had just received half his winter's stock, about $4,000 worth, but his insurance had expired a couple of days before the fire and he was awaiting the imminent arrival of the remainder of his goods before renewing it.

Even Premiums Went Up

Even the $400 he had earmarked for the premiums was consumed. Green immediately took off for New York, however, obtained more goods on credit and came back to relaunch a long and prosperous career.

The destruction of the Advocate, the area's only newspaper, would have left the town with the prospect of a dull winter but for prompt action by the mother of the Robinson brothers. Mrs. Robinson, a woman of decision, hurried to Buffalo where she procured a new press and type, won the race against the approaching freezeup and put her boys back in publication six weeks later.

Of inestimable loss to historians was the destruction of Burley Follett's papers. Follett being borough treasurer, all village and borough records prior to 1853 were kept in his safe and all were destroyed.

Indians Suspected

Nobody was ever certain how the fire started but a party of Menominee Indians was suspected. Since the band had kindled a fire near the old shack earlier that night it was assumed that the Indians, either carelessly or deliberately, were responsible.

The stricken town was a long time recovering. Some of the charred ruins stood where they were for years while the country pulled through the Depression of 1857 before their once prosperous owners were able to rebuild. The "burnt district" carried its scars as late as 1859, when the last vestiges of the disaster were finally erased.

First Hard Realities

County Sends Its Sons to War

December 2, 1961

One hundred years ago this month the hard realities of war were being felt in Brown County. For the first time in its brief history the county had learned what it was like to send its own men off to combat.

In mid-November, 1861, the Brown County Rifles and the Green Bay Union Guards, the first complete military units ever raised in Green Bay and De Pere, were called into active service. It was to be a long time before they came home again, and some were destined never to return.

It had taken the region the entire summer to wake up to the facts of life in that confused and somber summer of '61. Not that Brown County wasn't as patriotic as any other part of the state. It was simply that the Civil War was a long way off and still had an atmosphere of unreality that hadn't quite dissipated.

Like the rest of Wisconsin Brown County had followed closely the events leading up to Secession and the firing on Ft. Sumter. Being solidly Democratic — the region gave Stephen A. Douglas a heavy majority over Abraham Lincoln in the 1860 election — the county didn't really believe open conflict would or had come about.

Patriotic Outburst

Sumter's capitulation was a shock that triggered an outburst of indignant patriotism. There were war meetings, fiery oratory and high sounding resolutions, parades and a certain amount of casual drilling; then everybody simmered down again.

The weather was partly responsible. Spring came early and beautifully in 1861 and as the summer advanced, surrounding farms bloomed with the finest and heaviest crops the settlers had ever seen. It seemed much more to the point to cultivate and harvest them.

Martial ardor flared again briefly on July 4 when the new fairgrounds near the corner of Porlier and Webster (actually there wasn't a Webster Avenue yet) were opened with pomp and circumstance and a rousing oration by Gov. Horatio Seymour of New York. Two days later there was another celebration when the Oconto River Drivers, that remarkable company of lumberjacks raised by Joseph Loy of De Pere, passed through en route to Madison.

Back to Normal

Thereafter, however, everything was back to normal. A local military unit, the Bay City Guards, did a little drilling under the supervision of Capt. John Cotton, who had retired from the Regular Army in 1845 and who ran a haphazard farming operation from the mansion now known as Cotton House, but that was about all.

Shortly thereafter recruiting began in both Green Bay and De Pere as Milo E. Palmer and Joseph G. Lawton received state commissions to raise companies. Through the lovely summer the drive made little progress. A few individuals left town to join outfits already under arms and a number of well known citizens, including Morgan L. Martin, Charles D. Robinson and Dr. C. E. Crane, accepted commissions but nobody showed much enthusiasm for toting a musket.

In fact, recruiting in the county reached such a low ebb that early in the fall newspapers throughout the state, notably in Milwaukee and Appleton, began making snide remarks. Civic pride, especially the editorial variety, being extremely thin-skinned in those days, the Advocate reacted violently, particularly after the oddly-named Appleton "Motor" made an unflattering comparison of the activities in Green Bay and De Pere.

Indignantly denying that Bayites were only interested in wangling commissions (the "Motor" touched a sore spot there since Advocate editor Charles D. Robinson already had one), acting editor Frank Tilton claimed Brown County had actually sent over 100 men into the ranks of other outfits. His figure didn't jibe with Deborah Martin's estimate of only about a dozen.

Recruiting Picks Up

Whether the needling had anything to do with it or not, recruiting picked up noticeably. Possibly a greater incentive was the departure on Sept. 7 of 21 German recruits under the command of Lt. Arthur Jacobi. Made up of immigrants, many of whom could barely speak English, they were the first organized body of troops to leave Green Bay for war duty.

Eventually they became Co. H of the 9th Wisconsin and Jacobi rose to command of the regiment.

The departure was marred by the refusal of steamer agent E. A. Buck to move the group at less than regular fare. After considerable indignation the owner of the "Queen City" took the contingent, together with relatives, friends and escorting Germania and Guardian Fire Companies, as far as De Pere, where they continued to journey to the Appleton railhead by wagon.

Thereafter the county recruiting campaign became a spirited rivalry between Green Bay and De Pere to see which unit would be filled up first. The competition for members was countywide since neither city was big enough to raise a company by itself.

Race a Dead Heat

The race ended virtually in a dead heat, with both called together in early November, but the Green Bay Union Guards actually pulled out a week ahead of the Rifles. At the time of the call up, each had about 80 men.

The departure scene was strikingly similar to that of a few weeks ago when the 32nd Division went back into uniform, although on a more elaborate scale. Both companies were tendered public dinners and left by river steamer — Buck had reconsidered his position — amid the blaring of the town band, a salute from the guns of empty Ft. Howard, and the tears and cheers of those left behind.

The Guards went to Camp Randall where they became Co. H of the 12th Wisconsin and the Rifles to Camp Hamilton at Fond du Lac, where they exchanged their fiery title for the prosaic nomenclature of Co. F, 14th Wisconsin. As a unit of the "Marching Twelfth," Co. H didn't see Wisconsin again until four years and 3,700 miles later, including 1,600 miles of picking 'em up and putting 'em down again as it slogged with Sherman to Atlanta and the sea.

The 14th Wisconsin received its baptism of fire at Shiloh and distinguished itself at Corinth, where Co. F's commander (Capt. Lawton had resigned in the meantime), Capt. Samuel Harrison was mortally wounded and Color Sgt. Dennis J. F. Murphy won the Medal of Honor.

A colorful "morale boy" of F Co. was Henry Cady, whose story years later received national circulation when written by his friend and comrade, James K. Newton. Cady was killed at Shiloh while Newton finished out the war a lieutenant, eventually became a professor of English at Oberlin College and there wrote "Little Cady."

It Has Happened Here

When Green Bay Had Its Riot

September 3, 1966

You can't pick up a newspaper these days without encountering headlines about pickets, protest marches and National Guardsmen called out to prevent disorders —even in Wisconsin. So far, Green Bay has been spared.

The city needn't get too smug about it, though. It has already happened here.

That, of course, was a long time ago, more than a century, in fact. Nobody was hurt and the demonstrators dispersed peacefully, but not before they had scared the daylights out of the town, put the run on U.S. Sen. Timothy O. Howe and placing the stoutly Democratic Green Bay Advocate on an extremely uncomfortable spot.

The affair — it was called a draft riot at the time — had no racial origin, although there were nationalistic overtones. It was simply a hair-trigger protest by the Belgians in the Bay Settlement area against being drafted for a war in which they had no interest.

Followed Celebration

The riot occurred Nov. 15, 1862, only two days after the city had celebrated the completion of its first railroad. The earlier event, in fact, had a slight bearing on the outcome of the second since one of the first jobs of the newly completed Chicago and North Western Railroad was to transport a company of state troops to Green Bay to preserve order.

After the initial outburst of martial enthusiasm in 1861, enlistments in the Union Army began to fall off. As casualties and the needs for more and more men mounted, Congress passed, in the summer of 1862, the first wartime conscription law in American history.

The legislation set up state enlistment quotas which were then broken down by state governors to counties and towns. Sheriffs were designated the drafting agencies, and Nov. 10, 1862, was set for the first drawing.

City Not Affected

Green Bay itself wasn't affected since it had easily met its quota through volunteers, but a number of surrounding communities had not. This was the case in the Belgian settlements to the northeast.

The lack of enthusiasm there was understandable if not greatly appreciated. Most of the Belgian settlers were recent immigrants, isolated in forest clearings. Few had become citizens and only a handful could speak English.

They were busy trying to wrest a home from the wilderness, knew little of the issues of the Civil War and wanted no part of it. Furthermore, many had left the Old Country to escape military conscription and took a dim view of being hooked on it here.

They weren't disloyal; just disinterested. All they asked was to be left alone.

No Previous Trouble

There had been some muttering over the draft drawing but Sheriff Whitney had run the affair very well. When no trouble developed at the time of the drawing the Advocate congratulated itself there would be none.

It came as a shock on Saturday, Nov. 15, when word reached town that a large body of armed men was marching on the city from the Belgian settlements. Mayor Henry Baird tried to block them by ordering the draw of the recently completed Main Street bridge over East River to be opened, but somebody goofed or chickened out. The mob had no trouble crossing the river.

A mass of about 100 angry men, armed with rifles, muskets, shotguns, clubs and pitchforks and led by a fife and drum corps, was soon marching down Main Street to Washington. After reaching the main business corner, the marchers retraced their steps to the residence of Senator Howe near Whitney Park.

Howe the Target

Throughout the incident the senator, recently home from Washington, was the special target of the demonstrators. As draft commissioner for Wisconsin he was blamed for the whole thing.

Shouting and waving their weapons, the crowd swarmed over the Howe lawn and crowded around the front porch. Howe, surrounded by a crowd of anxious citizens, tried to talk to them but since he couldn't speak Belgian and few of them could understand English he got nowhere.

When the temper of the crowd began to look ugly, Howe was persuaded to retreat inside while John Last attempted to harangue the men in Belgian. Howe's friends convinced him it wouldn't be safe for him to remain where he was, and the badly shaken senator was sneaked out the back and driven away in a closed carriage.

Back Downtown

Finding the bird had flown, the crowd streamed back downtown to the Baird Building on Pine Street where the county offices were located. There they milled around uncertainly in the street while citizens who could speak Belgian began to circulate and talk to them.

After several tense minutes the crowd began to break up. Soon the men were heading quietly back out of town.

Nobody had been hurt although plenty of people had a good scare, and no damage was done except to Tim Howe's shrubbery. Nevertheless, nobody was certain the disgruntled men wouldn't be back.

Either Mayor Baird or somebody else had sent word down the valley asking for help. On Monday morning Company A of the 30th Wisconsin arrived via the brand new C&NW and everybody breathed a sigh of relief.

No More Incidents

Although the troops remained for

several days there were no more incidents. Indeed, when detachments went out to the Belgian settlements they were greeted enthusiastically and royally entertained.

When the farmers had calmed down, sincere efforts were made to explain to the disgruntled draftees what the war was all about. Once convinced, the Belgians contributed their full share of men to the armies, where they served with distinction. Subsequent draft calls were filled promptly and willingly.

The Advocate tried to brush the whole thing under the rug with an innocuous story, but word got around. Soon Republican papers in Northeastern Wisconsin and the Valley were pot-shooting at the Advocate and the Democrats.

Editor Charley Robinson was not only annoyed but waspishly on the defensive, snapping back at editorial barrages from down the Valley. Delighted editors there kept jabbing, just to watch him jump.

'Wisconsin Regulars'

De Pere Rifles Hardboiled Fighters

December 16, 1961

While the Green Bay Union Guards were acquiring blisters and military savvy as Company H of the "Marching Twelfth" Wisconsin in the Civil War their neighborhood rivals, the De Pere Rifles, were gaining an equally honorable reputation as a unit in another volunteer infantry regiment. As F Company of the 14th Wisconsin the Rifles did their share in winning for the outfit the title of "Wisconsin Regulars" at Shiloh and maintaining it through three more years of conflict.

The Rifles reported to Fond du Lac in November, 1861, about a week after the Union Guards left Green Bay for Madison. There they were incorporated into the 14th Wisconsin, which was slowly being put together. It wasn't until Jan. 30, 1862, that the regiment was complete and taken into federal service.

Joseph Lawton Commander

Commanded by Capt. Joseph G. Lawton, with George W. Bowers and Samuel Harrison as lieutenants, the Rifles mustered about 80 men. Unlike the 12th Wisconsin, the 14th was never recruited to full strength, and the company was never so numerous again. The 14th, made up of northern Wisconsin county companies, was called the "Northwestern Regiment" until it earned its more colorful nickname at Shiloh.

The regiment left Wisconsin early in March, 1862, being stationed initially at Jefferson Barracks, Mo. After a stay of only a month, it was sent to Tennessee to join Grant's army at Pittsburg Landing. Moving by transport to Savannah, Tenn., the 14th arrived there as the confused Battle of Shiloh was opening and was immediately dispatched to the scene of action.

Baptism of Fire

Arriving about midnight on April 6, the 14th was sent immediately into the line and received its baptism of fire early next morning with an assault on a Confederate artillery battery. The attack overran the guns but was immediately dislodged by a counter-attack. The process was repeated twice during the day before the regiment was pulled back, taking with it one of the disputed guns.

It was apparently an attempt to spike the guns after the first attack to which reference was made years later when Dennis J. F. Murphy was being considered for the Congressional Medal of Honor. After the battle the regiment was given the gun it managed to bring away with it in the withdrawal, at the same time being awarded the proud title of "Wisconsin Regulars."

Suffered Heavily

The regiment suffered heavily at Shiloh and never fully recovered from its losses. Casualties were 14 killed and 79 wounded and missing, those of Company F being Pvt. John D. Putnam killed and five wounded.

The 14th remained at Shiloh as part of the provost guard while the battlefield was being tidied up until late August when it was again sent to the front. Meanwhile, Lawton resigned as company commander after finding he was too old for the rigors of field service, Lt. Bowers was transferred and Harrison inherited the company and his captain's bars.

September found the regiment in the defensive lines at Corinth, Miss., where it was on the left flank when the surprise Confederate attack struck on Oct. 6. The Wisconsin outfits gave ground grudgingly under an all-day assault, during which Murphy, the regimental color bearer, displayed the heroism that later brought him the Medal of Honor.

Regimental losses at Corinth were 27 killed, 50 wounded, and 21 missing. Five F Company men were wounded, including Murphy and Captain Harrison, who lost a leg and died a couple of weeks later.

Culminated at Vicksburg

After Corinth the 14th took part in the complicated maneuvering of the fall and winter that culminated the following summer in the siege of Vicksburg. It fought in the battles of Champion Hill and Big Black River before moving into the trenches before Vicksburg on May 18, 1863.

Four days later it jumped off with the general assault that was beaten back with heavy losses, its casualties being 107 out of the 256 men engaged. The 14th remained in the lines until the surrender and was accorded the place of honor in its brigade when the Union army entered the city. John Munger and J. Bergman of Company F were killed in the Vicksburg campaign, 1st Sgt. J. D. McFarland was mortally wounded and 10 other members wounded.

Two Places at Once

Advancing rapidly on Natchez, Miss., the 14th was among the first troops to enter that city, then returned to Vicksburg where it remained until the following March. The year 1864 saw it involved in a lot of confused movements, including the disastrous Red River Expedition into Texas, during which it achieved the odd distinction of being in two widely separated places at the same time.

About two-thirds of the regiment re-enlisted in January and went on furlough. While they were gone the Red River force was organized and took off before everybody got back. When Company E and detachments from other companies reported in they were formed into a separate battalion under Maj. Asa Worden and sent east to Sherman, where they took part in the Atlanta Campaign as "Worden's Battalion."

Simon King Dies

One of this group was Simon King of F Company who died in front of Atlanta while his company was milling around in Mississippi, Arkansas and Missouri. After the fall of Atlanta the 14th Wisconsin men, with the exception of E Company, rejoined the outfit.

E Co. remained with Sherman, made the March of the Sea and didn't see the regiment again until the war was over, rejoining at Montgomery, Ala., in July, 1865.

Meanwhile, the bobtailed 14th took part in the Red River disaster, returned to Vicksburg and subsequently went on the Tupelo Expedition. It was almost annihilated in July when attacked by Confederate cavalry while guarding a wagon train but was rescued by the 33rd Wisconsin and turned the battle into a satisfying victory.

Ended in Alabama

After the Battle of Tupelo the 14th was sent back to Memphis. Thereafter it served in Missouri, was present at the Battle of Nashville in December and then went to New Orleans. The close of the war found the "Wisconsin Regulars" in Alabama, where F Co. suffered its last battle death at Spanish Fort, near Mobile, when H. Hill was fatally wounded.

Mustered out at Mobile in October, 1865, the regiment returned to Wisconsin, was paid off at Madison and quietly dispersed. At the time of the deactivation F Company was commanded by Capt. John P. Ryan, with Charles Beattie and James K. Newton as Lieutenants.

Newton, a young De Pere school teacher when he enlisted in 1861, afterward became an English professor at Oberlin College and achieved national recognition for his tear-jerker short story "Little Cady," in which he memorialized his wartime buddy, Henry Cady. Newton was careful not to let the facts interfere with a good story. He gave Cady his death wound at Shiloh; actually Cady died of illness more than a year later.

Battle casualties in the 14th Wisconsin were heavy, with 61 killed in action and 34 dead of wounds. An additional 191 men died of disease. The De Pere Rifles contributed a full share of the grim list, its losses being five killed in action, two died of wounds and 15 succumbing to disease out of an aggregate membership of less than 100 men.

Only Medal of Honor Winner

Dennis Murphy, Civil War Hero

November 25, 1961

Ever hear of Dennis J. F. Murphy?

Probably not; he's been dead for 60 years. But he enjoys the rarest distinction in American military tradition, one shared by less than 2,500 men in the past 100 years, including not more than 25 from Wisconsin.

He is also the only Green Bay resident ever to wear the Congressional Medal of Honor.

Dennis J. F. (nobody remembers what the double initials stood for) Murphy, won his Medal of Honor in the Battle of Corinth, Miss., Oct. 3, 1862. As color bearer of the 14th Wisconsin Infantry he was hit three times and wounded so severely he had to be discharged for physical disabilities that handicapped him the rest of his life. His citation reads "though wounded three times, carried the colors throughout the conflict."

Born in Ireland

Murphy was born in Cork, Ireland, July 28, 1830, and apparently came to Wisconsin with his family as a lad of 10. There is no clear record of what he did before the Civil War although Deborah Martin, in her "History of Brown County," referred to him as a farmer in the Town of Glenmore. His service record lists him in one place as a farmer and in another as a "hatter."

At any rate, he was 31 years old, married and the father of a family when Capt. Joseph G. Lawton of De Pere called for volunteers for his "Brown County Rifles" in the summer of 1861. Like any proper Irishman, Dennis couldn't let family responsibilities interfere with a good fight, and he enlisted as a private in what became Company F of the 14th Wisconsin.

When the regiment saw its first combat in the roaring hell of Shiloh, Murphy was slightly wounded and behaved with such bravery he was promoted to sergeant and made regimental color-bearer. What he did isn't clear — there is vague reference to an attempted spiking of some captured guns — but when he finally got his decoration Murphy was miffed because the citation ignored his conduct at Shiloh.

Defense Difficult

The post of color-bearer of a Civil War infantry regiment was one of considerable prestige but little future. As anyone who has ever carried the colors on parade knows, it's a two-hand job. In battle the bearer couldn't do much to defend himself.

Since keeping the colors flying in the front ranks and preventing them from falling into the hands of the enemy were points of great regimental pride as well as the targets of every enemy sharpshooter, the job was dangerous. In the Civil War, casualty lists testify, color-bearers were highly expendable.

Murphy was no exception. His number came up in his outfit's next big fight at Corinth where the Confederates partially surprised the Federals in a two-day battle that didn't rate such headlines as Gettysburg but yielded nothing in pure ferocity. Murphy was hit three times in the first day's fighting, taking a slug in the left hand, a charge of buckshot in the hip and a bullet through his side that lodged against his spine.

Kept on Soldiering

The last one finished his combat service but not his soldiering. Discharged for physical disability because of the wound, he got a commission as a second lieutenant in the 34th Wisconsin for gallantry in action. He served as a company officer for a few months at Camp Randall in 1863 but had to be mustered out again that September.

When the "Invalid Corps," Civil War version of limited service (its name was quickly changed to "Veterans Corps" because its initials had then, as they still do, a different meaning), was organized late in the conflict, Murphy got another commission, this time as a first lieutenant in the 51st Wisconsin. Transferred to the 53rd, he served until honorably mustered out in August of 1865.

He almost didn't make it. In June, while aboard the steamer Omaha (location not specified) he ran afoul of the lieutenant colonel of a cavalry regiment and was slapped in arrest. Nothing came of the incident, however, although it cropped up years later during some correspondence about his pension.

Home Still Stands

The war over, Murphy returned to Wisconsin and settled in Fort Howard in the heart of the old "Irish Patch." He built a house on the corner of North Ashland and Elmore that still stands and lived there until he died June 19, 1901, at the age of 71. He never worked again but apparently he had more than his pension to live on.

In 1891, when the government was belatedly awarding Medals of Honor for Civil War heroism, Murphy applied for one. He explained he had been told after Corinth that he had been recommended for the decoration, had never received it and would like to have it to pass onto his family.

Difficulty over Details

There was some difficulty since none of his old officers, including Lawton, could remember the details. After turning him down once the Army reversed its decision and awarded him the decoration in 1892. He was the eighth Wisconsin man (there were only 12 in the entire Civil War who got it) to receive the Medal of Honor, among the other seven being Gen. Arthur MacArthur, father of a subsequent CMH winner of note, Gen. Douglas MacArthur.

There was no trip to Washington for the presentation, with pictures of the President draping the ribbon around his neck. Instead, the Adjutant General sent Murphy his medal by parcel post and made him sign for it. The receipt is still in his file in the National

Archives.

Dennis Murphy has no known descendants living in Green Bay, but there are still a few old residents of the Patch who remember him. They were kids then and he was an old man, very erect, with white hair, who walked with a cane, slowly and with great dignity. They recall, too, that although he had been an officer he always made a point of wearing his old sergeant's stripes.

Married in 1853

As a young man Murphy must have been a typical "Black Irishman" with black hair, a dark complexion and blue eyes. He apparently wasn't a heavy man although he stood six-two. He was a real broth of a boy when he met Brigit (*Bridget*) McGinnis in 1852 and married her a year later.

The Murphys stood high in the estimation of the Patch because, despite being better off than most of their neighbors, they weren't "uppity" and were always friendly and helpful in the neighborly fashion of the day. There was an amused opinion, though, that old Dennis was a bit of a show-boat.

One neighbor, a youngster then, recalls how the old boy used to make quite a production of entering St. Patrick's Church on Sunday. He still chuckles about the time the church was set on a new foundation and settled unexpectedly during Mass.

Wild Rush Followed

There was a wild rush for the exits, including windows but Murphy gave the most amazing demonstration of all. In practically nothing flat he was at the foot of the altar and right behind the priest when the latter headed for the sacristy. Dennis would probably have explained that he was merely "protecting the good father" but he still had the old combat infantryman's instinct for the best avenue of retreat.

As befitted their station as pillars of St. Pat's the Murphys were definitely Lace Curtain Irish with touches of Cut Glass rank. Perhaps the most significant status symbol was their church pew.

That pew boasted the only red velvet kneeling pad and seat cushions in the parish. What's more, nobody in the congregation ever bent a knee to it unless they came to church as guests of the Murphys.

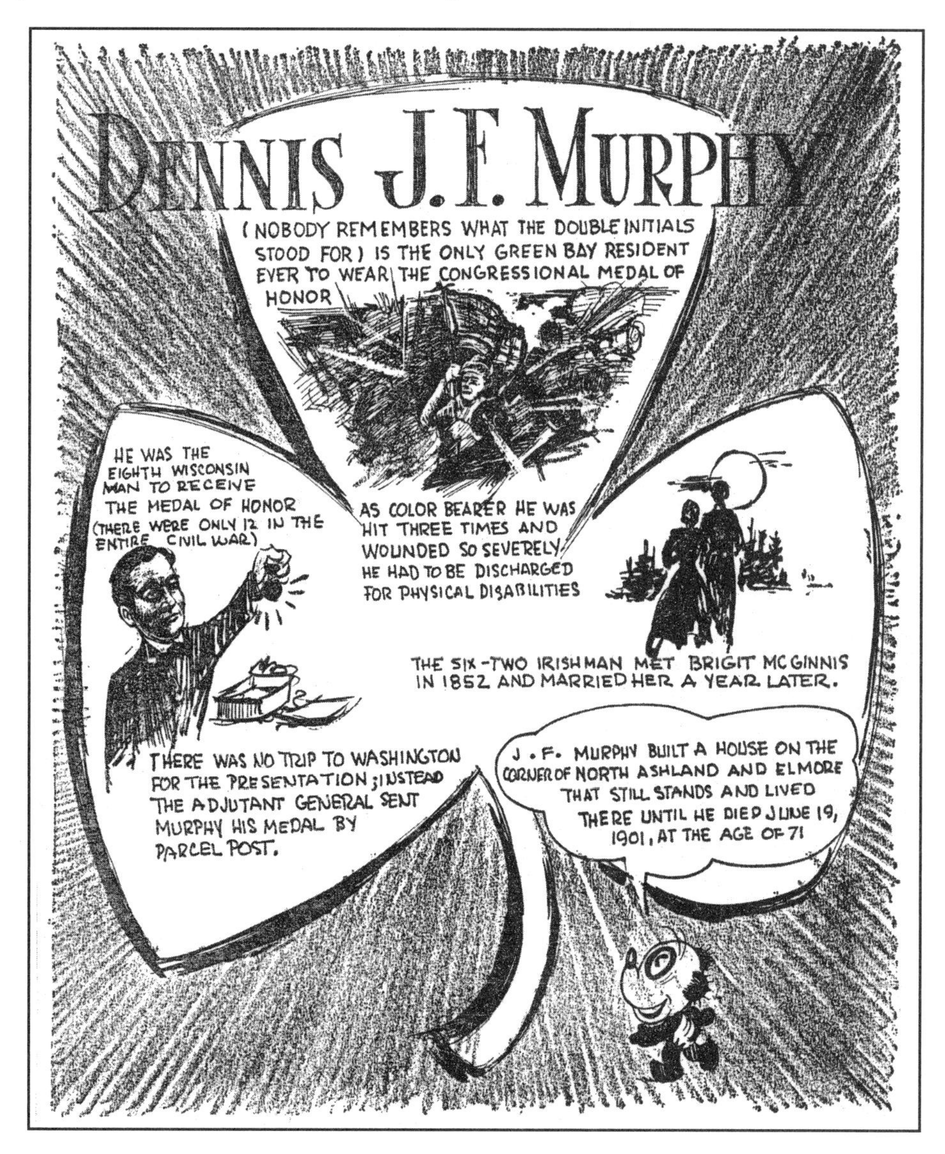

No Television Rites

City Held Own Lincoln 'Funeral'

November 30, 1963

Four times in a century Green Bay has been shocked by the assassination of a President of the United States. Each time the news fell like a thunderclap and each time reaction was similar-stunned disbelief, shock and outrage at a senseless deed. There has been grief, too, and the city has done what it could to express its feelings.

One each occasion the news came quickly on the heels of the act, although the killing of President Lincoln having taken place at night the little city didn't get the word until the next morning. Also, unlike last weekend *(John F. Kennedy assassination)*, people couldn't watch or hear the fantastic drama unfold in their living rooms via television and radio.

But in 1865 (and again in 1881) they did what they considered the next best thing as the nation buried its murdered leaders. They staged their own funerals, complete with hearse, casket, pall bearers and bands of music.

There is some confusion about how Green Bay got the first word of Lincoln's death, although it came chattering over the relatively new telegraph wire in the early morning of April 15, 1865. Deborah Martin, in her Brown County history, says the first inkling came in a War Dept. telegram to the district provost marshal, Capt. C. R. Merrill, warning him to be on the lookout for John Wilkes Booth, who had not yet been run to earth.

Advocate had News

However, since the message gave no particulars and was devoted largely to a description of Booth, the sender may have assumed — and probably correctly — that the Green Bay Advocate already had the news. A series of wires, datelined Chicago, were moving into the Advocate offices about the same time.

The very first one told the story, starkly and simply. With no wasted verbiage, it merely said: "President Lincoln was shot through the head in Ford's Theater last night and died this morning. The assassin is J. Wilkes Booth, the actor."

There is no record of the city's early reaction to the shock. The Advocate, a weekly, had been issued the day before the assassination and didn't appear again until April 20, the day after the state funeral in Washington. That issue devoted all available space to the actual crime and to the city's own observance of the funeral.

Word of Mouth

Since the telephone hadn't been invented yet, the news probably spread by word of mouth. Crowds most likely stormed both the telegraph and newspaper offices for details, which were read out as fast as they came in.

Hastily scribbled notes were probably displayed in the Advocate's front window or read to the crowd through the open door. At least, that's the way such things were usually done. There is no evidence that the paper issued an extra.

The Advocate coverage of the 20th merely printed all the wires received — a standard procedure — a ringing editorial by Editor Charles D. Robinson and a detailed description of the city's own "obsequies" on the 19th. There is nothing about what actually took place in Washington that day.

Black Column Rules

As was long the custom, the paper appeared with wide, black column rules, and the news from Washington was headlined simply "Assassination of President Lincoln" and "The Terrible Crime." In the local columns on the third page were separate stories of the preparation for the local observance and of the services themselves.

On April 17 a public meeting was held in Anderson Hall under the presidency of Henry S. Baird and with great punctilio a set of resolutions was offered by a committee consisting of U.S. Sen. Timothy O. Howe, Robinson, W. C. E. Thomas, Thomas Bennett and John Last. Unanimously adopted, these resolutions expressed the city's grief and renewed the "pledge of fealty" to the government.

It was also decided to hold appropriate ceremonies on the 19th, as close as possible to the actual time of the state funeral (time zones hadn't been thought of, either, and comparable times were always uncertain). A committee made up of Baird, Thomas, James H. Marshall, Paul Lawrence, J. S. Baker, John V. Suydam and Edward Crocker went to work at once.

'Vast Concourse'

At 1 p.m., April 19, a "vast concourse" of Green Bay and Fort Howard citizenry resplendent in tall hats and mourning emblems, assembled in front of the new Beaumont House. A funeral procession was formed under the marshalship of Col. W. H. Bugh, assisted by Charles E. Crane, Anton Klaus, M. J. Meade and C. J. Bender.

In line were the German band, a horse-drawn hearse containing an empty casket and lavishly draped in black (they took their "funerals habiliments" seriously in those days), the mayor and city council, the fire departments of Green Bay and Fort Howard, the Turners, Masonic Lodge, Odd Fellows, the German Benevolent Society — the German groups were always welcome in parades; they knew how to march — and many citizens on foot and in carriages. Among the latter were all the lawyers and clergy of the area marching together.

Pall bearers, wearing long frock coats and stove-pipe hats swathed in crepe that hung down their backs, marched on either side of the hearse. In these posts of signal honor were Sen. Howe, Capt. Merrill, Joseph Taylor and Fred S. Ellis on one side and Dr. H. O. Crane, Alexander Guesnier, D. M. Whitney and W. J. Abrams on the other.

Led by the mounted marshals, the arrangements committee and the band, the procession wound through a small town in which business was at a complete standstill and the largest crowd ever seen in the city lined the route. Virtually every shuttered business house and residence displayed a black crepe on the front door, flags "shrouded in mourning" were at half mast, bells tolled and the band's dirge was punctuated by the dull thud of a saluting canon fired at half-hour intervals throughout the day.

Parade Covered Ground

People didn't go through the motions of a parade a century ago. They really covered ground. The route of march went up Washington Street to Chicago, east to Adams and back to Main, thence to Monroe, back to the Washington-Main Street corner via Cherry, Adams and Main Streets.

It had been intended to hold the formal memorial services in Anderson Hall, but the crowd was too large. The site was shifted to the Harvey & Co. dock at the Fox River end of Main Street, where piles of shingles not only served as seats for the ladies but furnished protection against the chill wind of a dark, cloudy day.

The open air service was conducted under the threat of rain that held off until it was over. And a profoundly solemn program it was.

A clergyman opened with a prayer, after which C. D. Robinson delivered the principal eulogy. He was followed by another minister who spoke in German, none of which Robinson understood but which, he was informed, was very eloquent. There was another prayer by a third minister, and Mayor Myron P. Lindsley, like Lincoln at Gettysburg, made "appropriate closing remarks."

A motion was adopted to have Robinson's speech printed and five copies sent to the Illinois State Historical Society. The Advocate also promised to publish it in full in the next issue. Unfortunately, it didn't, so the only record is now probably yellowing in some forgotten archive at Springfield, Ill. Unless Charley's eloquent editorial in the April 20 issue is, in fact, the speech itself.

When President Garfield was buried 16 years later the scene was repeated in its essentials (some of the same gentlemen, including Howe, C. E. Crane and Abrams, again took major roles), although the procession was much longer and witnessed by a crowd of between 6,000 and 7,000 — double the city's 1865 population. The services were held in Baird Park, reached by another long and winding march.

The weather even repeated itself, being overcast and cloudy, with rain in the morning and again after the ceremony.

First of a Series

Flaming Holocaust of Peshtigo

October 11, 1969

The night of Oct. 8, 1871-98 years ago this past week-a large portion of the City of Chicago was destroyed by fire. That same night, 50 miles north of Green Bay, the Village of Peshtigo was also wiped out with many times the loss of life suffered in Chicago.

Yet for weeks thereafter the world, shocked by the Windy City disaster, was virtually unaware of the tragedy played in the "wings" of the Chicago "spectacular."

In sudden loss of life, the tragedy of Peshtigo has given it a high place on the list of the world's great natural disasters. Only one other forest fire, at Cliquot, Minn., in 1918, snuffed out more lives but not so quickly nor in such a concentrated area.

Community Obliterated

In minutes, a community of over 2,000 people was obliterated. While no accurate figures were ever determined, at least 600 died. Few caught in the flaming trap came out unscathed. For stark, raw horror, the Peshtigo fire has rarely been equaled.

Peshtigo in 1871 was one of the most prosperous lumbering centers in Wisconsin. The headquarters of the Peshtigo Lumber Co., which owned most of the heavily timbered pine lands for miles around, it boasted the largest and most modern woodenware factory in the United States, a large sawmill, a machine shop, four hotels, two schools and two churches, about 100 houses and the usual quota of stores, shops and saloons.

The main village was located in a forest clearing about seven miles from the mouth of the Peshtigo River, which flowed through its center. The factory and machine shops were north of the stream, while the residential area was on the south bank. A railway connected the town with the "lower village" at the river's mouth.

Despite its recent backwoods origin — Peshtigo was only about 20 years old — it was an attractive place with neat houses and wide, well planned streets. But the very reason for its existence also contained the seed of its destruction.

Everything of Wood

Completely surrounded by standing timber, everything was made of wood. The buildings were of wood, it had wooden sidewalks — even the streets were packed with sawdust several inches deep.

Since mid-summer, 1871, the town had been menaced by one of the most prolonged droughts in the history of Wisconsin. Fires raged in the surrounding woods, and several times the town had been narrowly saved from going up in flames. The population was emotionally and physically exhausted from the long, nerve-wracking siege.

Nobody knows how many people were in Peshtigo the weekend of Oct. 7-8. The 1870 Census gave it a population of 1,749, which had presumably increased. In addition, an estimated 300 railroad construction workers were in town, while about 50 Scandinavian immigrants had just arrived on Saturday.

Oppressive Day

Sunday, Oct. 8, was cloudless, sultry and oppressively hot. So dense was the smoke pall from the burning timber that by noon the sun had sunk out of sight in a dirty, bronze sky. A light wind in the afternoon increased briefly to a gale with a touch of the blast furnace in it, then subsided into an ominous, dead calm.

About 9 p.m., as the jittery village was preparing to call it a day, a dull, red glare was seen through the smoke pall above the treetops to the southwest. A few alert ears caught a low, rumbling moan from that direction.

As a sudden burst of hot breeze blew out of the south, the rumble grew into a steadily approaching roar. People gathered nervously in the streets to face an increasingly strong wind.

Accounts Jumbled

What happened next has been variously described by survivors, now dead, whose accounts are understandably jumbled and often contradictory. All generally agreed, however, that Peshtigo was instantaneously engulfed in a torrent of flame that poured out of the sky and burst from the side of the forest like a furnace door suddenly blown open.

"Slabs of fire" dropped on the streets and long tongues of flame shot down like lances. Buildings and streets seemed to explode into masses of flames all over the hapless town. A large boarding house in which an unknown number perished was suddenly wrapped in whirling coils of fire as if hit by a stream from a gigantic flame thrower.

There was a period of panic, during which many were struck down by the seething blast, then everybody raced for the river. Many never made it.

Scores, in panic, sought safety in buildings only to have them turn into raging funeral pyres. Between 35 and 100 — estimates varied and they didn't leave enough traces to tell — were trapped in the big company boarding house without a chance.

Those who reached the river were soon threatened by additional dangers. Stampeding horses and cattle trampled many under, while a rain of burning debris fell on the crouching mass. In addition, the air was so hot it was impossible to keep heads out of water to breathe. The greatest loss of life apparently occurred in the only place that offered any hope of survival.

Within half an hour the entire village was a seething mass of flames, and by midnight it had been completely burned out. Through the hideous night the closely packed crowd fought to stay alive in the river while scores sank from exhaustion. Not until dawn did the dwindling group dare leave the water, and even then the ground was almost too hot to walk on.

Just how many perished was never accurately determined, but the most generally accepted figure is in excess of 600. Sixty-odd charred bodies were found in the streets but those caught in buildings left little trace. Many were swept down the river or trampled into the bottom.

Unnamed Heroes

There were, as is usual in catastrophes of such magnitude, incidents of miraculous survival and freak deaths as well as acts of great heroism. Most of the heroes went nameless since few could remember exactly what they or anyone else actually did.

Of the dazed survivors who crept out of their river sanctuary next morning to wander aimlessly through the ruins, only one had presence of mind to do something decisive. Timber cruiser John Mulligan, in spite of his own exhausted condition, set off on foot for Marinette.

Most of the way Mulligan staggered along in the wake of the fire that had raced north after destroying Peshtigo, not sure of what he would find when he got there. He brought out the first news of the tragedy and led the first relief party back.

Second in Series

'71 Flames Swept Door Peninsula

October 25, 1969

While the tragedy of Peshtigo rose to its fiery climax the night of Oct. 8, 1871, 30 miles away across the smoke-shrouded waters of Green Bay another conflagration was sweeping up the Door peninsula. This one didn't claim as many lives (although more than 100 died) nor was the monetary loss as high, but the resultant suffering was probably greater.

Virtually everything in a 500-square-mile area was swept away. Timber, farms and small settlements, laboriously built up over a period of 20 years were wiped out in as many hours. The exact number of human victims was never determined, the total being eventually fixed at about 130. Property loss was estimated at $2 million, and every dollar represented the life's toil of hard-working, frugal people.

What is now (or once was) America's Cherryland was, in 1871, a typical backwoods farming district. It was a heavily timbered region of pine and hemlock, dotted with small farm clearings isolated from each other as well as from the outside. The population in 1870 was 7,857, mostly Belgian immigrant families.

Land Being Cleared

Few communities were large enough to be dignified as villages and these were located along the shoreline or about an occasional crossroads church. The land was excellent and was steadily being cleared under the impetus of lumbering and the demand for shingles and farm produce.

Like the rest of Northeastern Wisconsin, the peninsula had been hard hit by the drought of 1871 and harried by forest fires. Some districts had already been so thoroughly burned over by the first weekend in October there didn't seem to be anything left to burn. The fight to keep the flames from spreading had almost been won, and people figured the danger had passed.

It hadn't. Fire had eaten its way underground to break out periodically where least expected and with little warning. On the night of Oct. 8, 1871, at approximately the time the Peshtigo fire was leaping out of control...the same thing happened at the base of the peninsula.

Isolated Fires Unite

Isolated fires that had been smoldering beneath the surface for two weeks united into a roaring tidal wave of flame and rolled northward. In 24 hours it whirled over part of Brown, Kewaunee and Door Counties for 60 miles on a front varying from six to 12 miles in width.

The conflagration, although simultaneous, was distinct from that raging up the west shore of Green bay. The winds that fanned them were not noticeable on the water between, yet both followed the same general direction. Each fire apparently generated its own gale.

The same peculiarities characterized both. They struck without warning and with the same intense heat and fury. Frank Tilton of the Green Bay Advocate wrote the best description.

Tilton's Description

"The only warning was the ominous roar in the woods, followed a few moments later by the surging billows of flame, before which all human skill and strength was utterly powerless. The sturdy trees of the forest were torn up by their roots or twisted off; if they withstood the gale their blackened trunks attest the heat."

It was never possible to reconstruct a coherent account of what happened, particularly in the depths of the forest where none survived to tell the story. The fire apparently got its start in the Town of Morrison, gathered momentum as isolated outbreaks merged into a solid wall and moved up the peninsula at a rate of between five and seven miles an hour.

By the time the tardy rains beat it out during the night of Oct. 9, the holocaust had swept north to Jacksonport. The shoreline settlements, though damaged, were spared, but the interior of the peninsula was gutted. Desolation in the wake of the fire was almost complete.

Many Towns Singed

Singed in varying degrees were the towns of Wrightstown, Glenmore, Rockland, Preble, De Pere, Eaton, Humboldt, Morrison and Green Bay in Brown County; Franklin, Casco, Carlton, Pierce, Ahnapee, Red River and Lincoln in Kewaunee; and Union, Brussels, Forestville, Clay Banks, Gardner, Nasewaupe, Sevastopol and part of Sturgeon Bay in Door. The largest settlements destroyed were New Franken, Walhein, Robinsonville, Harris' Pier, Thiry Daems, Dyckesville, St. Sanveur, Rosiere, Williamsonville and Forestville.

There seemed to be no general pattern to the destruction. Buildings were consumed while adjacent fences weren't even singed; household goods stacked in the middle of clearings were swept away while the houses from which they had been carried remained intact; and many bodies were later found fully clothed and scarcely marked by the flames that had killed them.

A surprising feature was the proportion of livestock that survived. Hundreds of animals were killed but scores were saved by their instinct for self preservation while their owners died.

Horror at Williamsonville

Scene of the greatest horror was Williamsonville, in Gardner township about six miles south of Sturgeon Bay. Here three brothers — John, Fred and Thomas Williamson — had built a shingle mill in a 10-acre clearing and gathered a community of 80 people. Only 17 survived.

Panic apparently accounted for most of the lives lost at Williamsonville. Thirty-six people tried to crowd together in a shallow potato pit in the middle of the clearing and were smothered en masse, but individuals survived with scarcely any shelter a few feet away.

Mrs. Williamson, mother of the three brothers, was one. For five hours she crouched in the open, covered only by a blanket, not ten feet from the fatal pit. She was so close to the burning body of another woman she was in momentary danger of being set afire herself.

Listed 130 Dead

Tilton's account of the catastrophe, probably the most complete ever written, listed 130 dead, of whom 117 were killed in Door County; 271 buildings destroyed and 367 families, numbering several thousand people rendered homeless. Most of them lost everything they owned.

With winter coming on, the plight of the destitute survivors was desperate. But not hopeless. Soon the entire nation united in a great relief campaign that sustained them through the winter and gave them a start on rebuilding their shattered homes. Even their far-off homelands didn't forget them.

Last of Three Articles

Nation Aided Fire-Ravaged North

February 17, 1959

The tragically tardy rains of Oct. 9, 1871 halted the devastation of Northeastern Wisconsin but they also emphasized new dangers. With winter just around the corner thousands of people were homeless and destitute in a fire-ravaged wilderness with no place to go and little more protection than the clothes they wore. Everything was gone — homes, food, jobs, in some cases even the very land on which they had lived had been burned away.

Public reaction to their plight, however, was as prompt and generous as it was surprising in a country that had never faced such a crisis before. In the days immediately after the fires attention was fixed on Chicago's disaster, but as news spread of what had happened in the northern forests help began to pour in.

Although the United States had little previous experience in handling great natural disasters and such agencies as the Red Cross were not yet in existence, a vast relief program was improvised. Whether it was because the recent Civil War had given people some practical know-how or whether it was because those on the scene were used to taking care of themselves under pioneer conditions, that program was remarkably successful.

Almost before the smoke had cleared over Peshtigo and the Door Peninsula local relief efforts were afoot in Green Bay, Marinette-Menominee, Oconto and the cities of the Fox Valley. Soon local committees were functioning at nearly every crossroad in Wisconsin.

Resources were Inadequate

It quickly became obvious, however, that local and state resources were inadequate and Gov. Lucius Fairchild called for help. It came almost immediately and kept coming until the relief agencies had to yell halt.

Purses that had already opened to help Chicago were opened again, and contributions of money and supplies rolled in from all over the nation. Every state east of the Rockies donated, far off California wired money, and even Europe kicked in. Belgium, especially, remembered the sons and daughters who had deserted her for America.

Slowly at first, then in steadily increasing volume the flood poured in. Isolated wagon loads became carloads and finally full trains. As many as 15 trains arrived at Green Bay in one day at the height of activity. Supplies of every description threatened to swamp the small receiving communities, which had to create facilities as they went along. It was done with startling efficiency.

In a short time efforts were coordinated. Two central relief committees were set up, one in Green Bay and the other in Milwaukee, and the devastated region divided between them. These committees received and accounted for all supplies and money and organized their distribution and use.

Volunteers Worked

Volunteers sorted arriving supplies, repaired items when necessary and issued what was requested. The women of Green Bay took over two new store buildings, set up shop and worked around the clock for weeks processing the avalanche of clothing.

The central committees had surveys made of the stricken areas and issued appeals for specific needs. They also bought on the open market when they couldn't get them any other way.

The survivors, used to shifting for themselves, were willing and capable of building their own shelter when they had the necessary tools. These were provided, and everyone pitched into a cooperative effort. Before winter set in all had rough shelter. It wasn't very fancy but was probably as good and maybe even better than many of them had known in their pioneer beginnings.

The immediate requirements were food, shelter and treatment for the sick and injured. Supplying them was fairly easy at Peshtigo but a real job on the peninsula, whose population was scattered over an area deficient in communications.

Packed Supplies Inland

Boats were sent along the bay shore and men landed with medicines and cooked food to hike inland with supplies on their backs. These first rescue parties made surveys of conditions and their reports were the basis of relief committee planning.

Clothing was not much of a problem. It came from all over the United States, was sorted, mended and issued. The Army contributed 4,000 blankets, 1,500 overcoats and a like number of towels, jackets and trousers.

Some of the contributions would have been laughable if the situation had been less serious or the intentions of the givers less sincere. One box, from the ladies of a fashionable New York hotel, contained dainty kid gloves and slippers, embroidered underclothing, ribbons and laces. Another from Philadelphia had a brocade silk gown that must have cost when new several hundred dollars.

The daintiest baby apparel — little crocheted stockings, frilly gowns and the tiniest and most expensive shoes — was common. One woman contributed the entire layette of her long dead baby, white and frilled and perfumed, just as it had been carefully laid away years before.

Nation's Industry Contributed

Manufacturers of every type of staple goods sent liberal contributions. There were cottons and woolens, boots, shoes, underclothes, bedding, mattresses, axes and helves, shovels, finished woodenware of all kinds, hay forks — just about everything conceivable and all of it badly needed.

Ironically, the one critical item that should have been easiest to procure in Wisconsin *(turned out)* to be the hardest to get. Most of the sawmills had exhausted their stocks of logs and closed for the season, while those still working were tied to contracts-many of them to supply the needs of Chicago. Committees bought what they could, some mills reopened, and gradually enough lumber was scraped together to meet minimum requirements.

Hospitals for the badly injured were set up in Green Bay's new Turner Hall and at Marinette, and doctors and nurses donated their services. The Green Bay infirmary was used only briefly but at Marinette two-score injured victims of Peshtigo were still hospitalized months later. Surprisingly, relatively few of those who survived the horrors of the night of Oct. 8 subsequently died of their injuries.

Transportation costs would have been staggering, but railroads, shipping lines and draying firms threw in their services too. Everything labeled for disaster relief was moved free of charge.

Army Sent Wagons

A final fillip was provided by Gen. Phil Sheridan who sent 200,000 Army rations of hard bread, beans, bacon, dried beef, port, rice, tea, coffee and condiments. He also added an unexpected and slightly embarrassing bonus of 100 Army escort wagons, complete with tarpaulin covers, spare parts, tools and full sets of regulation harness.

The agencies were stumped momentarily by the latter but disposed of them by requiring that they be issued intact. Anyone who applied for a vehicle or a set of harness had to take a complete outfit whether he wanted all of it or not.

Charlie Robinson of the Green Bay Advocate was a trifle caustic about those wagons, but as a Civil War veteran he should have known better. Army quartermasters, saddled with warehouses full of war surpluses, weren't going to miss such an opportunity to get some of the stuff off their paper.

It was a long, hard job but by tremendous effort the crisis was met and everyone provided for. Frank Tilton, in his account of the disaster published in 1872, wrote that by Feb. 1 aid had been given to 1,534 families of 7,187 persons. By midwinter, all the fire victims were tolerably comfortable and free from the twin dangers of freezing and starvation.

Death of a Prowler

Crime and Punishment in 1876

June 13, 1959

Law enforcement, like organized crime, has become almost an exact science in the 20th Century. Crime laboratories, lie detectors, fingerprint techniques, microscopes and high powered squad cars have enabled lawmen from the FBI to the village constable to outdistance such fictional gumshoes as Sherlock Holmes and Philo Vance.

But there may still be something to the direct and simple approach. At least, citizens of Green Bay were eminently satisfied with Orson Avery's shot in the dark one summer night in 1876.

Avery, a member of the County Board who lived on Cherry Street, caught a burglar trying to break into his home early one Sunday morning and let him have it. He did such a thorough job that a series of burglaries which had plagued the city for months was summarily ended.

Hailed as Benefactor

Today there would be legal repercussions. Eighty-three years ago Orson Avery was hailed as a public benefactor who had saved the community time and money.

All through the spring and early summer of 1876 there had been a succession of bold and cleverly executed house breakings and robberies of well-to-do residents, so well conducted they were generally conceded to be the work of an organized gang. The police and everybody else were stumped until Avery rolled up the artillery.

About 2 a.m. the morning of June 18, 1876, Avery, who suffered from neuralgia, groped his way down to the kitchen in the dark for a sedative. On his way back he heard someone trying to open the bay window in the parlor.

Jimmied Window Open

Sneaking up to the bedroom, Avery got his revolver and crept back downstairs. By this time the intruder had successfully jimmied the window and was working on the drawn blinds.

Avery couldn't see anything but he let fly anyway. The burglar leaped back through the window and took off as Avery snapped a couple more blind shots in the general direction of running footsteps. He then returned to bed, satisfied that he had scared the daylights out of his visitor.

Next morning he was startled to learn he had let some daylight into the stranger. The body of a man was found draped over his yard fence, shot dead center through the heart.

Recognized Own Coat

The body was taken to the firehouse of the Washington Hook and Ladder Company where a post mortem was performed by Doctors B. C. Brett and L. Marchand, during the course of which Dr. Brett recognized the coat and underclothing as belonging to him. They had been taken from his home some weeks before.

Another macabre note was the fact that the instruments he used in the post mortem had been stolen at the same time but later covertly returned.

The victim was identified as one Antol Eckel, who lived in an area north of the East River then commonly referred to as "Mushrat City." A mason by trade with a wife and three kids, Eckel was rated as a competent man-when he worked. Just prior to his death he had been employed aboard a lake steamer under an assumed name.

Trunks of Stolen Goods

A police search of his home uncovered several trunks filled with stolen goods, much of it from the recently burglarized home of W. J. Abrams. Unfortunately for the future mayor, his prized watch — the Weekly Globe called it his "auriferous chronometer" — wasn't there.

Discovery of an open side door to the Avery residence indicated the presence of an accomplice in the attempted burglary. This was generally believed to have been a certain Thomas Wald but nothing was ever proved against him except that his wife left town hurriedly the morning after the shooting with a suspiciously large number of bundles.

Wald would have been hard to catch in any event. He had skipped town the year before after being indicted for the robbery of the Cadle Home.

Mass Meeting Called

What the citizenry thought of Avery's marksmanship was not long in coming. Monday afternoon a mass meeting was held in the city council rooms, attended by an impressive number of prominent residents.

Mayor Fred S. Ellis presided, and a series of high flown and commendatory resolutions were offered by his recent and unsuccessful election opponent, A. W. Kimball. Dr. Brett, himself a burglary victim, seconded them.

There was no argument about adopting them, either. The resolutions were unanimously carried by a rising vote, and it was directed that they be published in the Green Bay and Fort Howard newspapers, with a certified copy to be presented to Avery.

Text of Resolutions

The resolutions follow:

"Resolved, That while human life is precious beyond all estimate, and while all good men do naturally shrink from taking the life of another, still, there are times when, for the protection of life, family or property, it becomes a stern and solemn duty, public as well as personal, for evil-doers to be killed.

"Resolved, That our esteemed fellow citizen Orson S. Avery has and is entitled to the sympathy and thanks of the entire community for the summary judgment he inflicted upon the burglar Anton Eckel on the morning of the 18th inst., while said burglar was forcibly attempting to enter the dwelling of the said Avery, and contrary to the laws of God and man.

"Resolved, That the killing of said Eckel was not only justifiable, but, in this city during the past few months, Mr. Avery would have been unfaithful to his duty as a citizen and neighbor had he refrained from shooting the said Eckel.

"Resolved, That the sympathy and co-operation of all good citizens are hereby tendered our honored Mayor and all the vigilant officers of the law, and that we trust their endeavors to ferret out and bring to justice the rest of that infamous gang of burglars may be crowned with speedy and complete success, and that we as citizens stand ready to assist them in any way they may desire or direct."

Friends Harassed Him

Unfortunately, for all their flowery enthusiasm and the approbation of his neighbors, the resolutions didn't do Avery any good. Green Bay was a hard-boiled town and Eckel had friends among the toughest element who promptly launched a counter attack of harassment and terror against him and his family.

Green Bay had never heard of the telephone (it was only invented that same year) so the Averys were spared the modern tactic of the anonymous call, but they got it in other ways. Rocks were regularly thrown through their windows and threatening notes were pinned to the doors every few nights. Avery took it as long as he could, but when neither the police nor anyone else could give him any help he left town.

The Great Snow Blockade

1881 Blow Paralyzed Area

January 11, 1969

The average house-owner who surveys the lovely stuff — especially right after the city plows have thoughtfully deposited an entire block's accumulation in his driveway — may be excused for sneering at references to the Great Snow Blockade of 1881.

Don't knock it. The Blockade of March 2-6, 1881, was one of the worst blizzards in the history of a section that has endured some classic snowstorms in its time.

A succession of heavy storms that piled a deepening blanket of snow on Northeastern Wisconsin had apparently been climaxed on Feb. 13-15 by the meanest blizzard since 1860-61. Drifts were 12 feet deep in the county, while city streets were clogged by such windrows as the ten-footer that filled an entire block of Main Street between Van Buren and Webster.

Everything Immobilized

By the time that one blew itself out everything was immobilized. Scarcely had the section begun to move again when the Blockade swooped down.

It started during the night of March 2-3 (March 2 was a Wednesday) with a driving snow whipped by a northwesterly gale and raged without let-up until late Saturday. While it continued everything came to a stop as people simply refused to leave their homes.

As early as Thursday morning railroads abandoned operations. Trains arriving in Green Bay hours behind schedule discharged passengers, who fought their way through the storm to find whatever accommodations they could in the city's already filled hotels.

Never Suspended

By Friday, according to the Gazette, the only places showing any signs of life were the "saloons, reading rooms, hotel offices and places of public resort." The paper itself never suspended publication but nobody knows how it reached subscribers.

The storm began to subside sometime Saturday afternoon. By then the region was paralyzed under a snowfall unprecedented within memory.

Trains weren't running, rural roads were choked beyond the capacity of primitive equipment — basically strong backs and hand shovels — to open them, and city thoroughfares were barely passable on foot. There is no record of how much snow came down, but on top of what already existed the problem of digging out was prodigious.

The situation confronting the railroads is a vivid gauge of conditions.

Battle of the Drifts

A North Western snowplow leaving Oshkosh Friday morning with three locomotives and a shoveling crew of 50 men reached Green Bay Saturday evening after battling an almost unbroken succession of huge drifts. The biggest was a monster 800 feet long at Little Chute that averaged 14 feet in depth.

The Wisconsin Central was completely blockaded. In one 40-mile stretch six locomotives were off the track, and it wasn't until the 10th that the first train over the line made it into Green Bay.

Partial Service

Nearly a week went by before a Green Bay & Minnesota train got through. Agent Timothy Case described route conditions as the worst in his 31 years of railroading.

With hundreds of men shoveling the right of way the North Western partially restored service by Monday. Rural roads were re-opened by cutting fences and clearing across country, avoiding the worst of the 18 to 20-foot drifts. Many rural areas were isolated for days.

The first mail to reach the city in five days came in on Monday by sleigh.

With some trains running, stranded travelers began to pull out late Monday afternoon. A generally congenial crowd, the snowbound strangers had made their good natured best of things and even had a lot of fun.

Center of conviviality was Cook's Hotel, where most of the traveling salesmen holed up. The drummers organized a "Snowbound Travelers Association," rigged a lot of corny practical jokes and on Sunday attended Presbyterian services in a body. They donated a pot of $50 toward the fund to rebuild the church, destroyed in the great fire of 1880.

Food No Problem

The city was well stocked with food, but fuel posed some small problems. Fortunately (the firemen couldn't have made it to the firehouses, let alone get equipment on the streets), there were no fires and the weather never got very cold.

Good thing for Abel DuChateau it didn't; otherwise, he might never have survived his 30-mile journey from New London to Shawano at the height of the storm. DuChateau was two days making the trip through the shrieking blizzard, bucking drifts as high as 25 feet.

Barely Made It

Leaving New London Thursday morning, he reached Clintonville late that afternoon after leading his team much of the way, harnessing himself to the cutter and pulling with the horses. Although exhausted on arrival at Clintonville, he decided to try for Shawano on Friday.

Accompanied by a young man named Baker, he barely made it. On one occasion they were marooned in the midst of seemingly impassable drifts, but the horses found a way out and they eventually reached Shawano, where DuChateau decided not to push his luck any further.

Like most March blizzards, however, the Blockade had great early foot but no staying power. Although another brisk but brief storm hit on the weekend of March 19, the spring thaws set in shortly thereafter.

By the end of the month the storm and its huge drifts were just a memory. Those who went through it never forgot, but there probably isn't anyone alive now who remembers the great blizzard of 88 years ago.

75th Anniversary

1889 Fire Was De Pere's Worst

April 25, 1964

About 4 p.m. on April 20, 1889 — 75 years ago this week — fire broke out on the docks of the huge Meiswinkel Wooden Ware Co. in West De Pere. Before the wildest night in De Pere annals was over one of the largest manufacturing plants and the heart of the little west bank city's economy had been wiped out.

After three-quarters of a century the spectacular Wooden Ware fire still stands as *(one of)* the worst in De Pere's history. For a time the entire town — West De Pere was a separate city then — was in danger of being engulfed, too. With the blaze completely out of control, only a providential shift in the wind saved it. Miraculously, no one was injured.

The Meiswinkel plant was one of the largest in the Fox Valley. Founded on the east side of the river by E. E. Bolles and F. Holman in 1865, later moved across the river and subsequently purchased by R. A. Meiswinkel, the sprawling factory turned out over a million fish barrels, kegs, lard pails, butter tubs and similar articles a year.

Major Employer

Its products were shipped in its own double-sized boxcars, it needed four lumber camps to supply it with raw materials and used a force of more than 300 men. In a town whose population was only about 2,100, the plant was by far the major employer.

April 20 was a Saturday in 1889, and the plant was preparing to shut down for the rest of the weekend when sparks from the factory smokestack ignited piles of shavings, lumber and barrel staves along the docks. With a strong south wind blowing, the flames had a good start by the time the De Pere and West De Pere fire companies reached the scene.

Eating its way north, the blaze destroyed storage sheds, dry kilns and stacked lumber in its path and consumed 1,000 cords of wood in the adjoining Hooker brickyard. It was moving away from the main factory, however, and there appeared to be little danger following the arrival of Green Bay's Guardian Engine No. 2 after a five-mile gallop.

Double Blow

By five o'clock, when the fire seemed to be under control, disaster struck a double blow. First the De Pere fire engine broke down and had to be taken back across the river for repairs. A few minutes later the wind suddenly swung around to a northern quarter, increased in velocity and flung a revived wall of flame into the teeth of the two puny streams of water from the other two pumpers on the dock.

It happened so fast the engines were cut off before they could be pulled to safety and had to be abandoned. For the next couple of hours the disarmed firefighters could only watch helplessly while the conflagration raged out of hand.

An oil shed containing 100 barrels of kerosene went up with a roar, spewing flames onto a large pile of pine wood near the factory building. From there the fire leaped to the plant itself. In minutes the three-story structure, more than 300 feet long, was a seething inferno.

'Grand, Yet Terrible'

It was, according to the Green Bay State Gazette account, "a grand, yet terrible" spectacle. Flames shot hundreds of feet into the air, blazing shingles sailed off on the swooping wind and the glare could be seen for miles through the gathering darkness.

With nothing to oppose it, the conflagration slowly but steadily consumed the big factory, office building, cooperage, barns and surrounding storage sheds. Then it bore down on the helpless town in its path, jumped to a nearby row of houses and set an even dozen ablaze.

Shortly before 10 p.m., in response to a frantic appeal, Green Bay Enterprise Engine No. 1 arrived by rail. The company tried to unload too close to the fire, was driven back and lost nearly half an hour getting into action.

City Seemed Doomed

By now the entire city of West De Pere seemed doomed. Some families had already loaded what household goods they could cram into wagons and fled.

Others, unable to get transportation, stood grimly in the streets with full pails of water determined to do what little they could to save their homes. Flying sparks ignited the roofs of several houses but alert and desperate watchers quickly doused them.

About 10 o'clock the miracle occurred. Once more the wind veered abruptly, drove the flames back toward the burned out area and saved the town.

Returned to Scene

About the same time the De Pere engine returned to the scene and provided the necessary assistance Green Bay No. 1 needed to confine the fire to the factory area. Shortly thereafter, around 11 p.m., a special train pulled in from the south with two more fire engines from Appleton and Oshkosh. The pumpers weren't needed but the reinforcements brought hose to replace that lost when the other engines had to be abandoned.

Pushed back into an area already burned over twice, the fire lost its force. By 2 o'clock Sunday morning it was finally brought under control, although the nearly exhausted firefighters spent the rest of the night and all day Sunday wetting down the ruins.

Area Swept Clean

When curious crowds swarmed in from Green Bay, Fort Howard and De Pere on Sunday they found an area half a mile square swept so clean there was scarcely any debris. The brick walls of the boiler room and the main foundations were all that remained of the Meiswinkel factory.

Surprisingly, the two abandoned fire engines had not been destroyed.

The De Pere pumper was only slightly damaged, while Green Bay's veteran Guardian had its wheels burned off. It was saved from toppling into the river by the dock pilings, but extricating the heavy machine proved a difficult task.

Meiswinkel estimated his losses at more than $250,000, of which only about $70,000 was covered by insurance. Adjoining property damage boosted the bill to better than $300,000 a figure that would be multiplied into the millions today.

Green Bay Offer

The ashes were still warm when a group of alert business interests began to woo Meiswinkel into rebuilding in Green Bay. He was made an attractive offer of financial assistance and a choice site in Fort Howard, but despite his expressed interest the deal never went through.

Having been elected mayor of West De Pere only a couple weeks before the disaster, Meiswinkel finished out his term while winding up his affairs, then moved to Chicago. He remained there until his death about 1918.

Destruction of its major industry was a fatal blow to West De Pere, which had been, only a few years before, the manufacturing center of Brown County. The fire undoubtedly was a factor in speeding consolidation with De Pere, which was accomplished before the year was out.

Sunday Morning Tragedy

County's Worst Railroad Wreck

July 15, 1969

Although Green Bay has been a railroad center for more than 100 years, the area has been singularly free of spectacular and deadly railroad wrecks. But not entirely.

Sixty-eight years ago last month, on the morning of June 24, 1901, De Pere was the scene of the worst wreck in the history of Brown County and one of the worst in state history. The tragedy, which left six dead and 55 injured, was the more poignant for the fact that it could have been avoided.

About 9:30 a.m. that day a double-header freight train of 53 cars pulled out of the North Western yards at Green Bay headed south. At the same time a nine-coach excursion special carrying nearly 650 holiday passengers to the Turners' state saengerfest at Green Bay began to gather speed after passing Appleton.

Both Crews Aware

Both crews knew the other was coming. Orders were that whichever arrived in De Pere first was to pull onto a side track to let the other through. The meeting occurred as anticipated but not as planned.

Less than 45 minutes later — at 10:13 a.m., as nearly as could be determined — the trains met just south of the West De Pere station in a head-on collision.

As the passenger locomotive, traveling about 30 miles an hour, rounded the curve about a quarter mile from the station, the engineer got his first glimpse of a flagman racing down the track toward him, frantically waving a warning. Then he saw the head of the freight standing on the main track, dead ahead.

Fatal Freeze

For a fatal moment that may have been the difference between life and death for half a dozen unsuspecting passengers, the man froze in horror. With a shout of warning to his crew he slammed on the air brakes, realized his heavy train couldn't stop in time and jumped.

With suddenly slackened speed but slowly and inexorably, the special rolled on. In the crowded coaches startled passengers were still toppling into each other's laps when West De Pere's Sunday morning calm was shattered by the grinding crash of colliding engines and the distinctive, jarring sound of railroad cars violently slammed together.

A brief instant of shocked silence, punctuated by the deceptively gentle hiss of escaping steam, erupted into a pandemonium of screams and hoarse shouts as hundreds of frightened passengers untangled themselves and poured out of the cars. Quickly, the screaming took on a wail of horror as the crowd converged on the head of the train.

Gruesome Sight

The sight was gruesome enough to make anyone scream. The first two cars had telescoped, the leader — a combination baggage coach and smoker — being driven halfway through the crowded second coach like a gigantic ram. Seats, twisted pipes and passengers had been jammed into a tangled crush of wreckage and broken bodies that filled the back end of the coach.

There were shrieks of agony as well as panic and horror as injured men fought to escape the ghastly mess. Fear of fire (fortunately, unfounded) lent desperation to their efforts.

Slowly at first but with increased speed as panic subsided and the urgency of the situation dawned, rescue work began. Frantic men used bare hands and anything they could find to pry away the wreckage and free trapped victims.

All Pitched In

As the dead and injured were extricated under the level-headed leadership of Conductor Walter Roach — many had to wait hours before they could be freed — they were laid out in the shade of a nearby grove of trees. Meanwhile, the crowd was augmented by scores of De Pere residents attracted to the scene, most of whom pitched in to help. The job went faster after a wrecker arrived from Green Bay.

All the available doctors in Green Bay and De Pere were shortly at the scene. West De Pere High School was opened as an emergency aid station and the injured were made as comfortable as possible until they could be transferred to St. Vincent Hospital.

Eventually 16 were hospitalized. Except for cuts and bruises sustained by passengers tossed about in other cars, all the serious casualties were in the shattered second coach. Six men had been killed. For a time it was feared four others might die but all pulled through.

Investigation Launched

An investigation of the wreck was launched while rescue work was still going on. Since the engine crews had leaped to safety, all the key figures were available and it was quickly determined what had happened.

The probe uncovered a whole series of miscalculations, each relatively minor in itself but pyramiding into disaster.

To begin with, the freight was too long. When it pulled into the De Pere siding several cars could not clear the main line.

The engineer, thinking he had enough time, moved onto the line to clear his tail. He then cut off the first 15 or 20 cars, pulled them ahead and was preparing to back into another siding when the passenger train bore down on him.

Not Soon Enough

He had sent the flagman forward but the latter was only about half way to his normal post when the passenger train swept around the curve. A message from farther down the line, which might have alerted the De Pere station to the location of the special, was not received until two minutes after the crash.

The passenger engineer believed he had a clear track into the De Pere yards. The head of the freight had stopped just short of the next block, had not tripped the automatic signal and there was no warning that the right of way was occupied.

Running late anyway, the special's engineer assumed the freight was clear of the main line and waiting for him to go through.

Even so, had he reacted faster he might still have avoided the worst of the accident. Apparently, however, he froze just long enough to make the tragedy inevitable.

Curious Historical Twist

'Titanic' Sinking Shocked City

April 14, 1962

Fifty years ago tonight, on April 14, 1912, the White Star line "Titanic," the world's largest and most luxurious passenger ship, on its maiden voyage from England to the United States, sideswiped an iceberg and sank in the North Atlantic with the loss of 1,503 lives. The tragedy of the Titanic was and still is the greatest peacetime marine disaster in history and one of the most dramatic.

In 1834 John Jacob Astor foreclosed mortgages on the lands of the Grignon family, John Lawe and Jacques Porlier that gave him possession of half of what is now Green Bay. Among those drowned in the sinking of the Titanic was his namesake and great-grandson.

Just south of the North Western Railroad bridge over the Fox River, on the back slope of Woodlawn Cemetery, a lonely burial vault with the name "Minahan" above the door stares out across the lower De Pere road and the river.

The three items don't appear to have much in common but they do.

Within that tomb lies the body of William E. Minahan, member of one of Green Bay's most prominent families of half a century ago. Dr. Will Minahan also lost his life when the Titanic went down.

Shoulder to Shoulder

In fact, when last seen he was standing shoulder to shoulder with Astor's descendant after they had worked together placing their wives in the same lifeboat. But the coincidence doesn't end there.

Speeding through a clear but bitterly cold night at a speed of nearly 35 knots, the "unsinkable" Titanic swerved suddenly to avoid smashing head on into a huge iceberg looming in its path. The collision was averted, but in passing a 300-foot gash was ripped in the vessel's side, far below the waterline. The 2,207 persons aboard scarcely felt the jar.

A little more than two hours later the stern of the great vessel that "even God couldn't sink" rose high in the air and the Titanic went down by the bow, carrying all but 704 of its passengers and crew to death in the freezing waters. Even after 50 years the story of that tragic night retains the power to stir imaginations then unborn.

News of the disaster created a worldwide sensation, nowhere more than in Green Bay where it was known that a local woman and her brother were on board. Miss Daisy Minahan and her brother William were sister and brother of Drs. J. R. and R. E. Minahan and attorneys Hugh and V. I. Minahan.

Residents of Fond du Lac

Although Dr. Will was a resident of Fond du Lac, both he and his wife were widely known here. The sinking was front page news in the Green Bay Gazette for days after it was verified that Daisy and Mrs. Minahan had been rescued but that Dr. Minahan had been lost.

Mrs. Minahan, Daisy and Mrs. Astor were picked up from a lifeboat by the S. S. Carpathia, which arrived on the scene about daybreak, some six hours after the Titanic sank. They were brought to New York where Dr. John R. Minahan met the ship and escorted his sister and sister-in-law back to Green Bay.

Nearly two weeks after the sinking word was received that Dr. Will's body had been recovered and was being brought to Halifax. V. I. Minahan, who was deeply attached to his brother, went to Halifax to claim it. Identification was made by a letter of credit on the body and a valuable ring, although the two men looked so much alike there was never any question.

Meanwhile, the two women had reached home in a state of semi-collapse. Their story of the disaster was relayed to the Gazette through Dr. John.

Asleep in Cabin

According to Daisy, she had been asleep in her cabin when she was awakened by the screams of a woman — she thought it was Mrs. Astor — more than an hour after the collision. Rousing her brother and sister-in-law, she dressed and reached the boat deck in time to be placed in the last lifeboat to leave the ship.

Whether it actually was the last boat isn't known. For that matter, Miss Daisy's whole account was full of understandable errors. Neither she nor anyone else aboard the doomed ship was in an analytical frame of mind that night, and nearly all the survivors' stories were confusing and contradictory.

By the time she arrived back in Green Bay the badly shaken woman had apparently read the newspapers, which carried a mass of piecemeal and often erroneous information about the disaster. Consequently, in telling her version, she "verified" many of the stories which became legends of the tragic affair but were subsequently proven incorrect.

Among other things, she passed on one of the most persistent of all errors concerning the sinking. She told of hearing the ship's orchestra playing "Nearer, My God, To Thee" just before the Titanic's final plunge.

Never Played Hymn

Actually, the orchestra never played the familiar hymn at all. It was playing "Autumn" when the ship's last big lurch threw the musicians into a sprawling heap on the tilting deck.

Miss Minahan also said there had been a couple of great explosions and that the vessel had broken in two before it sank. That wasn't correct, either.

It was true, however, that she rode out the freezing night in the same lifeboat with the recent bride of Col. John Jacob Astor. Apparently all three women were helped into the boat by Astor and Dr. Minahan, whose last words before he waved them over the side were "Be brave."

Miss Daisy's account of getting into the boat is also somewhat at variance with that in Walter Lord's book "A Night to Remember" published several years ago. According to her she was lifted into it by Col. Astor and her brother. As Lord tells it, she was still hanging back when her mind was made up for her by the curt invitation of a harassed ship's officer to "Damn you, get in that boat."*

Can be Forgiven

But Miss Daisy can easily be forgiven. It had been a harrowing experience for all the survivors and she wasn't very well anyway. The trip to Europe had been taken for her health, and the night's experience eventually brought on a relapse that resulted in her death in Los Angeles seven years later.

Although Dr. Minahan did not live in Green Bay he was buried in Woodlawn Cemetery with his parents. The mausoleum, which has been because of its size and location, a structural problem ever since, was later built by his widow.

But there is an even more curious twist to the strange, last-minute intertwining of two families that had greatly affected the development of a city in which neither of the victims of the disaster lived.

Of the 1,503 persons lost less than 200 were recovered and returned to the United States for burial. The bodies of both Dr. Will Minahan and Col. John Jacob Astor were among those few.

* *According to a statement in Miss Daisy's affidavit for a Senate investigation into the Titanic mishap, the command to jump came when some passengers were transferred from one lifeboat to another with fewer survivors aboard. "I showed no hesitancy and was waiting only my turn," Miss Daisy stated. For a full account of the Titanic disaster, check the collection compiled in the Local History Department of the downtown Brown County Library, 515 Pine St., Green Bay.*

Ringing Call to Arms

America Goes to War

April 1, 1967

Fifty years ago tomorrow the United States entered the First World War. Officially, the nation was not at war with Imperial Germany until the afternoon of April 6, when President Woodrow Wilson signed the declaration of a special session of Congress that a state of war existed, but the sword was drawn between 8:35 and 9:10 p.m., April 2, when the President appeared before a joint session to call for it.

Today it is impossible for anyone under the age of 60 to appreciate the mood of exalted patriotism and lofty idealism with which America went to war half a century ago. The spirit was quite different, although no less determined, from that of the nation the day after Pearl Harbor.

For one thing, everybody was prepared for the step. The approach to conflict had been gathering momentum for two months, ever since the German government had resumed unrestricted submarine warfare and diplomatic relations were severed. America didn't want to go to war but was convinced it had to, and President Wilson, with one of the great presidential speeches, led the nation over the brink to make "the world safe for democracy."

Sounds Hollow

His ringing phrase may sound hollow in the light of the ensuing half century, but Americans believed it then. Press-Gazette editor John K. Kline echoed that faith next day in a sonorous editorial declaring that "Democracy must rule the earth. It is inevitable. The doom of tyranny and absolutism has been sounded."

News of the President's call to arms spread throughout Green Bay about 10 p.m. that Monday as a horde of newsboys, afoot and on bicycles with bundles of Press-Gazette extras under their arms, fanned out from the dingy little newspaper plant on Cherry Street. Virtually every porch light in the city was burning as residents waited anxiously for the approaching cry of "Extra! Extra!"

Radio hadn't been invented yet and nobody even dreamed of a day when such events would be brought directly into home living rooms on a television screen. So people waited for the inevitable extra. There was always something eerie about the newsboy's cry, first heard faintly in the distance, then getting louder and more insistent.

Took News Quietly

The city took the news quietly, knowing it was coming. Just the day before, Green Bay had officially and vociferously expressed its unqualified support of Wilson at a giant patriotic rally in the National Guard armory in old Hagemeister Park *(at the end of Cherry Street on the current site of East Green Bay High School).*

After a colorful parade through the downtown area and out to the park, 3,000 people had crowded into the armory. They heard stirring music by the Green Bay Concert Band and the Green Bay-De Pere Choral Society, cheered fervent speeches by Bishop Paul P. Rhode, the Rev. M. L. Eversz of St. Paul's Methodist Church, Judge Henry Graass and Mayor Elmer S. Hall and adopted an equally patriotic resolution by roaring acclamation.

Even so the news, when it came, added the thrill of accomplishment and release from mounting tension. Across the years that feeling can still be sensed in the Press-Gazette extra, the top third of the front page filled with screaming headlines and the added touch of an excited make-up man who put March instead of April in the date line.

Headline Eruption

There was little doubt at any time of where the P-G and the majority of Green Bay's citizens stood. Day after day, as events piled up through February and March, the Press-Gazette erupted in unprecedented banks of streamer headlines.

The action of Wisconsin's Sen. Robert M. LaFollette and a small group of colleagues in filibustering to death President Wilson's request for authority to arm our merchant ships particularly incensed the city. Editor Kline thundered dignified but bitter denunciations and hundreds signed petitions demanding that LaFollette either "do his duty" or resign.

Anger swelled again when LaFollette forced a 24-hour delay in the Senate vote on the war declaration but his stubbornness was soon forgotten in the fervor with which Green Bay accepted war. The final edition of the Press-Gazette for April 6, in huge, black type, announced that "War Is Declared!!" atop a bank of three eight-column and a pair of four-column, two-line heads.

Much important local news was crowded off the front pages, including the death of former Gazette publisher N. C. Pickard in an automobile accident, a municipal election in which a proposal to motorize the fire department was defeated and the organization of the Lawton (*Lawson*) Aircraft Co. to make war planes. People were more interested in the recruiting of Battery B to war strength and the formation of a cavalry troop.

Despite Green Bay's general acceptance of war, the decision wasn't easy for everyone. The area's large German population, including hundreds of immigrants, many of whom had become prominent and substantial citizens, was caught in the middle.

The great majority were loyal Americans as they subsequently proved, but they also had deep sentimental ties with their homeland. The mass of other, less emotionally involved citizens, however, was in no mood to accept or understand their predicament.

A major victim of war hysteria was former postmaster and congressman Gustav Kustermann *(spelled Kuestermann in Wright's 1915-16 City Directory).* A classic example of the American immigrant success story, and a highly educated, cultured and sensitive man, Kustermann was also a proud, stiff-necked individual.

His refusal to bow to the hysteria brought a mounting volume of abuse down on him. When he died shortly after the war the medical reasons for his death were serious enough, but those closest to him always insisted the real cause was a broken heart — not because Germany had been beaten but because people had doubted his sincere loyalty to the United States.

Historic Scourge

The 'Flu' Epidemic of 1918

December 28, 1968

You've read a lot about "Hong Kong flu" recently. To victims who have felt its discomforts, the flu isn't funny but to those who remember, the current epidemic is a cream puff compared to the "Spanish Influenza" scourge of 1918.

Fifty years ago Green Bay and the rest of the world were reeling from a "pandemic" of influenza (actually, the Italian word for influence) that in a few months swept unchecked around the globe killing an estimated 20 million people, including nearly 550,000 in the United States. The outbreak was one of the most destructive in history, ranking with the Black Death of the Middle Ages as an indiscriminate killer.

Such epidemics were not new in 1918, having erupted periodically since the 4th Century B. C. In this country there had been five between 1831 and 1918 but none serious since that of 1889-90. Green Bay had never experienced such a crisis.

Deadly Aftermath

What distinguished the 1918 epidemic was its extraordinary virulence. Previous sieges had been much like today's Hong Kong flu, but the 1918 brand — called "Spanish" because of its havoc in Spain, where 30 percent of the population was affected — had a nasty habit of developing into swift and deadly pneumonia.

Appearing first in Eastern Europe in the spring of 1918 the disease spread like a grass fire. Reaching the eastern coast of this country early in September, it erupted almost overnight all over the continent, reached a peak in late November, then subsided as quickly as it had come.

The flu hit Green Bay in late September. On Oct. 3 the city health commissioner Dr. C. J. Chloupek announced that a few cases had been identified and issued instructions about what to do and precautions to take.

Nobody Knew

His instructions were little enough. He had no real authority and anyway nobody knew anything about influenza (for which there still isn't any cure), what caused it, how it spread or how it could be controlled. With many of the city's doctors and nurses in military service, there were only 19 physicians to serve a community of 30,000, and shortly two of them were dead while others were out of action temporarily.

Within 24 hours of the initial warning the number of known cases had reached 100. The school board immediately closed all schools, Mayor Elmer S. Hall ordered theaters shut down and a West High football game was cancelled. That same day the first local death was recorded when Mrs. John P. Van Veghel succumbed to pneumonia.

From then on the crisis deepened. Medical people worked until they dropped, the sick roll skyrocketed and the death toll with it. Nothing seemed to work, not even the gauze face masks which Bill Van Beek made his Beaumont Hotel barbers wear and which were soon widely adopted. In many homes where whole families were down there was nobody well enough to care for the rest.

Frustrating Aspects

A frustrating aspect of the next three months was the unpredictable course of the epidemic, which rose, fell and rose again like a bouncing ball. No sooner would the harassed Dr. Chloupek announce that the worst seemed to be over and things were under control than it would break out again, worse than before.

By Nov. 1, after the number of reported cases had topped 500, there was a marked decline. Hopefully, schools were briefly reopened, the theater ban was lifted and the city breathed a sigh of relief — whereupon all hell broke loose again. A surge of new cases followed the riotous celebration of the Armistice and the death rate jumped alarmingly, hitting a late November crest of seven in one day.

December 1 saw the case load hit 800 — nobody ever knew the exact total — and there had been over 80 deaths. It was never possible to determine how many were down at any one time and many cases were not reported.

Council Finally Acts

The situation became so serious that the city council — hitherto reluctant to move decisively — finally reacted to Cr. Chloupek's pleas and imposed a quarantine with teeth in it. Part of the trouble was that nobody was sure of the legal authority of local governments to impose a quarantine and the council wouldn't do so until the State's Attorney General cleared the way.

The ordinance was a tough one. Every case had to be reported at once, infected houses were placarded and failures to report or violations of the quarantine drew an automatic fine of $100. Jail sentences were out of the question since the council didn't dare fill up the clink.

Having obtained the authority he had been pleading for since October, Dr. Chloupek — by this time the most unpopular man in town — lifted the orders closing theaters and other public assemblies. Schools, however, remained closed until Dec. 30, an unexpected 11-weeks vacation for the kids, who were strangely unaffected by the epidemic.

Danger Abates

Whether the quarantine was the answer or whether the epidemic had run its course was never determined, but shortly thereafter it began to abate. There was another flare-up in mid-December but cases were milder, and after Dec. 15 there were no more deaths.

By year's end the worst was over. From a high of over 200 houses quarantined the number had dropped to 20 by New Year's Eve and the date was celebrated in traditional style.

No reliable figures were ever compiled on the extent of the epidemic or death here but conservative estimate would be around 1,300, with another 400 or so in De Pere, where the flu had taken a parallel course. Up to Nov. 23 the death toll was 73 in Green Bay, with fatalities thereafter bringing the final count to about 100. In De Pere there had been about 15, with a number of young men also dying in southern army camps.

City in a Frenzy

When World War I Ended

November 16, 1968

Except for a lonely spot of life on Cherry Street, near the present back entrance to the Kellogg-Citizens National *(Associated)* Bank, Green Bay was asleep. There, in the brightly lighted editorial room of the old Press-Gazette building, a group of tired, sleepy men filled the air with smoke and desultory conversation.

The sudden chatter of the Associated Press telegraph cut through the talk, suspending it abruptly. The room came wide awake in tense silence as attention riveted on the A.P. telegrapher hunched over the instrument.

He looked up, nodded and grinned.

The word for which these men had been maintaining an around-the-clock vigil for four days had come through. World War I was over. It was 1:45 a.m. Nov. 11, 1918 — 50 years ago last Monday.

The Blast-Off

Amid triumphant yelling, Dr. Austin Olmsted, chairman of the Brown County War Board, grabbed a telephone and shouted into it. Moments later the whistle of the Northern Paper Mill shrieked, the fire alarm bell chimed in and soon other bells and whistles added their strident clamor to the rising tide of sound.

What happened after that isn't easy to describe. If the account seems confused and disjointed, so were the next 24 hours as Green Bay exploded in the wildest, most spontaneous celebration in its history.

The city was primed to flip its lid. It hadn't gone overboard for the "false armistice" of Nov. 7 largely because the Press-Gazette had stuck with the Associated Press in insisting the early rumor was premature.

Mounting Tension

Nevertheless, the end wasn't far off, and all through the intervening weekend — Nov. 11 was a Monday then, too — people waited in constantly mounting tension. When the word came they let go.

The newspaper's switchboard began to flash wildly as calls poured in. All over town lights snapped on. Isolated shouts merged into a swelling roar that rolled nearer and nearer to the newspaper plant where standby crews were replating a victory extra, as the joyous mob swept into the business district.

Within half an hour the streets were overrun with whooping, singing people, some of whom hadn't bothered to dress. Pajama trouser legs beneath overcoats testified to the haste with which many had headed for downtown.

Bedlam of Sound

By that time every bell, factory whistle and siren in the city was going in a sustained shriek that didn't stop for hours. To them were added automobile horns, band music, the crashing of drums and bugles and the hammering of pots and pans — anything that could conceivably make a racket.

Long before daylight the city's two musical outfits, the Northern Paper Mill and City Concert Bands, were in action, blaring up and down the streets at the head of impromptu parades that marched to every war song the musicians could play. These parades were a fixture of the entire day, breaking up as paraders thought of something else to do and promptly reforming with new recruits.

Happy, unruly human serpents were everywhere, swarming through hotel lobbies, restaurants and saloons. They even invaded sleeping quarters of the hotels, banging on doors and routing out anybody stubborn enough to try to sleep.

Reinforcements Arrive

At daylight the crowd was augmented by reinforcements from the country, converging from all directions. With them came the Oneida Indian Band and Duck Creek Drum and Bugle Corps to head additional snake dances.

With virtually everyone who could walk for miles around clogging the streets, businesses didn't even try to open. The few eager beavers who reported for work were told to go away and enjoy themselves.

About the only people on the job were bartenders, waitresses and the volunteer firemen who kept steam up for the incessantly blowing factory whistles. The Press-Gazette put out a regular edition that day in addition to the early morning extra but nobody remembers very clearly how it was accomplished.

Plans Collapse

A vague plan for some sort of formal observance quickly collapsed in the general confusion. The happy uproar went on, completely off the cuff.

The only organized incident of the day was a quasi-military one involving nearly 200 city and county draftees who had been ordered to report for induction that morning. The men assembled as instructed, were sworn into the army and marched to the Milwaukee Road station* through wildly cheering crowds.

By the time they got there word had been received that all draft calls were cancelled. After half an hour of milling around the contingent marched back to the courthouse and was formally mustered out after one of the shortest and happiest military hitches on record.

Traffic was a mess but no effort was made to unsnarl it, even if it had been possible. The police force simply resigned for the day and joined the fun.

Free Paddy Wagon Rides

The Black Maria was much in evidence but its function consisted of racing through the streets, siren wide open, giving rides to everybody who wanted them. Many took the opportunity to ride in a paddy wagon for the first and only time in their lives.

The most dangerous aspect of the

celebration was the flag-festooned trucks and automobiles, crammed with passengers, careening about the streets. Surprisingly, although there were a number of fender-bending collisions and several cars overturned, nobody was seriously hurt.

The bedlam continued all day and well into the night before it subsided from sheer exhaustion. A few diehards were still at it even after midnight. Next morning, a hoarse and bleary-eyed city made feeble efforts to get back to normal.

** The Milwaukee Road station at 400 N. Washington Street today houses the Green Bay Area Chamber of Commerce and is listed on the National Register of Historic Places.*

The Big 1922 Sleet Storm

February 24, 1962

There was a lot of griping about snow and wind this week and last weekend, but hardy "pioneers" of 1922 just sat back and sneered. To them the recent blow didn't even qualify as weather for a good snowball fight compared to the great sleet storm of four decades ago.

They were right. Forty years ago today Northeastern Wisconsin and the Fox River Valley, from Marinette to Fond du Lac, were reeling under one of the worst storms in history. For three days Green Bay was almost completely isolated, and conditions here didn't begin to approximate the devastation wrought farther down the valley.

The freak storm of Feb. 21-23, 1922, struck without warning and over a period of 50 hours dumped tons of snow, hail, sleet and rain on the area to the accompaniment of unseasonable and spectacular thunder and lightning. Physical damage locally was not excessive but the storm froze everything tighter than the proverbial drum.

It began innocently enough with light snow flurries shortly after noon of the 21st, a Tuesday. By 5 p.m. the snow, driven by a strong wind, had turned to hail and an hour later to sleet.

Sequence Confused

The sequence thereafter is confused, but a mixture of sleet, hail and snow apparently fell all night, with a violent electrical storm getting into the act shortly before daylight. Wednesday morning the sleet changed to freezing rain, which came down all day, switching back to sleet and snow late in the afternoon. This combination continued until Thursday noon, finally slacked off and cleared about 3:30 p.m.

All through the period the fall was driven into heavy, freezing drifts by the wind, which whipped it into windrows four to six feet high in the city and even deeper in the open country. Long before it ceased everything was coated with a casing of ice and sleet up to two inches thick. Whatever wasn't sturdy enough to bear the weight came down.

By Wednesday morning nearly all wire communication with the outside had been severed. One weak and sporadic telephone lie functioned to Oshkosh and there were only three telegraph lines open, two of which didn't go anywhere. One to Duluth remained in operation all through the storm but couldn't begin to handle the traffic.

The Wisconsin Telephone Co. made heroic efforts to keep lines open but with hundreds of poles down to the south it was a losing fight. City lines, however, were only partially knocked out.

Worked around Clock

Wisconsin Public Service Co. crews worked around the clock for three days keeping power lines functioning, and power failures in the city were held to a minimum. The situation might have been serious had heating systems then been as dependent as now on electricity, but thermostats weren't in general use yet. Everybody kept warm with hand-fired coal furnaces and wood stoves.

Not that the cold was ever a real problem. Temperatures remained below freezing but never fell much under 25 degrees, not enough to make Judge Henry Graass wear an overcoat.

With drifting sleet freezing in the tracks, rail service was quickly crippled and finally abandoned completely after a southbound passenger train, leaving here Wednesday afternoon, was derailed near Little Chute. From then until Friday afternoon nothing moved, and it wasn't until Saturday that a train managed to get in from the South.

About the only outside contact was through the lone telegraph line to Duluth and a new plaything of a few hobbyists like Emmett Platten, just beginning to be called radio. Thanks largely to Emmett, the city had some idea of what was going on in the world but not much.

A.P. Wire Out Early

The Press-Gazette Associated Press wire was an early casualty and was dead for three days, the longest news blackout in the paper's history. Platten tried to fill the gap by intercepting eastern broadcasts and telephoning bulletins into the paper, but the staff had to rely largely on local news. With the storm providing plenty of that the paper never missed an issue.

The Public Service Co. managed to keep street car tracks clear but the effort backfired. Unable to use the streets, automobiles and delivery trucks took to the tracks, packed snow and sleet solidly into the rails, and the street cars couldn't operate anyway.

Taxis had a field day until vehicles began to break down under the strain. So tough was the going that one cab, trying to make a call on the Duck Creek road, couldn't turn around and had to back a mile and a half to Washington Street.

The few remaining livery stables had floods of calls for rigs but all their horses were at work with shoveling crews. At the height of the storm more than 500 men were vainly trying to hold off the elements with picks and shovels.

Didn't Even Try

The county never attempted to open rural roads. Even the highways to De Pere were clogged, to the embarrassment of a couple of local swains who got hung up there sparking their girls and had to spend three days in the California House. They didn't have enough cash on them to pay the bill, but they had honest faces.

The county's pride, a brand new tractor plow, was loaned to the city and quickly conked out. Meanwhile, L. H. Barkhausen turned a new Northwest Engineering Co. crawler crane with a clamshell shovel over to the city in the futile battle to keep the streets clear. It wasn't nearly enough.

For the first time within the memory of veteran undertakers the city was unable to bury its dead. The only way people got to hospitals was through the efforts of a big Snavely Transfer Co. truck in breaking trail.

By the time the storm blew itself out nearly 3 1/2 inches of precipitation (equivalent to 35 inches of snow) had been measured, but the figure was not accurate. The weather bureau's snow gauge on top of the Minahan Building *(202-215 Walnut Street, now a parking lot)* froze up and had to be taken inside periodically to thaw out. Even that amount was more than double the normal precipitation for the entire month.

Not All Dismal

Everything wasn't dismal, however. There were no deaths due to the storm and the kids, with schools closed, had a field day. A Boy Scout troop actually made an overnight hike to a bay shore cottage and Curley (*sic*) Lambeau, the athletic director at East High, led a party of teenage skiers to Lily Lake. One local doctor used skis to get to his office.

By the weekend life was beginning to return to an approximation of normal. The first train in from the south on Saturday was greeted by a cheering crowd of hundreds of people.

Arrivals reported the valley a shambles. Those who had ridden out the storm here were inclined to be skeptical of statements that Green Bay "scarcely felt" the blow, but they happened to be correct.

Bad as it was, the local storm had caused more excitement and inconvenience than actual damage or hardship. The area between Appleton and Fond du Lac had been battered to the extent of over $2 million damages — and those were 1922 dollars.

Anniversary of Inferno

Barkhausen Fire Cost Three Lives

August 30, 1969

It was late in the afternoon of Aug. 22, 1929, when Ray Gaffaney, foreman of the Barkhausen Oil Company plant on McDonald Street, switched on the pump to fill a loading tank with gasoline up under the roof of the big warehouse. When he tried to turn it off a few minutes later the room blew up in his face, costing him his life and the lives of two others in one of the most spectacular and deadly conflagrations in Green Bay's history.

The city has known a succession of costly fires in its long existence, as is to be expected of a town whose economy was long rooted in forest products. Surprisingly, though, loss of life in those historic blazes has been small. In terms of death, the Barkhausen Oil fire of 40 years ago was the most costly until the Astor Hotel holocaust of 1966.

Killed, in addition to Gaffaney, were general manager Samuel Dexter Hastings Jr. and office manager Arthur J. Rollin. The latter's body, charred beyond recognition, was later found in the ruins of the plant. Gaffaney and Hastings were pulled from the inferno and lived long enough to give some account of what happened.

Three Injured

Three others were injured but recovered. Firemen Henry Bitters and Elmer Schoen were overcome fighting the blaze, while Elmer Aebischer, a Barkhausen truck driver, was burned trying to save Gaffaney.

The latter, who lived for three days, provided the most complete story. Hastings, one of the leading young business executives of the city, son of retired Judge S. D. Hastings and father of Dex Hastings, succumbed two hours after his rescue.

According to Gaffaney, he had turned on the pump to the 1,000-gallon loading tank, then went to the office to pick up a report blank to record the operation. On the way back he encountered Hastings, running toward the warehouse exclaiming: "Ray, I smell gas!"

Exploded in Face

Dashing into the building, Gaffaney found the loading tank had overflowed and the room filled with gas fumes. As he pulled the switch to turn off the pump there was a flash and the room exploded.

Actually, there were two explosions — one when the fumes ignited and another when the tank went up.

The blast was felt for blocks and the roar heard all over town. It was so powerful that people in the nearby North Western railway depot thought a locomotive had jumped the track and hit the building.

In seconds the section of the warehouse was a seething mass of flame. It was also a ticking fire bomb containing thousands of gallons of inflammable liquids, threatening to explode at any minute.

Thousands of Gallons

Three huge containers held 10,000 gallons each of gasoline, fuel oil and denatured alcohol, while two other 6,000-gallon compartmented tanks were loaded with various types of lubricating oils. Had any one of them exploded everything would have gone up with a force that could have leveled the whole neighborhood.

When the fire department arrived with its entire force, firemen had difficulty getting close enough because of the intense heat but were able to direct their efforts to keeping the still unexploded tanks cooled down and to drive back the flames. Their efforts were complicated by a steady barrage of exploding gasoline drums, spewing balls of fire, smoke and steel fragments hundreds of feet into the air and in all directions.

Most spectacular of the secondary explosions were those of two loaded tank trucks just outside the blazing warehouse, which went up with deafening roars. One of the latter almost got fire inspector Gus Joppe, who barely made it to safety in a dash for a protecting wall.

It didn't take long for word to flash through town, and on the heels of the fire department came a wave of spectators. Fortunately, the heat kept them at a relatively safe distance, but the Main Street bridge and street approaches to the plant were clogged by an impressive traffic jam.

Perched on Roofs

Hundreds of watchers perched on roofs throughout the city, where they had an excellent view of the pyrotechnics. The seething column of flames and its crown of black smoke could be seen clearly as far away as the West Side ridge.

Aebischer, who had just parked his truck outside the plant, ran to the fire in time to pull the unconscious Gaffaney clear but was painfully burned in the process. Bitters was overcome by fumes and Schoen suffered burns to his left arm and forehead.

Nobody knew how Rollin got into the blazing warehouse. He had been talking with Hastings in the office when the latter sensed that something was wrong and apparently followed him, although nobody saw him leave the office. His charred body was not found until the fire had been brought under control and it was identified by the remains of his wristwatch and wallet.

There were a number of narrow escapes. One office clerk risked his life to carry out vital company records, and Dex Hastings just missed the blast. He had been talking with his father in the office and was still on his way back to town when the explosion occurred.

Weather a Factor

The weather got into the act, too, but too late to do further damage. With a summer storm brewing, a strong wind blew up shortly before 6:30 p.m. By that time, however, the worst was over.

Had the wind freshened and changed direction half an hour earlier, it might have had even greater tragic consequences. A shower following the rising wind helped, instead, to dampen the flames.

At the height of the conflagration every member of the fire department and all equipment was fighting the fire, leaving the rest of the city stripped. More than 8,000 feet of hose was used, of which several lengths were burned, and the long coil spread over the railroad tracks held train movements up for over two hours.

1936 Deep Freeze Sets Record

January 17, 1970

The thermometer's sudden nose dive to 19 below zero a couple of weeks ago was a traumatic experience to the Press-Gazette editorial staff's Southern (Illinois) Belle. The way she shivered and her teeth chattered, our misnamed "snow bunny" obviously hadn't been "around" 34 years ago when the weather had all Northeastern Wisconsin shivering in the grip of the most prolonged deep freeze in history.

The Green Bay area has known some pretty rugged winters in its time but nothing to compare with the 35 days between Jan. 19 and Feb. 22, 1936. For pure, unadulterated cussedness, that was Winter's finest hour.

Although the weather bureau reckons the period from Jan. 19, the winter offensive actually got under way two days earlier with a blizzard that paralyzed highway traffic and severely hampered the railroads. Snowfall wasn't heavy but winds up to 36 miles an hour whipped it into drifts blocking all roads out of the city.

The winds continued strong for two days. Meanwhile, the temperature began to drop, finally slipping below zero on the 19th. By 6 a.m. the next day a 10 below zero reading marked the coldest of the winter to that point. It was only the beginning.

Mercury on Toboggan

It hit 18 below on the 22nd and 16 below on the 23rd, when 30-mile winds again swooped down to bring rail and road movements to a halt. Next day it was 24 below, coldest of the entire siege, thereafter rising gradually. By the 30th the reading was only two below and the cold wave appeared to be breaking.

The respite didn't last long. On Feb. 1 the temperature was down to 13 below and back on the front page of the Press-Gazette where it stayed for the next three weeks.

February 2, a Sunday, was the 15th consecutive day the mercury dipped below zero. The run was broken on the 3rd when the low was only four above, just four days short of the all-time record.

Temporary Setback

The setback was temporary, however, and merely seemed to goad the elements into more vicious reprisals. Beginning on the afternoon of Feb. 5, snow fell heavily and the winds cut loose again. By midafternoon of the 4th eight inches of new snow were being tossed around by a 30-mile gale and county crews had abandoned a losing fight to keep roads open.

It was 22 below next morning. Schools, which had closed briefly during the late January freeze, didn't bother to open again until the 7th. That day a temperature of one degree above zero snapped a streak of 68 consecutive hours of sub-zero temperatures.

At this point only nine of 24 county snow removal units were still working, but crews kept trying. By Feb. 8 they were beginning to see daylight, only to have their efforts wiped out by another weekend blizzard.

Worst since 1922

The ensuing tie-up was the worst since the famous sleet storm of 1922. Although main roads were reopened by the 12th, rising winds during the following 48 hours once more piled huge drifts on the restored highways and began to play havoc with the railroads.

Some communities, notably Kewaunee, were completely isolated for a time. Green Bay wasn't, although some supplies ran low and local bakers got yeast by airdrop. Shipments were dropped into the drifts at the snow-buried county airport.

Another frigid blast cracked down on Sunday, Feb. 16, when the temperature skidded to 18 below zero. It dropped to minus 21 on the 18th.

Highways were technically passable, although few tried them, but the railroads were badly choked. Both the Milwaukee and North Western roads brought in huge rotary snow plows for the first time since the Easter blizzard in 1929.

Back Broken

The back of the siege was reported broken on the 21st but nobody believed it here. The low reading of Feb. 22 was 13 below, to tie the record of 19 straight sub-zero days set in 1889. By then 19 inches of snow had been stacked in close-packed drifts that measured more than 14 feet in depth along some roads.

County Highway Commissioner E. Francis Brunette remembers that 35-day nightmare vividly. He was a snow plow jockey then, responsible for keeping 110 miles of road open with only one puny machine.

He recalls that conditions on the north-south roads weren't so bad at first but that after the winds had effectively blocked the east-west arteries they began to give the north-south connections a similar going over. With the equipment then available the task of keeping roads open was too great.

Emergency Conditions

As machines began to break down under constant use, emergency calls diverted what was left from the primary job of getting the road open. Although main highways were closed only temporarily, many town roads were hopelessly blocked for the rest of the winter.

Another big handicap was communication. When a plow went out in those days nobody knew where it was until the operator checked in by telephone.

If it went into a ditch a couple of hours might pass before the office heard about it. The boys simply operated on the principle that no news was good news and did the best they could.

Having proved its point, whatever it was, winter let up on Feb. 22. A half-hearted blizzard followed but didn't amount to much, and then a complete about face soon had streets looking more like canals than modern thoroughfares, but everybody was too relieved to care.

Set Persistency Marks

Although the unprecedented cold wave fell far short of the all time minimum of 36 below zero of Jan. 21, 1886, its persistence set a few marks that haven't been seriously challenged since.

Weather bureau files disclose that in spite of the warmth of the final week, February, 1936, was the coldest on record, exceeded overall only by January, 1912. Despite the last minute change February averaged only 4.6 above zero. Twenty-one days of below zero readings exceeded the old February mark of 18, established in 1904.

February 5, 1936, with a low of minus 22 and a top of minus nine, was the coldest February day since 1889 when a minimum of 33 below and a maximum of 10 below were recorded on the 10th. For the 35-day period between Jan. 19 and Feb. 22 the average was 4.3 below zero, the longest and most severe period experienced by Northeastern Wisconsin since 1865.

Fortunately, the wind chill factor hadn't been invented yet, so nobody realized how badly off they were. A chill factor of more than 70 below zero on Jan. 23 might have scared half the population to death.

Chapter Six

Green Bay's Social Side

Recreation, 1856 Style

Pioneers Had Fun, Too

May 27, 1967

Today's adult-ridden teenager may not think so, but he never had it so good. What with television, movies, travel, every conceivable type of participating and spectator sports the variety is bewildering — yet the constant complaint is there's nothing to do.

Such a squawk would get no sympathy from great-grandpa or anyone else who lived in Green Bay a century or more ago. Such things as TV, movies, radio, football and automobiles hadn't been invented yet and they had to provide their own amusement.

Not that gramps and grandma didn't have fun — they did all right. It may well be that a gang of teenagers in — say, 1856, to pick a typical year — got more kick out of a rousing taffee pull they organized themselves than a modern crowd whose recreation is so heavily supervised and planned for them.

Only One Troupe

Green Bay being small then and off the beaten path, there wasn't much in the way of professional entertainment. In fact, only one traveling troupe, the Barke Family Singers, played United States Hall in 1856 and they were the first professionals to appear in the city since the Lumbard Brothers nearly a year before.

Baseball was only a vague name in the wild west, being confined to a small group of amateur clubs in and around New York City. The first "world series" was played that year on Long Island between picked teams from Manhattan and Brooklyn but Green Bay knew nothing about it and cared less.

One circus did wander into town during the summer. That was Orton's Badger Circus, which had been making an annual visit ever since 1853 when it achieved the distinction of being the first circus ever to play Green Bay.

Historic Circus

The Orton spread was a typical, small horse-drawn outfit of its time, yet it secured a place in circus history by being the first show of its kind to come out of Wisconsin, once famed as the "mother of circuses." There was no wild animal menagerie, it had a single ring and trick riding was its principal stock in trade.

Like all circuses, there was nothing modest about its advertising, but one blurb probably wasn't meant the way it sounded. After detailing in glowing terms the wonders to behold, it wound up with the statement that the "New York Silver Cornet Band" would, throughout the performance, play all the latest popular hits to "relieve the tedium and monotony."

Benefit Dances

Otherwise, the tiny community was left to its own resources. There were several public balls during the year, all but one — which used the newly finished Klaus Hall — being held at the Astor House. Early in the spring the Astor was the scene of an elaborate masquerade which elicited a long and facetious account in the Advocate.

The Germania and Guardian Fire Companies staged benefit dances. Another was the main event of the Fourth of July, held in default of the usual civic celebration and parade, which was rained out.

In the fall and winter the more erudite settlers attended the Green Bay Lyceum, which put on a weekly series of lectures. This was largely a home talent affair but extremely popular.

It was quite a distinction to be asked to speak before the Lyceum, whose active membership included Henry Baird, Morgan L. Martin, John P. Arndt and other leading citizens.

There was a trotting course near the "upper square" in Astor (now St. James Park) where horse fanciers exercised their trotters and pacers, and a number of races were held there. A series of matches on the frozen river during the winter was a great success.

Hunting Paradise

On two counts the old timers had it all over their descendants. If it weren't for so much evidence down to the turn of the century, the quantity of fish and game would be unbelievable, but by every standard the bay area was a hunting and fishing paradise.

There were no game laws but by common consent hunting was confined to fixed seasons. Duck hunting was both a fall and winter sport.

So great were the flights of ducks that the man who couldn't knock down from 75 to 100 mallards and canvasbacks in a day simply didn't know one end of a shotgun from the other. In early summer tremendous flocks of passenger pigeons virtually darkened the sky. In May 1856, with beef selling at the outrageous price of 15 cents a pound, everybody thumbed their noses at the butchers and gorged on roast pigeon while the migration lasted.

Deer hunting was done mostly during the summer, although venison being a staple food for the farmers, a fat buck or doe was fair game any time. It wasn't necessary to go halfway to Canada to get one, either. On occasion, deer were actually chased down the main streets of the town, as was done one Sunday afternoon in September.

Fishing Equally Good

Fishing on the bay and nearby streams-including the Fox-was equally good. One party, returning from a two-day trip to Menominee, brought back 791 lake trout, all taken on hook and line. Lake trout of 20 to 30 pounds were unexceptional, one monster scaling a whopping 37 1/2 pounds.

Dinners and small parties in private homes were common but unpublicized. Henry Baird's old custom of holding open house on New Year's Day was being widely copied. The tradition of roaming from house to house on New Year's, destined to be a fixture of the Christmas season in the 1870s and 1880s, was taking hold.

Sailing on the bay and rivers was so common it hardly qualified as a diversion in a time when the ability to handle a boat was nearly as necessary as familiarity with firearms to live on the frontier. Nevertheless, sailors were as eager as trotting horse owners to match their skills for a genial side bet or two.

The gay young blade of 1856 may not have had a Mustang or imported sports car to tool around the neighborhood, but there was nothing wrong with a surrey, with or without a fringe. If he couldn't spring the family nag and carriage, there was always the livery stable where rigs were available at 50 cents an evening.

Not Like the Old Days

Holiday Celebrating Has Changed

December 21, 1968

When it comes to celebrating the Christmas season, freewheeling, party lovin' old Green Bay isn't what she used to be. Not that the city has abandoned the celebration, but the style has changed. Where the town used to go in for big public affairs in downtown restaurants and hotels, the trend nowadays is to private parties in neighborhood homes.

The week between Christmas and New Year is no longer a back-breaking succession of social affairs. The old hotel New Year parties have long been abandoned, largely because facilities are limited now and people aren't attracted to them anymore. Efforts to make old fashioned whoopee, with crazy hats and horns are usually forced and slightly embarrassed these days.

Green Bay has been celebrating the Christmas season with parties, however, since before the turn of the 19th Century. The original settlers were happy-go-lucky French Canadians who loved a good party, and Christmas was the best time of the year to throw big ones, but we have little more than hints about what they were like.

First Big Bash

The first big Christmas bash of which we have any detailed information was one thrown by the commanding officer of Fort Howard in 1823, to which civilian settlers and officers, families of the military garrison were invited. By all accounts it was quite an affair and it set a pattern that was followed for generations.

The early French Canadian pioneers were followed by a wave of New England and New York Yankees. The latter generally kept to themselves socially and soon developed their own methods of observing the holidays.

First to establish a custom that lasted for nearly half a century and gave Green Bay a reputation for unusual Yuletide hospitality was Henry S. Baird. Sometime in the 1830s Baird instituted an annual New Year's Day open house that was widely copied by friends and neighbors and gave a unique quality to the Green Bay social scene.

Held Every Year

Each year open houses were held all over town, eventually reaching such proportions that the newspapers regularly printed lists of locations and hostesses. It was one of the most charming customs the city ever enjoyed.

It was great for the men but probably not so much fun for the women, who had to stay at home and be hostesses and clean up afterward while their husbands roamed the town, dropping in for a nip at the homes of friends. Eventually the ladies got fed up and about 1885 the custom died out.

The first hint of change came a few years earlier when the ladies began to combine their efforts, several of them putting on the event in a single house. Once the combining started it was easier for individuals to drop out and in a short time the colorful and gracious custom was finished.

Public Celebrations

Meanwhile, as the town grew and public places became available, the holiday season became a time for many public dances and benefits to which everybody came. During the 1870s and 1880s the practice of forming social clubs got a foothold, reaching a peak in the decade before World War I.

As such clubs proliferated and larger hotels were built, partying moved out of private parlors and dining rooms. The period between Christmas and New Year was jumping with affairs.

During the 1880s and early 1900s the holiday season was one party after another, reaching the climax on New Year's Eve when hotels and restaurants were jumping with celebrants. The social pages of the Advocate and Gazette bulged with announcements of these affairs.

One of the big ones, between 1908 and 1922, was the annual Charity Ball given by the Sewing Club. It was always held during the holidays and was the biggest social event of the year.

Revived by Service League

For about a decade after the Sewing Club called it quits the Charity Ball was just a pleasant memory until revived in 1932 by the Service League. It has been going ever since, although no longer strictly during Christmas week.

Clubs put on their own parties, to which outside friends were invited, and many were very elaborate. Such organizations as the Neighborly Club (founded in 1911), the Powhatans, Wallacks and the Elks gave big dances, there were parties on New Year's Eve at Kaap's, DeLair's Café, the Beaumont Hotel and later the Northland *(212 N. Washington; 208 N. Washington; 201-213 Main Street near Washington; and 304 N. Adams and Pine, respectively. The Northland was rehabilitated as a housing facility for the elderly in 1979 and renamed Port Plaza Towers.)* In those days the social tone of individual events was measured by who got Tony Vandenberg's orchestra.

The advent of prohibition and the end of the Charity Ball diverted attention to the Elks Ball and area nightclubs (they were called roadhouses then) as the big downtown affairs closed out. During the 1920s the Elks Ball was the big social event of the season.

Social Changes

Meanwhile, the old family practice of dining out had also lapsed, the hotels closed their big dining rooms and didn't reopen them except for private parties. World War II put a further damper on the big events — the Charity Ball excepted — and when it was over old practices weren't revived.

One holiday trend that was highly pleasant for younger generations until wartime was built around returning college students. Starting with the arrival of the railroads' "student specials" the week was given over to a series of collegiate parties, including tea dances at the Woman's Club, the old East High Short Story Club's Holly Hops and others.

These holiday special trains were an experience in themselves. When classes suspended for the holidays students converged on Chicago and Milwaukee and the specials began rolling north, picking up and dropping contingents along the way. They were crowded and noisy but everybody had a whale of a good time.

Different Breed

They, too, are only a pleasant memory for an older generation. The modern collegian has his own car, he rolls home in his own good time and once checked in has a habit of disappearing again. If you want to find the college crowd during the holidays you head for the ski lodges.

In one respect there has been little or no change, however. Christmas Eve and Christmas Day have always been and continue to be family and religious days.

Families assemble, go to church together, then gather around the dinner table for a whopping meal and small talk while the children start breaking up their toys. Even today you can point a cannon down Washington Street anytime after 8 p.m. Christmas Eve and fire it without much danger of hitting anyone.

Off the Cuff Celebration

City Flipped Over Aquila Arrival

December 30, 1961

Green Bay is all primed to stage another civic celebration Sunday, assuming (naturally) that the Packers win the playoff. If history and anticipation are any guides it ought to be a good one.

Given a little time and any reasonable excuse the local citizenry have always been pretty good at cooking up a real rouser. They also demonstrated, at least once, that they weren't bad at working off the cuff when the necessity arose.

It did over a century ago, on June 16, 1856, when the steamer Aquila arrived in town to mark the completion of the Fox and Wisconsin River improvement that united the Great Lakes with the Mississippi in a single waterway.

Special Occasion

Of course, that was a pretty special occasion. When the awkward little twin-stacked sidewheeler nosed into the Goodell and Whitney wharf at the foot of Jefferson Street she had just fulfilled a dream almost as old as the chimera of the Northwest Passage.

Built in Pittsburgh especially for the Fox River trade, the Aquila had met her destiny by completing a 2,300-mile trip to the Great Lakes via the Ohio, Mississippi, the Wisconsin and Fox Rivers. Green Bay was not blind to the significance of the event.

Her arrival was not entirely unexpected but the timing left a lot to be desired. For weeks Green Bay and other towns along the Fox had been watching closely as the finishing touches were put on the 10-year task of completing the historic water route. Although none knew when the Aquila, already running between Appleton and Oshkosh, would try the passage, it was only a matter of days.

Rumor Started

Since the Aquila herself was about the fastest means of getting news of her coming down the river, nobody in Green Bay was aware that Monday morning that she was on her way. About 10:30 a.m., however, a rumor started that she was coming through.

Less than 15 minutes later a proclamation by Mayor Harry E. Eastman hit the streets calling an assembly of all citizens at the United States Hotel *(then at 40 Main Street)* at noon to plan a suitable welcome. Nobody ever told how Harry got his information.

At 12 o'clock the parlors and public hall of the hotel were jammed with excited Bayites, including just about everybody in town except those who, as the Green Bay Advocate put it, had gone home to tell their wives to forget about the week's wash and get prettied up.

Committee Picked

Since the public meetings were always conducted with much punctilio, Mayor Eastman was elected chairman and former Mayor Frank Desnoyers secretary. A committee consisting of Eastman, John P. Arndt, James H. Howe, John Day, Charles Tullar and Postmaster Edward Hicks was appointed to superintend the reception.

Another special committee of the mayor, Edgar Conklin and John C. Brown was deputized to meet the Aquila at De Pere and extend the official welcome of the city. With the Aquila expected around 4 o'clock, the latter had to get cracking.

Thanks to the "fleetest team and most experienced driver" in Munsan and McAllan's livery stable and failure of the Aquila to keep on schedule, the top-hatted and frock-coated committee reached De Pere at 4 p.m. with half an hour to spare. They found the village in an uproar and everybody converging on the river bank to greet the vessel.

Boat Already Loaded

Boarding the Aquila amid a bedlam, the committee found a large delegation of dignitaries already aboard from Neenah, Menasha, Appleton, Grand Chute and Kaukauna. The Menasha brass band was also noisily in evidence.

Capt. Steve Hotaling turned out to be the son of Capt. Peter Hotaling who, in 1841, had brought the first river steamer, the Black Hawk, from Lake Erie to the Fox River. Since his dad had failed in an attempt to run the rapids to Lake Winnebago, Captain Steve was fully conscious of the significance of his own trip.

After negotiating the locks at De Pere, the Aquila proceeded down river to the plaudits of a series of gatherings along the shore and the company of the tug Ajax, which met it at Point Chapman, about a mile beyond De Pere. Passing Hazelwood, the home of Morgan L. Martin, the man most responsible for the successful completion of the improvement, the excited passengers were treated to an elaborate display of banners, flags and other appropriate symbols which the vessel duly saluted with its whistle.

Triumphant Passage

The passage between Green Bay and Fort Howard was truly triumphant. Every dock, warehouse and lumber pile on both sides of the river was crowded with yelling people, as were the decks of all steamers and sailing vessels in port. Streets leading to the river were, again to quote the Advocate, "alive with a living mass of crazy humanity."

Rounding to at the mouth of the East River, the Aquila was saluted by a salvo from the guns of abandoned Fort Howard, whose caretaker, Maj. Ephraim Shaler, had thoughtfully recruited gun crews and taught them how to load and fire the cannon. At the docks of George Haywood and Goodell & Whitney at the foot of Jefferson Street, the unlovely little vessel completed her long and often interrupted voyage.

On hand to welcome her were a deputation of Green Bay's leading citizens, the Germania Fire Co. and Brass Band and the new Turner Society in full regalia.

Procession Formed

Here a procession was quickly formed under the direction of Nathan Goodell, perennial parade marshal of his day. Headed by the mayors of Green Bay and Menasha, Fire Chief Fred Lathrop, Germania foreman Henry Reber and H. Althrop and B. Rosenfeld, leaders of the Turners, the marchers moved up Jefferson to the combined music of the Germania and Menasha bands.

At the Astor Hotel the parade changed direction and returned north on Washington Street to the United States Hotel, in front of which a reviewing stand had been hastily raised. Here the parade broke up, the dignitaries took their places on the platform and the speechmaking began.

For once, almost miraculously in a day when windiness was a prerequisite of the polished orator, the speeches were short though eloquent. After a few opening remarks by Mayor Eastman, James Howe was introduced and launched into a flowery and fervent outburst extolling the future opening up of the Valley. He was followed by Judge S. D. Howe and General Turner, mayor of Menasha, who responded briefly.

Wound Up in Hotel

Eastman closed the enthusiastic rally with the news that Captain Appleby of the lake steamer Sultana had donated the services of his vessel for a dance that evening to which the "flower and chivalry of the Fox River Valley were cordially invited."

Said chivalry turned out en masse with the flowers in brilliant plumage and the dance went off as scheduled. The historic day ended with everybody adjourning to the United States Hotel at midnight where manager George Farnsworth served an "elaborate collation."

Last Excursion Boat

When the Nettie Plied the River

May 2, 1959

Forty years ago last week a story appeared in the Press-Gazette that must have read, to many, more like an obituary than the notice of a business transaction. The Nettie Denessen had been sold for scrap. With the sale of the little steamboat one of Green Bay's most beloved institutions, the old Denessen Line, came to an end.

For half a century Denessen boats had plied the water of Green Bay and the Fox and East Rivers, crowded with excursionists bound for Benderville, Little Rapids and Lawrence's Gardens. As far as veteran Bayites are concerned there never was anything like the Nettie or the John Denessen. When the Denessen boats stopped running something went out of the life of the city, never to return.

Capt. John Denessen established the Denessen Line in 1873. He had learned his business from boyhood on fishing boats working out of Green Bay and was later employed on a ferry that ran from the Beaumont Hotel landing to the west side, below the North Western station *(now Titletown Brewery)*. In 1870 he took over the business which was still profitable in spite of the recently completed Walnut Street bridge.

Carried Supplies

That year he put the William Denessen, named for his son, in operation. Three years later he replaced it with the larger William II. The latter didn't remain on the ferry run long, however, as Denessen turned that over to his employees and put the William to work hauling supplies for the railroad gangs building the North Western north to Escanaba.

About this time the practice of chartering steamers for excursions became popular, and the Denessen Line was in the business that made it famous. Early excursions were usually made to Point Comfort, up the East and Fox Rivers and to other spots as far away as the mouth of the Red River.

The line prospered. By 1876 the 50-passenger William II had been outgrown and was replaced by the Arrow, which could handle 65.

To De Pere on Christmas

The most famous feat of the Arrow was a Christmas Day run to De Pere in 1879, an event that grew with the telling through the years. Long afterward someone figured out that if everyone who claimed to have made that trip had actually been aboard, the battleship Missouri couldn't have handled the crowd.

The Arrow made the excursion runs for seven years, and in 1883 gave way to the best known of all the Denessen vessels, the John Denessen which, with the Nettie, continued in service until the company went out of existence in 1919. The John could accommodate 110 passengers.

The Nettie joined the John in 1891. Built in 1884 by Louis Schiller, who named it after himself, the Nettie was enlarged after Denessen bought her. The vessel was cut in two and a center section and more powerful engines added to increase her capacity to the same figure as the John.

Converted to Coal

They were much alike in appearance with a covered lower deck, an open top deck and a pilot house above the latter. Originally woodburners, the two vessels were ultimately converted to coal. While Capt. John Denessen had operated the early boats unaided, their larger successors required a crew of four. In addition to the captain-pilot each had an engineer, a fireman and a cook.

Every Sunday for decades the John made regular trips from the dock at the foot of Washington Street up East River to Hagemeister Park where East High School now stands and beyond to Lawrence's Gardens. The Gardens were a popular picnic spot in a noble grove at the east end of Crooks Street.

For five years the Nettie made three round trips a day to Benderville, as Red Banks was then called. Runs were also made up the Fox to Little Rapids, out to Point Comfort and to First and Second Lights.

Beer on Return Trip

Both vessels were extremely popular with the German Bathing Club, the Wednesday Bathing Club and the Friday group. Getting into their bathing costumes — roughly equivalent in those days to donning long-handled underwear — members would journey to beaches along the bay shore for an afternoon of fun and frolic, during which the more intrepid females might even risk becoming topics of town gossip by going into the water up to their pretty necks.

The German dunkers had a good routine. After holding their bathing party — you could hardly call it swimming — the gang would break out the beer and lunch on the return trip.

Sometimes stag groups would lay in a plentiful supply of edibles and liquids and be dropped off at a designated spot, to be picked up later. The boat crew and the more conservative members of the party would pour the rest of the boys aboard, salvage what was left of the beer and head for home. Long before the John or Nettie tied up to the dock, the singing of the happy revelers could be heard for blocks.

Moonlight Excursions

Such groups as the old Powhatans, Turners and Elks counted the summer lost that did not include at least one cruise on the John or Nettie. Church organizations, lodges and clubs of all kinds chartered the vessels for Sunday and holiday outings. Moonlight excursions were also extremely popular.

About 1904 "Cap'n John" was ready to retire and his sons bought him out. William, Theodore, Joe and Henry Denessen were splendidly qualified to carry on, as all of them had helped their dad since their teens.

Joe had even been born on a boat, the old George L. Dunlap, which used to run between Green Bay and Escanaba before the railroad was built. One winter, when his father was living aboard as shipkeeper, Joe arrived.

After purchasing the line from the old man, Theodore became captain of the John with Joe as engineer, and William ran the Nettie, assisted by Henry. William was only doing what he had done most of his life, having served aboard the Nettie from the time she was built. He stayed until the little craft was beached for good.

By 1915 the increasing number of automobiles and better roads began to cut deeply into the excursion traffic. More and more families were acquiring cars and preferred going out for week-end and evening "spins" in their own vehicles.

The Denessens gradually took to hauling freight instead of passengers, carrying hay, lumber, coal and cement between Green Bay and points along the eastern shore as well as to Menominee. Each spring and fall they enjoyed a big business in fish and fishermen's supplies although here, too, trucks eventually took over.

The John was the first of the two old vessels to go. Then, in the spring of 1919 the Nettie was sold, her engines removed and the hull broken up. She enjoyed the reputation at the last of having been in continuous service longer than any other boat sailing from Green Bay.

Fourth of July-1865

Rain Cuts Down Big Celebration

June 28, 1969

It has been more than 40 years since Green Bay staged an old fashioned Fourth of July celebration, with fireworks, a parade, oratory, a big picnic in the park and a ceremonial reading of the Declaration of Independence — which is, after all, what Independence Day is all about.

To most people nowadays, the Fourth is an excuse to hit the road for summer cottages, fishing or some other personal recreation. Americans are too busy having fun and smashing each other up in traffic accidents to listen to someone read a document most of them have never read themselves.

Rain can, to be sure, put a damper on the holiday. Not any more so, though, than it did more than a century ago when one of the most meticulously planned celebrations in the city's history went down the drain.

Pretty Special

July 4, 1865, was a pretty special day for most of the United States. The bloody Civil War was newly over, victorious and vanquished combat veterans were trickling home and, except in the defeated and prostrate South, the Fourth of July offered the first good excuse for a traditional celebration in five years.

Green Bay was no exception. Planning for the big day began early in June when Advocate editor Charley Robinson called a public meeting at the new Beaumont House to get the show on the road. The session set up an organization to bring off a real blast.

A general committee was appointed consisting of James S. Marshall, Henry S. Baird, Dr. Henry Pearce, George Strong, Anton Klaus, Charles E. Crane, Ephraim Crocker and James S. Baker. Marshall was elected chairman with Baker as secretary, and the committee took it from there.

Committees Proliferated

Special committees were named for every eventuality, including band and choral music, choice of speakers, toasts (a body whose importance was attested by the caliber of its membership, among them Sen. T. O. Howe, C. D. Robinson, Morgan L. Martin and J. C. Neville), fireworks, invitations, finances, public dinner, yacht races and a steamboat excursion.

Virtually every prominent man in town was tapped for some job. Since selection was both a civic honor and responsibility, nobody dreamed of refusing.

Such affairs were always carried out with great punctilio; consequently Mayor Myron P. Lindsley was named President of the Day, with the village presidents and town chairmen of every Brown County community on the roster of vice presidents. The Hon. James H. Howe was to be orator of the day, and the next most important post, that of chief marshal, went to C. E. Crane.

Sunrise Salute

The program was to open with a 13-gun salute at sunrise, fired from the remains of old Ft. Howard, the last time the old post ever figured in any public event; a mammoth parade, formal speechmaking, a national salute at noon and a public dinner at 2 p.m. The afternoon called for a yacht race on the bay and a steamer excursion, while there were to be elaborate fireworks after dark.

Everybody within commuting distance was invited and preparations made to handle a huge crowd of visitors. All stores were kept open — although that wasn't unusual.

Stores never closed in those days except on Christmas and New Year's Day, the only other general holidays then observed. A merchant whose doors were locked on the visiting farmers simply wasn't a good businessman.

Participating in the parade were to be drum corps, returned soldiers, the committee, mayor and city council, the clergy, legal profession, national and state officers, the medical profession, city bank, fire department, civic societies and Sunday school classes.

Outdoor Program

As was always the case, the official program was to be conducted from a speaker's stand on Washington Street. Opening with the national anthem, it would include a solemn reading of the Declaration, the oration of the day, prayers and the national salute at noon. Thereafter, those who shelled out $1 for a ticket could adjourn to Anderson Hall for a civic banquet and a series of fervently patriotic toasts.

With such careful planning it didn't seem possible that anything could go wrong, but nobody had taken the weather into account. Anyway, a weather bureau was still 20 years in the future, and the only weather prophet was some old Indian chief's rheumatism.

As might have been expected, the long awaited morning opened with a brisk shower. That was all right, since it settled the dust and put the streets in good shape for the parade, but the rain wasn't satisfied to leave well enough alone.

While the expectant crowd and the marchers ducked in and out of stores between heavy downpours and rolling thunder, parade time was repeatedly set back until just after noon, when the whole outdoor ceremony was reluctantly called off.

Banquet was Damp

Those who had tickets trooped through the rain to Anderson Hall on Adams Street for the banquet, nobly catered by Mitchell Resch and Theodore Noehle. Orator Howe relieved a little of his built-up steam with a "few remarks," toasts were solemnly downed and everybody took off for the yacht race.

The race was the only event of the day that came off as planned, and even that wasn't much of a contest. Fred Ellis' "Sirius" made a runaway of it, although there was a good battle for second place between the little "Star" and the "Eclipse."

An also ran was J. C. Neville's boat, on which his teenage son, Arthur Courtenay Neville, was a crew member.

The fireworks got wet, too, and the evening display had to be postponed until they dried out. It wasn't until July 14 that they were ready for use, but the display, when finally touched off along the river bank, was deemed a great success.

B.P.O.E. Birthday Party

Elks Celebrating Centennial

February 17, 1968

The "Best People On Earth" are throwing a party tonight. Green Bay Lodge No. 259, as others elsewhere throughout the nation, is celebrating the centennial of the founding of the Benevolent and Protective Order of Elks.

Coincidentally, although the local Elks aren't making anything of the fact, tonight's banquet comes only a month ahead of a milestone of their own. On March 15 Lodge 259 will mark its 75th anniversary as one of the senior lodges among the 2,100 all over the United States.

If the local lodge is a bit ahead of itself, it is a day behind the actual centennial of the Order. The B.P.O.E. dates its official existence from Feb. 16, 1868, when 15 "members of the Theatrical, Minstrel, Musical, Equestrian and Literary Professions and others" formally adopted a name and constitution for a society to promote their mutual welfare.

Born Earlier

More precisely, the Elks were born a few months earlier, in November, 1867, shortly after a 21-year-old English singing actor arrived in New York to try his luck on the other side of the pond. Charles Algernon Sidney Vivian was the son of a clergyman but he took a dim view of the blue laws that kept New York City buttoned up tight on Sunday.

Vivian and a few new-found theatrical friends solved the problem by gathering in the attic of his boarding house to ride out the 24-hour drought. Other bored actors took to dropping in, and soon there was a convivial group of about 15, who eventually succumbed to the American urge to join something.

They called themselves the Jolly Corks, because of an English trick Vivian imported to match for drinks in neighborhood bars, and Vivian was elected Imperial Cork. Shortly the gang got too large for the attic so they moved their Sunday night sessions to a place called Military Hall on the Bowery.

More Serious Aim

The death of one of the crowd, leaving his family destitute, sobered the Jolly Corks into forming a more serious organization for mutual assistance. This was the beginning of the Elks.

The matter of a name for the group aroused considerable debate. Vivian favored the term "Buffaloes" but the rest weren't satisfied. Eventually, a visit by a committee to P. T. Barnum's museum solved the problem. Here was found a magnificent elk's head, and a few days later, on Feb. 16, a formal vote adopted the now familiar name by a narrow vote of 8 to 7.

The new club was barely off the ground when it almost disintegrated in a fight over eligibility for membership. On faction wanted it restricted to theatrical professionals and got control long enough to expel the founder and other Jolly Corks who favored a wider membership.

Expulsion Rescinded

A few years later the expulsion was rescinded and some of the founders returned, although the record is silent about whether Vivian was one of them. Eventually, his part in the founding of the order was recognized but by then he had been dead for several years. He died of pneumonia at Leadville, Colo., while playing there in 1880.

Expansion of the B.P.O. Elks was slow for several years, during which it remained primarily a society of entertainers. It was not chartered as a national organization until 1871 and membership didn't hit 1,000 until 1880.

It was 1889 before the Elks chartered their 100th lodge, but with the advent of the Gay Nineties the dam broke. Shortly thereafter the Green Bay lodge was formed as one of the older groups, although the sponsoring Fond du Lac Lodge No. 57 predates it by several years.

23 Charter Members

Lodge No. 259 was instituted on March 15, 1893, with 23 charter members, including some of the leading citizens of the city. From the outset the Elks were active and prominent in many phases of community life, and their clubhouse was for many years as much a community center as it was a private men's club.

Early rooms in the Odd Fellows and Knights of Pythias Halls were merely meeting places, for which the lodge paid a nightly rent when actually used. As early as 1898 planning began for a place of their own, but it didn't become an actuality until 1902 when the old clubhouse was finished at Cherry and Jefferson Streets. There is no exact record of the date, but tradition always placed it on Washington's Birthday, 1902.

All Sorts of Affairs

The clubhouse, first in Wisconsin, was built and equipped at a total cost of about $25,000, probably the biggest bargain Green Bay ever got. From the outset it filled a civic need that may, at times, have caused the brotherhood to wonder just whose place it was.

Meetings, conventions and social affairs of all kinds were held in the red brick building with the white-pillared, two-story veranda. The total number of dances and parties held there — only a fraction by the Elks themselves — boggles the imagination.

Half a century of constant use took its toll on the building. As early as 1939 it was obvious that a replacement would be needed but it wasn't until 1957 that the project really got into gear. On Oct. 25, 1958, ground was broken for the present clubhouse at South Adams and Crooks Streets, and a year later the building was dedicated. *(The club later moved to its present location at 3195 South Ridge Road.)*

Over a period of three quarters of a

century the Green Bay Elks have made great contributions to the community as well as to their order. A rundown of all the major activities with which the Elks have been identified is impossible, but a few still command attention across the years.

Minstrels a Highlight

One was the series of Elks Minstrels, only a fading memory now but highlights of the local entertainment season from 1910 until the eve of World War I. Another was the annual Christmas party for the poor kids of the city that eventually reached astronomical proportions.

It is not generally realized, but the popularity of bowling among the women of Green Bay can be directly attributed to the Elks. In the early days, when alleys were adjuncts of saloons and pool halls, bowling was virtually a forbidden sport to women.

The Elks changed that. Their own alleys, being located in a private clubhouse, could be used by women, and the first female bowlers in the city learned the game there.

The Balmy Christmas of 1877

When Santa Claus Used a Boat

January 3, 1970

Forty years ago the Green Bay weatherman dug into his records and came up with the information that in the first 30 years of the 20th Century Green Bay had known only three Christmas seasons without ice and snow. Had he wanted to excavate a little further he might have stumbled onto the fact that as early as 1877 Green Bay set a "green Christmas" record that has never been surpassed.

In 1877 Bayites celebrated Christmas and New Year's Day with excursion boat rides on the bay and up the Fox River to De Pere. They sniffed pansies growing in their gardens and waded across Washington Street, whose pavement was ankle deep in mud.

On Christmas Day the steamer Union (Capt. Thomas Hawley) made two runs to De Pere with comfortable boatloads of passengers plus a brass band. Not to be outdone, his rival Capt. John Denessen matched him with excursions up the river and out on the placid bay on his steamer Arrow.

The winter of 1877-78 didn't begin that way. Late November was more typical, with chilly days, some cold nights, cold rain and an occasional snow flurry. By Dec. 1 navigation had closed and all vessels remaining in port were battened down for the season.

Mildest since 1861

Thereafter, nothing went according to the almanac. Not since the winter of 1860-61 had Wisconsin experienced such a mild December.

Instead of snow, Northeastern Wisconsin got rain and more rain. There were occasional light snow flurries but none of the fall lasted, while any skin ice that appeared overnight on the river promptly disappeared next day.

On Dec. 15 Green Bay basked in sunshine, with the temperature zooming to 57 degrees. That was enough to bring the boating enthusiasts out of hibernation. Sailboats began to dot the river and bay, an enterprising tug showed up from Sturgeon Bay and the Fox River bridges had to be re-manned and opened again.

The 18th witnessed a boisterous electrical storm, followed by more rain and thick fog. Any hopes for a white Christmas were dashed on Christmas Eve when a driving rain pelted down most of the day.

Bright, Clear Christmas

It stopped during the night, however, and Christmas day dawned bright and clear. There wasn't a fleck of snow on the ground, shrubs all over town were budding, and as the thermometer rose to 44 degrees stories began to circulate of intrepid pansies blooming in private gardens.

None were pinpointed exactly but there seems to have been something to the rumor. Such stories would normally be hooted down, but both the Gazette and Advocate reported the phenomenon in apparent sincerity.

With the temperature balmy and the sun shining brightly in the afternoon, the Union and the Arrow got steam up, tooted their whistles and welcomed cheering crowds aboard. There is no record of how the news got around but Green Bay and Fort Howard were small towns, and such news traveled pretty fast.

Hawley Got the Jump

Hawley's Union got the jump on the Arrow when the captain hired the German Cornet Band to dispense music from the upper deck during the runs. Everybody apparently had a lot of fun.

The unprecedented weather continued all through Christmas week, during which the Arrow made regular trips to De Pere. These, however, were windfall commercial runs, not excursions.

Warnings went up on New Year's Eve which was the coldest day of the season to that point, although the thermometer still didn't get down to freezing. When New Year's Day turned out warm (although not quite as pleasant as Christmas), Hawley, father of Green Bay's long time police chief Tom Hawley, made another excursion trip to De Pere.

The novelty had worn off by that time, however. The crowd wasn't very big and Hawley made only one run.

That night the temperature dropped and the river finally froze over. The crew of the Union had to break ice to free her next morning so she could be moved back into winter quarters.

Short Freeze-Up

Even so, the freeze-up was short. Ice went out of the Fox early in February and the river never froze again.

Residents may have enjoyed the novelty of the unusual weather, but it was a mixed blessing. It may have been easy to move up and down the river but getting around on land became a real problem.

The unseasonable and recurring rains made bogs of the country roads and unpaved city streets. Farmers found it hard to get into town, and if it hadn't been Christmas time they might not have tried. There was some concern among merchants about the weather's effect on Christmas shopping, but as it turned out, business was as lively as ever.

Washington Street, the city's principal business artery and the only paved street in town, was a mess. Vehicles coming in off the sloppy streets and country roads dragged huge gobs of mud on their wheels and horses' hooves.

Ankle-Deep Goo

These clumps, dropped off on the cedar block pavement, were churned up by following vehicles and soon Washington Street was almost as bad as any unpaved road, except that it had a bottom. The sloppy, slippery goo was ankle deep.

Since traffic was unusually heavy, the city wasn't equipped to handle the situation. Everybody finally got together and had the slop shoveled into piles along the curbings, but the piles froze before they could be hauled away.

The weather played havoc with country travel. Visitors to the country reported the roads as bad as they had ever been. If it hadn't been for the Christmas season, Green Bay would probably have been buttoned up tight.

Loggers Suffered

Loggers suffered acutely as the mild weather threatened to turn an anticipated profitable winter into a flop. Since it became impossible to move heavily laden wagons over the bottomless forest roads, many logging camps were literally starved out and had to be temporarily abandoned.

Fortunately, the weather posed no problems for the railroads. Traffic continued on schedule, bringing the usual run of outside entertainment, news and visitors.

One of the most curiously awaited visitors was the famous suffragette, Susan B. Anthony. Miss Anthony spoke at Klaus Hall on Dec. 17 to a small crowd but one that was large enough to cover her expenses. She didn't convince any of the men in her audience that women were entitled to the vote or equal rights, but she was courteously received.

Plenty of Parties

People 'Sociable' 75 Years Ago

December 3, 1960

In addition to the theatrical schedule which gave 1885 society plenty of opportunity to turn out in its best duds and shiniest carriages, Green Bay also enjoyed a full social season. Public balls were much more common than in previous years, sports were gaining ground and as for small functions, the city was "sociable" happy.

The charming old custom of New Year's open house, a feature of Green Bay's social life since Henry Baird started it over half a century before, had practically been abandoned by 1885, no doubt much to the disgust of the gentlemen who had all the fun but to the great relief of the ladies who did all the work. There was, however, plenty of other social activity.

Klaus Hall was the scene of a number of colorful balls, and the Bay City Cadets, a junior version of the now defunct Light Guards, kept the military-social tradition alive with a series of dances and drill exhibitions.

Biggest affair of the year, as it was until 30 years ago, was the pre-Lenten Turner Masquerade. The ball had to buck a snowstorm, but it took more than a blizzard to keep people away from Turner Hall on masquerade night in those days.

Sociables Popular

Church functions were frequent and popular, those held in church halls being called "socials" while those in private homes were designated as "sociables." With hostesses wracking their brains for new gimmicks, almost anything could happen at a sociable.

There were ice cream, strawberry, watermelon, straw-hat and coffee-and-doughnut sociables, necktie parties and many other versions. The exceptionally active temperance societies gave pink teas and "dime entertainments."

Oyster suppers were also popular with just about everybody but the Brown County Medical Society. The doctors showed what they thought of oysters at their annual summer luncheon, where the centerpiece was a mass of oysters frozen in a block of clear ice, topped by a human skull.

Other activities were popular in the summer, particularly excursions down the bay to Red Banks, Marinette and Sturgeon Bay on the steamer John Denessen, the sidewheeler Keweenaw, and the tug Resolute. Over 425 people crowded the Keweenaw for a trip to Sturgeon Bay, while the Resolute frequently accommodated over 100 passengers at a time.

Summer Activities

The German Bathing Club held weekly outings and the Green Bay Bicycle Club was active. Such enthusiasts as Louis Bender, Joe LaCourt and William Delwitch thought nothing of 15 to 25 mile jaunts over the primitive roads of the day. Another club organized that year was the Waubun Yacht Club with John C. Neville as first commodore.

Two circuses played to large attendances during the summer. The celebrated Adam Forepaugh Circus put on a spectacular street parade and was so well policed by its own detectives that it set some sort of a record for circus day decorum when not a single arrest was made. Later the Bur Robbins Circus came to town.

Hunting and fishing were as fabulous as ever, although the day was past when deer could be chased down the main streets of the city in cutters. The Sportsmen's Club, as the Peaks Lake fraternity was known, still titillated the town's tea tables with its bachelor duck dinners and subsequent drinking bouts, although the absence of Algernon Sartoris robbed them of an earlier international tone.

The city had a professional baseball team called the Greys but it rated short newspaper space. The opening game, in which they nosed out Kaukauna, 7-6, with a ninth inning rally, was well covered and so was a trip to Marinette that was washed out when the entire Marinette team was hauled off the field and jugged for playing baseball on Sunday.

Much Indignation

The visit of a touring female ball team was greeted with considerable indignation. The scheduled game with the Greys was banned by the police but the teams finally squared off at Cormier Park, outside the city limits. The Greys clowned to a 9-7 decision.

Horse racing, particularly harness racing, was avidly followed, and many matches were run at the Fox River Driving Park in West De Pere, now the county fairgrounds. The county fair, under new management, was held there that year and was a huge success, largely because of the excellent racing program.

The big rage of the day was roller skating. The Armory Opera House *(on the north side of Pine Street between Adams and Jefferson)* was used for it, but early in the spring of 1885 plans were announced by S. W. Champion, W. C. Wheelock, E. J. Collette and F. E. Teetshorn for an elaborate rink on the southeast corner of Jefferson and Cherry Streets, unoccupied since the destruction of the old First National Hotel.

It was later decided to build on the northwest corner of Adams and Doty, diagonally across from the Holland *(now St. Willebrord's)* Church. The congregation blew up a storm and the Rev. Norbert Kersten, its pastor, petitioned the city council to stop it. He charged the rink with being an immoral enterprise and cited six divorces in Chicago, allegedly due to hanging around skating rinks.

Petition Refused

The council refused the petition, however, and construction began in March. The Champion Rink, as it was called, was an elaborate affair and one of the finest in the state, with cloak rooms, a ladies' sitting room and a seating capacity of nearly 400 in the gallery and around the 124 by 50-foot skating floor.

The grand opening on April 9 was a big success in spite of some trouble with the new gas lighting. The rink continued to pack in crowds for skating and for many professional exhibitions.

After the fall reopening a new game — roller polo — quickly caught on. A Green Bay team was organized, consisting of Arthurs as point; Basche and Brooks, rushers; Vandenberg, half-back; Peterson, cover, and Joe LaCourt as guard. Roller polo as played in 1885 was a rugged, freewheeling sport and the crowds loved it, especially after the local boys got hot enough to lick some of the best teams in the state.

Anybody who didn't like what Green Bay had to offer for entertainment didn't have to stick around. The New Orleans Exposition was on in the spring and many Bayites went down to see it for the special rail and steamboat round trip fare of $30.90.

Impending Anniversary

The Monday Shakespeare Club

January 10, 1970

Green Bay's oldest women's study club and one of the two oldest feminine organizations in the city reaches a significant milestone Monday. The Monday Shakespeare Club will celebrate the 70th anniversary of its founding.

Small, exclusive and specialized women's study groups were once a familiar part of the local social scene. Today there are only a handful, and the Monday Shakespeare Club outranks them all.

The only group still functioning that predates the Monday Shakespeare is the Green Bay Woman's Club, which dates from 1895. The now defunct Marquette Club lasted longer, attaining the venerable age of 75 before it expired, but the way the Shakespeareans are going they're a cinch to beat that record.

Began in 1900

The Monday Shakespeare Club dates its beginnings to January, 1900. It is proud of the fact that it has met on a weekly schedule ever since during the period from October to May.

It grew out of a small circle of friends who had been getting together informally. They included the Mmes. J. P. Annen, Edward Van den Braak, S. D. Hastings, Joseph P. Hoeffel and L. C. Reber.

Other charter members were the Mmes. D. F. Smith, E. B. Warren, George D. Nau, H. W. Gosselin, T. G. Kraege, W. E. Smith, Rowland Burdon and Bertha Calkins. Mrs. Nau, one of the prime movers in the formation of the group, was elected first president and served for three years.

There was already a Shakespeare study club in existence, the exclusive and haughty Shakespeare Club, which dated from 1877. Why another was felt necessary isn't known, but it is possible that one or more of the Monday group's founders had been unsuccessful in cracking the older circle and decided to form a club of their own.

Combined Activities

Like the Shakespeare Club, the Monday Shakespeares were and are a combination study and social group. Initially they confined their activities to a study of the plays of the Bard of Avon but after a few years branched out into opera, other dramatists, music, travel and even social and political problems of the day.

Unlike the woman who has a Size Seven foot but is so comfortable in Size Eight shoes she habitually wears Nines, the Monday Shakespeare Club title means exactly what it says. The club started out meeting on Mondays and has never changed.

The club was also active socially in its early years. It usually threw two or three parties a year, including one Christmas holiday dance, but abandoned that sort of thing years ago.

Began Shakespeare Gardens

Perhaps its most permanent contribution to the cultural atmosphere of the city are the Shakespeare Gardens at the corner of Shawano and Oakland Avenues. An adaptation of the formal Elizabethan gardens on the site of the old Shakespeare house in Stratford-on-Avon, England, the Green Bay plot behind the West Side branch of the Brown County Public Library*, was begun in 1930 by the late Mrs. Charles Smith, then a member of the club.

Patterned on a combination of formal English gardens of the Tudor period, the garden contains plants and flowers common to such plots as well as flowers frequently mentioned in Shakespeare's plays. Spotted through the beds are benches, a sun dial and a shelter house, given to the garden as memorials to deceased members.

The garden was maintained for over 20 years by the club itself. Since 1951, however, it has been kept up by the city park department as a semi-civic project.

Surprising Durability

The most surprising thing about the Monday Shakespeare Club has been its durability through the years. Scores of such groups which once flourished here, including the original Shakespeare Club, foundered on inability to find a formula for the infusion of new blood.

The Monday Shakespeare Club has solved the problem uniquely. When a vacancy occurs, the junior member has the right to nominate a replacement. In this way, younger members are brought in instead of contemporaries of the more senior members.

Through the years membership has varied from 15 to 20, never more than the latter figure. The current quota is 20 with four associate members. *(Active members today number 26 with eight associates.)*

Former Regulars

The club maintains three types of membership — regular, associate and honorary. To hold regular status a member must attend a given number of meetings each year and must entertain and present one program a year.

Associate members are former regulars who no longer wish to work on programs but who can entertain the club. Honoraries are aged members who are no longer able to do either. At present the club has no honorary members.

Oldest member in length of membership is Mrs. R. F. Gronzo, now an associate, who joined in 1926. Next is Mrs. Earl Fisk, a regular since 1935, followed by Mrs. A. B. Brightman, an associate, whose membership began in 1938.

In addition to Mrs. Fisk, present regular members are the Mmes. W. C. Buermann, E. N. Clough, Sandy Duket, John H. Evans, Glenn Evjue, Edith Fontera, David Fountain, William Harker, Marvin Houghton, Ernest E. Jones, Frank Kellerman, Walter Larsen, Gorden S. Meyrick, Crane Murphy, Herman Parks, Robert Raymakers, Milton Schwarting, Carl Thiele and Emil Zapfe. Associates are the Mmes. Brightman, Gronzo,

William Lance and C. E. Manthey.

The Bard Will Preside

Presiding over the festivities next Monday at the Grace Lutheran Church parlors will be an equally venerable bust of William Shakespeare. There is some question just now as to who is responsible for Will.

According to senior members of the Monday Shakespeare Club, the bust was a gift of the club to the Kellogg Public Library. There is, however, evidence that it was a gift of the original Shakespeare Club as early as 1902, shortly after the library was opened.

The bust caused library director Jerry Somers some uneasy hours last week. When the club asked for its loan to grace the anniversary, Somers couldn't find it and had to do some tall scrambling before it was located in the Neville Public Museum.

** The Fort Howard branch library at this site closed in 1980.*

Thrilling 1902 Premiere

'Brilliant' Audience Saw 'Lazarre'

March 28, 1964

Green Bay's long and checkered theatrical history has had its ups and downs. Local marquee lights never blazed more brightly, though, than the evening more than 60 years ago when the city celebrated its first and only premiere of a play starring one of the finest actors in the annals of the American stage.

The lights of Green Bay (Vic) Theater* did not gleam in vain that night of Sept. 8, 1902. What was described as one of the "most brilliant audiences in the history of northern Wisconsin" packed the now venerable house to cheer Otis Skinner in "Lazarre."

A five-act melodrama in the romantic vein of the turn of the century, "Lazarre" doesn't stand today as a monument to Skinner's long and illustrious career. Nevertheless, being based on the Lost Dauphin pretensions of Eleazer Williams, one-time Green Bay resident, the play had great historical interest here, and the descendants of some of Williams' former neighbors loved it.

"Lazarre" was a stage adaptation of the popular novel of the same name by Mary Hartwell Catherwood. Its title, supposedly, came from Williams' boyhood nickname among the Mohawk Indians.

Romantic Tear-Jerker

In her highly romantic tear-jerker, published in 1901, Mrs. Catherwood adopted the premise that Williams actually was the Lost Dauphin, tragic son of Louis XVI and Marie Antoinette who, but for the French Revolution, would have been King of France. Out of the mystery of the fate of the innocent boy and Williams' claims to his identity she built an adventurous and melancholy tale of royal intrigue, Indian loyalty, unrequited love and noble renunciation.

The book enjoyed a long vogue in northeastern Wisconsin and was being read in Green Bay as late as the mid-1920s. In fact, the Kellogg Public Library *(now Brown County Library/Nicolet Federated Library System)* still carries at least one copy on its fiction shelves.

"Lazarre" had stage possibilities for a romantic actor like Otis Skinner. With the aid of Aubrey Boucicault, a top "play doctor" of the time, he wrote his own adaptation and came up with a picturesque book which followed closely the plot of the novel, for his major vehicle of the 1902-3 season.

Clever Gimmick

Nobody remembers who concocted the idea of opening the show in Green Bay, but it was a clever publicity gimmick. Significant, of course, was the city's association with Williams more than half a century earlier.

Williams' old home, scene of the last act, was still standing in what is now Lost Dauphin State Park. *(The Town of Lawrence acquired the park from the state in 1997. The house is gone now but a historical marker remains.)* A few old timers had vague and fading recollections of the man, and you could still trigger an argument about whether he was or was not the Dauphin. *(DNA testing announced in April 2000 debunked the claim.)*

Skinner had also played Green Bay before and was very popular here. Furthermore, he didn't have to squeeze his new production onto a tanktown stage. The Green Bay Theater, only two years old, was one of the finest playhouses in Wisconsin.

Area in Tizzy

The announcement that Skinner's new play would be premiered here threw the area into a tizzy. The actor cleverly fostered the feeling by showing up during the summer on "research" trips, during which he presumably inspected the Williams cabin and soaked up local tradition by talking to area historians.

Interest began to peak a couple of weeks before the opening, particularly after the announcement that Mrs. Catherwood and her family were coming for the performance. Ticket orders poured in from all over the state. A Skinner premiere being an important theatrical event anywhere, critics checked in from cities throughout the Fox River Valley.

The demand for seats, even at $2.50 top, was unprecedented for a local attraction. By the time Skinner company and its carefully packed scenery and costumes arrived two days early only a handful of tickets remained. Theater manager John B. Arthurs announced he was holding all out of town orders until local residents were accommodated.

Society Out in Force

Valley society turned out in force for the performance, with parties present from Oshkosh, Appleton, Milwaukee and as far north as Sturgeon Bay. There were individual seat holders from Chicago and even Minneapolis.

Among the prominent local figures in the audience were A. M. Murphy, David W. Britten (*sic*), H. O. Fairchild, Dr. J. P. Lenfesty, W. E. Kellogg, George Rice, Dr. J. R. Minahan, Henry Rahr and J. P. Dousman of De Pere. Presumably in the house, although not mentioned in reports, were the A. C. Nevilles and the Misses Deborah and Sarah Martin, whose father, Morgan L. Martin, had once been Williams' lawyer.

Skinner hadn't spared the horses in mounting a lavish production. Costumes were rich and elaborate and so were the six sets, which ranged from a forest scene on the shore of Lake George to the Tuileries of Napoleon, a Russian palace and back to the Williams cabin at Little Rapids.

Scene Drew Raves

The Lake George scene was especially effective and drew raves from all the newspapers. So did the Paris scene, when Lazarre told off Napoleon in a third act climax which raised such a storm of applause that Skinner had to make a curtain speech, in which he spoke of the appropriateness of opening in Green Bay and ended by introducing authoress Catherwood from her box.

Judging from extant reviews the production was pretty much a one-man vehicle for Skinner, who was onstage most of the evening. A sound showman, he was not afraid to take his chances with competition and had surrounded himself with a strong supporting cast that included his wife, Maud Durbin, in the principal feminine role.

Critics Enthusiastic

Critics were generally enthusiastic about the quality of Skinner's portrayal of Williams, especially his graceful and dignified bearing, his carefully modulated voice and the manner in which he built the role to a climax. A lone dissenter was S. Palmer Morse of the Milwaukee Sentinel, who qualified an otherwise favorable review with the opinion that the role was not up to Skinner's stature.

Morse also felt the book needed some pruning and that action moved somewhat ponderously. In other words, "Lazarre" was a good, colorful melodrama, elaborately staged and acted by a strong company headed by a great actor but still a lightweight story.

One of the most interesting and — presumably — most interested spectators was Mrs. Josephine Phillips, Williams' adopted daughter. Either the newsmen present neglected to ask her or she refused to talk; unfortunately, her opinion of the play was not recorded.

Another colorful party was a group of Oneida Indian children chaperoned by the Rev. F. W. Merrill, Williams' missionary successor several times removed. They took it all in with such deadpan calm nobody could tell what they thought of the show.

In contrast to other newspapers covering the event, the Green Bay Gazette was positively blasé about the whole thing. "Lazarre" rated merely a couple of short advance stories and the review was not only guarded but buried in the back pages.

The Elks Minstrels a few days earlier had received much greater coverage. The Elks also ran a bigger ad.

** Located at 217 E. Walnut Street, the Vic later evolved to become City Center Theatre; today the site houses a night club and an unrelated business.*

Historic 'Messiah' Performances

Old Choral Society Outstanding

January 25, 1964

Green Bay's musical horizons have been expanded greatly in the past half century. The city has developed its own community symphony orchestra and between a variety of organizations has welcomed (not always effusively) many of the great artists of the day, from Fritz Kreisler to Ernestine Schumann-Heink and Birgit Nilsson.

In one category, however, the city has failed to keep pace with what was once a rich heritage-community choral singing. A few small and dedicated groups have accomplished some fine things under discouraging handicaps but it has been a long time since the community has boasted an organization like the old Green Bay Choral Society of the turn of the century.*

The ranks of the society's survivors are thinning now, and so are those who heard it perform. Those who remember, however, insist that Green Bay has not since heard anything to compare with the magnificent performances of Handel's "The Messiah" put on by the Choral Society between 1905 and 1910.

The Green Bay Choral Society was formed in the fall of 1903. Its founder, sparkplug and director through most of its existence was a "Professor" William Boeppler (most professional musicians were called "professor" in those days) of Chicago, who had wandered into town and sold the idea of a community chorus with himself as director — for a fee, naturally.

Probable Free Lancer

Nobody recalls why Boeppler picked Green Bay. Best guess is that he was a free lancer who set up similar choruses in several cities and earned a living by commuting from one to another on a regular schedule to direct rehearsals and an occasional public concert.

A thoroughly trained and competent musician, Boeppler, as his name implies, was German, very serious about his work and a perfectionist. He was something of a tyrant but he got results and people liked and respected his sincerity and ability.

Ruined by Overstrain

Survivors of the society remember him as a stocky man of medium height with a bristling grey moustache, a singing voice like a crow and a murderous approach to the English language. The latter was a phoney though. When he wished, which wasn't often, he could speak excellent English but cultivated the vaudeville accent as part of his "stock in trade," as he called it.

According to his own account he had been a famous boy soprano in Europe whose voice had been ruined by overstrain. As a grown man he couldn't carry a tune in a bass fiddle but when he got worked up during a rehearsal would forget the fact. Listening to him mangle the soprano part in the "Alleluia" Chorus during a workout often helped lighten the burden of his choristers, whom he drove relentlessly.

Boeppler commuted between Green Bay and Chicago, conducting weekly rehearsals and planning elaborate concerts for which his meticulously trained and disciplined ensemble eventually became noted. He was very proud of the chorus, although he rarely let them know it, and lavished on it his enthusiasm and skill as a director.

He remained as its leader until 1910 when he became director of the Milwaukee conservatory of music. He ran the latter with distinction until his death.

Got Chorus Ready

After two years of careful training and a number of successful public appearances, Boeppler figured his group was ready for bigger things. In the fall of 1905 he came up with the scheme of presenting a full scale performance of "The Messiah" during the Christmas season.

It would be the first performance of "The Messiah" in Wisconsin north of Milwaukee. As such it was to be no pipsqueak, amateur job but a real spectacular with huge chorus, imported soloists and a 30-piece orchestra.

The chorus, expanded to 150 voices, worked for five months on the score, professional soloists were engaged and an orchestra hired consisting of carefully selected players from Chicago, Milwaukee and Green Bay. Expenses were budgeted at $800 (actually, it cost closer to $1,000), roughly comparable to an outlay of between $3,000 and $4,000 today *(1964)*.

Seven Selected

The chorus was made up entirely of area talent but the orchestra presented problems. Boeppler finally selected seven Green Bay players he considered up to his exacting standards and imported the rest.

Local musicians were Miss Pearl Brice and Louis Vilim, first violins; John Andre, second violin; Frank Vilim, viola; W. S. Parker, string bass; Jules Grognet, trumpet, and Mike Heynen, clarinet. The others were personally chosen from the Theodore Thomas Orchestra (today's Chicago Symphony) of Chicago and the Milwaukee Bach Orchestra.

Vocal soloists were Miss Grace Elliot Dudley of Chicago, one of the leading oratorio sopranos of the middle west; Miss Katherine Clarke, Milwaukee contralto, and a pair of male singers from New York. The latter were tenor Edward Strong and Frederic Martin, bass.

Theater Packed

At $1.50 a ticket across the board, the then new Green Bay Theater (now the Vic, *then at 217 E. Walnut Street, later, City Center Theatre and currently a night club and an unrelated business)* was packed for the performance on the night of Dec. 19, 1905. George L. North, who reviewed the historic event somewhat breathlessly for the Gazette, called it the most "brilliant" audience the theater had enjoyed since its opening night in 1900.

Although the out-of-town participants only arrived that morning, in time for a single complete rehearsal, everybody outdid themselves that night. North wrote — and there is no reason to doubt his judgment — that the performance was the greatest musical event Green Bay had ever heard. It was, undoubtedly, a magnificent "Messiah."

Not the least satisfying aspect of the evening was a handsome payoff on the gamble. The society netted a profit of $116, and everybody was so thrilled it was decided to make "The Messiah" an annual event.

The 1906 repeat was another resounding artistic and financial success, matched the following night in Appleton. Others followed in 1907 and 1909. No production was attempted in 1908.

1907 Tops

The 1907 performance was, by general admission, the finest of the series. The chorus, now thoroughly experienced and in full command of the music, was expanded to 160 and for the first time local soloists took part.

Contralto Helen Jane Waldo and tenor Harry Annen interrupted local studies in New York to come home for the event. Miss Shanna Cumming of Chicago was a hit in the soprano role and basso Martin was back for the third time. The orchestra was pretty much the same Chicago-Milwaukee-Green Bay ensemble.

The 1909 revival was another smashing box office success but the chorus had shrunk to 100 and the handwriting was on the wall. When the season of 1910 came around Boeppler was gone, and the Choral Society quietly folded after a brilliant existence of seven years.

** Various choral groups have picked up the slack in recent years-The Dudley Birder Chorale and Michael Rosewall's Green Bay Community Choir, as well as other St. Norbert College and UW-GB choirs.*

Venerable Tradition

How the Charity Ball Began

December 23, 1967

The Green Bay Service League is throwing its 34th annual Charity Ball tonight.

Some of the most active workers in the year's premier social whing were still in three-cornered pants when their mothers began the custom in 1934 but for the past three and a half decades the League has been carrying on a tradition much older than that. Actually, the Charity Ball has been the city's top social event for the better part of 60 years.

The original Charity Ball was held in old Turner Hall (which was razed about the time the present ball got under way) during Christmas week in 1910. A highly successful venture of a group called the Sewing Club, the ball was an annual event thereafter until 1921, with the only break the 1918 war year.

Those earlier balls were, like their modern counterparts, the big whing of the Christmas season. At one time they rated coverage as front page news in both the Press-Gazette and its predecessor, the old Green Bay Gazette.

Pre-War Organization

The sponsoring Sewing Club was a pre-World War I organization of about 40 of the city's leading debutantes. Essentially, it was a fore-runner of the Service League, with the girls-anxious to be more than social butterflies-working just like their granddaughters in the League.

Nobody remembers exactly how or where the club got the idea of putting on a fund-raising dance for charity. Probably, that seemed the easiest way of building up a kitty, and it was unusually effective. Over the years the annual events raised more than $6,000 for the Associated Charities.

Putting on a Charity Ball, as Service League veterans can testify, isn't as easy as it may seem, and it wasn't any simpler half a century ago. The girls work-and worked-like *(busy bees)* for months, but they got results.

Routine Publicity

The first Charity Ball, under the general chairmanship of Miss Helen Glynn, received only routine publicity in the single column that then passed for society coverage in the Gazette. By 1912, however, it had boiled over onto the front page and stayed there through 1917.

The 1913 ball, of which Emily Murphy was chairman, got almost sensational treatment when its traditional dignity was overwhelmed by the wave of new dance fads then sweeping the country. Before the night was over — sometime around 3 a.m. – Turner Hall was jumping to a series of tangos, hesitation waltzes, castle walks and other dances either brought home by the college crowd or deliberately insinuated into the program by the Sewing Club itself.

It was quite a switch from the 1912 ball, whose big promotion number was a grand march led by Emily with Edward Bach, Arleen Joannes and Milton Larsen, Helen Glynn and Eugene O'Keefe, and Eleanor Washburn and Will Elmore. Everybody was fox-trotting that season, so a number of quadrilles on the program were pointedly sabotaged.

Moved to Armory

By 1916 the crowds were overtaxing Turner Hall. When the old Hagemeister Park pavilion at the east end of Cherry Street was converted into a National Guard armory that year the ball was moved out there.

Despite special street cars to the end of the Walnut Street line and special parking arrangements for some of the city's few automobiles, the armory was too far out. In 1917 the Charity Ball was back at the old stand.

That 1917 affair provided the Sewing Club with one of the few embarrassing moments in its history.

Because it was a war year, the club decided the dance would be informal. When the hostesses arrived that night, however, they discovered they were the only ones in the place wearing short dresses. Everybody else showed up dressed to the teeth as usual.

Suspended in 1918

The war caused suspension of the ball in 1918, but it was revived in 1919. However, a number of factors were at work to take the edge off the affair.

Most of the Sewing Club members were married by now and many had moved out of town. Those remaining had growing families and were finding it increasingly harder to devote the time necessary to the ball. Also, there were more and more dancing parties encroaching on the Thanksgiving and Christmas holiday periods, and attendance at the Charity Ball was slipping.

The 1920 and 1921 balls were not as successful as their predecessors. Even the 1921 spectacle of Harold Joannes, Jack Hundley and the Mmes. Robert L. Cowles and L. H. Barkhausen jiving up a mixed quartet performance of "Mellow Cello" couldn't ignite the old spark.

Quietly Dropped

There was some talk of going ahead in 1922 but the Sewing Club couldn't generate the necessary enthusiasm. The Charity Ball was regretfully and quietly dropped after a colorful history of 12 years.

Mrs. Cowles, incidentally, was general chairman of more Charity Balls than anybody else. She headed four — in 1912, 1913, 1920 and 1921 — while Helen Glynn directed three (1910, 1911 and 1914).

Other chairmen were Mrs. Fred Hurlbut (1915), Mrs. Perry Wagner (1916), Mrs. Joseph Horner (1917) and Mrs. A. J. McCarey (1919). The late Mrs. Horner, then Lorraine Weise, was unable to attend her own ball and Amanda Schuette stepped in as a last minute substitute.

Turner Hall and Armory

From 1910 through 1915 the balls were held in Turner Hall, on the northwest corner of Monroe Avenue and Walnut Street. It shifted to the armory in 1916, back to Turner Hall in 1917 and then ran out the string in the armory.

With one exception, too, the orchestra was always the same. Except for 1915, when the Green Bay Concert Band under Dennison Wheelock furnished the music, dancers whirled and dipped to the tunes of the area's top "name band" of the period, Frank Vandenberg's "full orchestra." A couple of times Frank even augmented his ensemble with a harp and went in for dreamy "harp waltzes."

For more than a decade after 1921 the Charity Ball was only a fading memory. Then, in 1934, the recently organized Service League inaugurated a Christmas ball to raise funds for its welfare projects. It adopted the old title of "Charity Ball" in 1939.

Birth of a Symphony Orchestra

October 26, 1968

Tomorrow night in West High auditorium the Green Bay Symphony Orchestra is launching its 22nd season. It is also passing another milestone in the musical history of the community — 55 years of home grown symphonic music in the city.

Although the present symphony is now approaching a quarter century of existence, its beginnings can be traced back to 1912-14 when the first ensemble of the name was born. In the fall of 1913, under the leadership of the late Alex Enna, an orchestra of nearly 40 pieces was organized which gave its first public concert at the Orpheum Theater the evening of March 4, 1914.

Today's symphony, of course, does not claim direct and unbroken descent. There have been, in the intervening 55 years, at least three separate organizations with two good sized breaks in continuity. But there has always been an overlapping of personnel and up until a few years ago at least two members of the present orchestra also played in the first.

Back to 1850s

The city's musical history, however, dates even further back. As early as the 1850s, with the influx of German immigration into Wisconsin and the subsequent organization of the Turners and other Germanic clubs, there was an upsurge of interest in choral singing and band music — in fact, Green Bay has enjoyed good wind band performances for more than 100 years.

In the 1870s and early 1880s, under the leadership of Mrs. Mather Kimball, a Philharmonic Society was formed that gave elaborate public concerts for several years. Since the city had few string players, these were largely vocal events, although they sometimes included excerpts from popular operas.

By 1913, however, the supply of musicians was becoming more varied. There were still shortages, of course — the first symphony contained only one cello, a single oboe and but one string bass.

Two Young Arrivals

Organization of Green Bay's first community symphonic ensemble was preceded by the almost simultaneous arrival of two young men in town who were destined to have a long and continuous impact on the city's musical life. Walter E. (*L.*) Larsen and Alex Enna both came here from Marinette in 1913, and for years thereafter bucked each other energetically as operators of rival music schools — the Larsen Conservatory and the Enna School of Music.

To Enna, a native of Denmark and a fine singer, goes the honor of organizing the original Green Bay Symphony Orchestra. Formed late in 1913 from a 16-player nucleus, the ensemble of nearly 40 pieces made its public debut the following March.

Larsen occupied the concertmaster's chair with Otto Kaap as tympanist and the late Ernest Stiller playing viola. Stiller continued to play with the orchestra's successors almost to the day of his death, while Kaap, who dropped out after the first year, returned decades later to the present orchestra and continued to play until three years ago.

Larsen Takes Over

A highly successful opening concert was followed by several more that first season. During the off-season, however, there was a reorganization in which Enna stepped out and Larsen took over the podium. He held it until the orchestra disbanded about 1921.

Since there weren't enough local players to satisfy his exacting standards, Larsen annually beefed up his ensemble for concerts by bringing in players from the Chicago Symphony. Only one or two programs a year were given at the Orpheum Theater, always big social as well as musical events.

Bringing in a flock of outside pros was expensive, and with dwindling interest and box office receipts the orchestra couldn't crack the nut. After about seven years the project collapsed, although Larsen and J. I. Williams made an unsuccessful attempt to revive it.

Taste Buds Opening

The city had developed a taste for symphonic music, however, and the existence of two excellent music schools whetted the appetite. A number of local string players kept their personal interest alive by getting together for informal sessions for their own amusement. Eventually they became the nucleus of a second orchestra, the pre-World War II Polyphonia Society.

In 1929 Ludolph Arens, a member of the Lawrence College Conservatory faculty, got wind of their activities and took charge. Shortly he had them organized into a combination choral-orchestral group which lasted until 1942.

Although the Polyphonia Society presented many combined events, emphasis was on the orchestra. At full strength it numbered about 40 players. Concerts were given in various churches, in which regular features were performances of works by Mrs. A. J. (Eugenia) Goedjen, orchestrated by Arens. Some of the latter's own music was also presented.

Scuttled by War

The Polyphonia was a solid, popular and successful venture but World War II scuttled it. Many members went into service, replacements were unavailable, and in 1942 it reluctantly disbanded for the duration.

Arens died before things had settled down, and it remained for Herman Daumler to take up the torch. Concertmaster for most of the Polyphonia's existence, he recruited 16 string players in the fall of 1946 and formed a chamber music ensemble. The Green Bay Symphonette made its bow at Whitney School auditorium in November, 1946.

The success of the Symphonette was immediate. By the following season it had expanded into a small chamber orchestra about the size of its predecessor through the addition of percussion, woodwinds and brass. Many of its members were veterans of the old Polyphonia.

Death a Blow

By 1952 the Symphonette was a balanced ensemble of 52 pieces and a going concern when it suffered an unexpected blow in the sudden death of Daumler. Concertmaster Ralph Holter picked up the fallen baton and swung it until two years ago.

With symphonic size and balance, the orchestra had outgrown its name, originally adopted to describe a chamber music group. In 1960 there was a reorganization and the title of Green Bay Symphony Orchestra was reborn, nearly half a century after it was initially used.

In 1966, the Symphony again ran into the familiar obstacles of declining interest and funds. There was another reorganization, the decision was made to engage a full time, professional conductor, and Oleg Kovalenko was chosen to lead the ensemble out of the wilderness. Today the Green Bay Symphony is larger and better than it has ever been.

Deserted and Forlorn

Woman's Club Stirs Memories

December 1, 1962

The historic Green Bay Woman's Club building *(at 345 South Adams Street),* once so dignified and alive with activity, is a dilapidated derelict these days. About to be sold, the century-old structure on South Adams Street has been stripped of its furnishings and stands empty, forlorn and lonely.

It wasn't always thus. Forty years ago, when it was a shiny new possession of the Woman's Club, the old Morrow home was something to be proud of, the scene of many important civic and social events.

Whatever its fate — present indications are that the original portion will be restored — the auditorium is doomed. Added to the building after the club acquired it, the hall has outlived its usefulness and has become such a safety hazard it will have to be removed.

The passing of the auditorium will pull many a nostalgic heartstring. For nearly four decades the little auditorium was the heart of the building, whose pleasant memories will linger long after it is gone. At least three generations have cause to remember.

Built by Pioneer

Built by an eccentric Green Bay pioneer, Elisha Morrow, in 1856, the house was acquired by the Woman's Club as a clubhouse in 1920. Before it was purchased from Morrow's daughter Helen, however, the building touched off one of the most bitter fights in the history of the organization, a donnybrook that threatened to blow the club wide open.

When the club was forced to vacate the old county office building on Walnut Street, its headquarters from 1912 to 1920, the choice of a new home quickly narrowed to two sites. One was the Morrow property and the other the old Weise mansion which stood north of the *(former)* public library, on the present site of the WBAY building.

Both had strong support, and the argument eventually drifted into another battle between two factions which periodically split the city in those days. Leaders of both were strong-willed, aggressive women, and the showdown promised to be a dandy.

It was finally settled in a tense, animosity-loaded general session that is still regarded with awe by survivors. The Morrow house won, but only after the supporters of the Weise home walked out of the meeting and left the field to the opposition, a tactical error that blocked later efforts to set the decision aside.

Girls Closed Ranks

Once the choice had been made and tempers simmered down, however, the girls closed ranks to make the new clubhouse a model. The home was completely renovated and the auditorium added. When the clubhouse was ready for occupancy in the fall of 1921, everybody was proud of it.

The auditorium, originally intended for club meetings, soon became a civic and social center. Surprisingly as it may seem today, it was practically the only place of its kind in the city.

At once the hall began to fill a need. Shortly it was being used for numerous affairs that probably hadn't been contemplated when it was built-large public and private receptions, teas, dances and meetings of all sorts, provided they met the exacting standards of the club.

Social organizations like the Neighborly Club began to hold their winter dancing parties there. Throughout the 1920s the clubhouse was the scene of many such affairs, notably those for returning college students and high school teenagers during the Thanksgiving, Christmas and Easter vacations.

Proper but Fun

These were always very proper but thoroughly enjoyable. The clubhouse was dignified without being stuffy and youngsters liked to go there. The kids may have raised a little hell elsewhere, but they behaved themselves at the Woman's Club. A whole generation of Green Bayites, most of them grandparents now, will remember them with nostalgia.

The high-ceilinged parlors were pleasant for resting between dances, the narrow hallways ideal for whispered conversations and the tiny balcony overlooking the dance floor a cozy place, especially during the "moonlight" waltzes which used to be so popular. Many a youthful romance got a major lift in that balcony, and some of them are still glowing.

The clubhouse was also a great place for homing collegians to ruffle their plumage. Such capers could backfire, though, as one cocky college freshman discovered when he came home for Christmas flourishing a brand new pipe.

He had no intention of smoking it, but some of his friends, probably jealous of the swath he was cutting among the girls, maneuvered him into a corner where he had to light up or chicken out. He accepted the challenge (what else could he do?) with near disastrous results.

I haven't really enjoyed smoking a pipe since.

'Twilight Musicales'

Here, too, during the early 1920s were held a series of winter "Twilight Musicales" on Sunday afternoons under the direction of the late Miss Janet Merrill. Local and area musicians were recruited for these soirees which, if the Press-Gazette society editor can be believed, were always sensational.

Actually, they were pretty good. With the Larsen Conservatory, LeBaron Austin and Prof. Alex Enna active in those days, the city had a large corps of well trained musicians who put on very fine programs.

Among the remembered performers were the old Larsen Trio, the Fulinwider Quartet from Appleton, a promising teenage violinist named

Julius Vieaux who really could play a fiddle, and a pretty blonde cornetist with long curls named Bernice Lee. Pianists included the Mmes. W. O. Bielke, John Whitney, Walter Larsen and Miss Lucille Meusel, a very fine pianist before she discovered she had a voice that would carry her through a long and successful operatic career.

Little Theater Active

The auditorium was also headquarters for the old Little Theater, forerunner of the present Community Theater. The hall's tiny stage was the setting for a long line of one-act plays, some of them written by the group's own playwriting wing and in many of which so many current civic and social leaders acted that a roster of them would fill half this column.

Many of those unpretentious productions were outstanding. One that still looms memorably across nearly four decades was an outstanding performance by the late Mrs. George Ellis in "The Old Lady Shows her Medals."

But time caught up with the old hall. Bigger ones were needed and they came — the Columbus Community Club, the Hotel Northland with its Crystal Ballroom, and high school gyms and auditoriums. By the mid-1930s the Woman's Club auditorium had served its purpose, and the lights, the music and the youthful laughter died away. *(The house has been restored and is used now as commercial office space.)*

Grandpa Wouldn't Trade Shows

When 'Pickles' Packed the House

March 11, 1967

When Premontre's big, splashy version of "The Music Man" opened Friday night at least one first-nighter had some trouble keeping his mind on the stage. The faint, half-forgotten aroma of pickles kept intruding.

Memory kept slipping back 40 years to another high school first night-to June 7, 1926, when the East High class of 1926 presented "Pickles" as its senior production in the then brand new Columbus Community Club auditorium. "Pickles" was no "Music Man," but its cast wouldn't trade shows.

"Pickles" was the first musical comedy (actually, it was a Victor Herbert type operetta without the mythical royalty and fancy uniforms) East High had attempted in many years, the most elaborate high school production in the city up to that time and a whale of a gamble. It also turned out to be a spectacular success, but none of the aging members of the cast can tell you why.

Written specifically for high school production, "Pickles" had no Broadway or movie reputation. The show's format followed the prevailing musical comedy style of its time — picturesque scenery, a series of tuneful songs and dances only nominally related to the action, and a fluffy, romantic plot to tie them together.

Fluffy, Romantic Plot

The story, minus Balkan royalty but crawling with colorful gypsies, was straight out of Lower Slobovia, with assists from Franz Lahar and Herbert. Set in the courtyard of a "Vienese" inn and a nearby gypsy camp, it was all about a party of tourists and a band of gypsies.

Leading roles were those of an American pickle salesman, a beautiful gypsy girl who turned out to be the long lost daughter of a wealthy and titled English dowager, and a sinister gypsy "king," who had kidnapped her years before. Naturally, the dowager recovered her daughter, who promptly picked off the pickle peddler.

Curtain, with the high stepping chorus and cast belting out the show's theme song — not inconsistently about pickles.

Lois Schilling was originally cast as the ravishing gypsy. Ten days before the performance, however, she was taken ill and Eleanor Heicher was drafted from the chorus.

Came through Magnificently

Eleanor came through magnificently to earn a solid success. It was tough on her and everybody else but the leading man, who had been carrying a torch for her all through high school, only to have it doused regularly by Bud Drace. He loved every minute of the extra rehearsals, especially since Drace, a member of the chorus, had to stand helplessly by and watch him make time.

Lois finally got to sing some of her songs, though. Twenty-five years later, when scenes from "Pickles" were revived at a class reunion, she assumed her original role while Leon Gerlach (who had shared bit parts with Abe Alk) pinch hit for the absent hero.

The "heavy" was played by Gordon Maes, something of a switch for the suave haberdasher, the reigning matinee idol of East High following his resounding success as the hero of "The Charm School" the year before. Gordon's earlier leading lady, Dorothy Howlett, was the soubrette of "Pickles," carrying on a secondary love affair with Clud Sargent only a degree or two less torrid than their off-stage romance.

Third Romance

A third romance involved Euleta Webb as the gypsy girl's mother and George Burridge as Dorothy's father and the leading man's boss. Bob Kaftan played an oily innkeeper whose gemutlichkeit concealed his connivance with the gypsy king and the police chief (Gerald Carpiaux) to fleece his unsuspecting guests.

Comedy standouts were Harold Pfotenhauer and Jonathan Adams as a pair of inept Keystone Kops, Alp style. Harold and Johnny had a ball, practically stopping the show every time they stuck their dead pans on stage. Mildred Aronin rounded out the speaking cast as an imposter the Kaftan-Carpiaux-Maes trio tried to palm off as the missing daughter.

In addition, there was a singing-dancing chorus of about 25 (among them Max Murphy, Marty Burke, Burton Ashley, Fred Burrall, Brick Dolan, Maxine Brostrom, Violet Schefe and Verda Cradek), trained by Geraldine Reis and Anita Klaus, who worked out the dance routines. Ernest C. Moore, Green Bay's "Music Man" of the 1920s, assembled a 24-piece pit orchestra, although he needed help from West High.

Putting "Pickles" together was trickier than anybody had counted on. Since the Columbus Club wasn't available until a few days before the show, everything was done piecemeal (nobody seems to have thought of using the gym).

When the whole company finally got together on the Columbus Club stage, the youthful cast had the shock of its life. The orchestra and chorus couldn't get within a city block of each other on cue, the principals were equally befuddled, and the rehearsal staggered along to an obbligato of hammering from Charlie Byrnes' stage hands putting the sets together.

The show was set for Monday night and the first full stage rehearsal was held on Saturday. After stumbling around most of the day the cast hadn't managed to get into the second act by the time director Henrietta Ley called a halt until Sunday.

When Sunday's rehearsal was even worse, she scheduled a desperation workout for Monday morning. That was a shambles, too, and when Etta quietly sent everybody home at 2 p.m. to get what rest they could before curtain time her calmness barely concealed the fact that she was a hairline candidate for suicide.

Makings of a Dog

At this point the Class of 1926 had the makings of the mangiest dog in East High's history. Faced with a sold out house — the audience of 2,000 was the largest ever to see a high school show in Green Bay to that time and may still hold the single performance record —"Pickles" had never enjoyed a complete run through and the opening number was the biggest turkey in the barnyard.

So what happened? The curtain went up that night, the chorus pranced out, hit that first number smack on the nose and "Pickles" took off like a Gemini rocket. The final curtain fell on a smashing success.

The leading man, a tall, slim youngster (Would you believe 140 pounds and a mop of thick black hair?) hasn't figured out yet how it happened. All he recalls is that he got through somehow, although his voice was pretty wobbly on the high notes. As for his dancing, you'll have to ask Verna Clabots (she was Verna Mannebach then).

August 9, 1934

F.D.R. Climaxed Tercentennial

August 8, 1959

Aug. 9, 1934 — 25 years ago tomorrow — was one of those still, brassy days that seem even hotter than they are. A broiling sun beat down out of a clear sky, its heat unrelieved by the slightest breeze. Very early it was obviously going to be a scorcher.

Yet from the earliest daylight people converged on the city from every direction. Even before they arrived it was already so crowded that latecomers of the day before had spent the night cruising the streets in automobiles or simply pulled over to the curbs and snatched what sleep they could.

Aug. 9, 1934 was a big day in Green Bay's history. Franklin Delano Roosevelt, President of the United States, was coming to climax the colorful Tercentennial celebration. Although his visit was not going to be much more than a whistle stop everybody for miles around wanted to be in on it.

The sun, the temperature and the size of the multitude rose steadily together. By 8 a.m. the streets were choked by the greatest assembly the city had ever seen — more than 60,000 people packed behind ropes along the route to the Tercentennial grounds at Bay Beach — with additional thousands milling around the North Western station and at the beach.

That is, they would have been milling if it hadn't been so hot. Instead they sweltered quietly under hastily contrived sunbonnets made of newspapers while the tension of waiting built up.

Right on the stroke of eight the 10-car presidential special slid into the yards and halted with the President's observation car opposite the station platform. A crowd of about 6,500, kept at a distance by a strong guard, set up a welcoming shout, punctuated by a 21-gun salute from Battery B and the City Concert Band under Prof. Mike Heynen playing "Hail to the Chief."

Although the crowd had been waiting for hours, its patience was due for additional strain. For almost another hour nothing happened. Nobody left or entered the car, whose windows remained tightly curtained. A few minutes before nine, however, everybody perked up as a handful of political figures were allowed to go aboard.

Then at exactly 9 o'clock, the back door opened and F. D. R. appeared on the rear platform on the arm of his son, John. He was dressed in one of his famous white seersucker suits and carried a wide-brimmed Panama hat which he waved at the cheering throng before disembarking to enter an open touring car waiting at the steps.

Still Dynamic Man

He appeared tired after a month-long trip to Hawaii via the Panama Canal and a long rail journey back across country from the West Coast but he was far from the haggard, careworn figure of the last stages of World War II. He had been in office only 17 months, the crushing burdens of the war years were far in the future, and he was still the handsome, dynamic man whose leadership and personality had electrified the nation at his inauguration.

Preceded by a phalanx of motorcycle police, many "on loan" from other Fox River Valley cities, the 25-car cavalcade swung over to Broadway, south to Walnut and across the bridge, then down Washington and out Main and Irwin to the beach. The convoy sped through flag-bedecked streets jammed with wildly cheering people and lined by National Guard troops.

It swept along at a good clip but not too fast to prevent everyone from getting a good look at Roosevelt, who acknowledged the constant applause by smiling and waving. There was no way to count the crowd lining the route, but police estimated it at about 60,000.

Meanwhile, at the beach another multitude had been gathering since daybreak. When the presidential party entered the grounds a tumultuous roar went up from more than 35,000, many of whom had been standing in the blistering sun for hours. The cheers increased in volume as the President mounted the speaker's stand in front of the pavilion and continued until he raised his hands for silence.

Typical Pot Boiler

His speech had been heralded as a major policy statement for the mid-term congressional campaign, but the 30-minute talk reads tamely today across years punctuated by such eloquence as his "Day That Will Live in Infamy" and other war messages. It was a typical Roosevelt pot-boiler in which he pledged expansion of the New Deal and defied its critics. While he was speaking the White House announced an important policy decision but he never mentioned it.

The speech concluded, the crowd dispersed quickly and Roosevelt returned to his car, pausing just long enough in the pavilion to accept an Indian headdress. At this point the only hitch of the day developed.

Under the impression that Mrs. Roosevelt was coming too, local society women had arranged an elaborate reception for her in the second floor "Governor's Room." It had been beautifully set and the girls, dressed to the teeth, were out in force.

Roosevelt didn't have time to see it and couldn't have negotiated the stairs in any event, but he made amends by inviting the committee to his car where he greeted each one personally. The ladies had to be satisfied with an introduction, a brief handshake and a jolt of the great FDR charm, but the reception was not a complete loss. After he left everybody trooped upstairs and had their party anyway, with Mrs. Schmiedeman (*sic*), the governor's wife, acting as Eleanor's stand-in.

Blackout Came Down

Arriving back at the railroad station, Roosevelt paused briefly on the rear observation platform to receive a few gifts and greet some more privileged individuals, including 11-year-old Mary Vogue, whom he had met at his nominating convention at Chicago in 1932. Then he disappeared inside and the blackout came down again.

For another half hour nothing happened, there was no perceptible movement in the car and nobody got in. Just before departure time a number of area politicians filed in to pay their parting respects.

At 11 o'clock the train began to move, and as the wilted band struck up another tune Roosevelt again appeared on the platform to wave goodbye. He was still there, smiling broadly and waving cheerfully as the train pulled out of sight.

The entire visit had lasted only three hours but it had been exciting and satisfying to the 100,000 people who had seen, heard and cheered the President. Everything had gone off like clockwork, so successfully that the famed White House security chief, Col. E. W. Starling, was most complimentary. He had been less than diplomatic at Bay Beach, however, to one prominent dowager who was trying to hold up the departure from the grounds.

There had been one exceptionally remarkable feature about the visit.

Although everybody knew vaguely that Roosevelt was a polio victim, a nation-wide and voluntary censorship had suppressed all details of his case. It would be a number of years before the veil was removed and people took his condition for granted.

In the next two days the Press-Gazette devoted a good 25 columns of type to describe every detail of the event but one. Not by a single word was the slightest hint or reference made to the fact that FDR couldn't walk.

Chapter Seven

Sites and Landmarks: Some Saved; Some Gone

'Must See' Vacation Sites

City's Historic Buildings Open

May 7, 1960

Three of Green Bay's — and Wisconsin's — most important historic buildings opened for another season last weekend. From now until early November the quaint Roy-Porlier-Tank Cottage, Fort Howard Hospital-Museum and stately Cotton House will welcome interested visitors from all parts of the United States.

All summer the flow will continue — children's groups, women's clubs, convention visitors, historical societies and history and antiques addicts from far and near. In fact, they'll come from just about everywhere but Green Bay itself. Unfortunately, local residents either don't realize what they have in these places or they don't care.

Green Bay is lucky it still has them. All were nearly destroyed years ago and were only saved by the cooperation of private owners, civic groups, city government and a number of energetic women, notably the late Mmes. R. C. Buchanan and Francis T. Blesch.

A "must" for every visitor interested in places historic will be the Roy-Porlier-Tank home in Tank Park *(now at Heritage Hill State Park)*, more familiar locally as Tank Cottage. Built in 1776, the cottage is *(one of)* the oldest structure*(s)* in Wisconsin and has been a tourist attraction for half a century. *(Later research established that the structure was built between 1800 and 1805.)*

Erected by one of the area's early fur trading settlers, the French-Canadian Joseph Roy, the cottage served as a residence for a series of prominent local people for nearly a century and a quarter, the best known being Jacques Porlier and Nils Otto Tank. According to Roy's sworn testimony, he built it early in 1776, prior to the Declaration of Independence and about the time of the Battles of Lexington and Concord, which kicked off the American Revolution. *(Roy's — or Roi's — affidavit states he lived on the land since 1776 though there is no mention of any buildings on the property.)*

Challenged by Neville

Roy's statement *(about when the house supposedly was built)* was not seriously challenged until 1909 when Arthur Courtenay Neville, president of the Historical Society, advanced the theory, based on structural conditions found when the building was moved a couple of years before, that the cottage could not have been built prior to 1795. His thesis promptly drew heavy fire from Miss Deborah Martin.

Maybe he put it out just to see Debbie shoot off sparks, a tactic in which he delighted and at which he was very good. Anyway, he never insisted on it, and the earlier date is now accepted as authentic. *(As noted, later research proved Neville was correct — the building was NOT built in 1776.)*

For many years the building was believed to be a log structure. However, when it was moved to its present location in 1907 *(then on the west side at Fifth and Tenth)* the original portion was found to be of "wattle" construction. A covering of logs with clapboard facings had been added later. *(The building's middle section is what is called "piece-su-piece" construction. When the building was moved in 1907, it was said the addition was made of wood planks.)*

Originally the cottage stood on the west bank of the Fox River, directly across from another famous old home, Morgan L. Martin's "Hazelwood." In 1805 Roy sold it to Jacques Porlier who lived in it until his death in 1839....Its record of tenancy for the next several years is obscure, but it is believed to have been occupied by some of Porlier's family.

Purchased by Tank

When Otto Tank bought a large West Side tract for his unsuccessful Moravian settlement in 1850 the purchase included the cottage. Tank remodeled and enlarged the house by adding wings to each side. After his death in 1864 his widow continued to live there until she died in 1891.

The old house then became the property of the Eldred Lumber Co. and was acquired by George Rice. The Rices put it in excellent repair and made it their home, but in 1907 it was learned that the historic structure was to be pulled down to make room for a factory.

Rice notified the South Side Improvement Assn. and the Green Bay Historical Society that he was anxious to save the house and would give it to the city if some scheme could be worked out to move and preserve it. The two organizations hit the city council for an appropriation to move it and Rice made the presentation. It was decided to place it in the park donated to the city by Madame Tank, then called Union Park but fittingly renamed Tank Park.

The move, which began late in 1907, was an extremely delicate operation and took almost a year. The wattle *(?)* walls were in imminent danger of collapse every foot of the distance. One of the Tank wings did fall off but was rebuilt....

Good for Many Years

Relocated on solid foundations and greatly strengthened, the old building appears good for another century. Just to be on the safe side, however, entry is limited to no more than 25 persons at a time, and the city engineer watches it carefully. Necessary repairs and maintenance are at city expense. *(Not since the building was moved to Heritage Hill.)*

The cottage has been a museum for over 50 years under the supervision of the Tank Cottage Committee, a self-perpetuating group of dedicated women who were originally appointed by Mayor Winford Abrams but who select their own replacements as needed. This committee, presently headed by Mrs. John Arvey, furnishes and operates the building. Proceeds from the operation are used to purchase more furnishings. *(No longer applicable.)*

Except for the wings, which have been part of it for over 100 years, the cottage looks much as it always did, although it is now surrounded by a low stone wall, pierced by a pair of old-fashioned gates. The enclosure has an effective Dutch garden of the type maintained by Madame Tank and a small bake house contemporary to the early Tank occupancy period. *(A summer kitchen at Tank Cottage's Heritage Hill location is not the original.)*

Owners Recognized

Because of its long association with the Tanks the home was known for years simply as "Tank Cottage," but eventually Jacques Porlier's ownership and Roy's construction were also recognized. It is a quaint, charming little place, carefully furnished, preserved and maintained.*

The rooms are small and the furnishings include only a few items belonging to early occupants, although they are trickling back. The latest to return was the handsome and valuable marquetry cabinet that stood unnoticed for years in the Kellogg Public Library *(and is now at Heritage Hill).* All contents are authentic, contemporary antiques.

Other outstanding pieces are an inlaid bureau in its old place in Madame Tank's bedroom, several examples of Tank china and pewter, Otto Tank's surveying instruments, and a sketch book drawn by his daughter Mary. The book was rescued from a bonfire following the auction of Madam Tank's possessions.

Admission prices are 50 cents for adults and 10 cents for children. The cottage is open daily except Mondays from 10 a.m. to 4:30 p.m. and from 3 to 4:30 p.m. on Sundays and holidays. Mrs. Viola Van Lishout is the caretaker. *(Information now obsolete.)*

From now until the close of the school the tiny home will experience its busiest period of the year. Virtually every day groups of school children, Girl Scout and Brownie troops will file through its dignified rooms for a glimpse at the way their great-grandparents lived when they were also young.

* *Tank Cottage underwent extensive restoration beginning in 1989 and reopened to visitors in December 1991. Further work followed and the building reopened again in 1993.*

Historical Treasure

Old Hospital Unique Museum

May 14, 1960

On a shady corner of Kellogg Street and Chestnut Avenue a cluster of three plain wooden buildings nestles under the great trees. They are very old and two of them, with their wide, deep verandas, look like simple white cottages of long ago. *(Fort Howard Hospital and company kitchen are located now at Heritage Hill. Another building on the west side is still in use.)*

A large sign identifies the trio as the Fort Howard Hospital Museum. In a city that owes little to England, this is almost a British understatement — for here is one of the most remarkable historical treasures in the Middle West.

These are authentic, original buildings, not reproductions. Two of them formed the hospital of the old Army post of Fort Howard and were located just outside the walls, while the other stood inside the stockade where its purpose is still a matter of considerable controversy. No one is exactly sure how old they are but they have been standing for at least 130 years. *(The hospital was built between 1834 and 1835.)*

They have been restored and spruced up with such modern gadgets as electric lights but otherwise they are just as they used to be, even to the door hardware, handmade stair rails and old window panes. The fireplaces have been rebuilt but this work was done with stone known to have been part of the military post.

It was a long struggle for recognition these old buildings endured. Ignored and used for other purposes for many years, they were almost lost at least once, but they have at last come into their own. The story of the development of the hospital museum is not only fascinating but a tribute to a small group of devoted women, most of them now dead, who fought and worked for years to make the place what it is.

Age Unknown

Nobody knows when the buildings were constructed, but it was sometime between 1817 and 1825. *(See note above.)* Originally the hospital was a T-shaped affair, the two large structures forming its parts. They were separated when moved to the present site and remodeled as distinct units.

The smaller building, traditionally called the "scullery" although nobody knows why, was part of the interior of the fort. It has probably seen a wide variety of uses through the past century and a half but most of its history has been lost.

Ft. Howard was established as an important frontier stronghold in 1816 and was garrisoned until the Mexican War. Reoccupied for a short time after that war, it was placed in caretaker status in 1855 and finally abandoned entirely in 1862 *(or thereabout).*

In 1868, when the North Western Railroad acquired the property *(another source puts the year of purchase as 1863),* the hospital buildings were bought by Andrew Elmore, who either moved them to their present location or resold them to Frederick Wohlfarth, who made the transfer. Just when the "scullery" was moved isn't known, but it must have been about the same time.

The Wohlfarth family lived in the Kellogg Street house and apparently rented the other. Eventually they were inherited by a daughter, Mrs. Mary Hein, who used them as rental units. In 1928 Mrs. Hein decided to dispose of them, a big "For Sale" sign went up and things began to happen.

Drums Began to Beat

Fearful that if the now dilapidated and unsightly structures were sold they would be demolished, Harold T. I. Shannon and Mrs. F. T. Blesch began to beat the drums. They worked up so much interest that in March 1929, Mrs. Hein presented them to the city on the condition they be moved.

She indicated, however, that she was willing to sell the lots to the city as well. The council bought the entire package and the buildings remained where they were.

Restoration began with city funds. When they ran out money was raised by other means and the work went slowly forward. At one time interested groups were reduced to holding public teas in the larger building to get enough money to paint the woodwork. Finally in June of 1931, Gov. Phil LaFollette officially opened the museum.

It didn't have much to show at first but as the year went by a collection of furnishings has been assembled of which any larger institution would be proud. Sparkplug of the furnishing was the late Mrs. R. C. Buchanan, who made it the principal mission of her last years.

Jessie Buchanan knew what she wanted and she spared neither herself, time nor money to get it. In addition to outright purchases for the museum she loaned many of her own things....For years she supervised the operation of an antique shop in the "ward" building facing Chestnut Avenue and used the profits to buy more pieces.

Amazing Collection

The result is an amazing and valuable collection of relics of old Green Bay. Every piece is either an authentic local item or something that once belonged to a family or individual associated with the city's past.

Space does not permit a catalogue of the exhibits, but in interest, value and authenticity they are unmatched. Equally fascinating is the manner in which they are displayed.

It should be pointed out that, despite the name, this is not a medical museum. The title merely honors the original status of the main buildings.

Virtually every old family or personage in Green Bay history is represented, including the DeLanglades, Dr. William Beaumont, the Martins, Bairds, Eleazer Williams and many others. An interesting room is the little "office" of Dr. Beaumont, which contains many more of his personal professional items than are displayed in his memorial at Mackinac.*

Equally charming is the Deborah

Beaumont Martin room, honoring Miss Martin, who died 30 years ago in one of the chairs now in the museum. A crowning touch to this lovely bedroom is a set of toy dishes with which she played as a little girl. Also on display is the Sheraton dining table belonging to her family, on which was planned and written the Wisconsin state constitution. *(The table, only part of which is Sheraton, is now at Hazelwood. There is no documentation to prove the constitution was written here.)*

Gillespie Gave 'Scullery'

Initially the hospital wings constituted the entire museum. In 1953 the late Lee Gillespie bought the "scullery," which had been used for years as a dwelling, and gave it to the Brown County Historical Society. The society presented it to the city and it was moved to the museum property. It was opened last fall as a separate unit of the museum after a long period of restoration and furnishing by the Antiquarian Society.

The opening as a memorial to Charles DeLanglade kicked up a fuss, the argument being that DeLanglade, who died long before the establishment of Ft. Howard, had no connection with the post or its surviving buildings. The point, while well taken, foundered on the fact that no one knows what the building had actually been used for, much less how it acquired the designation of "scullery," a place for the storage of dishes and cooking utensils adjacent to a kitchen.

There is no evidence it ever was used as a kitchen adjunct although it could have been, just as it also might have been utilized as a headquarters office. The size, shape and interior mark it as a standard bachelor officer's quarters in an early 19th Century frontier military post, but it probably was used in many other capacities. Frontier garrisons habitually ignored official designations if the space was needed for something else. *(The buildings at Heritage Hill are interpreted as hospital and company kitchen.)*

* *The Fort Howard Hospital at Heritage Hill no longer functions as the museum Jack Rudolph describes here. Most of the artifacts of pioneer people, including Dr. Beaumont's office, therefore, are not among the furnishings which now depict the building's earliest use as a military post.*

Another Treasure Saved

Cotton House Is Impressive

May 21, 1960

Rising in lonely grandeur on the crown of Allouez Ridge, a short distance north of the reformatory, stands a large white house. From the lower De Pere road its classic columns are almost as impressive as the magnificent view from beneath the pillars themselves. This is "Cotton House" *(now part of Heritage Hill State Park),* the third of the Green Bay historic buildings to open to the public during the summer months.

Built about 1840 *(probably between 1840 and 1845),* and named for its owner, retired Army Capt. John Cotton, the home is not as significant historically as Tank Cottage or the Fort Howard Hospital Museum, but its location, great dignity and authentic furnishings give it much charm and interest. Of greater importance is its stature as the "finest, purest example of Jeffersonian architecture in the Middle West." *(The architecture later was identified as Greek Revival.)*

Like the other two local museums, Cotton House had its bleak, neglected days. For years it was unoccupied and permitted to become so run down that it came within an ace of being razed. Then, as in the case of Tank Cottage and the fort structures, it was saved and restored.

Built as Gift

Cotton House was built by John Penn Arndt, reputedly as a belated wedding gift for his daughter Mary, who married Captain Cotton in 1825 when he was a young lieutenant just out of West Point and stationed at Fort Howard. Cotton, a descendant of the famed New England colonial divine, Cotton Mather, was retired for physical disability in 1845 *(1847)* and the childless couple* returned to Green Bay.

For 20 years before that, however, the Cottons led the usual gypsy existence of an Army family. Part of the time, when Cotton was stationed at remote frontier posts his wife returned to her Green Bay home. It was probably during one of these periods of enforced separation that her father built the home for her.

Not Original Name

It was not originally called Cotton House, but Beaupre Place, a title bestowed by Mrs. Cotton. She had always coveted the site and when she got it she named the property for its original French owner, Louis Beaupre. From the beginning of her occupancy, however, it was popularly known as "Captain Cotton's House."

Neither is its present location the original one. The home was built and stood for 90 years on a lower point of the ridge facing the Fox River and further north, just to the left of the road leading into St. Joseph's Orphanage. *(Though the orphanage is long gone, the complex of administrative offices for the Green Bay Diocese remains in the area Rudolph describes here.)* It was moved to its present site 19 years ago.

A plaque in the central hallway dates the home from 1840 a date found painted over the door at the time of the move. A slight controversy over its accuracy has been settled by an invitation in the possession of Mrs. Charles Simpson to a social affair at "Beaupre Place" in the spring of 1841. It is signed by Mrs. Cotton. *(Heritage Hill welcomes information about this invitation or a copy of the original if available as it would help determine date of occupancy.)*

Center of Society

From the date of its occupancy by the Cottons until the captain's death in 1878 the house was a center of social activity. His wife, who became a much loved personality and widely known as "Auntie Cotton" before she died in 1896, was a gracious hostess and liked to entertain.

After her husband's death, however, advancing age forced her to give up the big and isolated house, which was sold in 1893 to J. W. Woodruff. The Woodruffs occupied it until 1896, when it was purchased by Bishop Joseph J. Fox, apparently to be used as an annex to the orphanage.

Deserted for Years

Whatever plans the bishop may have had never materialized. The old house remained deserted thereafter, at one time being relegated to the lowly status of a grain storehouse.

In 1933 Bishop Paul P. Rhode quietly presented the dilapidated building to the Brown County Historical Society and plans were made to move it to the site of old Camp Smith, where it stands today. The next five years witnessed a series of mysteriously unpublicized maneuvers which finally culminated in the reformatory giving the society permission to use the hilltop.

Tough Moving Job

The move, which began in the late winter of 1938, proved to be a tough job, not because the building was in poor condition but because of its great strength. It was found to be so sturdily built that not even decades of neglect had materially affected its soundness. The rehabilitation phase was completed in 1941 and the old house was reopened as a museum.

Meanwhile, a legal snarl developed over the authority of reformatory officials to permit use of the site. The problem was solved in 1953 when the Legislature passed a bill introduced by the late Assemblyman Robert E. Lynch approving what had been done and confirming the Historical Society's ownership and right to operate it as a museum.

Although not so old nor so historically important as Tank Cottage and the fort hospital buildings, Cotton House, because of its site, architecture, and spaciousness has become one of the most attractive institutions of its kind in Wisconsin. Tastefully furnished and decorated and immaculately clean, the high-ceilinged, airy rooms house a fine collection of period furniture and other pieces. Many of them *(about 15 percent of what is currently in the house)* are Cotton originals occupying the same places they did when the house was a social center of the town.

Cotton Items Displayed

Among the Cotton items are Auntie Cotton's own big four-poster bed, which stands again in her old bedroom *(the bed there now is not Auntie Cotton's)*; a Cotton sofa, several chairs, some family china and a number of pictures given to the couple as wedding gifts *(speculation)*. Although they had no children,* Auntie's love for youngsters is fittingly memorialized in a charming child's room, complete with miniature furniture, toys and dolls.

Another significant item is Polly Lawe's piano, the first ever brought into the western wilderness. Although it was saved when the old Lawe mansion was destroyed by fire in 1903, the instrument was permanently damaged and is no longer playable; however, it is a handsome piece....

Impressive Vault

Another little publicized feature of the grounds is the tomb of Green Bay's own Unknown Soldier. This is the grave of an American soldier who apparently died at Camp Smith in the early 1820s, was buried and forgotten until his remains were found when the foundation for the house was being dug. He was placed in an impressive limestone vault only a few paces from but out of sight of the building.

If present plans work out the grounds will eventually contain another historic Green Bay structure owned by the Historical Society. The county board is anxious to have the Baird Law Office removed from the rear of the courthouse, and it is hoped the little building can be transferred to the vicinity of Cotton House...*(It was transferred. It should be noted that among the buildings described, Hazelwood remains the only one still owned by the Brown County Historical Society.)*

*** Not Childless - Correction: May 28, 1960**

In last Saturday's Cotton House feature Capt. and Mrs. John Cotton were described as "childless." Actually, they had five children, all of whom lived to maturity. One daughter became Mrs. W. B. Gueinzius and the mother of J. Bernard Gueinzius and Mrs. Charles (Elizabeth Gueinzius) Simpson.

The Cottons did have five children-John, Elizabeth, Priscilla, Mary and Charles. Heritage Hill records do not show any of the daughters as Mrs. W. B. Gueinzius. Elizabeth married Charles Tyler; Priscilla married James Howe who later wed his sister-in-law Mary after Priscilla died.

Dowager Queen

'Hazelwood' Green Bay's Treasure

May 20, 1961

Whether the recently restored Wilcox home in De Pere *(at 707 North Broadway)* or Green Bay's "Hazelwood" is the older is a question that will probably never be determined. One thing is certain, though. It would be beneath Hazelwood's quiet dignity to argue the point. *(Research has since determined the Wilcox home was built in 1836 and Hazelwood in 1837.)*

She just sits there regally, back on her spacious, tree-covered Monroe Avenue domain, for all the world like a prim New England dowager accustomed to dominating all about her. She does, too. Like a dowager, she can even be a little vague about her age and get away with it.

There's something about Hazelwood other than its great age. The house is, in its own right, as much of a personality as the proud man who built, lived and died in it. Morgan L. Martin was one of the outstanding Wisconsin leaders of his time and he imparted something of his stiff-necked, indomitable self to his home that it has never lost.

Here was written the constitution of the Commonwealth of Wisconsin. Through its doors for nearly half a century passed most of the leaders of the state's early history. *(Because Martin served as president of the second constitutional convention, it is possible he might have scribbled some thoughts about the document in his home. The constitution itself, however, was written in Madison. How many of the state's political leaders actually visited Hazelwood is debatable also.)*

Exactly when Martin built Hazelwood is uncertain. A neat sign facing the street carries the date 1835 *(that sign is no longer there)*, but this is apparently earlier than actual completion and occupancy. Martin bought the property on which it stands in that year but did not marry until 1837, and his daughter Deborah often stated that the house was not occupied until a year later. *(See note first paragraph.)*

Center of Society

Martin lived in Hazelwood for 50 years, during which time it was a center of society and state politics. In 1846, in what was then his study and is now the dining room, the preliminary draft of the state constitution was drawn upon the fine Sheraton table that now graces the Fort Howard Hospital Museum. *(The table, part of which is Sheraton, can be found at Hazelwood. There is no documentation to prove the constitution was written here.)* Every visiting dignitary was proud to accept the hospitality of the place, although Martin being what he was, that hospitality probably wasn't very riotous.

Martin died in 1887. Following the death of his widow his two spinster daughters, Deborah and Sarah, continued to occupy Hazelwood until the former died in 1931.

The later years of this period were hard on the old home. The once considerable Martin fortune was gone, the house was aging and needed repairs the sisters could not afford, but the way they clung stubbornly to the only home they had ever known was as magnificent as it was pathetic.

After Deborah Martin died Sarah went to live with a brother in Detroit. For a time the house was rented and for a couple of years was vacant entirely. Then, in 1936, Hazelwood passed out of the Martin family, just a century after its construction.

New Owner Died

The new owner was Mrs. Flora C. Clisby. Before she could do much in the way of badly needed rehabilitation she also died and her grandson and heir, the late John M. Walter, sold it to Dr. Ralph Carter. To him the city and Hazelwood's present occupant, Mrs. R. E. Lambeau, will be forever grateful, for it was Doctor Carter who restored it to its present beautiful condition.

Doctor Carter's first task was to move the house 20 feet to the south. In doing so he had to destroy the long unused and once famous basement fireplace that had been the original kitchen, but the move was necessary to strengthen the building and correct a snarl over its location. When Mrs. Clisby bought the house it was discovered that, due to faulty surveying years before, several feet of the structure extended onto the next door property.

Having set it on a new and firm foundation, the doctor made Hazelwood's complete restoration a labor of love, into which he poured many times the price he originally paid for it. He had barely completed the job, however, when he, too, died and Mrs. Carter sold to the Lambeaus.

Today, from the street, Hazelwood looks almost exactly as it did when built, except for a north wing that collapsed many years ago and was never rebuilt. Inside there have been numerous changes, but the main portion of the house is the same, with all the original woodwork and hardware that Martin brought from the east. One of the huge, old fashioned brass door keys is still in use.

"Back" Is the Front

The front door, incidentally, does not face Monroe Avenue. That is the "back entrance," the front opening out onto a beautiful lawn and flower garden that slopes down to the river. *(The "front-back" question is controversial. Some experts argue that staircases typically descend to the house's front. Hazelwood's staircase faces Monroe suggesting this, in fact, is the front entrance.)* The garden is relatively new and replaces a tangled thicket of hazel bushes from which the house derived its name.

Entering by the "back" or street door, one steps into a wide, cheerful hallway that runs the full depth of the house and is crowned by a magnificent walnut stair rail on the steps to the upper floor. The walls are covered with a reproduction of their original paper *(paper of the period, as what was there originally is not known)* and still hanging there is a unique hall lamp, its hand-painted Chinese silk panels now covered with glass to protect what is left after a century and a quarter of use.

To the left *(coming from the river)*, at the foot of the stairs, is the entrance to a formal drawing room, in which stands one of the black marble fireplaces that Martin bought from Daniel Whitney and which the latter imported for his never-completed "Whitney's Folly." *(Another is in the dining room.)* A great crystal chandelier is suspended from the ceiling, and behind the room is a small library, once Mrs. Martin's sewing room *(not established)* but now lined to the ceiling with book shelves.

Fireplace Incomplete

Across the hall is the dining room, originally Martin's study, which contains another of the black fireplaces. This one is incomplete, however, the front of it having disappeared during the restoration. The south wing, which once housed a bedroom and combination dining-sitting room, has been converted into a garage and maid's quarters.

All the downstairs rooms are high-ceilinged with tall windows, upon which the original inside shutters still hang. Those shutters were designed to be closed from the inside in case of Indian attack and could probably stop an arrow though not a bullet. *(Later research shows the shutters served no such ulterior purpose.)*

The upstairs bedrooms are cheerful places, their low ceilings slanting down along the roof beams. All have recessed dormer windows that are delightfully quaint today but had a more sinister original purpose. They were built as firing platforms in case of attack and recessed to protect the room's interiors. *(Not so)*. The closets, which are really openings into the space under the roof, reveal the huge, hand-hewn beams with which the house was built.

Hazelwood came into the ownership of the Neville Public Museum Corp. from the Lambeau family about 1964. The Neville Museum maintained the home as a museum until ownership was transferred to the Brown County Historical Society in December 1989. Between 1993 and 1995 the house underwent major restoration including reconstruction of the south wing. That effort also created office space in the building's lower level which serves as headquarters for the Brown County Historical Society, a gift shop and the Kellogg Preservation Library. Due to the reconstruction based on more recent research, Rudolph's room descriptions are not completely compatible with the house as it exists today.

*A controversial point.

Burned Down in 1857

Ornate Astor House City's Pride

September 6, 1958

Every community as old as Green Bay has cherished legends of its early days, not all of which stand the test of historical research. Green Bay has one that can — the story of the fabulous Astor House.

A product of the fertile imagination of James Duane Doty, there wasn't much excuse for the Astor House. If John Jacob Astor hadn't gone for one last try at taking a fall out of Daniel Whitney, it probably never would have been built. For 20 years, until it went up in flames just over 100 years ago, it conferred on a straggling frontier town the distinction of possessing one of the most elaborate hotels west of New York.

When Astor decided in 1835 to develop the village named after him adjacent to Whitney's village of Navarino, he hired Doty as his agent and promoter. Since Navarino had a hotel, Doty wanted one so far superior to the primitive Washington House that it would be a frontier sensation.

Accordingly, he bombarded Astor with plans for a luxury hotel, the likes of which the Lakes region had never seen. Old J.J. wasn't enthusiastic but the persuasive Doty wore him down.

Astor having given a reluctant green light, construction began in the spring of 1837 at E. Mason and S. Adams Streets. The two communities watched with enthusiasm, considerable amusement and even greater astonishment.

Miss Fanny Last, in a paper written years ago for the Brown County Historical Society, described the three-story frame structure with crowning cupola and widow's walk as "very large, very square and quite guiltless of any adornment or frivolous device." Her description was borne out in a sketch drawn from memory by A. C. Neville, who had seen it when he was a small boy.

Painted white, relieved only by bright green shutters, the building was a startling contrast to the small cluster of log cabins and unpainted frame houses that huddled between the river, a swamp and the forest.

But if the exterior was no architectural gem the interior was something else. No one knows how many rooms it had, but there were more than enough for the time and place, plus a large dining room, a ballroom with stage and elaborate crystal chandeliers and several pleasant parlors. A feature of the central hall was a graceful staircase to the second floor.

Doty spared nothing — after all, he was spending Astor's money — to decorate and furnish it in the latest mode. Local residents, many of whom had left well-to-do homes in the east to emigrate to the wilderness, were bug-eyed at the quality and quantity of mahogany furniture, fine linen, glassware and silver he shipped in. There were two — not just one — sterling silver tea services.

The bill for furnishings alone came to $8,048.44. All told, the project cost Astor well over $20,000.

Doty also talked an experienced New York innkeeper, one Charles Rogers, into taking over the management. Rogers stocked his new establishment on Astor's cuff, and the Astor House opened with great fanfare in August 1837.

There is no existing account of the festivities, but the guest list probably included such local notables as Morgan L. Martin, Doty, Henry Baird, John Lawe and certainly Daniel Whitney. There was also an unbidden, unexpected and invisible guest, shortly to cast a pall over all of Doty's ambitious schemes — the Panic of 1837.

The depression, breaking almost simultaneously with the opening, promptly brought development of the settlement to a standstill. For several years the hotel was a white elephant. Rogers got discouraged after a couple of lean seasons and left, owing Astor $4,111.11 which he never paid.

Doty met the crisis by luring Thomas Green, manager of the rival Washington House, to the Astor. According to Doty's biographer, Alice E. Smith, he practically had to give Green the place to get him, but he blandly brushed off Astor's outraged bellow by pointing out that it was "much more pleasant to see the Navarino house closed than our own."

Like so many of Doty's promotions, the Astor House was premature. Yet it filled a community need that kept it limping along, especially after the consolidation of the rival villages.

Except for the overshadowed Washington House, the Astor was the town's only public assembly place and soon became the center of activity. All large social and political gatherings were held there.

The ballroom was the scene of elaborate dances, masquerades, local stage entertainments and such itinerant shows as found their way to the slowly growing settlement. Public and private banquets filled the dining room, including two testimonials to Territorial Delegate Morgan L. Martin. The officers of Ft. Howard were also partial to its attractions, particularly the ornate bar.

The hotel established and kept a reputation for lavish hospitality, although its comforts left something to be desired. One traveler, marooned there during a severe blizzard, complained that its hasty construction with unseasoned lumber had caused much warping. Snow and cold blew steadily in through cracks and poorly fitting window frames.

The Astor also got a prestige shot in the arm from the Prince de Joinville. The son of the King of France stayed there when he held his mysterious conference with Eleazar Williams in 1841.

Gradually, time caught up with the hotel and it began to justify Doty's vision. The rising lumber industry and the tide of immigration during the late 1840s and '50s turned it into a highly profitable venture.

In 1854 a hotelman named Ira Stone bought the place. He completely redecorated it, added rooms, enlarged the stables and imported a "Troy coach" that became Green Bay's first public transportation and which he used to transport guests to and from the ship landings.

But the Astor House's long delayed prosperity stuck in somebody's craw. Several times in 1856 and 1857 an unknown firebug tried to get rid of it and finally succeeded.

During a night in late August 1857, the hotel was completely destroyed by fire. The speed with which the flames swept through the building pointed to arson, but no one ever collected the large rewards offered for the apprehension of the culprit.

Just Faded Away

Klaus Hall, Once a Landmark

October 8, 1960

"Tonight. At Klaus Hall."

It has been nearly 70 years since that announcement — once as familiar to readers of the Green Bay Gazette as proceedings of the city council — last appeared. There aren't many left who remember it, but there was a time when Klaus Hall was so much the hub of the city's social and entertainment life it's a little shocking to find the old place so completely forgotten.

Maybe that was the trouble. Klaus Hall was such an established landmark that people just took it for granted. When it began to fade the process was so gradual they didn't notice it. Then, one day, the hall went dark forever, and nobody realized it was actually gone.

The story of Klaus Hall begins in 1856 when two enterprising brothers, Charles and Philip Klaus, built a small dry goods store on the south side of Pine Street, between Washington and Adams, and fitted up the second floor as a public hall. The exact location has been forgotten but it was probably just a couple of doors east of Washington Street.

The hall wasn't very big, measuring only 24 by 60 feet, but it was the first room in the city ever specifically designed for public use. Previously, most public gatherings had been held in the ballrooms or dining rooms of the Astor House, the Washington House or the United States House around the corner.

Popular Meeting Place

While Philip Klaus ran the dry goods shop, Charley managed the hall. The latter was an enthusiastic promoter, and in a short time he had made Klaus Hall the most popular place in town for public meetings, dances and the infrequent appearances of such theatrical companies as found their way to Green Bay. It was used so often by the city's two socially-minded volunteer fire companies that it was commonly called Firemen's Hall.

The early success was short lived. In 1858 Henry Baird built an imposing three-story brick and stone building across the street that contained a slightly larger and more attractive hall. Baird stole the play from the Klaus boys, who shortly sold the property and established their store elsewhere. The structure was appropriately remodeled into a fire station.

A year later, however, the brothers were back on Pine Street, erecting a larger place on the present site of the *(former)* Stuebe Binding and Printing Co. *(which was located then in the area of the former Boston Store in Port Plaza mall, now called Washington Commons)*. This hall, 30 feet wide and 70 feet deep, quickly recovered most of the lost patronage. Until the fire of 1864 wiped out the entire block, including both the original and the new structures, Klaus Hall was the city's leading meeting place.

Philip Klaus' business had prospered meanwhile, and he was no longer charmed by the headaches connected with running a public hall. Charley liked it, however, and in 1866 he rebuilt on the same site.

Still Dimly Remembered

This was the Klaus Hall still dimly and nostalgically remembered, a brick building with several ground floor store spaces and an auditorium above. A wide stairway between store fronts led up to a hall 80 by 40 feet, well lighted and ventilated, with a 17-foot ceiling. It is still there occupied now by the printing plant of the Stuebe company. *(See note above.)*

Equipped with a large and well appointed stage, it had a dining room adjoining and dressing rooms for both ladies and gentlemen. Charley kicked it off with a big dance on Aug. 30, 1866, and from opening night the new Klaus Hall was a greater success than its predecessors.

For the next 30 years Klaus Hall was the entertainment center of the city. Four out of every five touring theatrical troupes played there, many returning year after year. Minstrel shows, opera companies and individual artists of all classes were familiar with its peculiarities from long and repeated association.

How many times that popular and perennial comedian John Dillon convulsed full houses nobody knows. Dillon probably couldn't have told you himself, but he appeared there shortly after it opened and was back as an old man as late as 1893.

Variety of Uses

All big political rallies were held in Klaus Hall, whose rafters rang to the stirring oratory of such figures as Senators Tim Howe, Matt Carpenter and Charles Spooner. Masquerade balls and Christmas dances were winter fixtures, with ice cream and strawberry socials in the summer.

Leading lecturers followed minstrel shows and in turn were replaced by church bazaars and public testimonials. Close to 600 people dined there during the railroad celebration of 1862.

Through the years Klaus Hall had competition but was never seriously threatened. Gus Crikelair built an elaborate opera house on Cherry Street in 1871 but he couldn't lick Charley Klaus. The Bay City Light Guards armory, remodeled as the Armory Opera House after the militia unit folded, might have made it but burned down in 1885, just as it was gaining a solid foothold.

Charles Klaus died in 1884. Who owned and operated the auditorium after that isn't known, but it was as popular as ever for several more years. Whoever managed it, it was still Klaus Hall. In 1894, apparently as a last gasp attempt to regain failing prestige, it was renamed Klaus Opera House, but the change never caught on.

Finally Slipped

Klaus Hall was still going strong in 1893 but thereafter began to slip. The place was getting old, outmoded and probably dingy, and its accommodations could no longer compare with those of newer establishments.

When Turner Hall opened *(on the northwest corner of Monroe and Walnut),* its biggest feature was an excellent auditorium with one of the best equipped stages in the middle west, and after the society made it available for public performances most of the theatrical companies preferred to play there. Shortly, many other activities followed.

Then the Music Hall went up in Fort Howard *(at the southeast corner of Main/Dousman and Chestnut),* giving the west side its own show house. By this time, too, church congregations and fraternal societies were fitting up social halls of their own where bazaars and small social affairs could be more easily managed. Gradually the lights of Klaus Hall were turned up less and less frequently.

Just when they went out for the last time is unknown. The hall's name appears only spasmodically in the press of 1894, then disappears entirely the following year. The last reference found is for a lecture late in November, 1894, indicating that the old landmark may have locked its doors early in 1895.

For an institution that rated so much ink through the years, not a drop seems to have been spilled at its obsequies.

Time Runs Out on Venerable Hotel

January 19, 1963

Time has finally caught up with another of Green Bay's historic landmarks. After a century of service the Beaumont Hotel is to be torn down and replaced by a modern motor inn.

Although one of the city's last direct links with the era of the Civil War is thus being broken, two other traditions associated with the Washington-Main Street corner will be preserved. The venerable Beaumont name will be retained and the corner will remain a hotel site.

It has never been anything else.

When Daniel Whitney platted his village of Navarino in 1830 one of his first projects was a hotel which he named the Washington House. He built it on the northeast corner of Washington and Main, then much closer to the river bank than it is today.

Indian Battle Site

A century earlier the site hadn't been so hospitable. It was then occupied by an Indian fort which became, in 1733, the scene of the only pitched battle between white men and Indians in Green Bay's long history....

Whitney's Washington House, one of the first hotels in Wisconsin, lasted nearly 25 years. It escaped destruction in the disastrous fire of 1853, which wiped out much of the Washington Street business district, only to go up in flames a year later.

Most of the time it was owned by the famous Army surgeon Dr. William Beaumont, who bought the property from Whitney about 1834. Beaumont leased the hotel to a succession of managers, including one Thomas Green, who was eventually lured away by James Duane Doty when he built the legendary Astor House in the rival village of Astor.

Passed to Son

When Dr. Beaumont died in 1853 the hotel property passed to his son Israel Green Beaumont, who came to Green Bay to manage his late father's extensive land holdings. Israel, popularly known as "Bud," remained the rest of his life and died, a highly respected citizen, in 1901.

Bud had barely arrived on the scene when the Washington House burned to the ground. With the hard times of the 1850s just getting under way, he let the corner remain vacant until 1860.

In that year Beaumont and his brother-in-law partner, Alfred Pelton, began construction of a new hotel there. They named it the Beaumont House in honor of Bud's illustrious father, and the name has been carried ever since.

Although A. C. Witteborg and his son Carl, owners and operators of the Beaumont for nearly half of its existence, date the beginnings of the establishment from 1860, there is considerable confusion about when it actually opened for business. It was scheduled for completion early in 1861 but failed to meet the target date.

Construction Delayed

Beaumont and Pelton were in a lot of deals, spread themselves too thin and ran out of ready cash. Construction of the hotel had to be suspended, the outbreak of the Civil War complicated the situation and the project limped along throughout the conflict. As late as the beginning of 1863 the Green Bay Advocate was appealing to progressive businessmen to get behind the hotel, put up the necessary money and finish the job.

Apparently the hotel was finished piecemeal, portions being opened as completed. The building was finally finished in 1865 but by then the hotel had been in partial operation for some time; consequently, no formal opening was ever staged.

The four-story hotel was an immediate success. Until the construction and elaborate opening of plush Cook's Hotel in 1875 the Beaumont was the city's ranking hotel.

For a while even Cook's swanky establishment didn't cut appreciably into the Beaumont's business. Principal reason was the latter's manager, Arthur Cozzens.

Maintained Prestige

One of the best hotel operators in the state, Cozzens maintained the Beaumont's prestige largely through its dining room cuisine, which was famous all over the middle west. Shortly, however, the competition sneaked a page out of Doty's book, hired Cozzens away from the Beaumont, and the older house began to slip.

Bud Beaumont, unable to find a manager to match Cozzens, finally had to take over active operation himself. He even moved his family into the place one season to keep a closer eye on it.

Carl Witteborg still has old account books showing withdrawals from the till of nickels and dimes by Bud's young daughters, May and Sophia. Ostensibly the girls raided the cash register for their Sunday school collection plates.

Beaumont was a likeable and popular man but a bust as a publican. The hotel sank deeper into the red until he was finally forced to borrow $7,500 from his friend Henry Furber, president of the Charter Oak Life Insurance Co. That was a staggering debt in 1876.

Mortgage Foreclosed

Furber took a mortgage on the property, made out to the insurance company, as security. A few years later, when Beaumont was unable to pay, he foreclosed, and Bud lost the hotel.

Change of ownership didn't help. Furber couldn't find anybody to make a go of it, either, so he placed it with Philip Klaus for sale.

The deteriorating hotel was a white elephant on Klaus' hands. It was finally shut down, and in 1885 Klaus announced that if he didn't get a buyer soon he was going to remodel it into a business block.

Found a Buyer

Fortunately, he didn't have to resort to such drastic measures. Mr. and Mrs. Henry Bertram picked it up, remodeled and enlarged the house, and the Beaumont entered a new and long period of prosperity.

The Bertrams knew their business. They quickly restored the Beaumont's old reputation and by the turn of the century it was again one of the finest hotels north of Chicago.

About 1909 the Bertrams were ready to retire and sold out to Frederic G. Hall. A former superintendent of the Harvel railroad chain, Hall gave the Beaumont dining room a national reputation.

In 1912 Hall brought A. C. Witteborg from Chicago to manage the hotel. When Hall died a few years later Witteborg formed a group of employees to buy the Beaumont from the estate.

Long Association

Witteborg has been connected with the establishment ever since, although failing health in recent years has forced him to turn active management over to his son Carl. A. C.'s association of half a century gives him the distinction of having been in the same business on the same downtown site longer than any other local man.

Through its long history the hotel has been periodically modernized and enlarged until it is now several times its initial size. Most of the original structure is incorporated in the present building.

Until the Northland was built in 1923-24, the Beaumont was the city's premier hotel, a distinction it continued to share with the newer house for many years. The celebrities it has entertained and the civic and social events held there during the past century are a story in themselves.

The Beaumont Motor Inn was sold in 1973 to become the Beaumont Ramada Inn. The Days Inn chain took over the business in 1986, at which time the new owners dropped the familiar and historic Beaumont name.

End of an Era

Time Kayoes Broadway Hotel

May 12, 1962

One of the oldest hotel names and the oldest family hotel operation in Green Bay's history reached the end of a long and prosperous road together recently when Jerry McGinnis locked the doors of the Broadway Hotel for the last time. With the razing of the familiar landmark at Broadway and Dousman Street now under way, the book is closing on more than 75 years of colorful existence, most of it under the management of three generations of McGinnises.

The Broadway Hotel dates from about 1885, when Constantine McGinnis — familiarly known as Con McGinnis —opened the establishment. With the exception of about 15 years at the turn of the century, it was always under family management.

Goes Back Further

The name itself goes back even further. There was a Broadway House in Fort Howard as early as 1874, although not on the same site. The original Broadway House was on Dousman Street, a few doors south of the corner, and was operated by a man named Ed Lawlor.

Con McGinnis, founder of the family hotel dynasty, was born in Ireland in 1823 and came to this country in the 1840s, his family acquiring a homestead at Bay Settlement. His sister Bridget married Dennis J. F. Murphy, Civil War veteran, Green Bay's only Medal of Honor winner and a pillar of the old "Irish Patch" and St. Patrick's Church.

Ran McGinnis House

Exactly when Con got into the local hotel picture isn't known, but it was at least 90 years ago. The first city directory, compiled in 1872-73, lists him as proprietor of the McGinnis House, a small hotel on Broadway, and he was in and out of the business until he opened the Broadway House in 1885. He bought the corner property in 1881 and apparently built the place in the next few years.

Con and his wife Hannah were a couple of enterprising characters, not above bucking each other openly in business. While he was running the Broadway she was in active competition with a large boarding house a short distance west on Dousman Street, which she operated for many years.

After Con's death in 1893 Mrs. McGinnis leased the hotel to a succession of managers, among them Nicholas J. Terry and Joseph P. Fry. In 1909 she sold the property to the Hagemeister Realty Co., which still owns it.

Surprisingly, sale of the hotel also brought the McGinnis name back into its management. James McGinnis, Con's son, promptly leased it from Hagemeister and ran it until he died in 1941, at which time it passed to his son Jerry.

One of Three Brothers

James was one of three brothers long prominent in Green Bay's business, professional and political life. An alderman for many years, a suave and courtly personality with a keen knowledge of psychology, Jim also served for a time as vice-mayor of the city.

The other brothers were William and John E. McGinnis. John was a doctor and generally known as Ed, while Billy enjoyed a varied career as a baseball player, manager and umpire, saloon keeper and politician.

A catcher, Billy was a mainstay of Green Bay semi-pro teams in the 1890s and later managed the "Salvators" and "Savages," among the crack independent clubs in the state prior to the advent of the old W-I League. After his playing days Billy became a prominent umpire, did a hitch as alderman and operated one of the city's most plush saloons on Washington Street.

Most Prosperous Era

Under James' management the Broadway Hotel entered its most prosperous era. The house was remodeled and enlarged in 1912 when a third floor was added, and until the erection of the Northland shared with the Beaumont the distinction of being one of the two top hotels in Northeastern Wisconsin.

The Broadway was larger than it appeared, with 71 guest rooms on the two upper floors. The street level housed a large lobby, a billiard room, a bar, a barbershop run for many years by Johnny Kuypers and the general offices of the Larsen Canning Co. Two well-known day clerks of the era were Ed Sheehy and Henry Bohan.

Near North Western

Its location near the North Western station made it a natural railroad hotel and it was always popular with railroad men and traveling salesmen. The "drummers," as traveling men were called then, used to travel with large trunks for their display wares, and it was one of Jerry McGinnis' job as a youngster to wrestle the bulky things over from the station.

In those days a hotel's quality was measured by its dinner table, and the Broadway's dining room was one of the best. Jerry, whose whole life has been intimately associated with the house, has vivid memories of that appetizing oasis.

Appetizing Menu

He recalls that its menu presented a variety of entrees, always headed by three unvarying house specialties. Number One was broiled beef tenderloin with mushroom sauce, followed by prime ribs of beef and roast loin of pork with applesauce. The hotel baked its own pies and offered four kinds daily, of which one was always apple.

The dining room operated on a semi-formal basis in which a coat was mandatory attire for men, even at breakfast. McGinnis kept two or three well cut jackets available for anyone who showed up without one and nobody got in in shirtsleeves.

Saturday afternoon was doughnut time in the kitchen, when fresh doughnuts were made for Sunday breakfast. For decades, the rich, tantalizing aroma of frying doughnuts had the whole neighborhood drooling.

Until the dining room was closed in 1924 it was supervised by Miss Julia Foley, the housekeeper. Jerry also remembers a head cook named Anna, a Polish woman whose name he can still pronounce but which even today he couldn't spell.

Bow Tie Artist

Another chef was a Greek, Theodore Checkiras. "Checkers," as everybody called him, was not only a top hand with a skillet but also an artist at tying bow ties, a gift upon which Jerry leaned heavily and effectively in his high school days.

Jerry took over the hotel after his dad died in 1941 and carried out a large scale renovation in the next couple of years. One project was the remodeling of the long closed dining room into a banquet hall called the Rose Room, which enjoyed quite a vogue in the early 1940s.

Business boomed during the war years, but thereafter the hotel went into a slow decline. The building was beginning to show its age and finally reached a point of no return where repairs and renovation no longer justified the cost.

When Jerry's lease expired this spring it was not renewed. A few weeks ago he called it quits, and the building went under the demolition hammers. In a short time another famous old name and landmark will be just a fading memory of Green Bay's rich and colorful past.

Nearly Three-Quarters of Century

Kellogg Library 74 Years Old

March 30, 1963

The Kellogg Public Library celebrates a birthday next week. On Tuesday the dignified if somewhat bedraggled Old Lady of Jefferson Street will be 74 years old, 60 of those years having been spent in the present Carnegie grant building.* She has come a long way since her humble birth in an upstairs office suite at the corner of Adams and Cherry Streets on April 2, 1889, and physically she's beginning to show her years.

The story of the founding and growth of the Kellogg Public Library is that of the dedication, conviction and enthusiasm of a small group of individuals, often in the face of public apathy and indifference if not outright hostility. Rufus B. Kellogg made it possible, but his contribution might have been lost without the devoted years given to it by Judge S. D. Hastings, the A. C. Nevilles, George Fields, E. H. Ellises, Deborah Martin and Sybil Schuette.

Especially Deborah and Sybil. Between them their service spans 66 of the library's 74 years, with Miss Martin serving as librarian for 31 years and Miss Schuette 28 more as her successor.

The beginnings of the story go back to the winter of 1883-84 when a small group began beating the drums for a public library in a city just emerging from its crude frontier origins. Actually, the seed was probably planted a few years earlier.

Opened Reading Room

In the early 1880s, exact date not specified, the local WCTU *(Women's Christian Temperance Union)* chapter, disturbed at the thought of teenage boys hanging around the city's 90-odd saloons, opened the town's first reading room on Adams Street. It had a measure of success, but more important, it attracted the attention of Rufus Kellogg.

When the 1883-84 movement began Kellogg offered to give $2,000 toward a library fund if the city would match it. The fund-raising drive got almost enough pledged but only $200 in cash, and $189 of that went down the drain when Strong's Bank failed in 1885.

Kellogg did manage to get the library question on a city referendum. However, his proposal to add half a mil to the tax rate to support such an institution was overwhelmingly defeated. The scheme died.

In the fall of 1887, Mr. and Mrs. A. C. Neville, recently returned from a European honeymoon, suggested a series of descriptive talks called "Evenings in Italy," illustrated by stereopticon views, proceeds to go to a library fund. Crikelair's Opera House was secured for the lectures in the winter of 1887-88, but producing the series turned out to be more complicated than expected.

Not So Simple

Getting material for the talks wasn't easy and obtaining a projector was a major task. Since such equipment was complicated to run (it operated on gas and needed more know-how than merely plugging into a light socket), Neville not only had to dig in to his own pocket to get fuel tanks from Milwaukee but wound up operating it himself. Nevertheless, the 12-lecture series was so successful it was repeated the following year with England as the pictorial locale.

Meanwhile, Kellogg stepped back into the picture. In the spring of 1888 the city issued $15,000 in bonds to rebuild the Walnut Street bridge. He bought the entire issue, then offered to return them to the city on condition that interest he would normally receive ($900 a year) be used to maintain a public library for 50 years.

The offer, put to another referendum, was accepted. The Nevilles had made a few hundred dollars on the lecture series, which was tossed into the pot, and the show was on the road.

The first library board, consisting of *(Mrs. Kellogg),* S. D. Hastings, Mrs. Neville, Adam Spuhler, A. H. Reynolds, E. K. Ansorge, Oliver Libbey, Mrs. E. H. Ellis and J. H. Flatley, met on Aug. 28, 1888. Judge Hastings was elected president, Mrs. Neville, vice president, and Reynolds, secretary, in which posts they continued to serve for many years. As secretary, Reynolds missed only four board meetings between 1888 and 1906, a period of 17 years.

Inaugurated in 1889

Rooms were acquired in the Weise block at Adams and Cherry Streets, now the site of the new Kellogg-Citizens National Bank *(now Associated Bank)* and Miss Annie McDonnell hired as librarian. On April 2, 1889 the doors opened for business in the former law offices of the firm of Greene, Ellis & Merrill.

From the moment Miss Julia Beaumont signed as the first card holder, the Green Bay Public Library began to fill a need. By July there were 400 card holders and the initial stock of 1,511 books was moving in and out at the rate of 13,205 withdrawals the first year.

By 1895 the library had outgrown its cramped quarters and moved to the first floor of the McGunn Building where the Northern Building now stands, early in 1896. More accessible facilities and consolidation of Green Bay and Fort Howard sent business skyrocketing. The book collection, which now had 4,993 volumes, was circulating at a rate of over 40,000 withdrawals a year and over 6,500 people used the reading rooms.

Wanted New Building

Rufus Kellogg died in 1891. Five years later his vital contribution to the library was permanently recognized when it became the Kellogg Public Library. The step would have been made much earlier but Kellogg had stoutly resisted it while he lived.

In March, 1899, agitation began to house the library in its own building. A committee to investigate the possibilities was appointed and the city council got into the act but nothing happened.

In December, 1900, Annie McDonnell died. Her successor as librarian was Deborah Martin, who had joined the staff in 1897. Miss Martin served until her death in 1931, at which time Sybil Schuette moved up. Miss Schuette remained in charge until she retired in 1959.

The turn of the century was a tough period for the library. The city council went on a retrenchment kick, library funds were cut, and hopes for a new home apparently went dwindling until a dramatic turn of events altered the whole picture.

Carnegie Offer

At a board meeting of Feb. 22, 1901, the Mmes. E. H. Ellis and George Field produced a letter from Andrew Carnegie's secretary stating that Carnegie would give $20,000 for a new building if the city would provide a suitable site and agree to maintain the institution for not less than $2,500 a year thereafter. The two women had quietly been working on Carnegie for some time.

The band wagon immediately began to roll. The city council accepted Carnegie's offer (subsequently increased to $30,000) and Bishop Sebastian G. Messmer donated one of the two lots *(on Jefferson Street)* on which the library now stands. On Feb. 16, 1903, the spanking new building opened with considerable fanfare as the first Carnegie grant institution in Wisconsin.

The once proud structure, a classical showcase in its day, has gradually outlived its usefulness. Barely able to house its 1903 collection of 10,000 volumes, the structure and three branches now contain 205,676 books, card holders have mushroomed from 2,500 to more than 34,000 and circulation has climbed from 49,600 items 60 years ago to over a million in 1960.

** The Kellogg Public Library became the Brown County Public Library in 1968. The central library moved to its present location at 515 Pine Street in 1974. A partnership made up of attorneys Jim Sickel and William Hinkfuss with the Economy Tool Co. bought the vacant library and museum from the city in 1982. After extensive interior renovation for use as office space — the external facade remains unchanged — the attorneys moved into the building, now known as Jefferson Court, in December 1984. The site is listed on the National Register of Historic Places.*

City's Oldest Restaurant

The Story of 'Chili John' Isaac

May 4, 1963

In Green Bay's prosperous, business-as-usual atmosphere of 1913 the opening of a tiny chili parlor at the east end of the Main Street bridge attracted no more attention than a mild curiosity about its not-so-mild specialty. Had the dignified Business Men's Association known that 50 years later, long after the organization had been buried and forgotten, the little hole in the wall would still be going strong as the city's oldest restaurant, its product enjoying a nationwide reputation, the membership might have regarded John Isaac with considerable awe.

With a business established solely on a personally concocted recipe for chili con carne and a borrowed $40, "Chili John" did all right. His was a success story of which the Lithuanian immigrant boy and one-time coal miner had a right to be proud.

John Isaac was born in Lithuania in 1874 and came to America with his parents as a child of four. Isaac wasn't his real surname but an anglicanization of his nearly unpronounceable family name, adopted by his father on arrival in the United States.

Settling originally in Pennsylvania, the father went to work in the coal mines, and so did young John as soon as he was big enough to do a man's job. By the time he was nine he was handling a mule deep in the spreading mine galleries.

Headed West

A couple of years later, however, John's father pulled himself out of the pits and headed west. He reached Wisconsin sometime around 1885, acquired and cleared a homestead in the forest and eventually founded and named the community of Krakow in Oconto County. Young John did his share of the work, an experience that was to be a vital factor in his subsequent career.

As a young man, however, John returned to the coal mines — not in Pennsylvania but in southern Illinois. He worked in them for several years, got married and began to raise a family, but followed his father's example when mine work became too unsteady.

His first independent venture, shortly after the turn of the century, was opening a saloon in Auburn, Ill. As a come-on for his bar John and his wife dispensed homemade chili. It was John's favorite dish.

Having been exposed to the Mexican delicacy as a boy, Isaac loved chili and made a point of learning how to make it. Not only that, over a period of several years, he experimented with the recipe, playing with ingredients and their proportions until he had hit on a dish he thought was just right.

Never Changed Again

Once he had developed it to his own enthusiastic taste he never changed it. That recipe, a family secret, is still being used, exactly as John specified over a half a century ago.

Isaac's chili soon became more popular than his suds, especially among traveling men. The latter used to kid him about turning off his taps and concentrating on this hot stuff.

John brushed the idea off with a grin, but one day it didn't sound so silly. Auburn went dry about 1912, and Isaac suddenly found himself out of business and broke. Cutting his losses, he took his friends' advice, left Illinois and came to Green Bay.

Why Green Bay, which had never heard of chili except as a possible term in the weather report? The decision was more one of sentiment than of cold-eyed business.

Loved Wisconsin

As a boy in Krakow John had loved northern Wisconsin. An avid hunter and fisherman all his life, he had always wanted to come back. Green Bay was the city closest to his ideal of a happy hunting ground.

When he arrived he had his chili recipe and exactly $15 to his name.

The story used to be that it was only 15 cents, but his family insists the amount was actually a more reasonable 15 bucks. John, who loved to talk about his business to anyone who would listen, was the last man to spoil a good story.

With a borrowed stake of $40 he adopted the trade name of "Chili John" and set up his chili parlor near the Main Street bridge. It was a crude little place, with kitchen and small serving counter all crowded into one room.

His equipment was so limited that he had to wash dishes as fast as they were used to be ready for the next customer. In rush hours patrons ate standing up in any convenient corner.

Had to Expand

His old salesman friends soon found him, began flocking to his stand, and others followed. Soon he had to expand, and by 1923 boasted the longest eating counter in town, a horseshoe affair with 31 stools and a completely equipped kitchen.

For a time Chili John included short orders on his menu but eventually dropped them to concentrate on his specialty. Today, as for nearly 50 years, the restaurant offers only chili, coffee, soft drinks and a few desserts.

Chili con carne is a Mexican dish, its translation literally being "beans with meat," highly spiced with chili pepper. It is a fairly common dish today and widely sold, but Chili John's variety is his own and his family's secret. For more than 50 years it has been made carefully to his formula.

From the beginning John offered it in three grades, "mild," "medium" and "hot," and with beans, spaghetti or both. The proportion in which the highly seasoned meat sauce is added to the spaghetti or beans determines its strength — the more sauce the hotter it is. The dish is still served in exactly the same manner today.

Outsiders Wanted Chili

Soon after his restaurant opened, John began getting requests for his product from out of town and developed a means of shipping the meat sauce in pound bricks, like butter. Later he began shipping it in waxed paper cartons. (I have a vague recollection of John once telling me that these cartons, now in general use, were developed originally for him.)

One thing is certain. The tiny oyster crackers now widely sold and which have been served with his chili for decades were invented for him. Early crackers were much larger and hard to handle on a spoon, and it was at John's suggestion that one of the major biscuit companies first began making the small ones.

As satisfied customers spread the word, the reputation of Chili John's dish expanded, first through Wisconsin and then across the nation. The sauce is now shipped all over the country and even overseas, while periodic visitors to the city, from floaters to business executives, make Chili John's one of their first stops when they get to town.

John's son Ernest has helped spread the tidings with his own restaurant in Burbank, Calif., where he has dispensed the same recipe for nearly 30 years.

Fourth Location

The local restaurant's present location on Pine Street is its fourth. It remained next to the bridge until 1930, subsequently occupied two other Main Street spots and settled in its present quarters in 1947. *(A second store opened on the west side in 1973; urban renewal closed the downtown site not long after. In 2003, Chili John's opened in the renovated Lambeau Stadium complex.)*

The sauce is no longer prepared in the restaurant but in a special kitchen at the home of John's daughter and present operator, Mrs. Alden Spofford. Lillian Spofford makes it at the rate of about 500 pounds a week, still adhering meticulously to John's precise recipe.

A sociable man who loved and took pride in his business, John Isaac personally ran his restaurant until just before he died in September 1946 at the age of 72. Since then it has been operated by his daughter *(who sold the business to her sister and brother-in-law, Dorothy and Harry Hoehne, in 1970. A son, Dan, has owned and operated Chili John's since 1980).*

Cherished Institution

Kaap's Celebrates an Anniversary

May 23, 1964

While the Green Bay Free Press was launching its short career half a century ago another now famous local enterprise was also getting under way. The Free Press didn't last on its own, but the other did, and today it enjoys the reputation of being one of the city's most cherished institutions.

Fifty years ago this month — on May 1, 1914, to be exact — Kaap's Restaurant opened on N. Washington Street.

Initially, it wasn't a restaurant. When Otto Kaap shifted around the corner from Pine Street he merely continued his candy shop and ice cream parlor. Through a series of gradual expansions the business grew to its present dimensions, including a restaurant, cocktail bar, candy shop and bakery.

Typical Development

That's been typical of Kaap's from the beginning. Otto never intended to get into the candy business in the first place but being the enthusiast he is, one thing simply followed another.

Running a candy business was the furthest thing from Otto Kaap's mind in 1909. Had he followed original plans he might have become a banker like his brother Albert.

Otto was working as a teller in the Bank of Green Bay in those days and picking up a little moonlight money on the side by playing traps in both the old Orpheum and Bijou Theater orchestras. That's what got him into the completely unrelated business of making candy, wiener schnitzel and apfel kuchen.

Needed a Trumpeter

The Orpheum orchestra was hurting for a good trumpeter. There was one down in Oshkosh but he insisted he wanted to run a candy store, and the band finally got him by agreeing to set him up in business in Green Bay. Otto made it possible by advancing his own savings to the venture.

The guy may have blown a hot horn but he was no candy merchant. It wasn't long before he had ridden his new business into the ground, and Otto, who could only vaguely tell one end of an all-day sucker from the other, was forced to step in and take over to save his investment.

Early Going Rough

The going was rough at first. The shop was a little affair just east of the Main Street bridge, in which is now the Gordon Bent Building *(a sporting goods and cycling shop then at 125 Main Street)*, and strictly a shoestring operation. Otto used to spend part of the night there following theater performances whipping up the candy supply for the next day's business, which didn't take him very long.

He had to do it more or less in secret, too. As Otto tells it, he was afraid to tell his mother the box he had gotten into, and had a hard time cooking up plausible excuses for staying out so late.

Either Mrs. Kaap was sharper than he gave her credit for being and already knew about it, or Otto needn't have worried. When he finally worked up enough courage to tell her she promptly lined up behind him to make a go of the job.

Shifted to Pine

After about a year in the Main Street location Otto shifted to 211 Pine St. He says he made the move because the rent was $5 a month less, and with the show he had going that was important dough.

Slowly the Pine Street establishment caught hold. In a few years he added a soda fountain and set up a small ice cream parlor (he still has a couple of the old metal chairs he used there).

By 1914 he needed more room, so he rented the center portion of the "New Home Building" on Washington, where he was flanked on the south by Grunert's jewelry store and on the north by Slip Allen's saloon. Eventually, he absorbed both.

Much Smaller

Kaap's initial Washington Street site included only the front section where candy and bakery goods are now sold, plus the first portion of the modern restaurant directly in rear. His candy kitchen occupied the space now a part of the restaurant.

The shop was still only a candy store and ice cream parlor, but shortly thereafter he added sandwiches, and it wasn't long before Kaap's "Tea Room" was born. By that time he needed more space, so he picked up the southern section of the building behind the saloon. When prohibition came and Allen closed out, he acquired the rest. The Grunert jewelry store was purchased later.

Otto Kaap has never revealed where or how he learned to make candy, but it wasn't long before his product had achieved a reputation. He has never lost it, either, and one of the charms of becoming re-acquainted with Kaap's candy is the discovery that it hasn't changed in years.

One Facet

The unchanging quality of Kaap's candy is only one facet of an aura of comfortable permanence that has made Kaap's a unique institution. The interior appointments may not send decorators into the streets babbling in admiration, but the customers prefer it that way, as Otto discovered for himself a few years ago.

During a period of slow business some years back Kaap was toying with the idea of redecorating and canvassed a number of his regular customers for suggestions. When they almost unanimously informed him that if he changed so much as a light bulb they would go away and never come back, Otto happily junked the whole scheme.

By the middle 1920s Kaap had acquired the whole building. For a few years the entire ground floor was used for his retail sales and restaurant, but he later closed out the southern front portion and leased it to a hat shop and later to J.C. Penney's, which now occupies it. * When prohibition was repealed he remodeled the former Allen saloon into the cocktail bar.

Larger than Expected

Today's operation is much larger than it looks, with a staff of more than 100 people, including restaurant and sales staff, kitchen workers, cooks, candy makers and bakers.

The entire second floor of the building is divided between the bakery and candy shop, where a force of over 20 people concoct, dip and pack his famous "Old Fashioned" chocolate creams and a wide variety of other sweets under the direction of Florent DeCramer, Kaap's chief candy maker for 43 years. DeCramer is proud of the fact that Kaap's is one of the few candy makers still dipping candies by hand.

Otto Kaap now enjoys the unique distinction of being the only businessman on Washington Street still operating on the same premises. A couple of other businesses are in the same Washington Street locations but their ownership has changed through the years. Otto still runs his own show as enthusiastically as ever.

Not a Native

Although Otto has lived all his life in Green Bay he wasn't born here. His mother was a Green Bay native who moved to Manistee, Mich., shortly after her marriage. The stay lasted long enough for Otto to be born there, after which the family returned to Green Bay while he was still an infant.

A man of untrammeled enthusiasms who takes off like a runaway locomotive once he gets his teeth into a hobby, Otto Kaap's principal interest outside his business has always been music. There were many years, though, when he couldn't indulge in it.

Away for 40 Years

As his candy business prospered Otto had to give up his early place in the Orpheum orchestra pit, as well as the post of tympanist in the original Green Bay Symphony Orchestra. He didn't come back until the present symphony was formed as the Symphonette, since when he had been one of the orchestra's most faithful members.

When he left the Orpheum Theater pit he didn't return for 40 years. He finally came back in 1954 when the Symphonette furnished the pit orchestra for one of Russ Widoe's operetta productions there.

A few years ago Otto slipped and fell in the restaurant kitchen, suffering a fractured arm and leg. The accident slowed him down only briefly, and as soon as he could swing a drumstick again he was back behind his battery of kettle drums. He moves with a limp, now, but there's little distinguishable slackening of his speed and none in his ability to cover ground.

Now a supercharged 76, Otto is presently on a round-the-world tour with Mrs. Kaap. They passed through Hawaii en route to the Orient recently but didn't stop, although Otto has been anxious to visit the islands for years. He's saving them for a later trip.

** Penney's later moved to Port Plaza Mall, now called Washington Commons, as part of the 1970s Gregby-Greater Green Bay Urban Renewal Project. The downtown redevelopment effort also closed and razed Kaap's despite the establishment's popularity and listing on the National Register of Historic Places.*

Forgotten Anniversary

Green Bay 'Y' Has Long History

August 15, 1964

The Green Bay YMCA had an important anniversary a couple of weeks ago but nobody made anything of it. Forty years ago, in the midsummer of 1924, the cornerstone of the present "Y" on the corner of North Jefferson and Pine streets was laid.

The rugged old structure was, in its day, one of the finest and most costly buildings of its kind in the nation. It still maintains the dignity of indestructible quality and carries on proudly, although it has taken a steady battering for nearly half a century and is no longer adequate to the needs of a community that has more than tripled in size since it was new.

Actually, the history of the Young Men's Christian Assn. in Green Bay goes back much farther than 1924. In only a few more years the local YMCA will observe its centennial.

Beginnings of the movement locally are traced to old Fort Howard about 1870. Prime mover in that pioneer effort was the minister of a West Side church, the Rev. D. C. Curtis.

Popular Pastor

The Rev. Curtis headed a small Congregational Church on Third Street in Fort Howard's South Side. A popular pastor and a strong figure in the rowdy little town (still several years short of the dignity of a city), Curtis was genuinely interested in the welfare of the youth of the community.

He had good reason for concern. Both Fort Howard and Green Bay were different communities than they are today. A lake port, manufacturing and lumber center, the towns were wide open, rough and ready places where almost anything could happen.

Although Fort Howard could boast of a saloon for about every 25 inhabitants, social programs were non-existent except for what each church congregation could maintain for its own members. Slum conditions were appalling by modern standards, there was no compulsory school system and there were more kids roaming the streets than sitting in classrooms. There was plenty of trouble for young men and teenagers to get into, and they often made the most of it.

Talked up Program

In an effort to combat some of these conditions, the Rev. Curtis talked up an organization to get some of the youngsters off the streets. He interested several businessmen and Madam Tank in the idea and they contributed money for a small clubhouse.

The building, a recreation center of limited facilities and reading room, was built on church property and about 25 young men enrolled. The bulk of the program consisted of debates, prayer meetings and some social activity directed by the group's first president, George W. Wright.

The club was called the "Young Men's Christian Assn." but it was not formally affiliated with the state and national movement. It did, however, enjoy some supervision by the state YMCA secretary and periodically sent representatives to state meetings.

Interest lapsed after a few years. In 1887 a new organization was formed but operated only spasmodically.

Another Group

Early in 1890, however, a more dynamic group of young Fort Howard civic leaders took charge and in April a Young Men's Christian Assn. of Fort Howard was chartered. Signers of the articles of incorporation included Otis R. Larsen, William Miller, F. S. Marshall, J. H. Tayler, J. K. Ford, A. Anderson, Henry Bailey and William Hood. Six years later the name was changed to the YMCA of Green Bay.

Fruit of this revival was a permanent headquarters on the corner of West Walnut and Chestnut Avenue. The organization raised enough money to purchase the site and William J. Fisk sparked the rest with a dramatic contribution of $5,000 (subsequently raised to $7,500).

This was enough to construct a small gymnasium, meeting hall and bath facilities. As the only gym on the West Side the little plant long served a variety of needs and gave West High School a big jump on East High in basketball. The Wildcats were playing the game in the YMCA gym long before East had any place to play.

Damaged by Fire

In 1908 the building was badly damaged by fire and although rebuilt it never was so active again. In 1915 part of the building was rented to the Kellogg Public Library as a branch. The board of education ran an open air school and later its west side manual training department there. Just before World War I the property was sold to the school board to liquidate the organization's debts.

The sale raised enough to pay all the bills, with about $1,000 to spare. This was carefully set aside for future use, and when the campaign for the present YMCA was launched the fund was tossed into the kitty.

Felt Time Ripe

The passing of the old YMCA disturbed William Larsen and Mitchell Joannes, who felt the city needed such a facility. The two men got together and were ready to give it a starting push when Larsen died. Joannes went quietly ahead with the scheme.

Late in 1922 Joannes felt the time was ripe to get some sort of show on the road and called a meeting with J. H. Tayler, several other prominent citizens and the state YMCA secretary.

A number of the men at the meeting made substantial advance gifts, including Frank Murphy, Judson Rosebush, Tayler, Herman Greiling, J.T. Phillips and Mrs. Agnes Jorgensen. Joannes himself eventually emerged as the major contributor.

After careful preparation a fund raising campaign was launched in April of 1923. With promotional ideas in the talented hands of Harold T. I. Shannon, the YMCA drive was one of the most spectacularly successful in the history of Green Bay.

In one week between April 6-16, the sum of $426,000 was raised. A total of 4,109 local citizens contributed to the project.

Opened in 1925

Money or pledges in hand, a new YMCA organization was set up, the Jefferson-Pine Street site was purchased, and work began. The present YMCA, in its day a national show case, opened its doors in September, 1925, and they have never closed.

It would be virtually impossible to enumerate the varied contributions the YMCA has made to the life of Green Bay since then. Through its long history it has played a significant role in the lives of hundreds of local citizens, many of whom enrolled in the Y when it first opened and who are still using its facilities.

A major bulwark in the continued existence of the YMCA is the Y Men's Club. Formed in the spring of 1926, only a few months after the building opened its doors, the Men's Club has held a strong and enthusiastic rein over the numerous YMCA programs conducted there ever since.

Chapter Eight

Sports and Some Who Starred

Diamond Donnybrook

1891 Season a Baseball Thriller

June 17, 1961

Green Bay has seen a lot of exciting baseball since the original Stars first took the field in 1866. Few games have equaled the 23-inning marathon of 1907,* of course, but there have been free-wheeling donnybrooks, no-hit classics and all the other clutch performances that make baseball what it is.

But for sustained excitement, the fans here have never enjoyed another season like 1891. That year had everything, including a wild finish unmatched in the town's long diamond history. Everything, that is, except a pennant.

Although Green Bay had been a hotbed of baseball for a quarter of a century it had never had a league team before. In fact, there had only been one other league in this part of the country-the old Northwestern League of 1884-until the formation of the original Wisconsin State League in 1891 with Green Bay, Appleton, Marinette, Oshkosh, Oconto and Fond du Lac in the circuit.

Enthusiasm ran high in all cities. There was some dissatisfaction with the league's salary limit of $500 a month, but as it turned out nobody paid any attention to that.

Off to Good Start

A 90-game schedule was arranged, club president Frank Murphy lined up a strong club and things started well. The "Dock Wallopers," as they were called, were in the middle of the fight, which saw Appleton, Green Bay and Oshkosh setting the early pace.

On July 4, with a third of the schedule completed, Green Bay was in the lead by a slim margin, but there was trouble ahead. The next road trip saw the club dropping a number of games in which the players apparently could not find the handle on the ball and were shellacked by lopsided scores.

The Dock Wallopers were a good but irresponsible outfit with a weakness for what the Gazette called "sporting tendencies." At home they kept their noses fairly clean but on the road they let themselves go with results that showed up at the ball park.

By Aug. 1 Green Bay had skidded to fourth, attendance was falling off and rumors of a housecleaning were flying.

It came on Aug. 4 with the announcement that the entire team except one pitcher had been fired and a new one was en route from Terre Haute, Ind. Murphy had quietly visited the Indiana city, where the club was about to fold, and signed up the whole lot.

Great Diamond 'Angel'

Murphy was like that. A rabid fan who would have cheerfully traded his status as a millionaire in those days to be a big league ball player, he was the backbone of city baseball for years. No town ever had a better diamond "angel." Whenever things got tough Murphy was always on hand to pick up the tab.

Frank's importation was a classy outfit. Managed by George Brackett, one of the best known minor league managers in the business with a record going back to 1872, the team had started the season at Peoria, Ill., in the Northwestern League.

Playing at a .712 clip it was far out in front with a record of 42-17 when a league reorganization tossed Peoria out in the cold. Shifted to Terre Haute the team had won seven and lost four when Murphy waved his checkbook.

When the "Hoosiers" came to town (the Dock Walloper title was promptly forgotten), Green Bay was eight games off the pace with 38 to play. They proceeded to set the league on fire, sweeping seven straight before dropping a decision. By Sept. 1 they were in second place, having won 15 of 20, and had cut Appleton's lead to 4 1/2 games.

Meanwhile the Oshkosh Indians began to fade while the Marinette Logrollers moved up. Then the league-leading Papermakers started to crack. Things got complicated when Oshkosh took three straight from the Hoosiers while Marinette was splitting a pair, but the Bay bounced back with two victories over the faltering Papermakers as the Logrollers forfeited to Fond du Lac.

Down to Wire

With only 12 games to play the Hoosiers were tied with Marinette, two games behind Appleton. Four of the final contests were with Appleton, two with Fond du Lac and the last six with Marinette.

By sweeping the Appleton series Green Bay vaulted into first place but came a cropper against the underdog Fond du Lac Webfeet. With Appleton out of contention, Marinette was leading by one game. The pennant rode on those last six contests, three of which were to be played here and the last three in Marinette.

The Hoosiers promptly regained the top slot by taking the first two here but the pressure told. They blew the home finale to move on to Marinette for the showdown with everything tightly knotted for both clubs on records of 48 won, 39 lost.

The cards were stacked in the Marinette opener, however. An unruly crowd of 3,500 jammed the park, including some of the "toughest mugs" in the lumber country as well as hundreds of kids armed with foghorns, rocks and pea shooters. The din was incessant and so was the barrage of rocks and pea shooter pellets.

The Green Bay infield was pelted every time it took the field. Even Murphy, who was present, caught a few rocks during the afternoon.

The umpiring was malodorous, but when Brackett protested the ump frankly informed him he wasn't going to risk his hide by any decision against the home club. Under the circumstances, the result — a 7-1 defeat — was inevitable. At the hotel after the game Murphy and Brackett decided to pull the team from the field and return home at once.

As news of what was going on up north filtered back to Green Bay local enthusiasts, who included just about everybody in the town of 9,000, began to blow their stacks. When the team arrived home that night it was greeted at the station by a howling crowd and escorted triumphantly to Cook's Hotel with a parade unmatched until the return of the champion Packers nearly 40 years later.

Next afternoon at Marinette the home team took the field and when Green Bay failed to appear claimed the game and the championship. With the season over, four of the six clubs promptly entered claims for the pennant.

Appleton, which had edged into the runner-up spot on the basis of the final games, demanded forfeiture of several contests with Marinette for alleged crooked umpiring. Green Bay claimed the crucial series intact because of the unfair tactics of the Marinette crowd.

Oconto, which finished in the cellar, made its bid on the grounds that it was the only club in the league to abide by the salary limit. Marinette, a trifle sheepishly, stood on the record.

Thus matters stood until the league meeting at Oshkosh a month later. After a series of heated arguments, all the forfeiture claims were thrown out, but when it came to awarding the pennant nobody wanted to stick their necks out. The mess was finally sidestepped by the unanimous adoption of a resolution that, because of unfair practices of "some" clubs, no pennant would be awarded.

** The 23-inning marathon referred to here is described in detail in Rudolph's column of June 3, 1961.*

The Pastime Cycle Club

When Bicycles Ruled the Roost

May 2, 1970

Seventy-five years ago there weren't any hot-rodders, motorcycle demons or sports car buffs, but that didn't mean great-grandpa wasn't preoccupied with fads of his own. Throughout the decade of the Gay Nineties, enthusiasm for speed was worked off by the proliferation of bicycles.

Bike riders were all over the place, discoursing on the virtues of the Stearns, Columbia, Victory and other wheels with the same know-how as the present generation compares motorcycles, snowmobiles and sports cars. Most of this knowledge and practice was encouraged through the League of American Wheelmen and a host of local cycling clubs.

In Green Bay the manifestation was the Pastime Cycle Club.

Organized in the spring of 1895, by a handful of cycling enthusiasts led by Art Fontaine, the Pastime Cycle Club dominated the scene for the remainder of the century. The idea caught hold, and by the spring of 1896 the Pastime could boast a membership of about 150. By the end of the year more than 200 cyclists were in the fold.

Social Factor

Whatever the exact figure, there were enough of them to make the organization a major factor in the city's social and recreational life. For the next four years scarcely a week went by that the club activities didn't rate heavy ink in both the Gazette and Advocate.

Socially as well as athletically inclined, the Pastimes embraced both men and women members. By 1897 it had its own weekly newspaper, a well appointed set of clubrooms on Washington Street and was sponsoring a series of winter dances that never failed to make the society columns.

One of the biggest club whings for a number of years was an annual masquerade ball. Masquerades were happenings in those days and somebody was always throwing a costume party, but from 1896 to 1899 the Pastime masquerade ranked right with the Turners' party in size and popularity.

Summer Races

Every summer the club also staged a series of races and outings into the country, as carefully and formally controlled as a modern motorcycle or sports car rendezvous. As captain, George Schafer usually led these weekly events, which were enjoyed by large numbers of riders whenever weather permitted.

The Pastimes first major event was a road race to De Pere and back in the summer of 1896. Starting from the corner of Adams and Cherry Streets, the course followed the lower road *(Riverside Drive)* to east De Pere, across the river and back via the west side and Main Street bridge to the starting point.

That first race with stripped down wheels without brakes or other safety devices over a rough, unpaved course was a thriller, spiced at the outset by a number of spills and crackups. Bert Groesbeck, a local bicycle salesman and all-around athlete who also played on Green Bay's first state championship football team in 1897, won the race over the 11-mile course in slightly over an hour.

Shot for State Meet

Having received a charter from the League of American Wheelmen, the Pastimes began casting covetous eyes on the annual state racing meet. Since this was a LAW-sanctioned affair carrying points toward the national championships, the meet attracted top riders from all over the country, whose records were as familiar to the faithful as the batting averages of Muggsy McGraw, Willie Keeler and Ed Delahanty were to the baseball buffs.

The club was talked out of making a serious bid for the 1897 meet but apparently received encouragement for 1898. At any rate, the club drew a bead on the latter show, only to discover that Oshkosh and Racine were secretly maneuvering to euchre Green Bay out of the plum.

The Pastimes, who had John Rose on the state LAW board, immediately set up a cry of foul. It soon became obvious, however, that Oshkosh wasn't kidding and that the Pastimes had a fight on their hands.

Long Deadlock

The site selection meeting, held in Milwaukee early in December, 1897, developed into a regular political convention, with impassioned speeches, considerable bitterness and backstage politicking. A deadlock between Green Bay and Oshkosh required 46 ballots before Green Bay broke the line and got the prize.

The news, flashed by railroad telegraph to anxious Pastimers gathered in their clubrooms, touched off an impromptu celebration. The victorious cyclists poured into the streets for a noisy parade through the downtown area, after which many of them returned to the clubrooms to drink and talk it over.

When the local delegation, headed by Mayor Frank Desnoyers, returned the following evening, it was met at the station by a huge swarm of cyclists who escorted them through the business district with appropriate signs, torches and a great deal of noise. An augur of the future to which nobody paid any attention was the presence of 15 automobiles in the line of march.

Petered out in Rain

The 1898 meet, staged at Hagemeister Park racetrack *(where East Green Bay High School now stands)* Aug. 16-18, began auspiciously, only to peter out in a steady, drizzling rain. All the big riders, led by world champion E. J. Bald and including a then relatively unknown character named Barney Oldfield, showed up.

The first two days drew large crowds and was a huge success. Rain on the big and final day, however, made a mud hole of the racetrack and the last events had to be cancelled. Calling them off meant that a potential profit was converted into a considerable loss, which the merchants of the city had to make good.

The effort expended on obtaining and staging the meet and the anti-climax of canceling the last day seems to have taken most of the fizz out of the Pastime Cycle Club. It held its fourth annual masquerade as usual in the spring of 1899, but it wasn't very successful. By the end of the year the club had collapsed as quickly as it had flowered.

The Astors Buck the Navarinos

March 2, 1968

Whatever else it may or may not be, Green Bay has always been a sports town. From earliest days when hunting, fishing and horse racing were the rage until the current reign of the Packers the city has taken a fling at every imaginable form of sport, and the list of flourishing teams and clubs ranges from gymnasts (the old Turners), baseball and soccer to hockey, basketball and football.

Most were short lived but at least one sport spawned a club hard to kill off. The longevity of the Astors and Navarinos outmatches even that of the Packers, although the latter are closing in fast.

The Astors and Navarinos were bowling teams — the members called them a "league" — which were, in their long day, the most unique kegling outfit in Wisconsin if not in the entire nation. They were exclusive, too; almost as bad as the Euchre Club *(an elite woman's club)*, which they resembled in more ways than one, although the stately members of the latter shuddered at the thought of being seen just walking past a bowling alley.

Formed in 1895

Organized in 1895, the Astors and Navarinos lasted at least half a century. They weren't so hot on the lanes and they couldn't have cared less. Formed initially for fun and frolic they remained true to their original purpose to the end.

The gang, a group of congenial young men looking for a little fun, got together for the first time at the old Hagemeister Park clubhouse at the east end of Cherry Street *(where East High School now stands)* the evening of Feb. 4, 1895. That happened to be a Thursday, and for the next 50 years they remained faithful to the day, the game and the fun of bowling and needling each other.

Initially they bowled the then popular but now forgotten three-pin game with a ball about the size of a grapefruit. Each team recruited eight "regulars" plus a pair of substitutes for a total of 20, and league membership remained fixed at that number.

Only by Invitation

To join, one had to be invited and such invitations were not only rare but highly prized. Members were added only when somebody dropped out, few did, and they turned out to be a remarkably long-lived group. For at least 40 years it was the boast of the club that it had never lost an active member through death. Eventually, replacements were confined to the sons of members.

There is no record of the complete charter membership but among them were Frank Van Laanen, Nic Bur, George Schober, Fred Gehr, Henry Klaus, J. B. Theisen and Henry A. Foeller. Four decades later Van Laanen and Bur were still active and enthusiastic regulars.

Fun and Fellowship

Since the early roster was largely German, beer and pretzels were as important as scores — probably more so, since the "league" never kept track of games won and lost. The secretary maintained a record of total pins toppled and at the end of the season the "championship" was determined on the total score. In 1928, for example, the Astors took the honors by a margin of only 578 pins-60,027 to 59,449.

Fun and good fellowship being the primary purpose of the club, there was a lot of horseplay and practical joking. In 1898 the boys threw a banquet at the end of the season that was so much fun they made it a fixture thereafter.

The Beaumont Hotel eventually became the traditional site for the yearly whing but the party moved around in the early years. In 1916 it was held at Schwalbe's Restaurant on North Washington Street.

For the first decade the gang remained true to the three-pin game but the increasing popularity of ten-pins eventually converted them, especially after they shifted base to the new Elks Club alleys in 1903. *(The club then was located on the northwest corner of North Jefferson and Cherry Streets behind what is now Associated Bank.)* The league went to ten pins in 1905.

1900 Membership

By 1900 the membership had settled down. In that year the Astor regulars included Van Laanen, Klaus, H. Michaal, Joseph and Frank Kaster, George and Louis Schober, Foeller and Matt Bingen, with the Navarinos lineup consisting of Gehr, E. Bank, David Nys, Theisen, Herman Forst, Frank Bender and Bur.

Five years later Gehr was sporting Astor colors with Klaus, Forst, Nys, Ed Barth, Jacob Nick, Bur, Ed Shepeck, George Gazette and Dr. T. J. Oliver. Navarinos were the Schober brothers, Bill Brenner, Theisen, Van Laanen, Joseph Rothe Sr., A. G. Kurz, Bender, Foeller and George F. Reeke.

In 1928 the Astors included Van Laanen, Bur, Nys, Oliver, Bender, Forst, Gazette, John J. Rothe and Barth. Shepeck, Joe Rothe, Nick, Louis Schober, Klaus, Joseph Foeller, Brenner, Joe Bur and Tony Hoberg were throwing gutter balls for the Navarinos.

By this time the fame of the old club was spreading. Each year the banquet drew a lot of ink in the Press-Gazette, usually with old photographs and a full account of some of the gags played on each other.

Party Highlight

The high spot of the 1928 party came in the middle of the dinner when a couple of "traveling salesmen," complete with merchandise trunks, invaded the private dining room and ordered the club to vacate so they could set up displays for which they had rented the room. Things got pretty noisy before the hoax was revealed.

The last big public splash for the Astors and Navarinos came in 1934 when the state bowling tournament was held in Green Bay. The two venerable teams, which outdated the tournament itself by almost ten years, were given the honor of rolling the first shift as the oldest bowling organization in the state.

Lining up for the Astors were Van Laanen, Louis Schober, Gazette, Bur and Henry Foeller, while the Navarinos consisted of Joe Rothe Sr., Joe Foeller, Hoberg, Reeke and Bender, Rothe at 74 being the oldest bowler in the tournament. The Navarinos not only outscored their ancient rivals, 2,147-2,057 but both beat the teams with whom they were paired.

The two teams continued to chaffer and compete with each other for at least another decade. Nobody remembers when they finally called it quits and all the records have long since disappeared, but Tony Hoberg, the last survivor, is quite sure they were still at it until about 20 years ago.

Long Sports History

Golfing Fans Around Here Early

July 17, 1965

Pairing Green Bay with sports automatically means the Packers. But while the city loves football and practically idolizes its Packers, only a thimbleful of the crowds that jam Lambeau — oops! City — Stadium can actually take part in a scrimmage.

Football here is primarily a spectator sport, but Bayites, being as active otherwise as they are vocal about football, like to play games, too. Of all the participating sports now flourishing in the neighborhood, golf probably ranks second only to bowling in the numbers who play it regularly.

The rise of golf's popularity is a relatively recent trend, but the game has been played hereabouts for nearly 70 years. What began in the Gay Nineties as a hobby among a few well-to-do gentlemen is now eagerly pursued with a year around passion by thousands from the age of eight to 80.

The year 1895 is usually given as the date the first set of golf clubs appeared in Green Bay and Atty. H. O. Fairchild is the man credited with bringing them. Fairchild had learned to play the game in Chicago, talked it up with his cronies and finally got a few interested.

Imported First Clubs

In 1895 Fairchild and a couple of others imported some clubs and golf balls. Since they had no other place to swing they got into the habit of going out to Astor Park to hit a few.

The park was then just an open field with almost no foliage and practically out in the country. Since nobody made any fuss the enthusiasts sank three holes and started to bat around.

That's all they were, too — just three tin cans sunk in the ground, with no tees or greens. When the boys got tired of fooling around their informal three-holer and had a yen for real competition they had to go to Appleton or Oshkosh.

Since there were no automobiles or highways on which to drive them, they had to travel by train, and a golf date up the valley was an all-day safari. The only obvious answer was a golf course at home.

In 1903 Fairchild and eight friends, three of them from De Pere, organized the Wau-Be-Nuk-Qua *(sic)* Country Club, first in the Green Bay area. A 57-acre tract at the north end of De Pere, between Webster Avenue and Broadway, was leased and a nine-hole course laid out on both sides of the Green Bay-De Pere interurban street car tracks, between Webster and what are now the residential subdivisions of Daviswood and Urbandale.

An unused amusement park pavilion in a beautiful grove of white pine (now long gone) was converted into a clubhouse. For the next decade the Wau-Be-Nuk-Qua (*sic*) Country Club was a social mecca and membership an eagerly sought status symbol.

Flourished with Capital C

For about eight years the country club (always spelled with capital C's in the Gazette society column) flourished. By 1910, however, interest began to flag and the club started to wane.

The recession was rather abrupt and nobody seems to know why, but part of the trouble may have been the failure to interest the women in golf despite all efforts to promote competition. The girls liked to play cards on the clubhouse veranda and indulge in a spine-tingling game of croquet now and then but they had little time for golf. The cumbersome clothing they wore may have a lot to do with their indifference.

When the lease on the property ran out in 1913 it was not renewed and the Wau-Be-Nuk-Qua (*sic*) Country Club quietly died. For the next three years the hard core golfers had no place to play.

Fox River Club Next

You can't keep a golfing nut down, however, and in 1915 some of the veterans got together to form a new club. The Fox River Country Club was organized and a new course built along the lower De Pere road.

Technically the Fox River course (it was called a golf links in those days) was far superior to its predecessor but had one basic fault. There were only nine holes and no room to expand.

Predictably, the club followed the same path as its predecessor. By 1925 it was in trouble and three years later, after several of its most prominent members pulled out to form the Oneida Golf and Riding Club, it folded.

The spread was sold to the Chicago Landscape Co. which operated it as the first public fee course in the area until 1935, when Vince Hendrie bought it. The course, with some modifications, is now *(the defunct)* Town and Country *(on Riverside Drive in Allouez).*

Not Original Clubhouse

The present T and C supper club, however, is not the original clubhouse. That was located on the knoll across the highway and for a number of years flourished as a plush night club (the story is that it was also a gambling casino) until it burned down just before World War II.

Under the leadership of A. B. Turnbull, the Oneida corporation acquired land nostalgically remembered by a generation of aging Boy Scouts as Sullivan's Flats. Here, in the summer of 1928, one of the most picturesque and sporty championship courses in Wisconsin opened for play.

Oneida had a tough time during the Depression but, thanks largely to Turnbull, rode it out. It retains its reputation as a difficult and scenic course and has been the scene of many regional and state tournaments in the past 35 years.

In 1930 another group of enthusiasts tried to sell the city council on a municipal course, failed and established Shorewood on the bay shore. Originally only nine holes, it was lengthened to 18 in the early 1940s *(or late 1930s. The University of*

Wisconsin-Green Bay took ownership in 1969 to build the then new university on Nicolet Drive and reduced the 18-hole course to nine. Currently it remains a nine-hole course and continues as a public facility).

The municipal fee course idea was 25 years maturing but finally came to fruition in 1956 when the Brown County Course was opened. Green Bay now has three top notch 18-hole and one nine-hole spreads, yet interest in the game has outstripped facilities and already there is pressure for more. *(Within Brown County, there now exist two private clubs and at least 16 courses open to the public.)*

Major Boost

General participation in the game received a major boost in 1930 when the Press-Gazette sponsored the first county tournament. The annual event has been a fixture ever since, although it was boiled down to a women's competition during the war and when there weren't enough men around to make a field.

Surprisingly, when the women, who weren't interested in golf 50 years ago, finally took to it they overshadowed the men. Although Green Bay has never produced a state men's champion, several local women have taken the crown since Virginia Gittins blazed the way in 1923.

Best known was little Mary McMillin, who dominated the state field after the war. Mary, who played golf like she had veins full of ice water achieved national recognition as a teenager when she upset the great Babe Didrickson in the Women's Western Open in 1946.

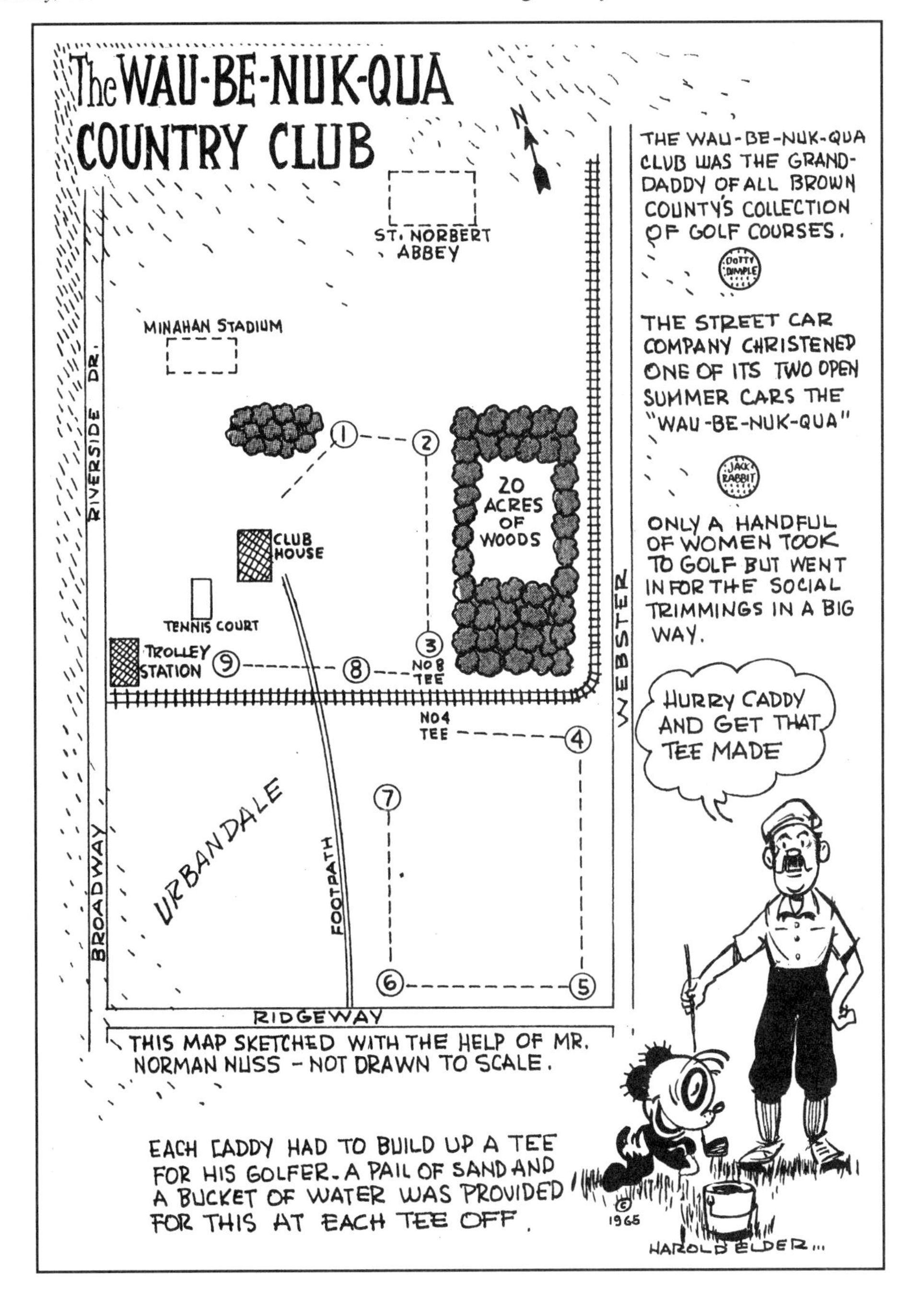

Social-Sporting Group

The Gentlemen's Driving Club

September 9, 1967

Green Bay has spawned over the years a succession of social organizations whose activities have enlivened the social scene and enriched the city's colorful history. Most of them have been exclusive women's groups, such as the Euchre, Sewing and Shakespeare Clubs, but one male stronghold that matched the girls was the equally prestigious Gentlemen's Driving and Riding Club.

During the first decade of this century, between the decline of the bicycle and the advent of the automobile, the horse was king of the road. A matched pair pulling a gleaming brougham, cabriolet or Victoria was a pretty sight, and Society was as conscious of the effect as are the proud owners of Jaguars, Continentals, Thunderbirds and Cadillacs today.

A top status symbol of the time and trend was the Driving and Riding Club, which added tone to the horsy set between 1899 and 1908. Membership was highly prized and prominent men of the city angled for it as avidly as their wives and daughters finagled for a bid to the Euchre and other exclusive circles.

Formed in 1899

The Gentlemen's Driving and Riding Club was organized at a meeting of about 30 owners of fine horses in the city council chambers the night of May 16, 1899. Among the instigators of its formation, all business, professional and civic leaders, were Dr. R. C. Buchanan, F. J. B. Duchateau, Frank B. Desnoyers, H. A. Barkhausen, M. J. Corbett and John L. Jorgensen.

Originally called the Gentlemen's Driving Club, it was purely a social — and therefore exclusive — organization, patterned after one in Milwaukee. The purpose, within the stated social framework, was to encourage interest in owning, raising and driving blooded horses.

Albert M. Murphy was its first president, a post he held until 1904. Other officers were J. L. Wilcox, vice president; William J. McCormick, secretary; and Herbert Camm, treasurer.

Purpose Expanded

At a second meeting, held at the Hotel Felch (the once plush Cook's Hotel on the present site of Catlin's Shoe Store *located then at 131 N. Washington Street)* the mission was expanded to include riding as well as driving and the name was changed to reflect the expanded program. Riding always remained a secondary consideration, however, and the club never showed any interest in flat racing.

Throughout its existence the main activity of the club was staging an annual series of "matinee" sulky races — Sunday racing was out — solely for trophies. Money purses were never offered and the meets were held only for social purposes, but that didn't mean the members were discouraged from privately putting a bob or two on the noses of their own nags. Indeed, it is highly unlikely the club would have flourished as long as it did without behind-the-scenes betting.

Joannes Bros., which then owned what was called Washington Park, including the present site of East High School and old City Stadium, offered the free use of the park race track and the club hired a man to maintain it. Almost at once Joannes sold the part of the area later known as Hagemeister Park to the Hagemeister Brewing Co., but Henry Hagemeister let the arrangement stand.

First Outing

The club staged its first "matinee" on June 29, 1899. Preceded by an elaborate downtown parade, the card of three races was a huge success, witnessed by more than 1,500 people.

Led by the Trombone Band, the parade passed through the downtown business district, across the river to Broadway and back along Walnut Street to the track. The first procession of its kind ever held in the city, the parade included a group of mounted men as well as nearly 50 driving outfits featuring a surprising variety of carriages decorated in the club colors of black and gold.

People who could afford it in those days took great pains to be costumed and outfitted with the correct vehicle and team for every social occasion. While nobody around here pretended to match the show then being put on at such summer citadels of wealth and society as Newport and Bar Harbor, they did pretty well. As the Gazette remarked next day, the parade was a "revelation to those who under-rated the number and quality of the town's stylish turnouts."

'Gracious' Salute

Arriving at the park, the parade passed in review in front of the grandstand. A popular section was the mounted group, led by President Albert Murphy and Mayor Simon J. Murphy, all outfitted in white canvas trousers and caps. To the appreciative cheer that went up when introduced as the "Rough Riders of Green Bay," they all "doffed their caps and smiled graciously."

Despite a spectacular spill in the first race, in which no one was hurt, the races were excellent. Owners, as was the custom before rivalries led to the hiring of professional drivers, drove their own entries in all events.

The success of the inaugural was so impressive it set the pattern for the future. Thereafter, the first matinee of each season was preceded by a similar parade.

Number Varied

The number of matinees each season varied. At the height of the club's activity there were four but the average was three. A couple of winters the club also revived the once highly popular races on the ice of the Fox River on a straightaway course laid out from the Mason to the Main Street bridges.

How much effect the club had on the improvement of the breed of horses locally it is impossible to tell, but developing rivalries led to the importation of some fast steppers. In 1903 the annual meeting had to be postponed because so many key members were out of town buying race horses to carry their colors during the coming season.

However keen such rivalry became and whatever money changed hands among the members, the Gentlemen's Driving and Riding Club always maintained its strictly social façade. There was no racing for money prizes and no Sunday racing. In fact, when it was planned to hold the 1902 inaugural on Decoration Day the idea raised such a storm it was called off.

Social Prestige

As a social club, membership carried considerable prestige and was closely regulated. The initial membership goal was 100 but there is no evidence the group tried very hard to reach it. In later years season tickets were sold which automatically carried membership status but they weren't available to just anybody.

The club reached the peak of its popularity and activity in 1904, then gradually declined as the horse began to lose ground to the motor car as a status symbol. The "in thing" thereafter was to chug out to the Wau-Bu-Nuk-Qua (*sic*) Country Club for a round of golf and a couple of tall, cool ones on the clubhouse veranda. In 1908, faced with dwindling interest in horses, the Gentlemen's Driving and Riding Club quietly tossed in the reins.

Old Time Hunting Was Fantastic

October 10, 1964

At noon today the shores of Green bay erupted in a fusillade of gunfire that will be repeated at regular intervals for the next 40 days. The duck season opened, and every hunter who can sneak into a blind will be blazing away in search of his daily bag limit of four ducks.

Some will make it and a few will succeed more than once, to brag about the wonderful shooting as long as anyone will listen. If, in the middle of their most choice tales, they hear an eerie razzberry or two they needn't be surprised. The shades of Green Bay's old market hunters will probably be giving them the ghostly bird.

To the old timers who hunted the shores of the bay until well past the turn of the century a limit of four ducks would have been unthinkable. In their time the hunter who couldn't bring down 100 birds in a day's shooting simply didn't know one end of a shotgun from the other.

They had some real tales to tell. Only a dwindling handful can recall it but there was a time when the shores of the bay were a hunters' paradise. Some of the accounts of hunting on the bay would be fantastically unbelievable if they weren't so well authenticated.

Claflin Told Stories

One of the veteran sportsmen who preserved many of these stories 35 and more years ago was the late Bert Claflin. Bert wasn't noted for letting the facts stand in the way of a good story, but he had known and hunted with most of the old "market hunters," outdoorsmen and crack shots who made a good living killing wild ducks and selling them to local meat markets. Besides, Bert couldn't have dreamed up any stories to compare with the truth.

For more than half a century the local market hunters piled up fantastic bags year after year. Such characters as Jock Poirier, Maishe Basche, Pete Salvas, the Barlament and Gross boys, Chris Seims, Jack Parish, Bill Conley, Charley Brunette and Sam Lindley, to name only a handful, counted the day lost when they didn't bring in a minimum of 100 ducks at a time.

Writing for the Press-Gazette in 1930, (when the daily limit was 15), Claflin told of seeing the entire bay carpeted with wildfowl from the mouth of the Fox River out over the Point Sauble sand bar. He claimed the flocks actually blotted out the sun when they rose from the water. There was no such thing as a limit in the days when the shooting began more or less by mutual consent on Aug. 20 and lasted until the freeze-up.

Basche Most Successful

Probably the most successful of all the Green Bay market hunters was Basche, who enjoyed the reputation of having bagged more wild ducks than any other man in the city's history. A colorful character, Basche shot and sold an average of over 2,000 ducks a season for more than 50 years.

His favorite hunting area was Peak's Lake, in its day a fabulous shooting stand and site of the notorious Green Bay Sportsman's Club lodge. From its inception in 1875 until after 1900, the club was the refuge of many of the town's top shots, stand up drinkers and convivial souls, among them General Grant's hell-raising son-in-law, Algernon Sartoris.

Pete Salvas was another legendary market hunter, who did most of his shooting outside the log boom across the mouth of the Suamico River. Pete's outstanding feat and one he bragged about for years was his record of 600 canvasbacks and mallards in six consecutive days of hunting. At 93 Salvas paddled his canoe from five to 15 miles out to his stands and back and he was still a crack shot.

Conley's Exploit

There may be a small knot of aging veterans whose own hunting days are behind them who remember Bill Conley, one of De Pere's top guns. On one occasion, with a vicious "nor-wester" keeping everyone else off the water, Conley raised the movable combings on the sides of his 18-foot canoe and headed for a large flock east of Grassy Island light.

With no competition except the wind and high seas, Bill shot 214 ducks that day. He then paddled back to town through rough seas with his craft loaded with 500 pounds of game, 35 decoys and his own 240-pound frame.

Another time Bill and his brother Lincoln Conley killed 240 ducks without even getting their feet wet. They hunted from a blind on the site of the Public Service Corporation's Pulliam Plant.

How it was Done

In one of his articles, Claflin described how the old time hunters did it. They always used canoes, sometimes paddling as far as Little Tail, some 18 miles down the bay. They usually hunted all the way down and back, customarily bagging more ducks on one trip than the present day hunter gets in an entire season.

Open stretches of water were often covered by thousands of birds, which would rise before the oncoming canoe, circle around and resume feeding after the boat had passed. Hunters poling through the grass along the shore flushed mallards every few yards.

As is the case today, mallards and canvasbacks were the prized game and many hunters never drew a bead on anything else. Canvasbacks and mallards sold for 25 cents apiece in the local markets, red heads went for 20 cents and bluebills brought a quarter a brace. Teal were too small to bring a decent price and were usually ignored.

Filled a Wagon

On one notable occasion, Claflin wrote, a party came in from Point Sauble with a lumber wagon loaded to the top. Parking in front of Martin Barth's saloon *(214 Pine St.)* they proceeded to dispose of more than 300 ducks, selling them in bunches of half a dozen for a dollar a string.

According to Claflin, as late as 1905 at least 50,000 ducks were still being bagged on Green Bay each year. It was common at the height of the season to see wildfowl piled like cordwood on the floors of the city's meat markets. Much of this bag was packed in barrels and expressed to Chicago and Milwaukee.

All Kinds of Game

While ducks were the principal game, the Green Bay area abounded in all kinds. Annually, as far back as the arrival of the first white men, huge flights of now extinct passenger pigeons swept down over Door County in sky-darkening flights miles in length.

A century and more ago the area around St. Vincent Hospital was covered with beech trees where the birds came to rest overnight and feed on the nuts. A single charge of birdshot fired into the trees brought down more birds than a family could comfortably eat.

In 1854 the Green Bay Advocate noted that the whole town was gorging on roast passenger pigeon, much to the distress of the local butchers, on whom the editor wasted no sympathy. Served the highway robbers right for trying to profiteer on fresh beef at the unconscionable price of 15 cents a pound.

Sixty Years of Rivalry

The First East-West Game

October 23, 1965

By the time most subscribers receive today's Press-Gazette the East-West game will probably be all over, and who-ever wins the town will be going unconcernedly about its business. For a variety of reasons, not the least being 10 football-playing high schools within a 10-mile radius of city hall, the East-West game isn't what it used to be.

Time was when the Thanksgiving Day clash between the city's only two public high schools was the all-absorbing topic of conversation for a week ahead of time, and the whole town was in a dither until it was over. Now it is just another football game and not the climax of the high school season either.

Yet it is one of the oldest interscholastic rivalries in Wisconsin and today's meeting is the 60th in a string stretching back to 1905 when the two institutions met on the gridiron for the first time. There has been only one break in the long series — in 1906, when West High didn't field a team.

1895 Preview

Although the East-West series began officially in 1905, there had been an informal preview a decade earlier, in 1895 when both schools were taking their first toddling steps on the gridiron. Neither could muster enough players for full teams but they finally got together in a pick-up match with East fielding 10 players and West eight. The former's numerical advantage was too great and the Red Devils — a nickname still 35 years away — won, 22-8.

East High began interscholastic competition in 1896 and West joined the fun two years later. Almost at once the boys conceived a hankering to have at each other, but nothing came of it immediately except a series of florid challenges and sarcastic letters in the newspapers.

A game actually was scheduled for 1901 but the board of education turned thumbs down. East High was in the running for the state championship in 1902 and 1904 and coldly ignored West's challenge, a snub that caused the 1905 negotiations to be conducted in a frigidly formal atmosphere.

Touchy Pride

In fact, West refused to consider a game unless East made something of an apologetic gesture by issuing the challenge. Even then the preliminaries were so cool it wasn't until the Monday before the game that everything was ironed out.

So the long series began on Thanksgiving Day morning, 1905 (Nov. 30 was the exact date), in the old Hagemeister Park baseball park, now the site of East High School. The game had to be played in the morning because the city team had a game scheduled there for the afternoon and refused to relinquish the field.

Despite the lateness of scheduling, a good part of the city's population converged on the park for the 10:30 kickoff, coming on foot, riding the old Walnut Street trolley and driving teams — even in a couple of automobiles. At 25 and 35 cents a head a crowd described as probably the largest ever to see a high school game in the city was on hand.

Different Scene

The scene was quite different from today's formalities in 50,000-seat Lambeau Field. There were no stands then and spectators stood behind ropes stretching along the sidelines. Smartly drilled bands and cheerleaders hadn't been thought of, and the players looked like sandlot pickup teams in contrast to today's well equipped squads.

The game itself was a lot different, too. Football was played with eleven on a side even then, but it was a line-smashing game with no forward passing and head-knocking mass play the standard attack. Scoring values gave five points for an unconverted touchdown, an additional point for a successful conversion and four points for a field goal, usually a drop kick.

Those values are important to the history of the East-West series, since an error has crept into the record of that first score. It is set in the archives as 22-0 East, but, since East scored a field goal and three touchdowns but missed one of the conversions, the correct count should be 21-0.

West Outweighed

East took the field for the inaugural with a weight advantage of nine pounds per man, its lightest players being the two ends, Frank McGrath and Howard Merrill at 135 each. Will Elmore, regular left end, couldn't play because of illness but his place was impressively filled by 14-year-old McGrath.

Roy McGrath was at left tackle, with Jim Cook at right tackle, the guards being Fred Green and Elmer Houart. Claude Kelly played center.

The backfield consisted of Bert Schilling at quarterback, Capt. Roy Brunette and Ed Boaler at the halves and Fred Schneider, fullback. Charlie Lewis called signals for West, Buck Noland and Roy Coddington were the halfbacks and Jack McNerney was fullback.

There is considerable confusion over the West High front line. Walt Spooner, right end, suffered a broken shoulder en route to the park when he was scraped off the platform of the streetcar he was riding, and a lot of scrambling was necessary to make up for his loss.

As nearly as can be determined now, Bill Early took his place with Louis Bedell on the other flank and Henry Leaper and Jim Lally at the tackles. The guards were Johnny Burke and Theo Rieberg and Emmet McNerney was in the middle.

West won the toss and East kicked off, but neither team could make much early progress. East finally started a drive from midfield that reached the West 10 yard line before stalling and settled for Howard Merrill's 20-yard drop kick and a 4-0 lead.

The same pattern held for several

more minutes until East got another march under way. Roy Brunette was shoved across for the first touchdown. Cook kicked the goal and the halftime count was 10-0.

Schneider Starred

The second half belonged to Fred Schneider, who became the first great hero of the series with scoring runs of 30 and 75 yards. The second was a spectacular affair as Fred pounded through tackle and set sail with a convoy of three blockers, evading at least six tacklers on his twisting run.

He slipped the last one, safety Charlie Lewis, 25 yards out. This couldn't have been too tough since Fred outweighed Lewis by over 40 pounds.

Nearly exhausted by the time he reached pay dirt, Schneider fell down several times en route. Each time Roy Brunette hauled him to his feet and he kept going.

With Cook missing one conversion and making the other, the final score was 21-0.

The 1909 Blow

Summer Storm Wrecked Regatta

July 25, 1964

As the graceful yachts, followed by a large flotilla of spectator craft, bobbed jauntily out on the starting line on the bright sunny afternoon of July 22, 1909, conditions seemed ideal for a successful and exciting race. A stiff breeze was blowing steadily, the bay was only moderately choppy and the brilliant sunlight highlighted a colorful show.

Nobody, either in the fleet or among the throngs lining the shore around spanking new Bay View Beach *(now called Bay Beach)*, paid much attention to the scattered clouds lurking along the horizon. Yet before the afternoon was over those apparently harmless flecks would join forces and swoop down on the bay in a vicious storm that scattered and beached craft all over the south shore, killed two men and made a shambles of the most elaborate regatta ever staged on the waters of Green Bay.

The big event had been planned to climax the most successful season the old Green Bay Yacht Club had ever enjoyed. It ended, instead, in tragedy.

The club, organized in 1903, was one of the largest and most active groups of its kind in Wisconsin. With over 200 enthusiastic sail and power boat owners on its rolls, it was in flourishing financial condition and boasted a large and luxurious clubhouse just west of the amusement park.

Big Lake

In 1909 one of the biggest powerboat events on the Lakes was the annual reliability race staged by the Columbia Yacht Club of Chicago. The ambitious Green Bay yachtsmen decided to climax their season by inviting the Illinois group to end its race at Green Bay and the Chicagoans accepted.

Elaborate preparations were made to greet the visitors with a two-day celebration, to open with the arrival of the survivors of the grueling test and to end with a program of power and sailboat races. Invitations were sent to other yachtsmen all along Wisconsin's lakeshore.

Boats of every description converged on Green Bay from Marinette-Menominee, Sturgeon Bay, Oshkosh, Manitowoc, Oconto and other lake port cities. Practically everything locally that would float was turned out to welcome the Illinois visitors.

Alive with Welcomers

When the 14 or 15 survivors cruised proudly across the finish line near the breakwater west of the new Bay View Beach pavilion the surrounding waters were alive with flag-bedecked craft and the shoreline was black with interested spectators. A terrific din from sirens, saluting cannon and shouting people made it a gala occasion, highlighted by a banquet at the Yacht Club that night.

Another huge crowd of people and boats was on hand next day in seemingly perfect weather. Dr. R. B. Power, who had recently succeeded A. C. Neville as club commodore, was official starter for the race and he got them off to excellent starts.

Nobody remembers exactly how many boats were in the sailing race, headed by Neville's "Algonkin," one of the sleekest and fastest racing yawls on the Great Lakes. Counting those who just tagged along to watch the fun, there must have been close to 100 craft on or around the course.

Clouds Gathered Quickly

The powerboat race was quickly over and interest concentrated on the sailing event, staged far out on the bay. The race was to be an 18-mile run, twice around a nine-mile, triangular course.

Shortly after the race got under way the clouds began to gather. By the time the "Algonkin" rounded the buoy to lead the pack into the second lap the sun had disappeared and dirty weather was closing in.

Neville, an avid sailor since boyhood, had sailed the bay for 40 years and knew its tricks probably better than any other yachtsman on the Lakes. He didn't like the look of things and as "Algonkin" passed the officials' boat he megaphoned for instructions.

The officials, thinking the impending blow would be just a typical summer squall, quickly over, signaled him to proceed. "Algonkin" had just turned the first leg of the second lap when the storm broke.

Raging Gale

It wasn't a passing squall, but a raging gale that blew far into the night. The wind suddenly quadrupled in velocity and driving rain poured down in sheets. Spectators ashore and in the power launches scattered for safety like quail.

The sailboats, however, were too far out. Their only choice was to drop anchors and sheets and ride it out or to run before the storm. Some were able to haul in sails and remained out all night, soaked and chilled to the bone. Most of them ran for it.

The sudden blow, however, had raised the water level along the south shore so high that the lowlands were flooded far inland. Fleeing boats, probably blinded by the driving rain in any event, couldn't stop in time and about 20 were deposited high and dry after the storm had blown itself out and the water receded.

Far from Usual Haunts

When farmers and fishermen along the shore emerged next morning they were startled to see fields and back yards dotted with sailing craft far from their normal haunts. Some claimed to have found stranded vessels as far as three-quarters of a mile inland, although that appears to have been an exaggeration.

The two men who lost their lives were members of the Chicago flotilla, part of a crew of five in a large launch caught well out on the bay, where they had gone to get a closer look at the race. They apparently tried to run before the storm, their engine washed out and they gambled on dropping the hook.

When the anchor caught, the craft either swung around, broached and capsized or nosed under and flipped. The three survivors were understandably hazy about what actually happened.

Clung to Derelict

All were thrown into the water, where the trio survived by clinging to the overturned craft and helping each other. None could recall having seen their doomed companions once the launch capsized.

They were rescued during the night by the steamer Denessen, which headed a search mission after the launch was reported missing. Putting a rowboat into the water in heavy seas and hauling the exhausted men aboard was a dangerous feat, but the Denessen's crew accomplished it smartly.

The bodies of the two drowned men were recovered near the spot of the accident next day.

Aside from the drownings, nobody was seriously injured although everyone was thoroughly soaked and many, particularly those aboard the beached boats, were badly bruised. Damage to the yachts was considerable but, thanks to the high quality of seamanship displayed, none were a total loss.

Mayhem On Ice

Hockey's Roots Deep in City

February 8, 1969

With the Bobcats now in their 11th season and playing probably the best hockey they have ever produced, the game apparently has established firm roots in Green Bay. It has taken considerable time, but the Cats had a few things going for them from the outset, not the least being the fact that ice hockey has been played here in some form or other for more than half a century.

Things were a lot different than they are today in the comfortable and modern confines of the Veterans Memorial Arena when the first puck was dropped on local ice. That was 52 years ago last week, on January 28, 1917, and the man responsible for it is still around. What's more, the sparkplug of the early game here was, of all things, a fiddler.

Violinist Walter L. Larsen had a good thing going in his new Larsen Conservatory of Music in 1917 but he was getting itchy for the game of his youth. Raised in Hancock, Mich., Walter had played hockey almost from the time he could strap on a pair of skates and he missed it.

Had to Start Team

He wasn't going to get a chance to play in Green Bay, though, unless he started his own team. After several months of talking up the joys of ice hockey to a number of friends, he gathered a group of curious young men at a cleared spot on the ice of the Fox River on the afternoon of Jan. 18, 1917 (a Sunday) and they poked and skidded through an hour's play to a 3-3 tie.

For the rest of the 1917 season play was confined to intramural games, largely because there were few organized teams in the Fox River Valley and none of the players could afford the expenses of ranging farther afield. Still, they had enough fun to keep up their enthusiasm for the following winter.

When the time rolled around, however, the United States was deep in World War I and most of the original players were wearing another kind of uniform. The game had to mark time until after the war, when the originators were home again and eager to resume play.

First Hockey League

In the early 1920s, thanks to the enthusiasm of Larsen and the late George W. Calhoun, sports editor of the Press-Gazette and a co-founder of the Packers, hockey began to boom through the competition of an amateur city league in which teams were sponsored by various business firms.

Cal was crippled and couldn't play but he had been a fine goalie in his youth and he took over management of a Press-Gazette team in the league, which fought a series of hot campaigns against the Gordon Bents and the Larsen-coached Northern Paper Mills.

Games were played on an outdoor rink in Legion Park *(on Cherry Street)*, behind the present post office building, under a crude system of lights set up on the roof of the Elks Club across Cherry Street. *(In 1969, the post office was located at the northwest corner of East Walnut and Jefferson, now the Sophie Beaumont Building for county government offices.)* Perhaps the most historic battle of those early years was a marathon between the Bents and the Press-Gazette that went on for a month, lasted through four overtime games and 245 minutes of actual play before the Newsmen squeaked out a 2-1 decision.

That was in January-February, 1921. Beginning the night of Jan. 11, the two clubs played three overtime, scoreless games before a decision was reached on Feb. 7, in nine overtime periods.

Got New Rink

Landscaping of the park drove the hockey players out around 1926, but a couple of years later a new rink was built in the open space between the then new YMCA and the Elks Club *(then at Cherry and Jefferson)*. Here the industrial league flourished for several seasons until the rink space was converted into a parking lot.

There was no organized league play in the city during the 1930s but the game was kept alive by an independent club called the Ambassadors, led by Don Brueckner, John Torinus and other youthful enthusiasts. They built an outdoor rink on a flat space behind the old Polo-Resto Tavern on the lower De Pere road *(now Riverside Drive)*, across the highway from Minahan Stadium, and had a lot of fun there during the Depression.

Another war sent most of them flocking into fighting uniforms and the sport again went into the deep freeze (not that it ever was anywhere else, really, what with outdoor facilities and Green Bay's winters) until after World War II. By that time most of the Ambassadors were too old and too involved in careers to have time for hockey, but it wasn't long until a new crop arose.

Hornets Next Club

In 1949 an amateur club called the Green Bay Hornets was formed to play in the Wisconsin State Amateur League, competing with Milwaukee, Fond du Lac, Madison, Appleton and other cities. The Hornets are still going after 20 years, with two alumni now on the University of Wisconsin hockey squad and another, Mike Fund, playing with the Bobcats this year.

From the beginning the game was handicapped here by the weather. Nobody could ever be sure a given game could be played on schedule and even when it was it might be so cold nobody wanted to stand around and watch it, even though the rink in Fisk Park was better than anything the hockey nuts had ever had before. Some contests were actually "snowed out," when driving snowstorms covered the ice so deeply play had to be called off.

Then, in 1958-59, came the Brown County Veterans Memorial Arena, and hockey had, for the first time, a reliable home where fans could sit and watch games in comfort. The Bobcats were organized that year, playing their first home game in December, 1958, as members of the Mid-America Hockey League.

Still in League

The Cats are still members of the circuit, which has operated under a series of different names since then, although they were out one season and played independent hockey. Rivalries have grown up between Green Bay; Rochester, Minn.; Marquette, Mich.; and the Soo which are just as furious in their way as the Packer-Bear tradition.

The foundations for enduring interest were laid that first winter with the coming of Johnny Mayasich and Dick Dougherty from the University of Minnesota. The story of the past decade is too recent and too well known to merit repeating, but since that first slow and scrambling effort Green Bay has established itself as a good hockey town, producing Olympic and U.S. National players as well as the man who will coach this year's Nationals in the world championships.

The familiar Bobcat emblem has been seen on rinks all over the U.S. as well as in Europe. One national tournament has been held here and the Bobcats have one leg up on the national championship trophy as they continue to provide the finest hockey currently available in this country short of the full time pros.*

** During the 1979-80 season, the U.S. Hockey League, then a minor pro league, became a Junior A league, eliminating the Green Bay Bobcats. Except for a brief interval, Green Bay was without an ice hockey team until the Green Bay Gamblers were organized in 1994.*

The Champions of 1918

Unbeaten Pappy of the Pack

October 19, 1968

As everybody knows the Green Bay Packers are now well into their 50th season, dating their existence from the establishment of a sandlot football team by Curly Lambeau and George Calhoun in the early fall of 1919. Had the ball bounced a little differently, though, the Pack would be a year older and Art Schmael, rather than Lambeau, might be venerated today as founding genius of one of professional sport's greatest success stories.

When Curly and Cal decided to organize what became the Packers in 1919 they were actually sowing on ground that had been broken by Schmael and the Green Bay city team of 1918. In fact, Lambeau played one game with the club before going off to star under Knute Rockne at Notre Dame that fall, and many of the original Packers — the Zoll brothers, Nate Abrams, Abe Sauber, Dutch Dwyer, Gus Rosenow and Schmael himself — were regulars.

Even when they captured the state championship in 1919 the "charter" Packers were a "me too" outfit. Schmael's team swept through an unbeaten, once tied season to establish a strong claim to the unofficial title.

Repeat of 1917

Actually, the 1918 city team was a repeat from 1917 when Schmael and several former Green Bay high school stars first took the field as a team. They enjoyed a good season but not as successful as the eleven of a year later.

The 1918 crew started out as the "Skidoos" but soon changed their name to the "Whales." That didn't catch on either, and for most of the season the team was known simply as the Green Bay city team.

Schmael, a Chicagoan and member of the Coast Guard stationed here during and after World War I, was coach and fullback — he also coached East High that year while backfield mate Rosenow was West's mentor — while other members included the Zolls, Nate and Pete Abrams (Nate was team captain), Dwyer, Eddie Glick, Flatley, Martell, Ouster, Jirgeau, Schmidt, Dickey, Praeger and Howlett.

With the war rising to a climax and men constantly called to the service, manpower problems were constant. It is virtually impossible today to keep track of everyone who played at one time or another.

Schmael, incidentally, holds his place in Packer history for scoring the first Green Bay touchdown in the National Football League in the 1921 classic victory over the Minneapolis Marines.

De Pere Donnybrook

As the Skidoos, the team opened the season on Sept. 15 by downing the De Pere city eleven, 13-0, in De Pere. Lambeau and Schmael were the stars of the game, which almost broke up in a gang fight in the fourth quarter. Somebody on the sidelines took a poke at someone else, the crowd piled into the act and things were pretty lively before the police finally broke it up.

The following Sunday, Sept. 22, the club, renamed the Whales, took on Marinette. The latter, fielding virtually the full lineup of the state high school championship eleven of 1917, was figured to be tough but Green Bay issued a warning for the future by rolling over the visitors, 42-0.

Included in the lineup that day were Vern Leaper, Jens Gallagher, Charlie Mathys, Lurquin and Secord, although none of them remained long with the club. A large crowd turned out to stand along the sidelines and cheer as Schmael scored three touchdowns, one on a 30-yard breakaway; Nate Abrams got three and Schneider returned an interception 50 yards for a seventh.

The crushing of Marinette drew a challenge from the unbeaten Appleton Crescents, who had walked over Little Chute, Kaukauna, Oshkosh and Fond du Lac and were already claiming the Fox River Valley title. They met at Hagemeister Park *(where East Green Bay High School now stands)* on Oct. 13 before the largest crowd ever to see a Sunday football game in Green Bay up to that time, and the result was a 72-0 slaughter. Glick and Schmael crossed the Appleton goal line four times each while Abrams and Dwyer scored two apiece. Appleton never penetrated the Green Bay 40-yard stripe.

Kaukauna Got Clobbered

Kaukauna had its turn on Oct. 20 and the final score was 64-0. If the club hadn't run out of gas in the second half the count would have been even bigger, as the Bays led at intermission, 40-0. Schmael was again the big gun with three touchdowns and four conversions, Dwyer, Nate Abrams and Rosenow each getting a pair of TDs.

Unbeaten Oshkosh came up on Oct. 27 boasting four victories and a goal line that had been crossed only once. Despite a driving rain and a muddy field the Bays sliced through the visitors to deal Oshkosh its first loss in two years, 48-0.

Rosenow ran an interception back 60 yards for one of his four touchdowns and Abrams added three more. Because of the bad weather the crowd was small and the club lost $100, a financial disaster that nearly submerged them.

November opened with the Twin City A.C. of Menominee, self proclaimed champions of the Upper Peninsula, coming in on the tenth. Despite a patched lineup due to losses of players to the service and with Schmael out with Spanish influenza, the Bays got off to a fast start and a 25-17 win. It was also the first and only time that year the team was scored on.

Sauber Scored Twice

Sauber counted two touchdowns, Abrams once and Rosenow got the other. Doyle got away for 78 yards to count the first tally against the Bays that year but the score at the half was 25-6.

The Oshkosh Rail Lights, a railroad team from down the valley, were scheduled to come next but got cold feet at the last minute, so the Bays took on the Twin City A.C. a second time on the 14th. This time the visitors were loaded and the two teams battled to a scoreless deadlock before the largest crowd of the season.

A playoff for Dec. 1 was under discussion but collapsed when the city health commissioner called off all public gatherings *(due to the influenza epidemic that year)* just before Thanksgiving. Attempts to bring the Milwaukee city champions here to settle the state title were unsuccessful because they wanted too big a guarantee.

When Pack Met the Marines

October 21, 1961

Tomorrow afternoon in Minneapolis the Packers face a new league rival in the Minnesota Vikings. The schedule makers probably never realized it, but no opponent could be more suitable for this particular weekend.

Just 40 years ago Monday, on Oct. 23, 1921, the Green Bay Packers made their own debut in the National Football League. They won it by the narrowest of margins — and the opposition was the Minneapolis Marines.

A lot of footballs have been inflated in the NFL — which wasn't even called the National Football League in those days — since then, but none ever took a more significant bounce for the Packers than the one Curley (*sic*) Lambeau dropkicked over the crossbar in the closing minutes to give the Packers a 7-6 decision. How much of what has happened in the ensuing four decades rode on that kick no one can say.

Independent Two Years

The Packers had been in existence as an independent, sandlot semi-pro team for two seasons when the chance to get into the American Professional Football Assn., as the NFL was originally called, came in the late summer of 1921. In that time they had lost only two games, been tied once and were so tough in their own neighborhood they had about run out of playmates.

Even so, Green Bay had its nerve trying to edge into what then passed for the Big Time.

Still had Doubts

If $50 hadn't been real lettuce to the boys who were trying to establish professional football, Curley (*sic*) and his backers probably wouldn't have gotten the time of day from them. Even so, the promoters had doubts about letting Green Bay play in their back yard.

The story has never been verified — nor denied — but it was generally believed at the time that the Packers' membership in the league was conditional. If they didn't show well in their first effort against the fearsome Minneapolis Marines, out they went.

The Pack opened its 1921 season with much the same squad that had started the whole thing in 1919. The players were all local and regional products. Cub Buck was the only "big name" on the roster, but Cub was a neighborhood boy, too, hailing from Appleton.

Three are Signed

Although the team disposed of its first four opponents handily, Lambeau was sure that home talent couldn't meet the challenge of the Minneapolis pros. New men were gradually worked into the lineup, but it wasn't until the week before the game that well-known outside players were obtained.

That week Lambeau signed Billy DeMoe, former Syracuse wingman; Jigger Hayes and Paul Malone, both of Notre Dame. Hayes, another end, and Malone, a fullback, only joined the squad on Friday.

Not Full Strength

The club wasn't at full strength for the big test. Tubby Howard, the regular fullback and himself an import, had an injured ankle, and Lambeau had been ordered by his doctor not to play.

The Marines, on whom the Packers were expected to cut their teeth, were an awesome crew. Organized for 12 years and claimants of the Midwestern championship the past six, they were a smoothly blended mixture of seasoned pros and recent college stars.

Key man was Rube Ursella, the captain and quarterback. Rube never went to college, but in a dozen years of the rough and tumble of pioneer pro ball he had established a reputation as one of the canniest signal callers in the business — if you could call it a business.

3,000 on Hand

When the Packers took the field in old Hagemeister Park — now the site of East High School — that Oct. 23, the whole town was in a stew of enthusiasm, tempered by anxiety, and the largest crowd ever to see a game here up to that time was on hand. Official attendance figures were never announced but the turnout was later estimated at a whopping 3,000.

Only one "charter member" of the home club was in the starting lineup — Sammy Powers at right guard. DeMoe and Hayes were on the flanks, Buck and Jab Murray were at the tackles, Jim Cook held down the other guard slot and Fee Klaus was at center.

Backfield Lineup

The backfield consisted of Roger Kliebahn at quarterback, Malone and Buff Wagner at the halves and Art Schmael at fullback. Before the game was over Lambeau, Joe Carrey, Milt Wilson, Howard, Cowboy Wheeler and Toodie McLean saw action, Howard only briefly. Lambeau, Wilson, Wheeler and McLean were 1919 holdovers.

Shortly after the opening kickoff the Marines missed a field goal from 30 yards out, took over again at midfield and crunched to a first down on the Packer four-yard line. The Bays piled up three thrusts but on fourth down Dvorak burrowed through for the first score of the season against the Packers. The power and precision of the drive didn't make Art Sampson's muff of the conversion seem very important.

Hold on Four

Through the rest of the first half, however, the Marines enjoyed only a slight offensive edge until a partly blocked punt gave Green Bay possession on the Minneapolis 30. An interception squelched that threat, but the Packers marched back to the visitors' 35, only to be thwarted when a forward pass grounded in the end zone with less than a minute to go. (In those days an incomplete pass into the end zone meant loss of the ball.)

Early in the second half the Packers got the jump when Malone carted an interception to the Marine 20. Schmael plunged to a first down but Minneapolis braced and held on its four.

Marines Roll

Again the invaders opened a well-executed assault. With Sampson punching through the middle and Dvorak and Pete Regnier sweeping the ends or slicing off tackle, the Marines rolled to the Packer 25 as the third quarter ended.

Carey opened the final period by recovering a fumble but the Packers couldn't gain. The pattern was repeated as minutes ticked off, neither team being able to make much headway.

Time was getting short when Sampson punted over the Green Bay goal line. Once more the Packers stalled after reaching their 40 and, with only six minutes remaining, Buck kicked.

Dvorak tried to field the ball on the run, fumbled and Jigger Hayes gathered it in on the Marine 35. The crowd, resigned to just a good try in the big bid, came up roaring but two cracks at the line netted only a couple of yards.

Curley Obliged

With fans pleading for the obvious pass, Lambeau — who had been at quarterback most of the way in defiance of Doc Kelly — obliged with a bullet to Wagner. Buff made a circus catch and raced to the Minneapolis 14 before being pulled down.

Four line smashes netted ten yards. The distance was so thin, however, that a measurement gave the Packers first down with only an inch to spare.

The park was tense and silent as Curley (*sic*) barked his signals over the crouching lines — the huddle hadn't come into use yet. Schmael took a direct pass from center and disappeared under a huge pileup on the Minneapolis goal line.

When the stack peeled off and Art was found across the big stripe with the tying touchdown the crowd went crazy. Hats and cushions sailed into the air and staid businessmen hopped around like kids.

Lambeau's drop kick between the uprights for the winning point touched off a continuous din that could be heard for blocks. It hasn't stopped yet.

Historic Encounter

First East-West Cage Clash in 1922

March 10, 1962

When West High's basketball Wildcats crushed East High's Red Devils in their tournament meeting last week they may not have realized it but they were redressing a low moment in their school's athletic history on practically a historic anniversary. Just 40 years ago Friday, on March 9, 1922, the old rivals met on a basketball floor for the first time and East upended the West Siders in overtime by a whooping score of 12-10.

You won't find that first encounter listed in the long record of their rivalry for some unknown reason. The list usually begins in 1923 when both launched their charter memberships in the newly organized Fox River Valley Conference.

Although East and West had been butting heads in football for nearly 20 years they had never met in basketball. There were a variety of reasons but the principal one was that West had a place to practice and play and East didn't.

Never Taken Hold

West, a pioneer in state high school basketball almost from the invention of the game in 1895, had put a team on the floor for many years and had gone to the state finals as early as 1915. East, lacking a gymnasium, had made sporadic efforts to launch the game but it had never taken hold.

Periodically West would challenge East to a game, everybody would get all steamed up and nothing would come of it. In 1921 East had actually accepted the defi and a meeting was scheduled, but the Hilltoppers (that was the Red Devils' original nickname) couldn't find practice facilities and it fell through.

In 1922, however, East High's new principal O. F. Nixon obtained use of the old National Guard armory in Hagemeister Park at the end of Cherry Street for practice and games. Clifford Dice, a teacher, was appointed coach and basketball finally got its roots down at East.

Eight-Game Year

East only managed to get in eight games that season — a couple more being frozen out by the big sleet storm — and won five, while West split even in 16. Although no challenge was forthcoming from either school, outside agitation for a contest cropped up which Press-Gazette sports editor George Calhoun carefully cultivated.

Part of the reluctance came from school authorities who weren't sure what would happen if several hundred rabid supporters were crammed into a hall where they could get at each other. Cal recognized the possibilities on the eve of the first contest when he cautioned that "the future of interschool basketball in the city rests on the conduct of players and spectators."

Season Running Out

The '22 season was running out when both East and West were listed as possibilities for the state tournament. Oshkosh Normal stepped into the picture and offered a place in its sectional tournament to the winner of a game between them.

No time was wasted thereafter. The school principals got together on Monday, March 6, and scheduled the game in Turner Hall for Thursday, a quickie move that didn't leave enough time to plan any shenanigans. In any event their worries were groundless. The contest came off in an atmosphere of healthy excitement but no trouble.

To make certain, the former Wisconsin football and basketball star Alan Davey was engaged to referee. Regulation 20 minute halves were to be played (there were no quarter periods in those days) and tickets were priced at 25 cents for students and 50 cents for general admission.

Despite the short time remaining, interest mushroomed. On Thursday night a "mammoth" crowd of 800 packed Turner Hall to the rafters.

Little to Choose

As Cal saw it there was little to choose between the two teams. East had a slightly better percentage record but West enjoyed greater experience. East had a smoother passing game while the Purple (the name Wildcats was still years in the future) boasted a stronger defense.

Taking the floor for East in the historic encounter were Capt. Kenneth Shaw and Omer Chadek as forwards, Tom Hearden, center; and Ralph Silverwood and Bill Charbonneau, guards. Before the game was over Dave Grimmer, Vital Counard and Adolph Nejedlo also saw action.

With regular forward Ben Kemnitz sick in bed, West coach Nordby relied on Bill Rather and Claude Smith in the front line, Dick Bader, center; and Cyril Feldhausen and Verdette at guards. Kemnitz did get into the game in the second half and contributed a basket but wasn't at his best.

Basketball was radically different in 1922 from today's fire engine rat race, and an IBM computer wasn't necessary to keep score. Emphasis was on intricate passing to work the ball into scoring position, virtually every shot was a two-handed set, and there was no battling for rebounds. If a shot missed, the defending team practically automatically got the ball.

The game opened according to formula with West breaking the ice. Although the final score wasn't at all unusual for its day, both teams were off target and missed repeatedly on easy shots. East displayed the sharper passing but West was "playing the man" more closely.

Cy Feldhausen was the first to get his name into the misplaced record book by drawing first blood with a successful free throw. Charbonneau put East in front briefly with a field goal but a basket by Feldhausen and another gift shot by Bader made it 4-2, West.

Ken Shaw, destined to be the game hero, pulled East even with the first of four ringers. Just before halftime Rather canned a set shot that sent the Purple off the floor with a 6-4 intermission lead.

As the second half opened Shaw

sparked an East drive by sinking a pair of free throws and then hitting on two "sensational" baskets to give East a 10-6 edge. Kemnitz put the Purple back in contention with a bucket and shortly before the final whistle Bader tied the count with an "overhand toss" — probably the 1922 version of an outside hook shot.

Shaw Wins for East

Through four minutes of overtime neither team was able to crack the other's defense. Then, with only about a minute remaining, Shaw cut in behind Feldhausen, grabbed a long, gambling pass and drove in for the winning layup.

East didn't have long to enjoy its triumph. Going to Oshkosh the following week it was paired against Oconto in the opening round of the tournament there. Oconto, twice beaten by West in the regular season, was singularly unimpressed by the Hilltoppers' conquest and proceeded to clobber them, 33-8.

With the formation of the Valley Conference that year the East-West court rivalry prospered under the advantage of league competition. The overall record to date, including that first non-league encounter and a number of extra tournament meetings, now stands at 87 games, with East winning 49 and West taking 37.

If the total doesn't add up, there's a reason for that, too. One of the games ended up in an unprecedented tie.

That was in 1942 when East and West battled to a 24-24 double overtime deadlock because existing conference rules required them to knock off after two extra periods. In contrast to the initial attendance of 800, more than 1,700 sat in on the standoff 20 years later.

When Herber Haunted East High

September 17, 1966

A long overdue tribute is being paid today in Canton, Ohio, to one of the great names in Green Bay's illustrious football story. More than 20 years after he threw his last, soaring forward pass Arnie Herber is being inducted into the Professional Football Hall of Fame.

The first in the long roster of great passing quarterbacks, Herber is remembered primarily for his fantastic ability to throw a fast football phenomenal distances with pin point accuracy. His skill, especially during the years when he was the propellant of the Herber-to-Hutson combination, has obscured the fact that Arnie was a superb all around football player.

As a pro he was rarely called upon to do anything but throw, but Arnie could also run like a ghost, he was a splendid punter and, even as a kid, a deadly exponent of the now lost art of drop kicking from anywhere inside the 40-yard line. A team player above all else, Herber was equally gifted with the less spectacular skills of blocking and tackling.

Forty Years Ago

At no time in a playing career that spanned two decades did Arnie perform more wholeheartedly and effectively than at the very beginning when, a slender, black-haired kid who never scaled 165 pounds wringing wet, he led West High through one of its glory periods just 40 years ago.

As quarterback of the Wildcats (they were known simply as "The Purple" in those days) from 1925 to 1927 Arnie knew defeat only once. That was at the hands of East High in his sophomore year, and before he was through Herber had repaid that disappointment with interest. The three games he played against his cross-town enemy loom across the years as some of the most vivid memories of a generation now crowding the "Golden Age."

Herber and the "Hilltoppers" as East was then dubbed collided for the first time on Thanksgiving day in 1925 in then brand new City Stadium. Both East and West went into the contest with unblemished records, with East riding a 21-game winning streak and seven in a row over West.

Star at the End

When the game began Arnie was just a 15-year-old quarterback on an otherwise veteran eleven — at its end he was a star. East won but Herber hogged most of the glory, and the emotionally spent crowd of 7,000 — largest ever to see a football game in Green Bay up to that time — sensed that it had just seen the end of East's long domination of the series.

Early in the first quarter East got the jump when a blocked punt bounded over West's end line for an automatic safety. Leading 2-0 the Hilltoppers played cozy as Dave Zuildmulder and Herber staged a brilliant punting duel throughout the rest of the half in which Arnie stayed right with his bigger and more experienced opponent. His 14 punts during the afternoon averaged better than 40 yards.

West opened up with a passing attack in the second half, Herber's short snappers over the line and into the flat connecting regularly with Rasmussen and Joe Quinn. Twice West moved deep into East territory, East held, and the second time Herber drilled a drop kick between the posts from 35 yards out to put West in front, 3-2.

Quick Reaction

East reacted quickly, and as the final quarter opened Zuildmulder fired an arching pass to speedy Emil Saunders from midfield which Emil took in full stride on the Purple to go in standing up. Dave then converted to make it 9-3.

With less than a minute to go West moved to a first down on East's 11 yard line. Three running plays picked up only six yards, and everybody in the house knew what was coming next.

Once more Arnie fired a bullet over the line to Joe Quinn, all alone in the East end zone. Just as the ball reached him, however, Max Murphy came out of nowhere to knock it down with a desperation leap. There wasn't time for West to get possession again.

A year later Arnie made up for his initial failure but only after coming within a whisker of being the goat of the day. West sent another unbeaten, once tied team into the 1926 contest and had to come from behind to crack the inspired defense of a twice-beaten East team, 7-2.

Missed Three Goals

The Herber-to-Quinn air arm was West's big weapon that year, but East kept Joe well blanketed most of the afternoon and blitzed Arnie unmercifully. Only his superb punting kept East at bay, but Arnie missed on three field goal attempts.

East broke the ice late in the third period, and again it was with a safety. Attempting to punt in his end zone, Herber bobbled the pass from center and was buried before he could get the kick away.

With the goat horns beginning to sprout, Arnie coolly went to work. His first move was to bring a punt back 23 yards across midfield, and then he began to thread the needle to Quinn.

Quinn Goes In

Instead of throwing to Joe for the winning TD, however, he slipped the West captain the ball on an end around and Quinn swept the flank for the score that ended East's long string. Arnie casually added the unnecessary extra point.

The 1925 script was repeated in 1927 as two undefeated, untied teams again faced each other in the showdown. Arnie was West's captain that year, a robust 17-year-old who had grown to a sturdy 164 pounds and was generally considered the finest high school football player in Wisconsin.

Neither team threatened seriously until late in the third quarter when East cracked the stalemate on Shekore's 32-yard touchdown dash. The conversion was missed, but East's bristling defense made the omission seem unimportant to everybody but Herber.

Final Drive

Midway of the fourth quarter Arnie passed to Joe Borchers for 40 yards to reach the East 29 yard line. The Hilltoppers halted that threat, but Herber came right back with another bomb to Borchers which covered 50 yards before he was run out of bounds on East's ten.

With less than a minute remaining and the East defense keying on Borchers, Arnie pitched wide to Arnie Adams. The pass was low but Adams made a beautiful shoe string catch as he fell over the goal line to tie the score. Herber booted the conversion that gave West a 7-6 decision and the first perfect season in its history.

A 60-minute player, Herber did everything that afternoon except blow up the football. He carried the ball on 13 of West's 26 running plays for 54 yards, completed six of 18 passes for 151 yards and the tying touchdown and averaged 42 yards on his punts.

Will History Repeat?

The '29 Champs Come Home

December 17, 1960

The Packers are coming home to another civic welcome tomorrow night, and by the time most subscribers get around to unfolding today's Press-Gazette they will know whether it is a greeting to the city's first Western Division champions since 1944 or a club still facing a battle for the Little Casino. Jack Yuenger, chief drum beater for the airport welcome, is talking of the "greatest" homecoming in the team's history and hoping for a crowd of "10,000 or more."

I have news for Yuenger who, apparently, could use some of the "historical fact and fancy" he loves to needle me about. If he doesn't produce more than twice 10,000 he's fired a blank.

Although Green Bay was only about half its present size and the Packers hadn't attained the institutional status they now enjoy, a yelling mob of over 20,000 turned out in freezing weather 31 years ago when Green Bay's first pro champions came home the night of Dec. 9, 1929.

The city has staged a number of spectacular celebrations in its long history. None compared with the greeting to the first of its six world championship football teams. And the best thing about that 1929 welcome was its explosive spontaneity.

Green Bay had been a member of the National Football League since 1921 and had more than held its own in competition, but it hadn't been accorded big league status by the rest of the circuit. As the organization grew from sandlot to major league proportions the smaller cities had been shoved aside by metropolitan centers until Green Bay was the only little guy left.

Attitude Rankled

Gradually the Packers had been relegated to the status of country cousins, and the patronizing of the larger members rankled. The undefeated champions of 1929 changed all that — small wonder the citizenry was popping its shirt buttons all over the place.

Nobody — unless it was Curley (*sic*) Lambeau — had seriously entertained championship visions when the season began, but eyes began to open as the Packers bowled over one opponent after another. The town was in a fine frenzy when the club went east late in November, undefeated and headed for a showdown with the unbeaten Giants in New York.

As every fan old enough to recognize a picture of Vince Lombardi knows, the team met the challenge but the championship wasn't in the bag yet. Green Bay still had three games to play and the Giants five, and a single defeat coupled with a Giant sweep could still cost the Packers the title.

New York did win them all, while the Packers almost came a cropper against the Frankford Yellowjackets and were lucky to escape with a scoreless tie. The championship wasn't nailed down until the final conquest of the Bears in Chicago on Dec. 8. By that time the city was ready for a rousing whing.

The team was due home via North Western train at 8:30 p.m. Monday, Dec. 9. Long before then the crowd began to converge on the station *(now Titletown Brewery),* and by 8 o'clock every street leading to it was solidly plugged by an estimated turnout of 20,000 cold but cheerful citizens and 6,000 automobiles.

Immovable Mass

People were packed in an almost immovable mass around the station, overflowing into the yards and perching on top of roofs, box cars, in every available window — some even climbed telephone poles. The size of the crowd took the police by complete surprise and if it hadn't been for its good-natured cooperation things would have been an utter mess. As it was, traffic was at a standstill for blocks in every direction.

The train rolled into town through lanes of blazing red flares and an ever increasing bedlam of sound. People yelled at the top of their lungs, sirens wailed, locomotive and industrial plant whistles screamed, and every one of those 6,000 auto horns was going full blast too. Between Mason Street and the station the crowd was so dense the train had to crawl along behind brakemen and volunteers walking ahead to clear the right of way.

The press was thickest at the station, and police had a lot of trouble moving the players from the train to waiting buses. The platform lighting being no better than it is now, it is doubtful if more than a handful actually saw the players get off, but that made no difference. Every movement brought another round of cheers.

Finally the transfer was completed and with the American Legion band and Battery B leading the way the cavalcade swung slowly over to Broadway, south to Walnut and across the bridge. The parade turned down Washington to Main, over to Adams, back to Walnut and thence to city hall. The entire route was lined with cheering people.

At city hall, which was also surrounded by a whooping mob, the players were escorted to the council chambers where Mayor John V. Diener greeted them with the unprecedented gesture of the "freedom of the city" — whatever that meant — for 24 hours. There were congratulatory speeches back and forth, although the player spokesmen were so choked up the oratory wasn't very sparkling, and the ceremonies closed with a rising vote of thanks from the city council to the team for bringing the championship to Green Bay.

Only the Beginning

That was only the beginning of a round of celebrating that lasted for three days. The following evening the team was given an elaborate banquet at the Beaumont Hotel, attended by over 400 at which each player received a watch and $220 from a hastily subscribed purse of over $5,000.

There were, inevitably, more speeches, and this time the players gave as good as they received, especially the irrepressible Johnny Blood. The Vagabond Halfback's talk nearly stole the show, something of a habit with Johnny under most circumstances.

The banquet was also noteworthy as the first current events program ever broadcast live by radio station WHBY with Harold T. I. Shannon at the microphone. Harold still has the papier-mache football that topped the elaborate cake baked as a centerpiece by the old Bohemian Bakery — one of the very few if not the only souvenir of the event still in existence.

There wasn't much serious business transacted in town the rest of the week. People went through the motions but their hearts weren't in it. Everybody had more fun adjourning to the nearest oasis, there to assure each other they had known all the time the boys would come through.

The celebration even stopped the rugged Packers, whose ability to win football games was exceeded only by their enthusiasm for the roles of conquering heroes. Traveling jauntily down to Memphis, Tenn., the following Sunday for an exhibition game against a pick-up team, the new champions were dumped unceremoniously on their hangovers.

The score was 20-6, the same count by which the big boys from the small town had chopped down the Giants' beanstalk.

Most Under-rated Packer

'Old Reliable' Lavvie Dilweg

January 6, 1968

When news filtered up from St. Petersburg, Fla., this week of the death of former Congressman LaVern R. Dilweg, surprisingly few memory bells rang in Green Bay. After all, Lavvie had been gone from town for 25 years and it had been closer to 35 since he last took the field.

The half dozen men who stood beside his grave as honorary pallbearers this morning remembered, though. To Boob Darling, Mike Michalske, Verne Lewellen, Arnie Herber, Jug Earp and Whitey Woodin, Lavvie Dilweg was one of the finest ends who ever played professional football both ways for 60 minutes a game.

Darling, who lived with him for two years during their playing days, is even more emphatic. He states flatly that he never saw Lavvie's equal as a two-way wingman.

Old Timers Agree

The vast majority of old timer players who lined up with or against him would agree. It was Lavvie Dilweg's fate to be one of the most underrated players of his time, both as a collegian and as a pro.

He was often described in later years as an All America from Marquette, but he wasn't. He was named on Walter Eckersall's Chicago Tribune All America for two years, but Eckie did not rate with the better known Walter Camp, consequently Dilweg's name will not be found on the charmed roster.

It appears on only one all pro team. That was the first one ever selected in 1931, when Lavvie's career with the Packers was more than half finished. Had the selections been made earlier he would have made at least three.

Four Year Letterman

At Marquette he was a four-year letterman and captained the team in his junior year on the crest of the greatest glory period in the Warriors' gridiron history. Between 1922 and 1925 Marquette posted a record of 28-4-1, including two unbeaten seasons, but it was not a major power in those days and its heroics attracted little attention outside Wisconsin.

As a Packer Dilweg was a star for eight years, a bulwark of the only team in NFL history to win three straight championships until the present club matched it just 36 hours before he died. Yet you won't find his name in the now voluminous statistical records of the league. Such records weren't kept until after he hung up his pads, but he wasn't a record-shattering figure in any event.

His entire point production as a Packer was only 86, a figure most modern field goal specialists would blush to own for a season. But until Don Hutson came along ends weren't the touchdown hounds they have been ever since.

No Aerial Circus

In Lavvie's day a game in which both teams threw a total of a dozen passes was an aerial circus. The back who threw 40 in a season, let alone a single game, was practically a qualified astronaut. Anyway, other backs were more often the target when such quadruple threats as Lewellen, Johnny Blood, Bo Molenda and Red Dunn were in the same backfield.

What made Dilweg really great — a quality that can't be measured in the statistics — was his steady dependability. Darling can't remember a single spectacular play he ever made but he was always there to give help when needed-and he always made it look easy.

Dilweg himself could only remember in later years two games he considered outstanding. One was the classic 1929 victory over the New York Giants in the Polo Grounds when he spent the afternoon disputing parking space on the back of Bennie Friedman's neck with Michalske, Earp and Tom Nash. Rud Rennie, who covered the game for the old New York Tribune, wrote that any All America candidate could have learned his trade just watching Dilweg at work.

1927 Stand-Out

The other was the 1927 game here against Red Grange's New York Yankees. Lavvie was all over the field that day knocking down runners, piling up interference and collaborating with Eddie Kotal and Lewellen on a forward-lateral that blew the game open.

A native of Milwaukee where he starred in high school before entering Marquette, Lavvie remained in school to get his law degree after his football days were over there, meanwhile playing with the old Milwaukee Badgers during the season of 1926. He came to the Packers the following year when the Badgers folded.

He remained with the Packers as a 60-minute stalwart through 1934. Meanwhile, he hung out his lawyer's shingle while still playing football.

Story in Error

The story has long been current (an error which I must admit having a hand in perpetrating) and cropped up again in his obituary that he and teammate Verne Lewellen were law partners, but it isn't correct. Lavvie first practiced with Eben Minahan, Ed Duquaine, Vic McCormick and Art Thiele, and after the death of the former he went into partnership with the late Jerry Clifford, one of the Packers' fabled "Hungry Five."

His playing days behind him, Lavvie settled down to being a steady family man and a solid citizen. While holding his own in competition with some of the most colorful and competent legal eagles any city ever had he was an active member of Community Chest and Boy Scout work.

In 1942 he was nominated for Congress by the Democrats and beat incumbent Joshua L. Johns in a heated campaign. Just 25 years ago this week he took his seat in the 78th Congress, where he functioned quietly until his defeat in 1944 by John W. Byrnes.

Stayed in Washington

Dilweg never returned to Green Bay, remaining in Washington where he built a lucrative practice as a legal consultant on congressional legislation. In 1961 President Kennedy appointed him to the U.S. foreign claims commission, a post to which he was re-appointed only a few weeks before his death.

The question remains whether he could have cut it as a professional player today. Darling insists he would have been a great offensive end but at 210 would have been too light to play defense. That would have been his great disappointment, since Lavvie really preferred defense to offense.

Lavvie Dilweg would have been more clearly remembered had he been a more colorful personality. A quiet fellow both on and off the field, he was a physically powerful individual who liked people, enjoyed a good joke and was no panty-waist but not a boisterous character, either. What he lacked was the flamboyance of a Johnny Blood.

Gate Swings Wide for Cal

'Oldest Packer' Passes On

December 14, 1963

The death last week of George Whitney Calhoun snapped one of the few remaining threads still binding the proud Green Bay Packers to their humble, sandlot origins. Cal, with Curley Lambeau, was one of the founders of the football team that has made this city famous wherever sports fans gather.

The Packers were Cal's great love, and on their success he lavished a fervent loyalty and the best years of his lonely life. It may come as a shock, but Cal was only 29 when, as a result of a casual street-corner conversation, he and Curley launched the team. He was 73 when he died, yet his loyalty was as strong and fresh as in the days when he was barely keeping the club alive by passing the hat around old Hagemeister Park.

Through the years Lambeau has been given the lion's share of the credit for founding and building the Packers into one of the great sports traditions of America. It is taking nothing from him, however, and Curley would be the first to admit it, to say that without the selfless efforts of George Whitney Calhoun the Packers would never have progressed beyond their small town beginnings.

Calhoun was sports and telegraph editor of the Press-Gazette in 1919. He was a close friend of Lambeau, whose career at East High and for one season at Notre Dame he had watched closely and affectionately.

Street Corner Meeting

Lambeau had to drop out of college after his freshman year but he still wanted to play football. Thus it was that, one late August afternoon in 1919, he and Cal stood on a downtown street corner bemoaning fate. Nothing was more natural than the conclusion that if Curley wanted to keep on playing football he'd have to organize his own team.

Once the decision had been made the two enthusiasts wasted no time. They talked officials of the Acme Packing Co., Curley's employers, into putting up some money for equipment, thus insuring both the establishment of the club and its now famous name. A few weeks later, at a meeting in the old Press-Gazette editorial offices on Cherry Street, the Packers were launched.

Beat Drums Loudly

Cal had been a football player in his youth and a good one, but the game had given him the injury that crippled him for life. A sentimental softy beneath his irascible exterior, Cal still loved football, and the Packers gave him the chance to enjoy it second hand.

From the beginning he beat the drums loudly, creating interest in the team and eventually backing Lambeau's ambitions to put it into the fledgling National Football League. Once in he devoted most of his energy to keeping the club there.

With Nate Abrams, Lambeau and Joe Ordenz, Cal was one of the club's original incorporators in 1922. When, following a rough year that almost saw the experiment pile up on the financial rocks, A. B. Turnbull became interested and gathered the "Hungry Five," Cal remained an officer and member of the board of directors for many years. In fact, he was still a director, although inactive, to the day he died.

When the present corporation was formed in 1923, Cal was named traveling secretary and publicity director. He held the former post until 1940 and, with the exception of four years between 1946 and 1950, was publicity director until 1954.

As traveling secretary and chief tub thumper, Cal accompanied the team on all its trips until 1944. Most of that time he also covered the out-of-town games for the Press-Gazette. He wrote his last Packer story either in 1940 or 1941 (Cal himself was never quite sure of the date.)

Had Own System

For someone who couldn't get around very well Cal worked up plenty of ink whenever the Pack moved. He had his own way of accomplishing the trick, too.

Unlike run-of-the-mine publicity men, who haunt newspaper offices, Cal used the system of making the sports writers come to him. Arriving in another city, Cal would get a hotel room, fill the bathtub with ice and beer and then call the papers to let the sports writers know where he was.

They all came flocking, too. The best of their day, from John Kieran of the New York Times to Pat Gannon and Bill McGeehan of the New York Herald Tribune, all rallied around.

Most of the resulting ink went to Curley, but Cal didn't mind. In fact, he preferred it that way.

Among his traveling secretary duties Cal took over the guardianship of the pass gate, where he earned his greatest fame as the toughest man to get by in the country. To him trying to see the Packers play for nothing always was the most heinous form of treason, and he could spot a freeloader as far as he could see one.

Over the years, only one group consistently beat Cal at the game of getting by him. That was the Packer Lumberjack Band, which developed a system against which Cal, although he suspected what was going on, never quite figured a defense.

His best known nickname was "Gates Ajar" Calhoun, a title which, ironically, stemmed from the only time he ever abandoned his vigilance. That was the day in City Stadium Don Hutson began his spectacular career with the historic first play touchdown against the Chicago Bears.

Cal knew the play was coming and slipped away from the pass gate just before the kickoff. He missed the kickoff — as he missed every kickoff for many years — but reached the sideline in time to see the Herber-Hutson play click, then went happily back to the gate.

'Gates Ajar'

When Howard Purser, then sports editor of the Milwaukee Sentinel, heard about it he promptly dubbed Cal "Gates Ajar." Cal flaunted the title proudly the rest of his life.

From the first sandlot game of 1919 until the last game in old City Stadium, Cal never missed a Packer home game. When the new stadium was opened Cal had a lifetime pass but didn't figure he could negotiate the park's steep ramps and steps and was too proud to accept help. Thereafter he followed his club via radio and television.

As a sports editor and writer Calhoun had a great respect for statistics. The outcome was, over a period of more than 40 years, one of the most complete collections of statistics and records of professional football in existence. Nearly every book on the game written in the past 30 years had the benefit of Cal's knowledge.

He was always going to write one himself. It would have been a priceless account of the Pack's early days, full of stories only Cal and a few others knew, but he never got around to it.

Chapter Nine

Others Who Made a Difference

Father Mazzuchelli Got Around

February 22, 1964

The Santa Clara Convent of Dominican Sisters at Sinsinawa, Wis., tiny community in the extreme southwest corner of the state, will play host Sunday to the largest assembly of Catholic prelates and priests in the 115-year history of the institution. The inundation of ecclesiastical gold braid will crest there from all over Wisconsin, Illinois and Iowa to observe the centennial of the death of the Rev. Samuel Mazzuchelli, Dominican missionary in the Middle West, who established Catholic parishes and schools throughout the three-state area more than 100 years ago.

Included among the guests will be two from Green Bay, the Revs. Walter T. Williams and Norbert Rank, pastors of St. John's and St. Matthew's parishes, respectively. St. John's has the honor of being the first church established by the remarkable little Italian in what is now the territory of St. Matthew's.

Green Bay has more than a passing interest in the honors being paid the memory of Father Mazzuchelli. He began his missionary work here in 1830 and remained in the area for five years. The first book ever published in Wisconsin was printed for him here on the press of the old Green Bay Intelligencer, first newspaper published west of Lake Michigan.

Perpetual Motion

A sort of human experiment in perpetual motion, Samuel Mazzuchelli was born in Milan, Italy, in 1806. Being the 16th of 17 children, there wasn't much future for him in the fortunes of his family, and he drifted inevitably toward the priesthood.

He entered the Dominican Order at 17 and became a sub-deacon at Rome in 1823. Volunteering for missionary service in America, he was sent to Cincinnati, Ohio, where he completed his studies and was ordained on Sept. 5, 1830.

Almost at once he demonstrated his ability to move. Assigned to the mission field at Mackinac Island and Green Bay, he reached Green Bay in time to celebrate Mass on Nov. 15, then took off for Mackinac to get there before the freeze-up.

Roamed Wisconsin

From then until the winter of 1835 he roamed all over Wisconsin and northern Michigan. He was the only Catholic priest in the area and the first to serve it regularly in many years.

Father Mazzuchelli's first Green Bay Mass was celebrated in the attic of the Grignon home on the site of the *(former)* Wisconsin Public Service bus barn *(on South Washington Street)* because there was no church here (there hadn't been one since the destruction of the St. Francis Mission in De Pere at the end of the 17th Century). He was just the man to correct that oversight.

By October 1831 the first St. John's Church, an 80 by 35-foot structure on the river bank in what is now Allouez, was well under way. Father Mazzuchelli was architect, mason, carpenter and just about everything else for the tiny chapel.

For five years he swept back and forth over Wisconsin by canoe, on snow shoes, a horse and on foot-from the shores of Lakes Superior and Michigan to Prairie du Chien on the Mississippi. Everybody knew and liked the dynamic little priest, for he was as personable and intelligent as he was energetic.

Educational Programs

His most important work in the Green Bay area was his educational program among the Menominee, Winnebago and Chippewa Indians. One of his earliest projects was a curriculum for the Menominees that is remarkably practical today and which is preserved in the National Archives.

For the Winnebagoes he prepared a prayer book in their own language, which he had printed in Detroit in 1833 and which is now a prized rarity. His Chippewa Almanac, for which he paid $18 to have 150 copies printed in Green Bay in 1834, was the first book printed in Wisconsin.

The Master General of the Dominicans, summarizing his early career, wrote to Rome that he knew definitely that Father Mazzuchelli had baptized more than 1,500 Indians of different tribes as well as a large number of white people during his Green Bay-Mackinac years. The priest's own sermon diary lists more than 100 sermons in Green Bay alone and the list is admittedly incomplete.

Pioneer Wire-Pulling

In the spring of 1835, on his way down the Mississippi to St. Louis, Father Mazzuchelli stopped at the small frontier settlement of Dubuque, Ia., and Galena, Ill. His impact on the settlements was so dramatic they not only begged him to stay but pulled sufficient strings to have him transferred to the tri-state area of Wisconsin, Illinois and Iowa, where he spent the rest of his life.

Under his enthusiastic and dynamic leadership schools and churches sprouted all over the area, for many of which he served as architect, contractor, building superintendent, fund raiser and, on occasion, laborer. He had a hand, too, in the construction of many public buildings — the state capitol at Iowa City, courthouses in Galena and Fort Madison, and the Market House at Galena, to name a few.

In 1836 he served as chaplain for the first session of the Wisconsin Territorial Legislature at Belmont. His Memoirs, written in 1844, give a fascinating account of his work as a missionary and the personalities with whom he dealt.

Bought Property

Father Mazzuchelli obtained some funds from Italy in 1844, with which he purchased property at Sinsinawa Mound. His object was to establish both a Dominican convent and a "great college" there.

He did found the college, which he kept going practically singlehanded. It didn't survive him, though, as it was forced to close shortly after his death.

It took a little longer to get the convent under way, but the roots were planted in 1849 when four young women made their professions there. The convent of Santa Clara, grown sturdy from those roots, will be the site of Sunday's memorial services.

In February 1864 Father Mazzuchelli made a sick call in bitter winter weather. He contracted pneumonia, from which he died on Feb. 23, 1864. His passing went unnoticed in Green Bay, where he began his phenomenal career, but was reported at length in both New York and San Francisco.

Fascinated By America

A friendly, unflagging and eloquent little man, Samuel Mazzuchelli was fascinated by pioneer America, and the pioneer Middle West was equally fascinated with him. In the execution of his office, weather and distances meant nothing to him; he was equally at home in a river canoe, on the building scaffold of a wilderness church, in its pulpit or in a legislative mansion.

Father Mazzuchelli never mastered English very well, but he was a voluble sort who got his message across despite his picturesque mangling of the language. He was a highly intelligent and well educated man with a long range vision of the future of America.

Some tentative efforts have been made in recent years to nominate Samuel Mazzuchelli for sainthood. Nothing much has been done so far, but with such advocates on his side as Giovanni Cardinal Cicognani, former apostolic delegate to the United States and now papal secretary of state, the cause has possibilities. *(The process is under way; the Vatican bestowed the title "Venerable" to Mazzuchelli in 1993, a step toward canonization.)*

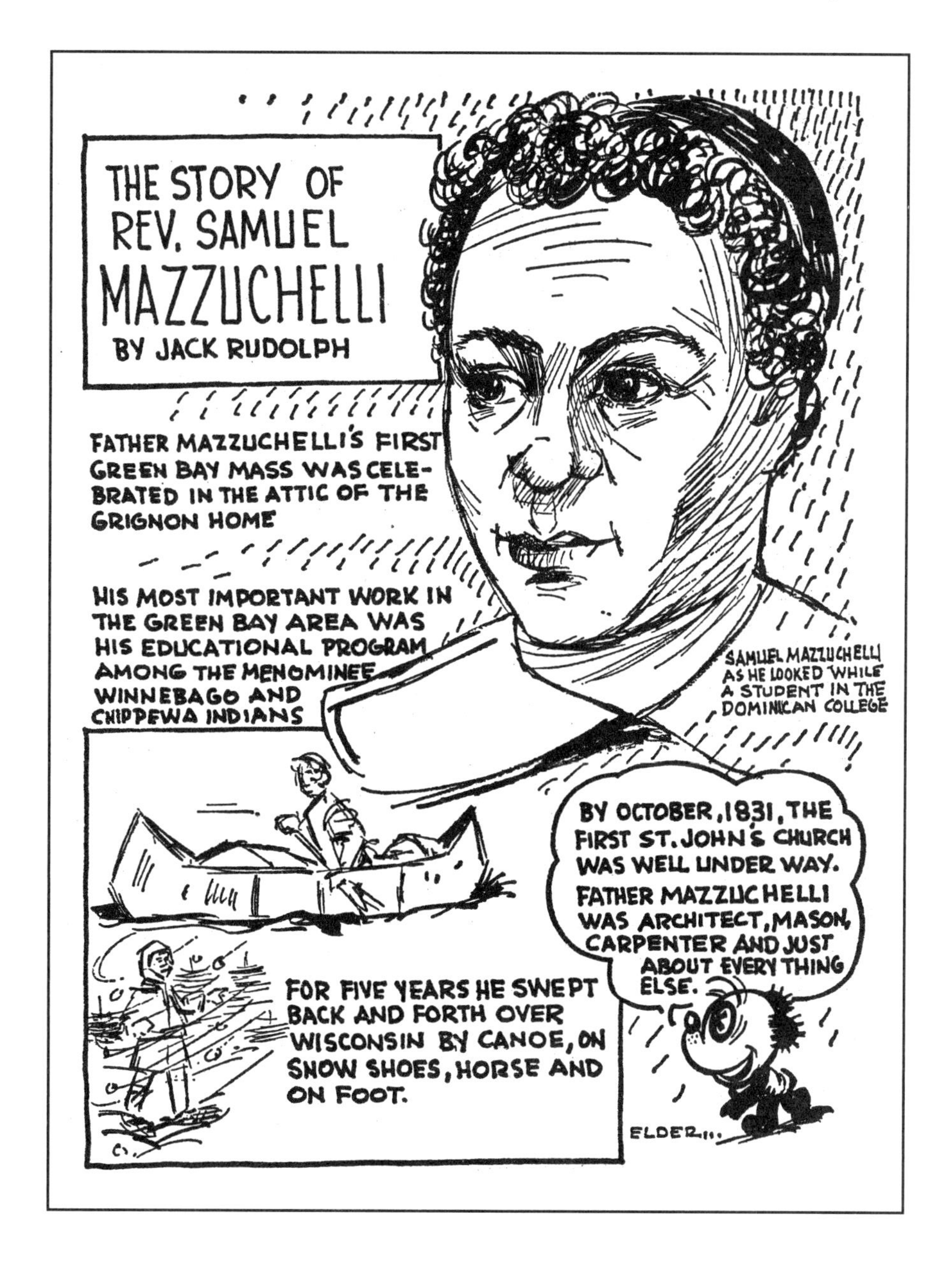

Legend of the Menominees

Side Looks Loved Morning Star

August 24, 1968

De Pere's Wau-Bu-Nuh-Qua Trail *(current spelling on area maps and in local directories is Waubaunuqua)* and the Town of Ashwaubenon are on opposite sides of the Fox River but they have a lot in common. The story has been largely forgotten, but the two place names recall one of the most charming romances in the legends of the Menominee Indians.

Most residents of Ashwaubenon have a vague idea that their town was named for a "famous Menominee chief." They're wrong. The town was named for an Indian but his name was not Ashwaubenon, he was not a Menominee and he was not a chief.

Ask anyone living on Wau-Bu-Nuh-Qua Trail where the street name came from and you're likely to draw a complete blank. Few even know that Wau-Bu-Nuh-Qua is the Menominee word for "Morning Star."

Stranger in Town

In 1795, according to the Indian legend, a tall, handsome young stranger named Little Crow, the son of a powerful Ottawa chief, visited the large Menominee village on the present site of the Northwest Engineering works at the west end of the Walnut Street bridge. *(The plant closed in September, 1990.)* He made quite a hit and was welcomed into the lodge of Chief Ah-Ke-Nee-Be-Way (Standing Earth).

Little Crow liked the set-up, too, and was in no hurry to leave. In fact, he never did.

Two years after his arrival, in the summer of 1797, a party of young women took the afternoon off for a berry-picking expedition in the surrounding woods. When they were ready to return, the youngest member of the group was missing.

After about an hour, when darkness was falling, the party returned to the village without her. Chief Standing Earth launched a widespread search that turned up no leads for several days.

Trail Discovered

Finally, a faint trail was discovered. A careful study of signs indicated that the missing girl had been kidnapped by a party of Chippewas from Shawano Lake, on the way home after a visit to the white settlement at La Baye.

The Chippewas and Menominees were at peace and Standing Earth was not eager to start a fight, but he could not brush off the incident. A council of all neighboring villages was called and a war party of 50 braves recruited to go to the Chippewas and demand the return of their captive.

Standing Earth hoped it could be brought off without violence but the expedition was fully armed and authorized to fight if necessary. At the last minute Little Crow was appointed to lead it.

Midnight Arrival

Moving rapidly, the party reached Shawano Lake about midnight after a march of a day and a half, hid out until morning and prepared to close in. First, however, Little Crow went ahead alone, instructing the rest to lie low until he gave the word.

Reaching the Chippewa village, Little Crow discovered all the men were away on a hunting trip. Cautiously entering the unguarded town, he moved from lodge to lodge, searching for the missing girl. He found her in a large wigwam surrounded by the Chippewa women to prevent her escape.

Silently and dramatically entering the lodge, he threatened the startled group with his tomahawk while motioning for the girl to come with him. His appearance so surprised the women they had no time to do anything but give him a barrage of murderous looks before Little Crow and the girl disappeared.

Wasted No Time

The Menominees wasted no time getting out of there. Runners were sent ahead to announce the rescue, and a strong force moved out to meet them about halfway home.

The return of the kidnapped girl, who had come to no harm, touched off a wild celebration. The next day Standing Earth convened another council to pay formal tribute to the young Ottawa brave.

Little Crow was highly praised for accomplishing the rescue without triggering an unwanted war. Then, flashing the sly Indian sense of humor, Standing Earth gave Little Crow a new name.

Henceforth, he declared, Little Crow would be known as As-ha-wau-bo-may (*sic*), or Side Looks in remembrance of the dirty looks he had received from the frightened women. As a further reward Side Looks was given the choice of two of the prettiest maidens of the village for his wife.

Gallant Side-Step

Not to be outdone in gallantry, As-ha-wau-bo-may (*sic*) replied that his only regret was that he wasn't twins, so he could marry both. However, since he could not and did not wish to offend either, he would like to choose a third, one whom he had long admired.

True romance would demand that Side Looks choose the rescued girl and that they lived happily ever after. Instead, he asked for Standing Earth's youngest daughter, a budding beauty named Wau-Bu-Nuh-Qua (Morning Star). Since Wau-Bu-Nuh-Qua had had an eye cocked on the young Ottawa anyway, she was willing.

Next morning As-ha-wau-bo-may (*sic*) and his bride ceremoniously left the village to canoe to establish their own lodge on the banks of a beautiful woodland stream not far away. Here they built a home where they lived happily and quietly for many years.

Peaceful

Although a proven warrior, As-ha-wau-bo-may (*sic*) was a peaceful sort who admired the customs and crafts of the white man. He remained all his life on friendly terms with the settlers of La Baye, had his children educated in white ways and eventually saw all of them intermarried among the French-Canadian settlers.

When As-ha-wau-bo-may (*sic*) died he was buried on the bank of the stream near his lodge. His wife outlived him many years and was long well known and highly respected by the white colony.

The stream was eventually named after As-ha-wau-bo-may (*sic*), although the whites gradually corrupted the spelling to Ashwaubemie and then to Ashwaubenon. In time the latter name was given to the town.

At the turn of the present century, when the first golf course in the area was laid out at the north end of De Pere, it was called the Wau-Bu-Nuh-Qua Country Club, after Morning Star, whose memory lives on in the street.

Once Local Celebrity

Dr. Beaumont Major Figure Here

January 6, 1962

Except for the Beaumont Hotel the name of Beaumont is a fading memory in Green Bay. Time was, though, when it meant something. In spite of its decreasing importance locally, the city has always had a proprietary interest in Dr. William Beaumont, although his personal contact here was short.

In his own right, however, Dr. Beaumont's place in medical history is secure. His series of experiments and observations on the digestive system of the human stomach produced the first American contribution of enduring value to medical knowledge.

He also lived in Green Bay briefly, bought property here, and his name was perpetuated for over 80 years by his son and two granddaughters. The Beaumont Hotel *(currently Days Inn-City Centre),* built by his son on property purchased by the doctor from Daniel Whitney, was named in his honor.

Who and what was this man who pursued his quest of knowledge with such singleness of purpose and success that he gouged a great niche in the history of medicine practically with his bare hands?

Fame Due to Freak

He was simply a run-of-the-mine military surgeon with an unusual knack for careful observation who, but for a freak accident, might have been just another unknown doctor. In fact, his medical training, by modern standards, wouldn't get him through the service entrance of a present day clinic or hospital.

The accident that started him on his road to fame occurred in the basement of the American Fur Company store on Mackinac Island the night of June 6, 1822. During a period of horseplay among a group of French-Canadian employees of the company a shotgun was accidentally discharged.

Eighteen-year-old Alexis St. Martin took the full charge in his stomach at a range of not more than three feet. When Dr. Beaumont, military surgeon on duty at Ft. Mackinac, was called he took one look at the mess, did what he could to make the victim comfortable and left with the remark that the youngster couldn't live out the night.

When, however, St. Martin was still alive the next morning, Beaumont took another look, decided he might pull him through and in the process began the long series of experiments that settled once and for all the chemical nature of human digestion. The work continued for nearly ten years, complicated by an understandable lack of cooperation from St. Martin, who made a miraculous recovery.

Experiments Intermittent

From 1822 until 1831 Beaumont carried on his intermittent experiments, usually when he could catch his elusive subject and make him hold still. St. Martin was superstitious, resented his savior and took off every chance he got.

Beaumont would track him down, lure him back and work on him until Alexis, literally, had a bellyful and disappeared again. St. Martin finally ran off for good in 1831 and refused to return, but by that time Beaumont had made 52 discoveries about the stomach that brought him enduring fame.

They brought him little else. It really cost him money since he had to pay St. Martin fancy wages out of his own pocket to keep him in line, and he remained in the Army until his retirement in 1840. His reluctant guinea pig outlived him by more than 30 years, sired 17 children and died of a heart attack while chopping wood at the age of 80.

William Beaumont was born on a farm near Lebanon, Conn., Nov. 21, 1785. His father, a Revolutionary War veteran, was a tough, old cookie who ruled his family with an iron hand and to whom daily church attendance was a must. Beaumont once explained his non-attendance at church in later life by saying he had endured enough in his youth to last a lifetime.

Left Home at 21

Always restlessly ambitious, Beaumont left home at 21, traveling through the New England winter with a horse and cutter, a barrel of cider and $100 he had earned and saved. He was already plagued by deafness caused when he stood too close to a cannon about to be fired, just to win a boyhood bet that represented part of the $100 stake.

He settled first at Champlain, N.Y., in the spring of 1807 where he taught school for three years. En route he had stopped at Burlington, Vt., and met a Dr. John Pomeroy who lent him a number of medical textbooks. Beaumont read them avidly and carefully during his stay in Champlain.

Having saved enough money to get him started, he went to St. Albans, Vt., in 1810 and joined a Dr. Benjamin Chandler for the required two years of medical apprenticeship. He got his license to practice in 1812, the certificate being signed by the same Dr. Pomeroy who had lent him the books. It was the only formal medical education he ever had.

The war of 1812 was on and Beaumont joined the Army as a surgeon's mate, serving throughout the conflict and gaining his practical knowledge of gunshot wounds the hard way — on the battlefield. He resigned in 1815 for private practice at Plattsburgh, N.Y., but re-entered the service in 1820 and was sent to Ft. Mackinac, where he was stationed when the St. Martin shooting occurred.

To Ft. Howard in 1826

He was already a celebrity when he came to Ft. Howard for a two year tour of duty in 1826. He liked Green Bay, bought the hotel built by Daniel Whitney on the site of the present Beaumont as well as other property, and was a frequent visitor here after he was transferred away.

On one of these visits he brought

his niece along. She met and later married Morgan L. Martin.

Upon retirement he settled in St. Louis, Mo., where he held the first chair of surgery in the medical department of St. Louis University. He died in 1853 from injuries received in a fall on icy pavement while making a professional call.

Following Beaumont's death his son Israel Green Beaumont, more popularly known in Green Bay as "Bud," returned here to manage properties inherited by his mother. He married a sister of Alfred Pelton, went into partnership with his brother-in-law, and in 1860 began construction of the Beaumont Hotel to replace the earlier structure which had burned down. Bud lived in Green Bay the rest of his life, dying here Oct. 16, 1901.

His daughters, May and Sophia, lived on in the beautiful home Bud built at the corner of Jefferson and Doty Streets, now the site of the Wisconsin Telephone Co. exchange, until the house was razed about 30 years ago. After destruction of their old home the sisters lived in De Pere, where May Beaumont died in 1934 and Sophia on New Year's Day, 1936.

Remarkable Pioneer Woman

Elizabeth Baird a Frontier Charmer

January 18, 1964

The name of Henry S. Baird looms large in the early history of Green Bay and territorial Wisconsin. He also had a remarkable wife about whom little has been written and less remembered, who deserves far more credit for his success than she has ever received.

That Elizabeth Therese Baird exerted a substantial influence on his career seems undeniable, although it is impossible at this distance in time to gauge it accurately. She was a highly intelligent woman with great charm and personality, and if she saw fit to remain in the shadow of her gregarious lawyer husband she knew what she was doing.

She was always there, standing quietly and smiling at his side for more than 50 years.

Elizabeth Baird came to Green Bay as a child bride of 14. Pampered, scantily educated and barely able to understand a little English, let alone speak it at first, she achieved a high place in the affections and esteem of the community she joined as a backwoods settlement and lived to see grow into a thriving city. She did it the hard way but with little apparent strain.

Born at Prairie du Chien

She was born Elizabeth Therese Fisher at Prairie du Chien, April 24, 1810, where her father, Capt. Henry Monroe Fisher, was an important cog in the American Fur Co. and the first American settler in the frontier outpost. On her mother's side she was a descendant of an Ottawa chief and always proud of her Indian ancestry.

Her family left Prairie du Chien when Elizabeth was only two. Her mother had taken her on a visit to Mackinac Island just before the outbreak of the War of 1812. They were caught there by the British occupation and stayed for the duration. The war broke up their Prairie du Chien home, and her father was transferred to Mackinac where he remained the rest of his life.

As the daughter of one of the fur company peers, she grew up in such luxury as the island afforded. Consequently, she was poorly prepared for the role of a frontier wife when she fell in love with Henry S. Baird, a poor but ambitious teacher-lawyer on the island.

Parental Opposition

The romance was not without parental opposition. Not that her age was much of a factor — girls married young on the frontier. Her parents weren't convinced the penniless though likeable young Irishman had much to offer but ambition and enthusiasm. They were enough, however, and the couple was married at Mackinac on Aug. 12, 1824.

On Sept. 20, 1824, Baird and his young bride arrived at Green Bay, where he had decided to hang out his legal shingle. Except for the Army post of Ft. Howard and a few homes scattered along the opposite bank of the Fox River, it was a crude and lonely place.

It wasn't an easy introduction to marriage for a girl who had never done a lick of housework in her life. Their first home was a former set of officer's quarters at abandoned Camp Smith (near the present site of Cotton House), that lacked just about every convenience of the day.

Couldn't Speak English

The place was somewhat isolated, too, and the young girl was alone most of the day. Since she couldn't speak much English it took considerable time for her to make contact with her distant neighbors. Being as resourceful as she was willing, however, Elizabeth learned fast and well.

Shortly she was an accepted and popular addition to the community. After the first uncertain days she was never to be lonesome again.

There were several moves in those early years, first to a new house in Shantytown *(near the river, in the area of what is now Heritage Hill in Allouez)* after the arrival of her first baby in 1825 and eventually to Daniel Whitney's newly platted village of Navarino. Elizabeth had built a friendship with Mrs. Whitney that endured until the two old women died within a fortnight of each other more than 60 years later.

As she matured Mrs. Baird developed great poise and adroitness as a hostess. Both she and her husband loved parties and liked to entertain, and Elizabeth could be gracious in a chicken coop. Among their innovations was the practice of holding open house on New Year's Day that for many years was one of the traditions of Green Bay social life.

Took Things in Stride

Elizabeth never saw a real city until she made her first trip to Detroit and New York in 1836, but by that time she could take anything in stride. A quick-witted woman, she was equally at home in John Jacob Astor's New York mansion or an overnight camp in the wilderness.

Having grown up among Indians and being fluent in several dialects, she understood and liked them. Unlike most white women on the frontier, she moved freely and unconcernedly among them and they in turn liked and respected her.

By the time she was 35 Mrs. Baird had traveled over much of Wisconsin and knew everybody of consequence in the territory. She was just as popular in Madison, Milwaukee and Prairie du Chien as she was in Green Bay, although she never courted popularity. She just had what it took.

Whether her physical attractions matched her personality can't be determined now. Her sole surviving photograph was taken when she was an elderly lady and there is no known description of her as a young woman. Nobody knows whether she was tall or short, plump or slender.

Brilliant Mind

In addition to her other qualities, Elizabeth Baird had a brilliant mind. By her own admission she never went to school a day in her life, but no less an authority than Dr. Lyman Draper, Wisconsin's first great historian, credited her with an "excellent" education.

If so, she did it herself — a truly remarkable feat for a woman who lived on the edge of the wilderness much of her life and was a frontier housewife and mother at 15.

Dr. Draper was in a position to know. The Bairds were keenly appreciative of history and their part in it and both contributed valuable reminiscences to Draper's research that eventually grew into the great Wisconsin Historical Collection. Mrs. Baird's writings on Indian customs and life on Mackinac Island and in early Green Bay are charming.

Written in 1880s

They were written in the 1880s and first appeared in the Green Bay Gazette under her initials. Apparently it wasn't considered proper for a woman of her unique position to write under her own by-line, although the Gazette made no bones about their authorship. *(The memoirs are available in book form, published by the Heritage Hill Foundation.)*

Baird died in 1875 but his widow outlived him by 15 years. In her last years she was something of an institution, moving in an exclusive and dwindling circle of original pioneers. Her graciousness and her prodigious memory never deserted her, and she was as popular with younger generations as with her surviving cronies of earlier days.

Henry Baird never became wealthy but he left enough for her to live in comfort and dignity until she died on Nov. 5, 1890. Her lifelong friend, Emmeline Whitney, had passed away just 11 days earlier.

"Madame" Baird, as she was called by that time, was buried beside her husband in Woodlawn Cemetery. Her pallbearers constituted a roster of many of the most influential men in the city.

Murder in the Morning

The Trial of Chief Oshkosh

February 6, 1965

Near the bank of the Fox River in Allouez, at the foot of the long slope reaching down from the ridge on which Cotton House stands today, a dignified monument marks the site of the first courthouse in Wisconsin.

The memorial is probably more impressive than the building it commemorates (which Judge James Doty described as "no better than a hovel"), but within the log walls of the crude structure were tried many cases that established the supremacy of civil law west of Lake Michigan.

One of them was the trial of Chief Oshkosh for murder.

Probably the most celebrated case ever tried in the cramped little cabin, the Oshkosh affair was once a popular item of local history, although its memory has dimmed in recent years. It is still a favorite pageant piece with Harold T. I. Shannon, in which the principal actors in the drama, costumed in the style of 1830, march down the ridge from Cotton House toward the old courthouse site.

The tableau disregards the fact that Cotton House was not then in existence, would not be built for another 10 years, and not on the same site. Still, it is a tremendously effective method of bringing the incident and its characters to vivid life for spectators.

A Triple Affair

The famous case, held before Judge Doty on June 14, 1830, is known as the trial of Chief Oshkosh. Actually, it was a triple trial in which the Menominee chief was jointly accused with two other defendants named Amable and Shaw-pe-tuk.

Oshkosh, remembered in history chiefly because the city of Oshkosh is named for him, was a principal war chief of the Menominees who presided over the large Indian village on the present site of the Northwest Engineering Co. plant. *(Located then at 201 W. Walnut Street, the plant closed in 1990.)* Although he really had no authority to speak for the entire Menominee tribe, it suited the purposes of the whites to regard him so in treaty negotiations.

The status was also convenient for Oshkosh in stalling off inroads on Menominee lands. It was largely due to his delaying tactics and refusal to be pushed that the Menominees today are the only tribe never driven entirely off their original holdings.

Impressive Figure

At the time of the trial Oshkosh was 35 years old, an impressive man whose fighting ability on the British side during the War of 1812 was still remembered. After the war he made his peace with the victorious Americans, kept it faithfully and held his own warriors in check at the time of the Black Hawk War. He died at Keshena in 1858, and nearly 70 years later his remains were moved to the city that now bears his name.

A remarkable aspect of the trial was the speed with which it followed the deed. Less than a fortnight after Oshkosh knifed O-ke-wa to death he was hauled before Judge Doty and the grand jury of the Circuit Court of Brown County on a charge of murder.

During the night of June 2-3, 1830, O-ke-wa, a Pawnee slave of the Menominees, accidentally shot and killed a Menominee hunter named Ma-ki-wa while hunting deer. O-ke-wa was paddling quietly along the East River near its junction with the Fox when he saw something moving in the underbrush on the shore.

Fatal Marksmanship

Thinking it was a deer, he got off a quick shot (the trial testimony doesn't specify whether he was using a firearm or bow and arrow), only to discover that his marksmanship was his undoing. Instead of a deer he had killed Ma-ki-wa, a relative of Oshkosh, who was also hunting.

The unfortunate young Pawnee (what he was doing so far from his own country was never explained, either) had little hope of escaping and apparently never considered it. He merely put the body in his canoe and headed back to the village to report and hope for the best. What he did not know was that Oshkosh, Amable and Shaw-pe-tuck had also been hunting nearby and had seen everything.

Under Indian custom, his own life was forfeit to the relatives of his victim if they chose to exact the penalty of blood vengeance. As a slave, his chances weren't too good, but it was a risk he had to take.

Never Given Chance

In any event, he never had a chance to explain. As his canoe grounded on the shore near the village just at dawn, Oshkosh and his two companions swooped down on him. Oshkosh drove a knife (later meticulously described as "of the value of six pence") into his neck, back and chest, killing him instantly.

In an isolated settlement starved for sensation, the killing caused a lot of talk but little concern. However, Circuit Court happened to be in session and Doty ordered the arrest and arraignment of the three culprits.

The young judge apparently saw an opportunity not only to affirm the supremacy of territorial and federal law in the region but also to set a firm precedent for his long held theory that such law could not be applied in opposition to long established customs among the Indians.

Colorful Trial

The trial, held on June 14, was a colorful affair. Nearly everybody who could make it was on hand. The courtroom was packed and the overflow stood around outside, Indians in full ceremonial dress mingling with white settlers in frock coats and buckskins. Significantly, the only persons missing were troops from nearby Fort Howard.

With Henry Baird as prosecutor, a jury of 21 men was impaneled to hear the case. It included many of the leading whites of the settlement, among them John Penn Arndt, Alexander Irwin, John Lawe, Ebenezer Childs, Joseph Jourdain, Albert G. Ellis, Paul Grignon, James Vieaux, Joseph Ducharme, James Porlier and Peter Charbonneaux. Witnesses called to testify included Bernard and Amable Grignon, Dominique Brunette, Joseph Redline and Daniel Whitney.

There were no Indian witnesses, although presumably they were the only ones with first hand knowledge of the facts. Being pagans and savages they would not and could not be forced to take a Christian oath and their evidence was legally worthless.

Long Indictment

The indictment, a long and involved accusation still difficult for a white man to follow, let alone an untutored Indian, charged Oshkosh, Amable and Shaw-pe-tuck severally and Oshkosh specifically. It specified that Oshkosh "not having the fear of God before his eyes but being moved and seduced by the instigation of the devil" had struck the fatal blows and that Amable and Shaw-pe-tuck were accomplices.

Oshkosh, in full Indian dress, conducted his own defense with much dignity. He readily admitted the deed, basing his justification on the traditional Indian right of blood vengeance.

The jury, however, returned a verdict of murder or manslaughter, leaving it up to Doty to determine the degree of guilt and the sentence. On the final day of the session the defendants were again brought before the court for the final judgment.

Careful Decision

In a carefully prepared decision, Doty reviewed the federal and territorial laws governing white residents of the territory, then declared they did not apply to Indians.

The laws, he reasoned, were not enacted for the Indians; the latter were unaware of their implications and could not be held responsible under them as long as the deed was consistent with Indian tradition and custom. His conclusion was that none of the accused had willfully or maliciously violated territorial law, the judgment of the jury was refused and the three defendants were released from custody.

Doty was proud of his handling of the case and sent a copy of his decision in a personal letter to President Andrew Jackson, expressing the hope that Jackson would approve his theory of separate codes for the separate races. Jackson did so, thereby establishing a precedent that henceforth governed relations between whites and Indians throughout the westward movement of the frontier.

Never Saw Green Bay

Astor's Impact Still Felt here

May 25, 1963

John Jacob Astor, immigrant son of a boozy German butcher, never learned to speak English very well but he was smart enough to parlay a handful of wooden flutes into America's greatest fortune. In the process he managed to exert an uncommonly durable influence on the development of Green Bay.

That impact is all the more remarkable for the fact that he never came within 1,000 miles of the city and wanted no part of it in the first place. Nevertheless, he once owned half the town; one of its original plats, a park and a street are named for him, and to this day nobody can buy real estate south of Doty Street without his name figuring in the transaction.

Astor, whose name became and has remained an American synonym for great wealth and social exclusiveness (although he personally had nothing to do with the latter development), was born July 17, 1763, in the German village of Waldorf, near the famed university town of Heidelberg. About the same time, in far off America, a notorious Indian leader and fur trader named Charles de Langlade was toying with the idea of moving from Mackinac Island to the mouth of a wilderness river now called the Fox.

John Jacob was the son of a happy-go-lucky village butcher whose cheerful improvidence kept his family in constant poverty. All his sons resented it and got out as fast as they could.

Last to Break Away

John Jacob was the last to make the break. At the age of 17 (De Langlade's trading post was already a thriving frontier settlement) he worked his way to London where he joined an older brother in the musical instrument business.

In four years he saved enough money to buy passage to America, where he landed at Baltimore in March 1784, with a stake of seven flutes and barely enough cash to get him to New York. He found the bustling little city, just emerging from the paralyzes of the Revolution, wanting many things, the least of which were flutes.

On the trip from England, however, a shipboard acquaintance had interested him in the fur trade and shortly after reaching New York he apprenticed himself to a furrier to learn the business. He was so unremitting in his ambition to learn all there was to know about it that within two years he had set up for himself in a tiny shop on Water Street. Working quickly and quietly, he was so successful that by 1800 he had a quarter of a million dollars.

Hard Work

He got it by hard work, the most rigid economy and knowing more about the fur trade than anyone else. It wasn't until he was worth several million that he left his cramped apartment above his old shop and built his first mansion.

In his rise he was ably assisted by his wife, who worked closely with him and whom he subsequently praised as the best and only real partner he ever had. It was true. In business Astor was strictly a lone wolf.

Following the Louisiana Purchase and the Lewis and Clark Expedition, Astor conceived the idea of a chain of trading posts from the Great Lakes to the mouth of the Columbia River. It was a grandiose project which only he had the resources to establish and maintain and through which he intended to achieve a monopoly on the fur trade.

He might have made it, too, if the War of 1812 hadn't intervened. It was during the early planning of the scheme that he got involved in the Green Bay region through the American Fur Co., which he organized in 1806.

War Time Killing

He made a further killing in the War of 1812, during which not a shipping venture in which he was interested was captured by the blockading British navy. One of his feats in putting a vessel through the tight blockade was as shrewd a bit of payola as he ever perpetrated.

After the war he secured a virtual monopoly on the Great Lakes fur trade and used his position — or rather, his agents Ramsey Crooks and Robert Stuart did — to get John Lawe, Jacques Porlier and the Grignons so deeply in debt to the American Fur Co. they could not hope to pay off. The only one he couldn't trap was Daniel Whitney.

By 1834 Astor was ready to get out of the fur trade. He was over 70 and had all he could handle just watching his vast New York real estate holdings. He sold the fur company to Crooks and Stuart and in the process foreclosed on the Green Bay traders and crushed them. In order to get clear they had to part with extensive land holdings in Green Bay and elsewhere in Wisconsin.

James Duane Doty, his agent at Green Bay, handled the unpleasantness of the foreclosures. Although Astor only wanted to dispose of the newly acquired land as quickly and profitably as possible, Doty talked him into setting up a rival village to Whitney's Navarino.

Not Enthusiastic

The old man wasn't very keen on the idea but Doty flattered him into it. Whitney had been a thorn in his side for years and he probably couldn't resist one more crack at the tough Yankee. He didn't succeed but the effort wrote the Astor name indelibly into the story of Green Bay.

For the last 20 years of his life Astor was in retirement. Through his vast fur trading empire and genius for picking up real estate he had acquired an estate estimated at his death at more than $20 million, then America's greatest fortune.

He died March 29, 1848, at the age of 84, after being nearly blind and almost a complete invalid in his last years. Other than his family and the impact of his death on financial circles, his death was not generally regretted. Astor was not the type to endear himself to anyone, especially a business competitor.

Iron Constitution

A powerful man in his younger days, he had an iron constitution that enabled him to work long and concentrated hours. Although in later years he became portly he was always an impressive figure whose penetrating eyes dominated everyone. Courteous and cordial, he had a kindly smile that was as dangerous as the bait in a mousetrap.

Punctual, a master of detail and one of the most efficient operators in American business history, he possessed uncanny accuracy of judgment. A tight situation always found him at his decisive best. Then he was calm and smiling, his cheerful advice to "keep cool, keep cool" being almost a trademark.

Great as were his gifts he had an unlovely side where his faults were equally glaring. Rigidly honest in business, he was tight-fisted, hard to deal with and utterly ruthless. He demanded great service for small pay and as he grew older his desire for more and more wealth became an obsession. Willing to risk great sums where there was a chance for equally great profit, he otherwise squeezed every dollar until the eagle howled like a banshee.

Not Generous

One biographer who despised him wrote that he never willingly performed a generous act in his life. Even his endowment of what became the great New York Public Library was only achieved by a combination of blackmail and playing on his weakness of never giving up anything once he had it.

Astor's private secretary, a poorly paid but highly trusted individual, was offered a better job by Astor's friend Washington Irving. Astor was beside himself — a condition, however, that never got so far out of hand the old skinflint was willing to meet or better Irving's offer.

The secretary and Irving knew their man, though, and the former — probably in cahoots with the writer all along — said he would stay if the boss would endow the city with a library. Astor promptly coughed up $400,000 to keep him — at the same old salary, naturally.

Gen. William Dickinson

De Pere's Forgotten Founder

June 15, 1963

General William Dickinson missed the boat.

Founders of cities usually have their creations named after them or at least achieve a statue in the park. Dickinson, founder of De Pere, had no such luck. He doesn't even have a tombstone.

In fact, he deserves double honors which he has never received. He was not only the founder of De Pere but also the second American settler in the Green Bay area — not that you'd know it from his place in regional history. Only in recent years has his city gotten around to remembering him at all by naming an elementary school in his honor.

Why he should be so completely neglected in the community he established — especially one as history-minded as De Pere — is a tantalizing mystery. Outside of a few recollections that De Pere's founder built a mansion that was never finished nobody remembers much about him. Even his house, torn down years ago, is better known than he.

Like so many of the Bay area pioneers, William Dickinson was a New England yankee. He came west from Middlebury, Vt., in the fall of 1819, just a few months behind Daniel Whitney, whom he bucked in business for years, and set up a rival trading post at Shantytown.

Shrewd Operator

Apparently as shrewd an operator as Whitney, he prospered. In a short time he was a well-to-do and substantial member of the growing settlement.

Nothing is known of his early years here, even how old he was, but he was apparently a young man, a bachelor and an acceptable sort. In 1825, at Ft. Howard, he married Elizabeth Irwin, daughter of Robert Irwin Sr., one of the most influential men in the community.

Fire destroyed his house and trading post in 1828 and the following year he joined Whitney, Morgan L. Martin and others in abandoning Shantytown. However, he turned a deaf ear to Whitney's plugs for the new village of Navarino and elected instead to stake his future on the possibilities of the Rapides des Peres.

A man of vision, Dickinson saw a great potential in the water power of the rapids, if they were properly harnessed. He lived to see his judgment vindicated, although he died too soon to get anything out of it for himself.

Built at De Pere

He built a new store and house near the rapids and on April 20, 1829, moved his reluctant wife to the new wilderness home. The City of De Pere was born that day but Mrs. Dickinson was not impressed.

The site was a long way from neighbors, completely surrounded by forest and isolated except by boat or wilderness trails. It remained that way until the following year when Ebenezer Childs moved in nearby and Mrs. Dickinson's parents came to live with her.

Dickinson and Childs formed a partnership which they called the De Pere Manufacturing Co. — first formal use of the city's present name — although they do not seem to have manufactured anything except a little lumber at John Lawe's old sawmill. Trade, however, was excellent. Helped by a ferry across the river, business prospered.

It really boomed when everybody else awoke to the possibilities of improving navigation on the Fox River and utilizing the rapids' water power potential. Randall Wilcox was brought from the east to build a dam and locks and the future seemed unlimited.

Riding High

Dickinson was riding high, probably higher than his old competitor Whitney, who was having his troubles with James Doty, Ramsey Crooks, John Jacob Astor and their promotion of the rival village of Astor. But Whitney was building an imposing mansion at Navarino and Dickinson wasn't the man to hold still for that. In 1835 he began construction of his own wilderness palace.

The house, a two-story, square pile on a large lot at the southeast corner of Lewis Street and Broadway, would have been an eye-popper if ever completed. But the carpenters got into a fight over one's attentions to the other's wife and walked off the job. Just about that time the Depression of 1837 struck and Dickinson was in trouble.

Never finished, the house stood as a ghostly shell for many years until torn down and its lumber sold for salvage. Its huge pillars eventually found their way to what is now Cotton House and the portico of old St. Willebrord's Church. Like Whitney's equally unsuccessful project, the place had early acquired the name of "Dickinson's Folly."

The depression caught Dickinson badly overextended in land speculation and hurt him badly. But he still had huge holdings around De Pere, and when times improved he began a comeback.

Died too Soon

He might have made it with his development of the Dickinson Road area but he sickened and died on Oct. 27, 1858. The issue of the Green Bay Advocate which undoubtedly contained a detailed obituary is missing from the files of the State Historical Society, thus depriving future historians of scarce biographical information.

Dickinson was originally buried in De Pere but his body was later moved to Woodlawn. There it lies today in a lost, unmarked grave.

Dickinson died land poor. What little cash he left was lost when the head of the De Pere bank absconded with all the funds, and Dickinson's widow, who lived until 1891, barely supported herself by gradually disposing of the real estate. Before she died that, too, was gone.

Like his contemporaries, William Dickinson was a courageous gambler. He was a good businessman who held his own with Whitney — who never operated on a shoestring.

Probably Well Heeled

It can be inferred that he was comfortably heeled when he first came west — contrary to legend poor men seldom struck it rich quickly on the frontier. It was the man with financial backing who made the big killing.

Also, he seems to have been well educated, if handwriting is a criterion. Specimens still extant show he was a beautiful penman in a day when merely being able to scrawl one's name was an accomplishment.

A mystery that long surrounded him was his right to the title of "General." Dickinson was no soldier but he was entitled to the rank. When Wisconsin became a territory Gov. Henry Dodge commissioned him a brigadier general in command of the 2nd Brigade of territorial militia, and he sported the title the rest of his life.

There is no indication that he ever actually served in that capacity, the only record of military activity being the organization of a company of Oneida and Stockbridge Indians during an uprising. It is possible that he saw some service back east during the War of 1812.

Randall Wilcox, 1797-1872

De Pere's Remarkable Citizen

November 14, 1959

When Mrs. Ellen Lawton Wilson died recently in De Pere her obituaries might have stirred a lot of pioneer memories if there had been any left to stir. "Aunt Ellen" lived to be a very old lady and was blessed with an extraordinarily long memory herself, but even hers didn't stretch quite far enough to embrace her great-grandfather, Randall Wilcox, although she lived in his shadow most of her 90 years.

Randall Wilcox, one of De Pere's earliest settlers and its first citizen for nearly half a century, was a remarkable man. Had he wished he probably could have become a highly successful Robber Baron, junior grade.

He had all the qualifications, including shrewd business sense, a forceful personality, willingness to take a long chance and the capital to seize the opportunities so plentiful on a frontier for men who had the wherewithal.

Technical Schooling

Wilcox was a New Englander, born in Lee, Mass., in 1797, but at an early age he moved to Lewisburg, Pa. There is no record of where he obtained his education, but he apparently enjoyed a pretty good technical schooling.

He had established a fine reputation as a civil engineer and accumulated a considerable fortune by the time he came to De Pere. He had built one large bridge and a set of locks on the Susquehanna River in Pennsylvania, and similar structures in Maryland.

Wilcox was invited to Wisconsin in 1835 by William Dickinson, Charles Tullar and John P. Arndt, who had just organized the De Pere Hydraulic Co. as one of the moves in the popular scheme of improving navigation on the Fox River. Offered the position of president and construction engineer of the company, Wilcox liked the set-up and accepted. He went back East, collected his family and started for Wisconsin that fall.

Wintered in Detroit

On arrival at Detroit, however, the family found the last boat of the season had already sailed for Green Bay and that they would have to remain there for the winter. Wilcox wasn't happy about the development, but he put the delay to good use. While marking time he ordered and supervised the manufacture of all the finished woodwork and hardware for the house he planned to build at De Pere.

The Wilcoxs had always lived well and saw no reason to change their style merely because Wisconsin was just a short jump out of the wilderness. They filled their new home with fine furniture, much of which is still there, and the place soon became a social center for both De Pere and the two villages of Navarino and Astor, which had not yet combined to form Green Bay.

First Dam on Fox

Wilcox went promptly to work on the river project and successfully completed the first dam and locks ever built on the Fox at the De Pere rapids. His dam went out in 1847 but by that time he was deeply involved in other things.

The Depression of 1837 temporarily killed interest in river improvements and might have discouraged the average man. But Wilcox had become an important figure in the area and he abandoned his engineering career to stay.

He had acquired extensive lands in and around De Pere and the Depression enabled him to buy more. He had also become involved in territorial politics and, since he was well off and not caught short by the recession, could do as he pleased.

Built Flour Mill

At one time he owned and operated a sawmill and in 1858 built a flour mill on the present Osen Milling Co. site *(now home to the James Street Inn),* which he ran profitably for years. A less successful venture was his presidency of the first bank in De Pere, which failed during the panic and cost him heavily. He was also an investor in the Fox and Wisconsin Steamboat Co., chartered in 1841.

His political activity was long and varied. He was chairman of the Brown County canvassers from 1838 to 1842, a member of the Wisconsin Territorial Council in 1845-46 and was first elected to the State Assembly in 1853.

When De Pere was incorporated as a village in 1857 Wilcox became the first village president. He served additional terms in 1861 and 1863-64.

He was for years a member of the County Board, served in the State Senate and in the Assembly of 1871 was the oldest and one of the most highly respected men in the Legislature. He also ran for Democratic presidential elector-at-large in 1864 but was defeated.

Like so many of his contemporaries who also became figures of wealth and prestige in the community, his personality has been obscured by laudatory biographical sketches. For all his success, Wilcox was an unpretentious man, cheerful, kindly and sociable with a keen sense of humor.

He was also exceedingly generous. In his day he was popularly known as the "bailmaster general" because every time someone got in a jam and needed bail he appealed to Wilcox. He usually came through and his bond was always good. In fact, at one time it was said that he was the only man in Brown County willing to admit he was worth anything.

Painted Face on Head

A sidelight on his kindly sense of humor involves a family story of his late years. It was his habit as he grew old to sit in his parlor each afternoon, looking out on the river. Frequently he would doze in his chair, his forehead falling forward to rest on his cane, held upright between his knees.

On one occasion a couple of his grandchildren sneaked in and painted a face on the top of his bald head. His wife was considerably put out, but Wilcox only chuckled and remarked that he was sorry he couldn't see it.

Physically, Wilcox was of medium size and height, very erect, with blue eyes and clean-shaven in an age of impressive whiskers. His hair, which disappeared in later years except for a fringe, was silver-grey. A portrait still hanging in his old home shows him to have been a strikingly handsome, alert old man.

In dress he was something of a dandy, affecting light tan broadcloth suits and wide, light felt hats. He invariably carried an ivory-headed cane.

Wilcox died Oct. 16, 1872, at the age of 79 after a long illness, and is buried in Woodlawn Cemetery. His widow survived him by several years.

As a personality in the early growth of De Pere and Brown County Randall Wilcox has been forgotten, but his name will be remembered as long as his gracious home stands at 707 N. Broadway.

Mistress of Cotton House

'Auntie' Cotton Colorful Figure

April 8, 1967

Last week's Hazelwood opening and the impending opening of Green Bay's other historic sites prompts the thought that three of them were for many years the homes of a trio of remarkable women, all of whom made their mark on the history of the city.

Miss Deborah Martin was born, lived all her long life and died in Hazelwood; Caroline Louisa Tank was for over 40 years the dignified chatelaine of Tank Cottage, and Mary Arndt Cotton presided for decades as the cheerful hostess of Cotton House. Most colorful of the three was the latter, beloved in her day as "Auntie" Cotton, a popular nickname no one would have dreamed of applying to her two contemporaries.

Green Bay's long procession of colorful personalities is by no means a masculine monopoly, and Mary Cotton marches well up toward the head of the column. She was not a political figure, although she had strong political opinions; neither was she a social leader in the usual sense of the term.

She took no formal part in civic affairs, yet she affected the lives of everyone around her. "Auntie" Cotton was simply herself, and that was a great deal.

Came as Teenager

Mary Cotton came to Green Bay in her early teens and left again a year later as a young bride. She returned to stay and for the next 40 years was one of the most widely known and best liked figures in the town. A gusty, forceful female, she liked people and enjoyed life with an enthusiasm she never lost until the day she died at the age of 86.

The daughter of John Penn Arndt, Mary Beitelmann Arndt was born in 1809 and came to Green Bay with her family in 1824. A year later, when only 16, she married Lt. John Winslow Cotton, West Point graduate and member of one of Massachusetts' earliest families, who was then serving at Ft. Howard.

For nearly 20 years thereafter she knew the nomadic existence of an Army wife, living in all parts of the country and raising her family in all sorts of places, always on the move. She loved it, though, and through the years developed into a charming and resourceful hostess, a woman without fear and a strong personality that overshadowed her amiable and mild mannered husband.

Twice Crossed Plains

Twice she crossed the Plains in a wagon train en route to frontier military posts and at least once she made the trip down the Mississippi when such a journey was not only arduous but dangerous. There is no record of all the places she set up housekeeping, but by the time she returned to Green Bay in the early 1840s she had pretty well covered the waterfront.

John Cotton resigned from the army in 1845, but at least four years before that — probably while he was serving in some remote wilderness outpost — his wife and children returned to Green Bay. Cotton joined them there after he left the service because of injuries received in a fall from a horse. *(John Cotton resigned from active duty in 1845 but did not retire from the Army until 1847.)*

Mrs. Cotton established herself in the beautiful home built by her father, now known as Cotton House but which she originally named Beaupre Place. For the next 40 years the Cottons made their farm home the center of congenial gaiety.

Even Farmed

They even did some farming, but, considering Auntie's liberal ideas of measurement, it couldn't have been very profitable. Not that they worried about it, particularly.

From the beginning Beaupre place was a popular spot for young people and children, whom Auntie Cotton spoiled shamefully. Like her mother, Mary was a born nurse and she was always available in any illness, regardless of her own time and comfort.

If she also inherited some of her mother's flair for sticking her nose into other people's affairs and bluntly telling them how to run them, nobody minded. She did it with such well-meaning kindness and practical good sense that nobody took offense and most took her advice.

Humor Helped

Her sense of humor helped, too. Auntie was the first to tell it on herself when she skinned her nose in the process.

At the outbreak of the Civil War, although she was then in her 50s, Mrs. Cotton joined the Army as a nurse, one of the few women officially accredited to the service. Nobody knows what Capt. Cotton thought about it when she marched off with the Oconto River Drivers but it probably made no difference to her.

She worked in Union hospitals for a year and came back home before the shooting was over only because her husband's health required her presence.

Tall, Strong Woman

A tall, rawboned woman of great physical strength, Mrs. Cotton was constantly on the go. Although Cotton house was considerably farther from De Pere then than it is today, she thought nothing of hiking the whole distance to argue politics with her brother. Both were strong Republicans but differed vociferously on how the party ought to run things.

There used to be enough stories floating around about Auntie Cotton to fill a book, but one of the best illustrations of her character and kindliness concerns her relationship with her housekeeper Veronica. The latter was a willing worker and excellent cook but she was also a periodic drunk, given to disappearing for several days whenever she went on a bat.

Each time she returned, shaky and contrite, Mrs. Cotton would light into her. Veronica would take it as long as her throbbing head could stand it, then announce she was leaving. Auntie would promptly fire her.

Regular Routine

Veronica would pack, icy farewells would be exchanged and out she would flounce. Come dinnertime, though, and there was an immaculate Veronica to announce the meal and that would be the end of it.

This went on for years. After Capt. Cotton's death in 1878, however, Veronica's sprees became more frequent and she often left the aging widow alone in the big house. Finally, she had to be hospitalized — Auntie paid the freight — and Beaupre Place, now too much for Mrs. Cotton to handle, was sold.

Auntie went to live with her son in Green Bay where she remained for years, a well loved and popular personality, until she died in 1896. Her funeral was one of the largest in the city's history, as people of all creeds and station crowded Christ Church to pay their last respects.

An Authentic 'Forty-Niner'

Gold Rush Story Finally Published

June 13, 1970

The name of Howard C. Gardiner rings no bells around here today. For that matter, it didn't peal very loud when he died in Green Bay more than half a century ago, although he had lived here for better than 30 years.

Yet Gardiner was a unique personality in this city at the turn of the century. An authentic "Forty-Niner," he was one of the early argonauts who followed the lure of gold to the Pacific Coast in 1849 and he was one of the last remaining survivors of the California Gold Rush when he died in Green Bay in 1917 at the age of 90.

Maybe he would be better remembered if he had struck it rich. He didn't, but the primary story of the Gold Rush is infinitely richer today because of him.

Just a couple of weeks ago the Brown County Public Library received a memorial copy of Gardiner's memoirs, written 75 years ago but only published this year. The book ("In Pursuit of the Golden Dream," Western Hemisphere, Inc., 1970) was presented to the library by Gardiner's granddaughter, Mrs. Harley C. Warner of Wallingford, Conn., in memory of her grandfather.

Gift to Library

The gift was made on behalf of Mrs. Warner by Mr. and Mrs. Crane Murphy, friends of many years standing. Lucilla Judd and Crane Murphy were childhood playmates when she used to visit her grandfather here.

The memoirs have been hailed by their editor, Dale L. Morgan, as a major contribution to the surprisingly thin literature of the Gold Rush. Because of their unique value *(then)* Brown County library director *(the late)* Gerald Somers indicates the volume will not be available for general distribution but will be kept in the rare book collection for serious study. *(Currently, the book is available through library interloan.)*

"Cal" Gardiner was born in Sag Harbor, Long Island, in 1826. His father was a minister there and the family had settled on Long Island as early as 1638. That young Gardiner, therefore, should take out on such a trek as the California Gold Rush wasn't surprising — he already had pioneer blood in his veins.

Self Reliant Youngster

A self reliant youngster, he was already engaged in his own trading venture in North Carolina at the age of 22 when he got first word of the discovery of gold on the Pacific coast in the winter of 1848-49. Settling up his business, he returned home as soon as possible and in mid-March, 1849, left for California by way of the Isthmus of Panama.

It was an extended journey, and not until July, 1849, did the youngster reach San Francisco. Even so, he was in the vanguard of the great tide of adventurous men — most of them young — that was to sweep into the far west country that year and the next.

Young, healthy and footloose as well as capable of taking care of himself, Gardiner quickly entered into the spirit of the time and place. He mined for gold both north and south of San Francisco in the years following his arrival. He never made a killing, but he did well enough to support himself and, judging by the tone of his reminiscences 40 years after the fact, enjoyed every minute of it.

Stayed Nine Years

Gardiner remained in California for almost nine years. In that time he came to know the gold fields and mountains so thoroughly that he could write knowledgeably about them off the top of his head decades later. He also enjoyed a wide acquaintance and-although this is not indicated — some prestige as one of the very early arrivals.

His was a story of small but colorful adventures, unspiced by high drama. At least, by the time he came to write about them the rough edges had been smoothed away and the principal spirit that comes through is one of pure enjoyment of the best years of his life.

In 1857, Gardiner returned to New York. He didn't intend to stay, having every intention of going back to California, but he never did. The beginning of the Civil War found him involved in lumbering in Wisconsin and after rejection from military service because of defective hearing he settled in the state as a lumberman.

To Green Bay in 1880s

Working at first out of Little Suamico, Gardiner operated lumber mills and camps throughout Northeastern Wisconsin, settling in Green Bay about 1881. He retired in 1892 and lived quietly in this city the rest of his long life.

In 1895, when he was on the threshold of 70, Gardiner wrote his memoirs of the Gold Rush days. He put it all down in longhand in a couple of ledger books, where they remained until turned over a few years ago for editing and publication.

According to Morgan, Gardiner evidently intended to publish them himself but never did. Why they remained hidden in the hands of his descendants for so long is something of a mystery, but it was not until nearly 75 years after they were written and more than half a century after the death of the author that they have finally come to light.

Splendid Job

Editor Morgan has done a splendid job with the manuscript as well as compiling a series of prefaces that are almost as valuable as the memoirs themselves, particularly his detailed analysis of the literature of the Gold Rush. He proves rather conclusively that the Gardiner memoirs will occupy a high place in that category.

The story itself is a charming one, written in the somewhat florid yet formal style of the late 19th Century but detailed and colorful. There is no indication that the author relied on anything but his memory but Morgan says he has checked the manuscript carefully and is astonished at its accuracy.

A big, beautifully printed volume, "*(In)* Pursuit of the Golden Dream" is an impressive tome and at $25 a copy not one that will hit the Best Seller list in the foreseeable future, but it is enjoyable reading and of inestimable value to the student of the Gold Rush. Cal Gardiner didn't fill his poke in California but he left a rich lode of history for others to mine.

Widow in a Strange Land

Lonely Life of Caroline Tank

December 12, 1959

If Otto Tank had been crowned King of Norway he never would have married Caroline Van der Meulen. He would have missed a good bet, because she would have made a first rate queen. She had all the necessary poise and strength of character — enough to keep the residents of Green Bay and Fort Howard in awe of her for over 40 years.

It was a pathetic performance, though, this dignified old woman living out her lonely life in a strange country, far from her native land and surrounded by the treasures of a greater day. But that's the way she wanted it, and what Caroline Louisa Albertina Tank wanted she got.

She was no stranger to courts and courtiers. Her mother had been First Lady-in-Waiting to the Queen of Holland and her maternal grandfather was a distinguished soldier. He was supposed to have been one of the few generals to defeat Napoleon in a pitched battle, but I can't find any reference to it.

Clergyman's Daughter

She was the only child of a prominent and wealthy Dutch clergyman, over whose luxurious home she presided as hostess for many years. Accepted in the highest circles of Dutch society, she knew her way around them. *(Caroline actually had two sisters, Claira Henrietta and Wilhelmina.)*

Caroline Van der Meulen was born in Holland early in 1803. The exact date isn't available, although obituaries after her death on April 1, 1891, stated she died shortly after her 88th birthday.

She enjoyed all the advantages of wealth and social position and was a well educated woman of her time. Nevertheless, she elected in middle age to start a completely new life in a frontier community in an alien land and, having made the decision, she stuck with it.

Met in Europe

Miss Van der Meulen first met Otto Tank sometime in the early 1820s when the young Norwegian was living the life of a traveling courtier through the royal courts of Europe. It doesn't appear to have been more than a casual acquaintance, although it would make a romantic story to say otherwise.

At any rate, she never married. Although she apparently was no beauty, she was an excellent middle aged catch when Tank reappeared in Holland in 1847.

They renewed their acquaintance and, although Tank was a widowed missionary with a small daughter and planning to return to Dutch Guiana, were married in 1849 when he was 49 and she was 46. Shortly thereafter Tank accepted an invitation to come to the United States.

Sold Dutch Property

Following their arrival at Green Bay and Tank's purchase of the west side land that included Jacques Porlier's old homestead, Madame Tank disposed of her property in Holland and had all her household goods shipped to the new home. Even though they expanded the old Porlier cottage by adding two wings, the house was too small to hold her treasures. Many remained packed away, not to be opened until after her death nearly half a century later.

There is no information on Madame Tank's part in her husband's abortive colonization project, but after it collapsed the family, which included Tank's daughter Mary, of whom Caroline was very fond, settled down to a rather secluded life. They remained aloof from their neighbors, made few intimate friends and were content to live to themselves.

Donated Tank Park

After her husband's death in 1864 Madame Tank (nobody ever dreamed of calling her anything but Madame) and her stepdaughter remained in the cottage, to which the aging widow had become deeply attached. Under the influence of Mary, who was a capable business woman, she began to take a greater interest in her surroundings. She opened two additions to Tank's plat in the Borough of Fort Howard and donated a park (now Tank Park) to the town.

Mary's sudden death in 1872 was a great shock to the old lady and she retreated back into her shell, becoming more and more of a recluse as the years passed. Although she had a reputation as an extremely charitable woman she was victimized a couple of times and became so annoyed with business complications she didn't understand that for a long period she was inaccessible.

For many years she was alone in the cottage, with even the companion she engaged required to live elsewhere. In spite of her wealth she was so frugal as to appear downright stingy. There are older people in Green Bay who remember visiting the cottage in the dead of winter when it had no heat and was about as cozy as a deep freeze.

Could be Lavish

But her penury applied only to herself. When she wished the little old lady could be a charming and lavish hostess, and on the infrequent occasions she entertained she went all out. She acquired a few close friends to whom she was very devoted and who were steadfastly loyal to her.

Madame Tank never learned to speak English very grammatically, although she was a forceful talker in her quaint accent. There is a hint of pathetic nostalgia in the accounts handed down by her small circle of friends of how, in her declining years, she would regale them with her court experiences as a girl.

Gradually, too, she resumed her contributions to charity, although so secretly that only her lawyer knew it. Not until after her death did the truth come out.

Over the years Caroline Tank had given away almost $100,000 to foreign missionary work and other religious activities. A principal beneficiary was a home for missionary children at Oberlin, Ohio, to which she gave over $10,000 and which was subsequently named in her memory.

The first Christian chapel in Peiping, China, was also built with funds provided by her. She didn't have much time for local causes, and the city's only share was Tank Park*, where the famous old home now stands. (The historic building was moved there from its original site on the river bank in the winter of 1908-9. *It was moved across the river to Heritage Hill by barge in the late 1970s.)*

Madame Tank left an estate valued at more than $100,000, which her will distributed among various charities. Her fabulous heirlooms, antiques, furniture, porcelains and fine china she ordered disposed of at public auction.

Attracted Many Buyers

It took nearly two years to inventory everything, including the long unpacked items, but word of the treasures got around. When the auction was held in 1893 it attracted buyers from all over the United States and Europe.

Her possessions were scattered far and wide, although a few items remained in Green Bay. Among the latter is the valuable 16th Century marquetry cabinet that stood for decades in the public library until returned recently to Tank Cottage. It was purchased with funds raised by the city's school children. *(Both the cabinet and Tank Cottage reside now at Heritage Hill State Park.)*

The library and the Neville Museum also own a number of brocaded court ball gowns of her youth which are now on exhibit in the museum as well as several pieces of rare china. *(The Neville Museum retains one of four gowns and one piece of Blue Delft china. The whereabouts or disposition of the other gowns could not be determined with certainty.)* In the last 25 years a few other pieces have also found their way back to the historic cottage.

** Caroline also donated $1,200 to construct the YMCA library, now located at Heritage Hill. In 1867 in her husband's name, Caroline donated her father's library to the State of Wisconsin. Shipped from Amsterdam, Holland, the Tank library included nearly 5,000 volumes, an especially impressive collection in that era. It is housed now with the Wisconsin Historical Society.*

Kindly Rolling Stone

Nathan Goodell Beloved Citizen

February 25, 1961

The career of Nathan Goodell was not a financial success. Not that he wasn't a hard worker. He poured the remarkable energies of a long and active life into everything he did, but he was always a shade too ready to sacrifice his own interests to help others.

Neither does he quite qualify as a Green Bay pioneer, although he arrived when it was just a small village in a swamp and lived to see it a thriving city.

It is doubtful, however, that the death of any of the community's early settlers — and that includes them all, from Daniel Whitney to Morgan L. Martin — left quite such a void as the passing of this beloved old man.

Goodell, who enjoyed the unique distinction of being one of the last links with the time of George Washington, having been born a year before Washington died, lived over half his life in Green Bay. When he died on June 2, 1883, just two months shy of his 85th birthday, he was one of the best known and most respected of the small city's citizens.

Born in New England

He was born on a New England farm in the Town of Pomfret, Windham County, Conn., Aug. 8, 1798. A restless, enthusiastic and sometimes overly optimistic fellow, he bounced all over the Great Lakes country before he put his roots down for good in Green Bay in 1840. That was 10 years after he first saw the place.

Goodell left his farm birthplace in 1819 and drifted into western New York. Here during the next nine years he displayed the restlessness that was to mark his whole life. He worked at a variety of jobs, being at different times a land agent, operator of a store, a distillery and an ashery.

Too young for the War of 1812 and too old for the Mexican War, he nevertheless had a flair for soldiering. While in New York he organized and drilled a company of "grenadiers" that was rated, under his leadership, as one of the best militia units in the state. Even his coming to Green Bay had a military background.

Drifted to Detroit

Between 1826 and 1828 he was steward on a lake vessel running between Buffalo and Detroit. In the latter year he shifted to Detroit where he went into the forwarding and commission business.

His first visit to Green Bay was in 1830 when he came aboard a vessel bringing replacements and supplies to the military post of Fort Howard. The little mud hole with the high-sounding name of Navarino couldn't have been very impressive, but he was back a year later as a sutler — forerunner of the modern post exchange system — to the army garrison.

He stayed only about a year that time, shuttling back and forth between Navarino and Detroit, jumping from one thing to another in a manner that must have driven his wife to distraction. Part of the time he was in partnership with Oscar Newberry as a commission merchant, a field he was in and out of half a dozen times.

Settled Here in 1840

Settling in Green Bay permanently in 1840, Goodell bought the property on the corner of E. Walnut and S. Adams Streets where the courthouse annex now stands. Here he built a comfortable house where he lived the rest of his life.

His first local venture was as a storekeeper, but he was soon back in the commission field as a partner of Joshua Whitney in the warehousing firm of Goodell and Whitney. Their headquarters was the old Astor warehouse on the river bank opposite the present waterworks *(which was located at 310 East Mason, almost beneath the current Tilleman/Mason Street bridge overpass).*

The business seems to have prospered but Goodell could not or wouldn't stay put, and he tried his hand at a lot of things during the next 20 years. In 1845 he had the agency for delivering government supplies to the Indians, he built and operated river boats, ran a sawmill at Duck Creek and even dabbled in truck gardening.

Had a Green Thumb

The latter seems to have been something he particularly liked. He had a green thumb, and for years his fruits and vegetables enjoyed a high reputation. Unfortunately, Goodell's generosity got the better of him — he was always giving stuff away.

For a number of years prior to 1860 he was local agent for the Astor estate and in and out of the commission business, in which he was engaged in 1847 and again in 1860. At the outbreak of the Civil War he wangled a permit as a sutler with the western armies but gave it up in 1863. Trying to keep up with Grant and Sherman may have been too much for a man of 65.

Returning to Green Bay, he was re-elected mayor in 1864, a post he had previously held in 1859. The last 20 years of his life were a repetition of his previous career as he tried his hand at what his obituaries lumped together as a "variety of pursuits."

Created a Job

For much of his four decades in Green Bay, Goodell was superintendent of streets. In fact, he practically created the job, taking it upon himself to put his own corner in the best condition of any street in the city. The City Council eventually recognized his service by establishing the street position and giving it to him.

Goodell worked hard and efficiently as street superintendent. After every severe storm he was on the job promptly setting things to rights, especially after blizzards when his own teams were usually the first to break trail through the drifts. Although he was 82 at the time, the great snow blockade of 1881 had scarcely stopped blowing before the indefatigable old man was out with his crews.

By then he was something of an institution, known by and knowing everyone. He loved young people, who responded in kind. There was not a kid in town who didn't call him "Uncle Goodell," a greeting probably used by many of their parents as well.

Didn't Show Age

Although he was an old man he didn't show or act his age. Throughout the winter of 1882-83 he was bothered by a lingering cold but by late spring had so completely recovered that just two weeks before he died he seemed as active and indestructible as ever. His death on June 2, 1883, apparently from pneumonia, was a shock to the city.

The local papers broke out with long and elaborate obituaries, the Gazette filling two closely printed columns, one a solid eulogy. Ordinarily such effusions are suspect, but there is a ring of sincerity about Nathan Goodell's lacking in most others.

All dwelt on his kindliness, his cheerful, even temper and his willingness to go out of his way to help others. The Weekly Globe defied anyone to recall ever having seen him angry or lacking in cheerful courtesy. Just about everyone in town turned out for his funeral, including the City Council, which passed a glowing resolution to his memory the night after he died.

That was Nathan Goodell's real success — the memory he left behind. It was a far greater memorial than the street which now bears his name.

Family Fireball

Anton Klaus' Success Story

October 15, 1960

Although Klaus Hall, in the days of its glory, kept the owners' name steadily before the public, the Klauses didn't need the publicity. During the 30 years between 1860 and 1890 the name of Klaus carried its own weight in Green Bay's political and business circles, thanks to the ability of three remarkable brothers.

Charles and Philip Klaus did all right after coming to the United States as young men, but the real fireball of this exceptionally gifted family was brother Anton. Within a decade after his arrival in Green Bay Anton Klaus was one of the leading young men of the little community.

He made and lost a fortune, then started all over again in middle age. Before he died suddenly at the age of 68 he was back on top again.

Born in Brutting, Prussia, Dec. 30, 1829, Anton was a year younger than Charles and two years senior to Philip. He apparently had all the solid qualities of his brothers plus a colorful personality and a flair for leadership they lacked.

Young Hotel Manager

Anton Klaus was a month short of his 20th birthday when he first saw Green Bay. What he did initially has been forgotten, but by 1853, when he was only 24, he was successfully managing the Green Bay House, a small hotel on Washington Street a few doors north of Astor Place. He also was active in village politics.

Green Bay became a city in 1854 and a year later Anton was elected city treasurer (the Klaus boys had a weakness for that job). He withdrew from the operation of his hotel, which he leased to Charles and Philip, but after one term in office he returned to the business and proceeded to make good money at it, at least enough to establish the foundation of his later fortune.

When the lumber boom began to roll again after the Depression of 1857 Anton was one of the early passengers on the bandwagon. He began by building a sawmill, acquired others and then branched into the special field of trading in shingles. He ultimately owned a large number of shingle mills and operated others under lease.

By 1870, when Green Bay was the primary shingle market of the world, Anton Klaus was the biggest shingle buyer, manufacturer and trader in the United States. Already wealthy and with the boom at its dizziest height, he was considered one of the most successful and prominent citizens of his adopted home. He had already served two terms as mayor and was working at the third.

An enthusiastic booster and firm believer in Green Bay's future, he reinvested his money in the city as fast as he made it. He bought or built all over town and was interested in many enterprises. He even owned another hotel.

Paved Washington Street

His pride was one of the largest business "blocks" in town on the corner of Washington and Main Streets, opposite the Beaumont Hotel. Among other things, in 1866 he secured the contract for and laid the city's first pavement on Washington Street.

Meanwhile he had gained a reputation for liberality and an interest in anything that promised civic betterment. For years his name automatically headed every public subscription list and he was always one of the most generous donors.

He entered the local political scene early, being city treasurer in 1855-56 and later county treasurer. He served three terms on the City Council and in 1868 capped his political career by being elected mayor. He was subsequently reelected in 1869 and again in 1870.

By 1873 he was loaded but also spread all over the place. Most of his assets were tied up in real estate, buildings and lumber mills. Then the Panic of 1873 struck, and Anton woke up one morning to find he was broke.

The sudden and complete cleaning discouraged even such an optimist as Anton Klaus. After all, he was 45 years old, he had been a big wheel and he had his pride. Even young men weren't setting the world on fire in the years immediately after 1873.

Headed West

Anton wasn't the kind to stay down long, however, and in 1874 he left Green Bay, heading west. He wound up in the new frontier community of Jamestown, N.D., where the only way to go was up. With the return of prosperity Klaus became a leader in the new town and quickly gained a position as a respected pioneer citizen.

In the next 23 years he recouped his fortunes, although he never again attained the pinnacle he had enjoyed in Green Bay. However, he was extremely well off when he died suddenly in Jamestown on July 22, 1897. Since he was a bachelor *(according to 1870 census records, Klaus was married and had several children)*, and all of his family was still in Green Bay, his body was brought back here and buried in the family lot in Allouez Cemetery.

A surprising quirk in Anton Klaus' career is the little known fact that in his early years here he called himself Antoine, later reverting to his German name. All references to him or his activities in the Green Bay Advocate of the 1850s call him Antoine, although by the time he began to flap his wings it was Anton again.

Why he adopted a Frenchified version of his name is a mystery. Maybe he felt that in a community where French influence was still strong he had a better chance as a hotel keeper if he sounded like a Frenchman.

Again, perhaps his experience was similar to that of Vitalus Joannes 20 years later. People mispronounced the latter's first name so persistently that he eventually settled for its most common corruption of Mitchell.

ANTON Klaus
By Jack Rudolph
WAS CITY TREASURER IN 1855-56.. HE SERVED THREE TERMS ON THE CITY COUNCIL AND IN 1868 WAS ELECTED MAYOR... HE WAS REELECTED IN 1869 AND AGAIN IN 1870
GONE!
KLAUS MADE AND LOST A FORTUNE, THEN STARTED ALL OVER AGAIN IN MIDDLE AGE. BEFORE HE DIED AT THE AGE OF 66 HE WAS BACK ON TOP
GET OFF
HEY, THIS IS SWELL FOR CARVIN' YOUR NAME!
YEAH!
IN 1870, ANTON KLAUS WAS THE BIGGEST SHINGLE BUYER, MANUFACTURER AND TRADER IN THE UNITED STATES.
IN 1866 ANTON SECURED THE CONTRACT FOR AND LAID THE CITY'S FIRST PAVEMENT ON WASHINGTON STREET.
HAROLD ELDER...

'Sage of Mukwanago' (sic)

Andrew Elmore Long Forgotten

March 25, 1961

When Miss Rose Vanderperren died last fall the last slender link binding Green Bay to the era of the Elmore family snapped. She was the last survivor of a household that once wielded great social and economic influence in the city but is now long forgotten.

About all that is left to remind the present generation of the Elmores are Elmore School and a number of West Side streets named for members of the family and friends. It was different 60 years ago when the venerable Andrew Elmore, his son James and daughters Mae, Gussie and Phebe were still alive. The name of Elmore carried weight in those days.

Andrew E. Elmore died in 1906. His affectionate nickname of the "Sage of Mukwanago" (*sic*) was singularly appropriate for a man of 92, and he had been answering to it with considerable pride for over 40 years. The "Sage" was not only a leader in the development of Fort Howard but also one of the foremost men in the early history of Wisconsin.

He was the last surviving member of the Territorial Legislature and the constitutional convention of 1846 as well as a pioneer in charitable and reform work. His influence is still felt in Wisconsin's system of correctional institutions.

Born in New York

Andrew Elmore was born at New Paltz, N.Y., a colorful little Dutch settlement that still flourishes in the Hudson River highlands, on May 8, 1814. After receiving what was then called a "common school education" he became a merchant and grain elevator and warehouseman.

In 1839 Elmore came west and settled at Mukwanago (*sic*), in what is now Waukesha County, where he opened a trading post and picked up bundles of real estate all over the Territory. Mukwanago (*sic*) was then known as the "Potawatomi capital" because it was the center of the Potawatomi Indian nation.

Elmore had the foresight to learn the Potawatomi language and thereafter cashed in handsomely. He soon had most of the tribal trade, which he held for almost 20 years after the Potawatomis had been moved to a distant reservation.

He became postmaster at Mukwanago (*sic*), serving from 1840 to 1849 and again from 1853 to 1857. In 1842 he went to the Territorial Legislature as a Whig representative of Waukesha and Milwaukee counties and served two terms.

Active in Politics

In the constitutional convention of 1846 Elmore was on the committee for the revision and adjustment of the articles of the proposed state constitution. After Wisconsin achieved statehood he was elected to the state Assembly, this time as a Democrat, where he sat from 1858 to 1860.

Early in the Civil War he became interested in welfare work when he was appointed a trustee of the new Waukesha School for Boys. He remained active until 1890 as a member and later president of the state board of charities and reforms, which supervised jails, poorhouses and asylums. Through the years he became a familiar and respected figure at national charitable and reform conventions.

As a member of the Waukesha school board he was responsible for the removal of the wall around the school, thus making it the state's first open institution. He was also the father of Wisconsin's system of county insane asylums, which was widely copied throughout the country.

Elmore moved to Fort Howard in 1863. He had probably been in on the ground floor of the maneuvers leading to the government sale of the Fort Howard military reservation and he acquired from Daniel Whitney's widow a large chunk of the most desirable portion along the river, just north of Dousman Street and the North Western Railroad grant.

Partner of Dousman

He went into partnership with John Dousman in the warehouse and elevator business as the firm of Dousman & Elmore, erecting docks, warehouses and an elevator on the river frontage adjacent to the railroad yards. Later known as Elmore & Kelly, the firm remained in business until 1878, when its facilities were sold to the North Western.

Elmore reserved a large portion of his holdings along the river north of Dousman Street for a personal estate, on which he built a handsome 16-room mansion. Construction, which began in 1863, wasn't completed until after the Civil War, when it was a center of Fort Howard social life. The home was finally sold in 1914 and razed about 1921.

The rest of the property was laid out in streets and lots and platted for development. Many of the northwest side's oldest streets were named by Elmore, including Elmore, James, Augusta, Mary, Phebe (although it is now misspelled Phoebe), McDonald, Mather and Bond — all honoring members of the family or old friends. He stood in so well with the Fort Howard village board that it officially named his private driveway Mukwanago (*sic*) Street.

Elmore stayed out of local politics, at least as an active office-seeker. He left politicking to his son James, who eventually achieved the triple distinction of becoming the first mayor of Fort Howard, mayor of Green Bay and finally mayor of the consolidated cities in 1895.

Retired in 1870s

The "Sage" retired from business in the early 1870s, turning the operation of the firm over to James, but he lived another 35 years as a sort of "elder statesman" around Fort Howard. He grew old gracefully and was always keenly interested in what was going on.

He traveled a great deal and kept

himself mentally alert and physically vigorous right up to his death. His advice on many matters was regularly sought and freely given.

Just how or when he acquired his nickname isn't known, although its origin is obvious. It was always a term of good natured kidding, something the old man could handle in stride with his keen but kindly sense of humor. There was much respect in it, too, and Elmore was proud of it.

Shortly after New Year's Day, 1906, the old man caught a cold. It didn't seem serious at first, particularly with two of his spinster daughters also down with colds, but he was 92, and pneumonia set in.

Died in 1906

On Jan. 13, 1906, he died. Two days later his daughter Augusta — or Gussie, as she was generally known — died too, her death being attributed to a broken heart and the shock of her father's passing.

The following year another daughter, Mary — her nickname was Mae — also died. That left Phebe, who lived on in the old house alone, attended by Miss Vanderperren, until it was sold in 1914.

Phebe, whose name was spelled without the O, was a frail wisp of a woman, a fine and gentle lady who was ill much of the time but who attained the age of almost 91 before she died in 1936, the last local survivor of her once prosperous and influential family. By that time the memory of its affluence was already fading.

When Andrew Elmore's will was probated the city was astonished to learn that the "Sage" was far from being as wealthy as everyone had thought, although he was still comfortably fixed. His estate was valued at about $80,000, more than $75,000 of it in real estate.

Nobody Remembers

Three Forgotten Pioneers

July 27, 1968

Implausible as it may seem, it is possible for a man to live in a community so long everybody forgets him.

Green Bay is no exception as a city, and over its long history a number of men once active and prominent in its affairs have "gone to their reward" without causing more than a slight ripple in the city's flow of life, simply because they had been around so long nobody paid any attention to them at the end. One was Dan King, another was Elisha Morrow and a third was Albert C. Robinson.

Daniel Webster King was Wisconsin's first druggist and at the time of his death in Racine at the age of 87 was, although long retired, the oldest druggist in the state. He had come to Green Bay as a young man from Detroit in 1833 and shortly thereafter established the city's first drug store at the corner of Washington and Walnut Streets.

Also Postmaster

In addition to operating the store for more than 50 years, King (he was often referred to as Doctor King but there is no record of where he got the degree) was socially and politically active and postmaster from 1849 to 1853. In the late 1880s he sold his business and retired, moving to Appleton where he lived for several years prior to going to live with a daughter in Racine.

Even after retirement King was a regular visitor to the city where he enjoyed visiting with his dwindling circle of old cronies, right up until a few months before his death in Racine on March 8, 1898. A son, Dr. Edward B. King, was a practicing physician in Green Bay and brought his father's body back here for burial.

In one of his sketchy obituary notices in local papers mention was made of his "jovial character," comparing him to his son Daniel W. King Jr. That may or may not have been a compliment, since Dan King Jr. was a young hellion, notorious for his escapades with Algernon Sartoris, President Grant's ne'er-do-well son-in-law.

Tragic End

After repeatedly scandalizing Green Bay, young King left town about 1888. He married a woman with considerable wealth but she shortly committed suicide and although he inherited her wealth, the tragedy shook him up badly.

Eventually he ran through the inheritance. When he died in 1904 in Detroit he was practically destitute, living in one room over a saloon while his second wife cooked in a hotel to support him.

King's contemporary, Elisha Morrow, outlived him by only a month dying April 7, 1898. Once a prominent businessman and political leader, Morrow was familiar to most neighbors in his last years as an eccentric old character who filled numerous barns around with hoarded, second hand junk.

Born about 1819 in New Jersey, Morrow made his own way by personal acumen most of his life and did pretty well at it. He went to work as a store clerk at the age of 15 but before he was 20 was farming a 100-acre tract at Peoria, Ill., which he had cleared himself.

Speculation Paid Off

Early in 1840 he sold his farm, bought a herd of cattle which he drove to Galena and sold at a tidy profit. Hearing about the garrison at Fort Howard Morrow bought another herd, drove it to Green Bay and did even better.

Following his arrival on Nov. 26, 1840, Morrow bought an interest in a tannery here and settled down. For the next 35 years he was active in a wide variety of enterprises, including real estate, lumber, farming and merchandising, at all of which he was successful.

He became an active and vociferous Democrat, serving two terms in the Territorial Legislature in 1845-46 and as a delegate to the state constitutional convention. From 1847 to 1849 he was receiver for the U.S. Land Office here.

Republican Leader

Morrow jumped the political fence in 1856, becoming a member of the fledgling Republican party and one of its organizers in Wisconsin. He was active in the nomination of John C. Fremont for President in 1846 and a delegate to the Chicago convention which nominated Abraham Lincoln in 1860.

After 1874 he withdrew from business and politics except for a couple of farms he owned and managed. In the 1880s, becoming somewhat eccentric, he was the instigator of a famous local rhubarb centering around a city ordinance prohibiting cows from roaming the streets. Elisha was agin it and pontificated loudly about denying Bossy her rights.

In 1856 he built a fine home at the corner of Adams and Stuart Streets that was a town showpiece in its day. The old house, still standing across from the new Elks Club *(since moved to 3195 Ridge Road)*, was for more than 40 years the headquarters of the Green Bay Woman's Club.

Career Forgotten

When Albert C. Robinson died in 1900 it had even been forgotten by the newspaper he had helped to establish that he was a co-founder with his brother Charles of the old Green Bay Advocate, first successful newspaper west of Lake Michigan. Born at Marcellus, N.Y., Nov. 1, 1824, Albert (nobody knows what the middle initial stood for) came to Green Bay with his brother and established the Advocate in 1846.

A quiet unobtrusive man, Albert worked obscurely as business manager for the paper while Charles was editor, publisher and general front man. He kept out of the limelight until the death of Charles in 1886, after which he got involved in a dispute with his brother's widow over ownership of the Advocate.

When it was decided against him by legal litigation in 1887, Albert sold his interest to his sister-in-law and in 1889 joined A. H. Lehman in the publishing of the German language newspaper "Der Landsmann." He was still a partner when he died on May 13, 1900, at the age of 75.

Courageous Widow

Rosamund Follett Carried Torch

August 9, 1969

Seventy-five years ago last week the name that had topped the masthead of the Green Bay Gazette almost from the beginning of its existence nearly a quarter century before disappeared. Rosamund Follett, widow of co-founder Dwight I. Follett and his successor as editor-publisher, had sold the paper and a new management took over.

Although Follett laid the foundations of the Press-Gazette in his struggle to put the old Gazette on a firm base, his effort might have been in vain without his wife. Rosamund Follett snatched up the torch when he died and brought her husband's work to a successful conclusion.

Any roster of Green Bay's distinguished women through the years would be incomplete without her name. She has been long forgotten — after all, she's been gone three-quarters of a century — but in her time few women were more widely known and more respected.

Professional Rarity

Through no desire of her own she became a professional woman in an age when such status was not only rare but socially tainted. She was highly successful, too, a strong individual who gave a full share of life and service to her community.

Rosamund Brown never intended to become a newspaper woman. Her husband's failing health gradually pulled her into it and when he died she stepped into the breach — which, in fact, she had been filling for some time — to continue as editor and publisher of the Gazette until shortly before her own death.

The daughter of a well-to-do New York family, she was born at Danville, N.Y., Jan. 1, 1847. She received an unusually complete education for a woman in her day and it was apparently while studying in Milwaukee that she met Dwight Follett. They were married in 1873.

Coming to Green Bay where her husband's position as editor of the only daily in Northeastern Wisconsin and the son of a local pioneer gave her entrée, she quickly took her place in the social life of the city. Just when she became involved in the paper is not clear, but she got into it originally as an addressor of out-of-town subscriptions. From that she progressed to reporting social and church news.

Shortly after Follett bought out his partner to become the sole owner of the Gazette his health broke, and from then until his death she found herself taking on more and more of the active management. After he died in 1888 she determined to go it alone.

It wasn't an easy decision but probably the only possible one if she hoped to salvage anything from her husband's work. The Gazette was shaky financially and his health had never permitted Follett to do what he wished. The widow buckled down to the task of rebuilding.

With all the handicaps she had certain advantages. Despite its weak financial status the Gazette was an influential paper, and by this time she knew what she was doing. She was well liked in town and everybody was pulling for her to make it.

Really Ran Paper

A forceful, determined woman, she really ran the Gazette. Every bit of copy went over her desk, she controlled editorial policy firmly and she worked hard and enthusiastically.

There were discouragements but no real setbacks. Gradually she worked from under her load of debt and began to establish herself as a competent force in state journalism.

By 1894 success was clearly in sight. The paper was prospering and she was an influential member of the State Press Association.

Then, suddenly, her own health, of which she had always been proud, began to slip. Early in 1894 she underwent exploratory surgery that brought her face to face with the fact that she wasn't going to get well. She had cancer, and her case was terminal.

Wouldn't Give Up

Although there was no hope of carrying on under the Follett name — her only son had already opted for the sea, eventually becoming master of large, ocean-going luxury liners — she refused to give up, but her decline was rapid. In July, 1894, she sold the Gazette to Walter E. Gardner of Milwaukee who assumed control on Aug. 1.

Less than four weeks later, on Aug. 27, 1894, Rosamund Follett died. Her funeral brought out most of the town and was attended by newspaper figures from all over Wisconsin. She was only 47.

After 75 years it isn't easy to assess her personality and abilities. Extant biographical sketches are so laudatory as to be largely worthless by themselves, while her old staff pulled out all the stops writing her obituary. More significantly, so did the rival Advocate.

Not Very Tall

She wasn't very tall, only about five-six, but she was strong and sturdy. Her photograph, an engraving done in New York at an undetermined date, shows a round, firm face with a large and generous mouth and determined chin.

Everybody liked and respected her for her pleasant, cheerful personality, modesty and kindness. Business associates held her in high esteem for her force of character and determination, which couldn't be shaken once she had made up her mind.

It is interesting to speculate how far she might have gone. She was only 47 and as an editor and publisher she had already attracted attention as far away as New York, where the prestigious New York Times had commented editorially and favorably on her competence.

ROSAMUND FOLLETT

75 YEARS AGO ROSAMUND FOLLETT SOLD THE GAZETTE TO WALTER E. GARDNER OF MILWAUKEE.

A FORCEFUL, DETERMINED WOMAN SHE REALLY RAN THE GAZETTE. EVER BIT OF COPY WENT OVER HER DESK.

HER WORK ATTRACTED ATTENTION AS FAR AWAY AS NEW YORK, WHERE THE NEW YORK TIMES COMMENTED EDITORIALLY AND FAVORABLY.

HAROLD ELDER... GREEN BAY PRESS-GAZETTE

Last Years Clouded

Keustermann Success Story

May 13, 1961

The story of Gus Keustermann *(spelled Kuestermann in Wright's 1915-16 City Directory)* was closed in Green Bay a short time ago. It came to an end when his comfortable old home on Cherry Street was razed and the big, beautiful linden trees in what was once Legion Park — trees that had grown from cuttings he transplanted from Berlin's famed Unter den Linden Boulevard — were destroyed to make way for the new post office *(northwest corner of East Walnut and Jefferson, now the Sophie Beaumont Building housing local government offices).*

It shouldn't have ended that way, but then Gus' life shouldn't have ended as it did either, his last years clouded by the anti-Germanism of World War I. His career is a heartwarming instance of the young immigrant who attained success in a new country, and there ought to be some way to keep the story alive.

Gustave Keustermann was a "Lipper," a term once familiarly applied to a group of remarkable young men who came from the Village of Detmold in the German Province of Lippe to Green Bay, where they all became successful and prosperous. He was born in Detmold May 24, 1850, the son of a German Army gunsmith.

Young Keustermann emigrated to America in 1868 and headed directly for Green Bay where a couple of old schoolmates had preceded him. A gregarious, ambitious and hard-working lad, he entered readily into the life of the little city and soon was well known and popular.

Spoke Fluent English

An exceptionally good education that enabled him to speak fluent English as well as French and German came in handy. A handsome, strapping youngster, he was also an accomplished musician, whose talents were frequently in demand.

After clerking in a hardware store for a few months he became a bookkeeper for the Green Bay Advocate, a job he held until 1872. That year Gus, Louise Neese and Erastus Root established their own stationery store and job printing business.

A year later Root took over the printing department while Keustermann and Neese expanded the stationery business by adding music and musical instruments. Keustermann bought Neese's partnership in 1876 and in 1880 was joined by his brother, Robert, who remained with the firm until 1894.

The establishment prospered during the 1870s and '80s until it became one of the largest of its kind in this part of the middle west. In 1882 the brothers erected the building at 127 N. Washington St., now occupied by the Vander Zanden jewelry store. *(Vander Zanden's opened on West Walnut Street in Fort Howard in 1893, moved to 123 N. Washington where it remained for eight years, and settled at 217 N. Washington in 1923. The store was heavily damaged by fire in August 1993 which closed several other businesses. Vander Zanden's re-opened later that fall but closed the downtown store three years later — November 1996 — to consolidate operations with its store in Bay Park Square.)*

Statue Pulled Down

Gus put a statue of "Columbia" in a niche above the second floor that remained there until 1918. It was pulled down during the war by a group of young hot-heads under the impression that the rather martial figure represented "Germania."

Meanwhile Keustermann, an ardent Republican, became active in local politics and served as a member of the City Council, the County Board and as city treasurer. A forceful speaker with an excellent voice, he was much in demand as an orator — he was an equally good spellbinder in English or German — and he also wrote political articles for Milwaukee newspapers.

For years, too, he contributed articles on the American scene to German periodicals. It was on one of his periodic visits to Germany that he brought back the tree cuttings which grew into the Legion Park lindens.

In 1892 he was appointed postmaster. When his name was first proposed there was some opposition to a "non-citizen" being given the post but Gus squelched that by quietly proving he had been a naturalized citizen for over 20 years. He served until 1896, then returned to his store, in which the music department had become predominant.

Elected to Congress

Keustermann had once been seriously considered as a Republican candidate for governor and had twice unsuccessfully sought the nomination for Congress, but he made it in 1906. That year he defeated E. S. Minor of Sturgeon Bay to become the second Green Bay resident and first local Republican to win a seat in the House of Representatives. He served two terms, giving way to Thomas F. Konop of Kewaunee after an extremely close election in 1910.

Gus retired from the music business after his Washington interlude but remained active in other enterprises. He was one of the organizers of the Green Bay Drop Forge Co., which began as a horseshoe factory, and of the Diana Manufacturing Co. Otherwise, he puttered around his yard, played the zither with old cronies, wrote music and gave speeches whenever and wherever called upon.

Tall and well built, with a proud, erect carriage, Gus Keustermann was a man of great dignity without being in the least a stuffed shirt. He was a kindly man who liked a good time and enjoyed music in any form. He was, among other things, an accomplished pianist, a fine singer and a capable composer.

Those who knew him do not recall ever having seen him angry, although he could be a stern as well as an indulgent parent. One daughter, now dead, once pictured him as a happy man who was always singing around the house and who always had a supply of candy in his pockets for any children who might waylay him, a tactic at which his four daughters were especially adroit.

Gus was not a rich man, although he lived comfortably, and he gave away a lot of what he had. After he died it was discovered that he had over the years advanced considerable sums to hard pressed friends, most of which never had been — and never were — repaid.

Respected Figure

He was a familiar and highly respected figure in the community until the entry of the United States into the war of 1914-18. The violent anti-German sentiments of that conflict were hard on the German residents of Green Bay and none more so than Gus Keustermann.

Throughout the war he was constantly badgered by insults and threats, both openly on the streets and anonymously by phone. The destruction of his statue was part of the campaign.

Keustermann maintained his dignity, however, never losing his temper and never complaining, even to his own family. Nevertheless, Gus, a thorough-going American but also proud of his nationality, was deeply hurt.

Had he lived a little longer he would have seen the trend swing the other way again. Unfortunately, he died before the antagonism did.

Gustave Keustermann died at his home on Christmas Day, 1919, after an illness of several months. The cause of death was given as Bright's Disease, but many who knew him well were convinced that a broken heart had a lot to do with it, too.

Belated Tribute

Library Honors Rufus Kellogg

November 18, 1961

On the south wall of the main reading room in the *(former)* Kellogg Public Library *(on South Jefferson Street)* a portrait of a dapper little man with iron grey hair, ruddy complexion and a walrus moustache was hung recently. Quite aside from the artistic merits of the painting — and it's a very fine one — putting it there and identifying it properly was a long overdue tribute to the nearly forgotten man to whom the library owes its existence.

Not that the library has ever been ungrateful or has forgotten Rufus B. Kellogg. The painting, by the once famous "painter of presidents" G. P. A. Healy, has been in the same room for over 30 years but has heretofore been displayed obscurely and without identification.

Rufus Bela Kellogg didn't live in Green Bay very long and his active business career was even shorter, but it was long enough to perpetuate his name in the library and the Kellogg-Citizens National Bank *(now Associated Bank).* Less spectacular but once equally important to the agricultural life of the era was his work in drastically improving the breed of farm work horses in Northeastern Wisconsin.

Unlike many of his friends and associates, Kellogg didn't get a street named after him. Kellogg Street on the West Side was named for someone else.

Kellogg came to Green Bay and established the Kellogg National Bank in 1874. He was forced into retirement by high blood pressure in 1882 and died, a victim of apoplexy, in 1891 at the age of 54. *(In fact, Kellogg remained bank president and involved in the bank's affairs until he died.)* He packed a lot of accomplishment into those 17 years.

Graduate of Amherst

He was born in Amherst, Mass., April 15, 1837, and died there while attending a college class reunion. When he graduated in 1858 he was president of his class although one of its youngest members.

An older brother, A. W. Kellogg, had established Oshkosh's first bank in 1852, and after graduation Rufus joined him there to learn the banking business from the ground up. He did, too.

Kellogg, always a careful and natty dresser, delighted in telling of his introduction to the dignified profession of banker. When he reported for work the first morning togged out in stripped pants, morning coat and flowing cravat his brother handed him a broom and invited him to get cracking on the floor and wooden sidewalk out front.

Started as Messenger

Starting as a bank messenger, Kellogg was an executive by 1873 and highly regarded throughout Wisconsin. That year Henry S. Baird and a number of other prominent men here decided Green Bay needed more than one bank. Kellogg was invited to come and start another.

He accepted and moved to Green Bay early the following year, becoming the first president after purchasing 290 of the first 500 shares issued. He put up a tidy bundle for them at $150 a share, receiving in return a salary of $100 a month.

The bank was successful from the start. Kellogg's nominal tenure as president ended in 1882 because of his health, but he continued to run things. It was he who personally gave John Rose Sr. his first job as a messenger in the institution to which Mr. Rose has devoted over 70 years.

Following his semi-retirement, Kellogg found time heavy on his hands and, so the story goes, fell into the habit of driving his buggy around the countryside to talk to farmers at work. Noting the spindly horses most of them were forced to use for lack of better animals he decided to do something about it.

He bought a 1,000-acre farm in Allouez and stocked it with blooded French percherons for breeding. To maintain the quality of his herd, which soon acquired a national reputation, he made annual trips to France to purchase prize animals.

It was on one such trip, in 1885, that he met Healy, then one of the most sought-after artists in Paris, and sat for the portrait now hanging in the library. How the library got the painting is a story in itself.

Library was Solution

An active and enthusiastic booster of his adopted city, Kellogg wanted to see it develop into something other than a roughneck sawmill and lake port town where culture was in short supply and less demand. His solution was a public library.

Startling as it may seem today, when a public library is considered as much a part of a community's life as its school system, the citizenry were not impressed. After several futile efforts to get the project off the ground, Kellogg got it put up for a referendum vote in 1886, promising a liberal donation if it went through. The proposition was soundly defeated.

Kellogg could have done the job alone but he was convinced that a privately endowed library was not the answer. It needed public funds and support to succeed and grow.

Bond Issue

His chance came in 1888 when the city issued $15,000 in bonds. Kellogg quietly bought them all, then confronted the city council with another proposal.

He offered to give the entire issue back to the city, to be put in a library fund from which $900 a year was to be spent on a public library. He further stipulated that when the fund was exhausted the city agreed to keep up the annual payment for 10 *(50)* years. He reasoned that by such time the city would be in too deep to get out even if the citizens would permit it.

The council bought the idea, and

the library was organized in 1889.

Not content with what he had already given, Kellogg also donated more than a third of the 3,000 volumes the library acquired in its first three years.

Death a Shock

Although his health was precarious few of his friends seem to have realized it; consequently, his sudden death on Sept. 24, 1891, was a shock. The library board hastily assembled and adopted a long, flowery but obviously sincere tribute to its benefactor. Five years later, in 1896, his name was given to the institution his interest and gifts had founded.

Rufus Kellogg was not a big man but he stood tall in the estimate of those who knew him. Rigidly honest, he insisted upon absolute integrity in any institution that handled other peoples' money, and he lived up to it.

The few who remember him recall that he was a slight, active man with great dignity but friendly and approachable. A kindly man, he apparently had a fiery temper but kept it under rigid control. Although the effort probably contributed to his hypertension, nobody ever saw him angry.

The city also retains another visible memento of his presence, although it is getting old and few people recognize it for what it once was. His big Victorian home on South Monroe Avenue is still standing as the oldest part of St. Joseph's Academy. *(The building was razed in June 1964.)*

The Kellogg Public Library became the Brown County Public Library in 1968. The downtown central library moved to its present location at 515 Pine Street in 1974 where Kellogg's portrait hangs on the second floor. Kellogg's biography, "In That Place, In That Time: Remembering Rufus B. Kellogg," is available in hardcover through the Brown County Historical Society.

* *Razed in 1964.*

Yachtsman, Historian

A. C. Neville Became an Institution

September 20, 1958

Arthur Courtenay Neville looked, in his later years, like a cross between a retired British army colonel and the dean of the local clergy. He was far from being either, although his tall, spare figure, white hair and moustache and high, stiff collars fooled a lot of people into thinking he was English.

Actually, he was an Irishman, with a suave charm, old fashioned gallantry and a sly sense of humor. He also coupled a monumental dignity with a vocabulary that could peel the hide off a muleskinner on the rare occasions he turned it loose.

A. C. Neville has been dead for almost 30 years and so nearly forgotten that probably half the city's present population never heard of him. But when he died in 1929 the city felt that one of the last links with its lusty youth had been broken.

The old man had become an institution after nearly 75 years. He had come to Green Bay when it was little more than a mud hole on the fringe of the wilderness and lived to see it a thriving modern community. His own contribution to the change had been considerable.

Born in Pottsville, Pa., Oct. 15, 1850, Arthur Neville came to Green Bay in 1856. His father, John C. Neville, was a native of Dublin and had been a highly successful lawyer back East before he decided to pioneer. He quickly became a leading citizen of the small Wisconsin city, was active in its professional, social and political life and prospered accordingly.

His son came naturally by his charm and personality. If anything, the senior Neville was even more colorful. John Neville was a significant legal and political figure throughout Wisconsin, serving as district attorney for 12 years, as city attorney for eight, and one term as mayor in 1880-81. He also served in the State Assembly from 1860 to 1861. When he died in 1898 at the age of 83 he was the oldest practicing attorney in Northeastern Wisconsin.

Arthur got his formal education in Green Bay's primitive public schools, which he left at the age of 17 to become a messenger and clerk for the Dousman and Elmore Co. Two years later he went to Chicago where he worked as a bookkeeper, returning home in 1871. The following year he entered his father's law office to read law and was admitted to the bar in 1874.

In addition to showing a natural aptitude for the law, young Neville was one of the town's social blades with a liking for good horses and fast yachts and always the gallant with the ladies. He was an enthusiastic member of the notorious Peak's Lake Sportsmen's Club in the heyday of Algernon Sartoris and one of the best yachtsmen on the Lakes.

Even after he settled down Neville never lost his love for sailing. He was a charter member of the original Green Bay Yacht Club, its commodore for years, and the skipper of a series of fleet yachts, all named "Algonkin." He sailed his own boats all over Lake Michigan until he became too old to handle a wheel.

His first wife died within six months of their marriage and in 1883 he married again. His second wife had been a widow, Mrs. Ella (Hoes) Peak, whose father was a nephew of President Martin Van Buren.

Mrs. Neville was a strong and civic minded woman who made significant contributions to the development of Green Bay, but even her dominant personality couldn't subdue A. C. She was highly respected but because of her aggressiveness never as well liked as her more easy-going husband.

In addition to a successful law practice, Neville followed his father into local politics and was elected mayor in 1888. He served until 1890. Meanwhile, too, he branched out into a variety of business and promotional activities.

He was an organizer of the Business Men's Assn., forerunner of the Assn. of Commerce, and its secretary for 12 years. Among the business firms he helped form and of which he was an officer were the Green Bay Iron Furnace Co., the Green Bay Water Co. and the Kendall Manufacturing Co.

He was the first president of Kendall, now the Green Bay Planing Mill. *(Then at 1599 University Ave., the company closed in July 1980.)* When the National Iron Furnace Co. of De Pere went into receivership, he took over and ran it successfully for two years.

Always deeply interested in state and local history, so much of which he had seen made, Neville was a longtime member of the State Historical Society and an organizer of the Green Bay *(now Brown County)* Historical Society. He was president of the latter group from its inception until his death.

Neville did a lot of historical research as a hobby and wrote a number of valuable papers for the historical society. There is suspicion, though, that some of his conclusions were advanced, not so much in the interests of accuracy as to get a rise out of Deborah Martin.

He and Miss Martin had known each other since childhood and were the greatest of friends. Both loved a good argument, and A. C. delighted in getting her riled up, an art at which he was charmingly adept.

When the Green Bay Museum was organized in 1915, Neville became one of its spark plugs. As he grew older and retired from active business the museum gradually absorbed more and more of his time until he naturally slipped into the job of running it.

He didn't know much about the technical phases of managing a museum and he made mistakes, but he tried hard. Without his interest the city might not today possess one of the best institutions of its kind in the state.

The Nevilles had no children but Mrs. Neville had a daughter by her first marriage who married George Grant Mason, a New York financier. When the local museum was looking for funds to finance a new building the Masons offered to put up the money on condition it be named the Neville Public Museum.

The offer was accepted and the present museum building *(then on Jefferson Street)* was added to the public library in 1927.* A. C. Neville was formally named director, a post he held until he died May 20, 1929.

His death of a heart attack was sudden and unexpected, although he was 79 and had suffered from a bad heart for years. He had had a severe attack while on a trip west during the winter but appeared to be slowly recovering. The night he died he had just finished winding his bedside clock while bickering good naturedly with his nurse. Five minutes later he was gone.

* *The present museum is located on the west bank of the Fox River, just off Dousman Street. It opened there in 1983.*

Ella Hoes Neville

Green Bay's 'Uncrowned Queen'

August 14, 1965

In any pantheon of women who have contributed heavily to the development and welfare of Green Bay the name of Mrs. A. C. Neville must be placed at or very close to the top. A torchbearer for civic progress for more than half a century, she yielded to none in her unflagging enthusiasm and devotion to her city, yet no one has received less credit for her efforts than Ella Hoes Neville.

If, in the 30 years since her death, the memory of Ella Neville has been less than blessed, it was largely her own fault. Haughty, dictatorial and sublimely indifferent to the opinions of others, she made a host of enemies and few real friends. The enemies never bothered her; she picked her own friends and was highly selective in the process.

While she lived nobody knew how old Mrs. Neville was and nobody ever found out. When she died in 1935 it was generally agreed that she was at least 90.

Until the last weeks of her life she was as physically and mentally active as most people half her age. Ella Neville was, to put it simply, an extraordinary individual and a complex, often baffling, personality.

Born in Illinois

She was born Ella Hoes in Ottawa, Ill., presumably about 1845. Her father, a federal district judge, was a nephew of President Martin Van Buren, a relationship she never let anyone forget. She received an exceptionally complete education for her time, first at a Miss Dutton's School in New Haven, Conn., and later at Sans Souci Academy, Balsam Springs, N.Y.

When, how and why Ella Hoes came to Green Bay has been forgotten but in 1869 she was married here to Marlin DeWitt Peak, cashier of the First National Bank. They had one daughter who married George Grant Mason of New York and subsequently provided the funds to build the *(first)* Neville Public Museum *(on Jefferson Street).*

Peak died in Paris during a European trip in 1877 but his widow returned to Green Bay. In 1881 she married a widower, Arthur Courtenay Neville. A colorful character in his own right, A. C. Neville was much younger (which probably accounted for her sensitivity about her age) but she survived him by several years.

Dominant Figure

From the time of her second marriage — if not before — Mrs. Neville was a forceful and dominant social and civic figure. A born leader, she ruled Green Bay's social and club life for more than 50 years.

She reigned with a heavy hand. Although there was scarcely a public institution or enterprise in the city 30 years ago that had not felt the touch of her powerful hand and shrewd mind, it was not a gentle touch. Once committed to action, Ella Neville brooked no opposition, ran roughshod over it and left a lot of scars in her wake.

A detailed list of all the activities she dominated would fill one of these columns. A founder and president of the Green Bay Woman's Club, she was also a founder of the State Federation and prominent figure in both the state and national groups.

Museum her Memorial

With her husband she was a prime mover in the Brown County Historical Society as well as the State Historical Society and president of the former when she died. Until a few months before her death she also headed the board of directors of the Neville Public Museum, which she helped launch and which remains as a memorial to this remarkable couple.

A woman of culture as well as action, Mrs. Neville was a leader in the fight for a public library, one of its organizers in 1889 and president at her death. She was equally devoted to the museum, to which she brought the first art exhibit in Green Bay's history.

Her home on "The Hill" was a cultural center and visited by more notables than any other in town. Relatively few local residents got past the front door, however. Mrs. Neville was exclusive and she issued invitations sparingly.

Active Club Woman

In addition to her prominence in the Woman's Club, which later created for her the title of "Honorary Founder," she was a member of the exclusive Euchre Club and founder and first secretary of the old Shakespeare Club. The latter yielded social precedence only to the Euchre Club and grudgingly at that.

Her most enthusiastic hobby, though, was city beautification, to which she devoted much of the last 20 years of her long life. She was a deadly foe of roadside billboards and fought them fang and claw. The present proliferation of neon signs would have driven her out of her mind.

Her principal weapon was the City Beautiful Committee of the Woman's Club which she formed in 1915, built into one of the most powerful departments of the organization and ramrodded to the day she died. One of the understatements of the first half of this century was the story on the society page of the Press-Gazette in the late 1920s that she had "consented to re-election as committee chairman."

Consented, my eye! Ella Neville would have publicly disemboweled anyone who tried to take the job away from her.

Honored by Ripon

A few months before she died Mrs. Neville was awarded an honorary Doctor of Literature degree by Ripon College for her work in city beautification. Descending on the unsuspecting campus, she dominated the presentation ceremony, completely astonishing everyone with her mental and physical alertness and charming them with a witty and forceful acceptance speech.

(She was one of the finest feminine public speakers in Wisconsin.)

In the fall of 1934 she made her annual trip to California to spend the winter, stopping en route to address a joint session of the State Legislature about the Nicolet memorial at Red Banks. She didn't live to see the completion of the project but she had a lot to do with its eventual success.

Shortly after her return in the spring of 1935 she came down with an infection that would have been serious to a much younger person. It was one enemy she couldn't lick, although she gave it a surprising fight before she died on July 7.

Not Kind to Memory

Green Bay has not been kind to Ella Neville's memory. Arbitrary and domineering she certainly was, but she had qualities as admirable as her faults were great. Without them she could not have accomplished what she did.

She possessed a youthful zest for life and was a staunch and devoted friend to a community that didn't always appreciate her concern for its welfare, completely honest and dedicated to what she believed to be right. She worked hard and selflessly for the betterment of the city and didn't give a snap of her fingers whether she got credit or not.

A ruthless fighter when aroused, she neither gave nor asked quarter, admiring and respecting anyone who fought back as implacably as she did. She knew when she was licked, could yield suavely and was, in fact, more gracious in defeat than in victory.

A charming hostess, she could be most thoughtful and generous, as many a young bride discovered. She was choosy about conferring her friendship but once she did was steadfastly loyal. She expected — and received — the same loyalty in return.

No Intimates Left

Her small circle of intimates is gone now, and there aren't many people left who knew her well. Those who do remember her were much younger and their recollections are tinged with awe. Most of her contemporaries either cordially disliked her, were afraid of her or both.

Mrs. Neville is dimly remembered across the gulf of 30 years as a stately, white-haired woman with an erect, regal carriage that not even a cane could alter in her later years. She simply converted it into a form of scepter.

Nobody can actually remember whether she was tall or just seemed that way. They think she was but aren't certain.

A local matron who had known her slightly as a teen-ager, probably came as close recently to describing this phenomenon as anyone could. She may not have been as tall as memory indicated, but it didn't make any difference. Ella Neville could always make anyone think she was.

Time Dims Memory

The Story of Abbot Pennings

April 2, 1966

Abbot Bernard H. Pennings has been dead for only 11 years but already his memory is beginning to dim in the community that knew, loved and honored him for nearly 60 years. Even on the campus of his beloved St. Norbert College he is, to all but a hard core of veterans who personally knew him, little more than the old geezer seated in marble majesty before the entrance to the auditorium that bears his name.

As that core dwindles with the passing years the memory will inevitably change, too, until it is encased in a mold as remote, as pale and as rigid as the cold, white stone of his statue. Exactly the fate, in short, the little abbot would have rejected with withering scorn.

In life there was nothing remote or shadowy about "Father Abbot." A cheerful, benign and kindly man who had lived long and found life good, Abbot Pennings was a vibrant, colorful part of his college and abbey to the day he died at the threshold of 93.

Precious Relationship

Shrewd, forceful and sharp, he watched the world with penetrating eyes whose twinkle ruined the stern façade he sometimes assumed, and his puckish sense of humor was likely to break out at the most unexpected times and places. Everybody around St. Norbert knew him and he knew everybody — a precious, intimate relationship rare in modern collegiate institutions.

Founder of St. Norbert College and of the Praemonstretension Order in America and oldest member of his worldwide order at the time of his death, Abbot Pennings spent the last 20 years of his life collecting a list of academic and clerical honors as long as his arm, but none of them impressed him very much. Years and ecclesiastical gold braid rested lightly on his frail shoulders.

The guns of the American Civil War had just begun to mutter when Bernard Henry Pennings was born in the small North Brabant town of Gemert on June 6, 1861, and they had been silent for only 14 years when, in 1879, he first donned the white habit he was to wear with distinction for three-quarters of a century. Ordained a priest at the age of 25, he had apparently settled down to the peaceful routine of a Norbertine abbey when far off America called.

Bishop Sent S.O.S.

In 1893 Bishop Sebastian G. Messmer of Green Bay, of which Father Pennings had probably never heard, was concerned about inroads being made in the ranks of Belgian Catholics of Northeastern Wisconsin by a remarkable character named Joseph Rene Vilatte, who called himself "archbishop and primate of the Old Catholic Church in America." Bishop Messmer wrote to Belgium asking for assistance.

Plucked out of his post of professor of philosophy and moral theology and master of novices in the ancient abbey of Berne, the 32-year-old priest and two other Norbertines were shipped off to Wisconsin. Arriving in November, 1893, Father Pennings was assigned to the little rural parish at Delwiche (now Namur), whose ramshackle church had recently been gutted by fire.

The little priest took hold firmly and performed so brilliantly that within five years Vilatte's influence had been wiped out. His *(Pennings')* parishioners never forgot him and for generations thereafter, whenever he turned up in the neighborhood, his arrival touched off an impromptu reunion.

Shifted to De Pere

In September, 1898, Father Pennings and his Norbertine colleagues, then numbering half a dozen, were pulled out of the Door Peninsula and assigned to St. Joseph's Parish in De Pere, which was named a priory with Father Pennings as its head. Within a fortnight he made his first move in the founding of St. Norbert College.

Convinced that the Wisconsin Belgians should have their own priests, he set out to supply them. St. Norbert dates its birth from Oct. 10, 1898, the day Father Pennings held his first "class" with one student. It was no accident that St. Norbert's first graduates (1903), all of whom became priests, were named Van Dyke, Vissers, Savageau and Marchant.

Thereafter the lives of Bernard Pennings and St. Norbert College are inseparable. The institution met a need that quickly outstripped the original goal of a training school for priests.

Raised to Abbey Status

Growth of both the priory and the college was so steady that in 1925 the former was raised to the status of an abbey — the first and still the only Norbertine abbey in the Western Hemisphere* — and Bernard Pennings was elevated to the rank of abbot. By 1952 he was presiding over the third largest Norbertine house in the world.

Abbot Pennings went quietly about his business until 1934 when honors suddenly began to descend on him. In the next 20 years he was honored with such cherished ecclesiastical symbols as the Cappa Magna, the purple biretta and pileolus (small purple skull cap reserved only for bishops), honorary degrees and other distinctions too numerous to mention.

Conservative Dutchman

A conservative Dutchman who had learned the hard way, Abbot Pennings was a cautious man with a dollar, no administrative fireball, and his desk drawer business methods were the despair of his subordinates. Through the years many stories of his tight-fisted operations accumulated around the campus and abbey, but nothing ever shook his firm grasp of the reins except great age.

There were other stories about him, too, as the old man became a living legend. You don't hear them any more — a sure sign that the legend is hardening — but all of them testified to his kindliness, humor and complete indifference to the dignity of clerical brass hats, his own included.

Through the decades Abbot Pennings enjoyed the truly great and unique experience of welcoming not only the sons but the grandsons — and eventually granddaughters — of earlier students to the college he founded. Not the least of his satisfactions was setting the feet of succeeding generations on the path of life and giving them a gentle but firm push forward.

Bernard Pennings died, loaded with but unbowed by years and honors, on March 17, 1955, and was eventually buried in the crypt of the great, new abbey he didn't live to see. He probably isn't too comfortable in his gleaming, marble tomb.

** St. Norbert Abbey provided the personnel that gave rise eventually to a second abbey, Daylesford in Pennsylvania, in 1971. Two decades earlier when a group of Hungarian Norbertines fled their communist-dominated country, the De Pere abbey helped the priest establish an abbey in California. Other De Pere initiatives include Norbertine houses in Jackson, Miss., Albuquerque, N.M., and Lima, Peru.*

Chance of a Lifetime?

Nobody Listened to Lawson

July 7, 1962

Alfred W. Lawson was a picturesque screwball but no fool. He may not have been the genius he blatantly claimed to be, but if his Green Bay associates had listened to him this city might be one of America's aircraft manufacturing centers today.

It has been nearly forgotten because the venture did not last very long but, thanks to Lawson, Green Bay once boasted the first airplane building factory in the middle west. It was strictly a wartime industry, that folded with the Armistice of 1918, but the demise wasn't Lawson's fault.

The Lawson Aircraft Co. was formed here in 1917, shortly after the United States entered World War I. It made a pretty good plane and had just wangled its first contract when the conflict ended. So did the company.

If Lawson had had his way, however, the factory would have converted to peacetime production, in which case Green Bay would have had the distinction of producing the world's first commercial airliner. Instead, the honor went to Milwaukee.

Rode Latest Trends

A personable, dynamic megalomaniac, Lawson had been riding new trends all his life and was already an established figure in the pioneer days of aviation when he came to Green Bay. Before he was through he had even established a religious sect with himself as its leader.

Not much is positively known about his early years, although he apparently came from somewhere in the east. As a young man he had played and promoted professional baseball, engineering the first barnstorming tour of Latin America. He also claimed to have developed John J. McGraw, who went on to become a diamond immortal as manager of the New York Giants.

When the Chautauqua lecture craze swept the country in the 1890s Lawson jumped into that. A top flight spellbinder, he built up a lucrative lecture circuit, discoursing on his personal system of the universe, which he called Lawsonomy and later developed into his religious movement.

Then came aviation. The Wright brothers had scarcely hit the ground after their first successful flight when Lawson was swarming into the tail assembly. By 1907 he was a well-known figure in the infant science as founder, editor and publisher of "Fly," the first popular aviation magazine.

National Figure

In 1909 he changed the periodical's title to "Aircraft," a term, incidentally, that he coined and copyrighted. He was nationally known and a somewhat glamorous aviation personality when he turned up in Green Bay with a plan to establish an airplane factory here.

Why he picked Green Bay is anybody's guess. Most likely, some of the city's free-wheeling promoters like George D. Nau twisted his arm a little. Today nobody recalls who was back of the project except the late J. H. Tayler. Nau was probably another because this was just the sort of scheme to get him all fired up.

Lawson brought along a young Texan, Vincent J. Burnelli, as his designer. Burnelli, who subsequently enjoyed a long and distinguished career in the field, more or less ran the show.

The Lawson Aircraft Co. was housed in a building at the corner of Pearl and Howard Streets, now part of the Northwest Engineering plant *(which closed in 1990)*. Lawson held forth at the Beaumont Hotel when he wasn't scooting off to Chicago and undisclosed points.

A wiry handsome fellow with a fetish for physical fitness, Lawson had great attraction for women which he enthusiastically reciprocated, although not to the extent of getting married. He was too smart to play the field in a city the size of Green Bay in 1918.

Made Good Machines

The Company produced several good military planes which were test flown from a field near Denmark and later from old Blesch Field, the city's first landing strip and site of the first Brown County airport. Although the planes were offered to the government at cost, the major problem was getting a contract.

Lawson and his backers finally succeeded but the break came too late. The ink was hardly dry on the contract when the war ended and it was promptly cancelled.

Burnelli, according to his own account in the June issue of True Magazine, had seen it coming and was already busy with plans for a revolutionary peacetime passenger carrier. He had little difficulty convincing Lawson but selling it to the local promoters was beyond even the latter's talents.

Green Bay was still nursing the most colossal hangover in history when the company directors gathered in the plant office on Armistice Day. Lawson made a rosy pitch for his "airliner" (he invented that term, too) and the city's golden opportunity.

Called it Off

The local men were possibly disenchanted with his genius by now. At any rate, they merely yawned and called the whole thing off.

On purely practical grounds they can scarcely be blamed. At the time nobody could see any peacetime future for flying, and the ship Lawson was trying to sell was simply a wild paper dream. There was no assurance such a monster contraption could get off the ground.

Undismayed, Lawson immediately pulled out of Green Bay, never to return. He obtained financial backing in Milwaukee where the visionary airliner, the first passenger cabin plane with an enclosed cockpit for the crew, was built in 1919.

Lawson then made a spectacular and highly publicized flight to

Washington, hilariously described in Burnelli's True Magazine piece. Having demonstrated that commercial flying was practicable, he got the first airmail contract in 1920.

Wrecked Carelessly

Lawson successfully carried more than 400 passengers in his 26-seat plane before it was wrecked through his own carelessness — fortunately, with no passengers aboard. A larger replacement wouldn't fly, and the Depression of 1921 wiped him out.

Thereafter he returned to writing. He turned out books and articles on history and religion in which his Lawsonomy theories were constantly expanded and from which he derived a considerable income.

In 1948 he founded and incorporated the Lawsonian religious movement with himself as the Supreme Head. He made a pretty good thing of it, too.

When he died in San Antonio, Tex., on Nov. 29, 1954, the movement collapsed. He was an old man then but only he possessed the vigor to keep it rolling.

Nobody knew how old he really was. His press obituaries said he was 85 but Burnelli insists he was at least 95 and probably closer to 100. In either case his was a long life, packed with drama.

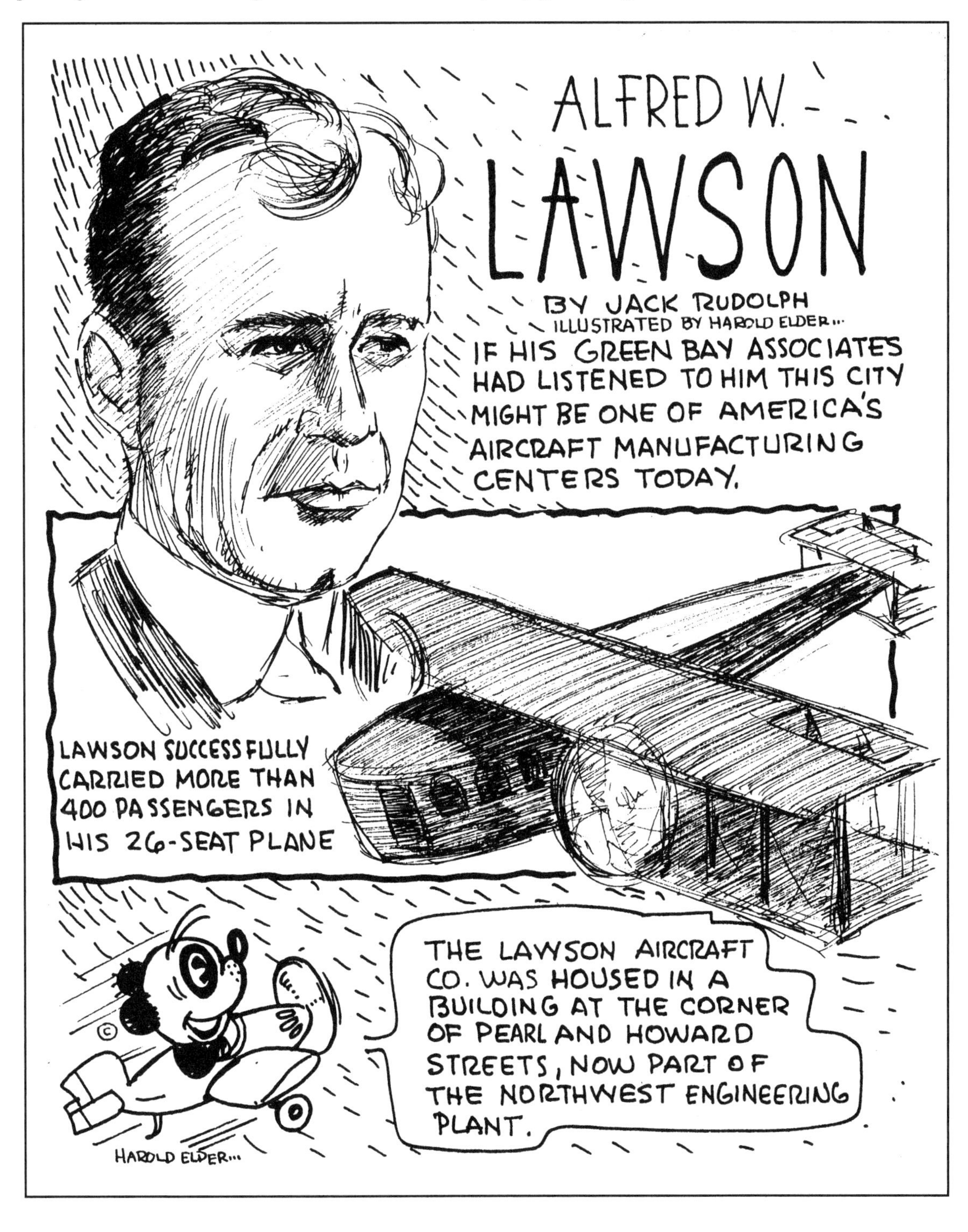

Dedicated to Home Town

A Tribute to Harold T. I. Shannon

October 17, 1964

Monday evening at the Hotel Northland* friends of Harold T. I. Shannon will gather at a testimonial dinner for one of the city's most remarkable figures of the past half century. It will be a belated but greatly deserved tribute to a man who has worked long and hard for his home town, who has neither sought nor received adequate credit for his efforts but whose achievements have made Green Bay a better and more interesting place to live.

Journalist, promoter, radio pioneer, advertising man, public relations counsel, historian — the list could go on and on. Indeed, the story of H. T. I. Shannon would be much simpler if you just stuck to the things he hasn't done. You name it — the "Bishop" has probably had a finger in it.

Not the least part of Harold Shannon's juggling act is the fact that he's done it under three-ply billing without having had to explain very often what all the initials mean. It is a bad trick, especially when none of them are really "official" in the first place.

Not a 'Native'

Somehow, it seems appropriate too, that technically Harold is not even a native of the city, although he has lived nearly 70 years in the room in which he was born. The son of Timothy J. Shannon, a North Western Railway conductor and later city treasurer, Harold was born on North Chestnut Avenue in the heart of Fort Howard's old "Irish Patch."

That was in February, 1895, two months before Green Bay and Fort Howard consolidated. There's at least one local milestone on record as a result in which Harold did not have a promotional hand.

He revealed his touch early enough, though. Because he didn't want to go to school he conned Dr. W. H. Bartran Sr. into letting him stay out and the doctor served as the boy's private tutor for several years. While other kids were hitting McGuffey's Reader Harold was absorbing detailed and eye witness accounts of the great battles of the Civil War from the doctor and his war veteran cronies.

Consuming Interest

The experience gave him a consuming and lifelong interest in history. In fact, the love of history, especially that of Green Bay and Wisconsin, has been the most important influence in Harold Shannon's life.

Once in school Shannon began to exert his flair for leadership by being elected president of his West High class all four years. Nobody had ever achieved that distinction before and few have matched it since.

When the diplomas were presented to the Class of 1914, however, the president wasn't in ranks. He was watching proceedings from out front as covering reporter for the newly established Green Bay Free Press. Harold quit school a month before graduation to take a reporter's job at a higher salary than his dad was drawing as city treasurer.

Reporterial Career

When the Free Press and Gazette consolidated in 1915 Harold stayed on as a Press-Gazette reporter. All told, he spent 21 years in the newspaper field, nearly all of it with the Press-Gazette as reporter and promotions man, although there were breaks in the continuity.

He left to serve in the Army in World War I, from which he came out a sergeant, functioned as advertising manager for the old Oneida Truck Co., and pioneered in the local radio field for several years before returning to his first love. He left his impact on all of them.

While with Oneida Harold conceived and carried out the "Tramp Truck" journey to the West Coast that old time truckers consider a major landmark in the early development of long distance hauling. One of the first to demonstrate the possibilities of commercial radio, his activities in that medium would make a story in themselves.

Biggest Coup

His biggest coup, though, was Green Bay's 1934 Tercentennial celebration, which he brought off in the face of almost unanimous opposition by persuading President Franklin D. Roosevelt to attend.

Harold's own story of how he swung that visit is a bit vague. All he will say is that he merely made a long distance call to F. D. R.'s press secretary Steve Early, explained the significance of the occasion and the next thing he knew Roosevelt was on his way. A simple enough explanation, except that the President of the United States doesn't come running at the beck and call of every unknown promoter who manages to get a line to the White House.

During World War II Shannon was information director for the 46-county Green Bay O. P. A. *(Office of Price Administration)* District, a job he took on again during the Korean fracas. One of his most cherished possessions is a personal letter from OPA chief Chester Bowles congratulating him for running the most effective information program in the nation.

Doesn't Take Credit

Harold doesn't take credit for that success, however. He frankly states the job would not have been done without his assistant and later business partner, Florence Schilling De Spirito. It was a spectacularly effective combination, good enough a few years later to put Green Bay second to Cincinnati in the fund raising campaign for the Voice of America.

After the war Harold and Florence continued their association as a public relations counseling firm. Harold remained active in it until a few years ago when a series of serious illnesses, climaxed by a fall that broke his hip, forced his retirement.

Over a span of nearly 50 years, Harold Shannon has been active in so many enterprises not even he remembers them all. A remarkably high proportion, furthermore, have been projects that brought small return to himself but lasting benefit to the city. He could have gone on to bigger jobs but refused to leave his home town, where he felt he could contribute something to its progress.

Priceless Contributions

In the historical field, particularly, Harold Shannon's contributions have been priceless. He served as president of the Brown County Historical Society and as a vice president and curator of the State Historical Society with enthusiasm and complete dedication. Thanks to Harold Green Bay has preserved vital portions of its rich historical heritage that might otherwise have been lost.

All but two of the area's principal historical buildings were saved primarily through his efforts. Tank Cottage came before his time and Hazelwood after, but he can still claim a share in the latter. Without his example and results for inspiration, Hazelwood's saviors might not have persevered.

But to get back to that name business. For the record, H. T. I. stands for Harold Timothy Ignatius, a three-way handle few people have ever known. Actually, it isn't important because, by Harold's own admission, that isn't his right name.

Depending on how you look at it, his real name is either Michael Timothy Michael or just Michael Michael Shannon.

His mother wanted him baptized Harold but Father Mike O'Brien, beloved pastor of St. Patrick's Church, couldn't see it as a proper name for a good Irish lad. Unknown to the family for many years, Father Mike substituted the name Michael for Harold on the baptismal certificate.

Later, when Harold was confirmed, the Sisters at St. Pat's pressured him into taking Ignatius as his confirmation name. Father O'Brien was gone by then but his successor was having none of that Ignatius business and again slipped in the name Michael. Harold (or Mike) insists that's the one the bishop actually used in the ceremony.

There's some confusion, too, over whether Timothy belongs in the list or not. Anyway, it stands for Harold's father.

Harold Shannon died August 5, 1965, less than a year after this tribute and the testimonial dinner honoring him.

** Located at 302 North Adams, the Northland was built in 1923-24, rehabilitated as a housing facility for the elderly in 1979 and renamed Port Plaza Towers.*

Postscript

Jack Rudolph, Harold Elder, and the *Green Bay Press-Gazette* retired the local history series after twelve successful years. Upon reporting the column's "demise" in June 1970, the *Press-Gazette* stated, "It isn't that Jack has run out of gas, or that Harold has run out of ink. It's just that the history features have caught up with current Green Bay history and to avoid repeating too many of the 600-plus episodes, Historian Jack and Artist Harold are going to get somewhat of a rest." The last column appeared June 27, 1970.

The entire collection is available in the Local History Department of the Brown County Library and in the library's newspaper microfilm collection.

Jack Rudolph (left) and Harold Elder, June 1970.
(Green Bay Press-Gazette photo reprinted with permission.)

Suggestions for further reading

Adams, Diane L; Graf, John; and Rucker, Della G. *On Washington Street - A Photographic Memory.* Neville Public Museum of Brown County, 1994.

Baird, Elizabeth Therese. *O-de-jit-wa-win-ning, or Contes du temps passe: The Memoirs of Elizabeth T. Baird.* Heritage Hill Foundation, 1991.

Baird, Elizabeth Therese. "Reminiscences of Life in Territorial Wisconsin." *Wisconsin Historical Collection*, vol. 15.

Baird, Henry. "Recollections of the Early History of Northern Wisconsin." *Wisconsin Historical Collection*, vol. 4.

Burridge, George Nau. *Green Bay Workhorses - The Nau Tug Line.* Manitowoc (Wisconsin) Maritime Museum, 1991.

__________________. *La Mystique de Renard: The Fox River and the Passage to the West.* Brown County (Wisconsin) Historical Society, 1997.

Catherwood, Mary H. *Lazarre.* Bowen-Merrill Co., Brooklyn, New York, 1901.

Childs, Ebenezer. "Recollections of Wisconsin Since 1820." *Wisconsin Historical Collection*, vol. 4.

Commemorative Biographical Record of the Counties of Brown, Kewaunee, and Door, Wisconsin. J. H. Beers and Company, Chicago, 1895.

Draper, Lyman Copeland, Editor. *Collections of the State Historical Society of Wisconsin.* Wisconsin State Historical Society, Madison, 1903.

Foley, Betsy. *Green Bay: Gateway to the Great Waterway.* Windsor Publications, Woodland Hills, California, 1983.

__________. *In That Place, In That Time: Remembering Rufus B. Kellogg.* Brown County (Wisconsin) Historical Society, 1999.

French, Bella. *The American Sketch Book: History of Brown County, Wisconsin.* Green Bay, 1876.

Gilsdorf, Gordon and Zimmer, William. *The Diocese of Green Bay: A Centennial 1868-1968.* St. Norbert Abbey Press, De Pere, Wisconsin, 1968.

Green Bay Historical Bulletin, Volumes 1 - 9. Green Bay Historical Society, 1925-34.

Green Bay Press-Gazette Tercentennial Edition, July 1934.

Grignon, Augustin. "Seventy-Two Years Recollections of Wisconsin." Collections of the State Historical Society of Wisconsin, vol. 3.

Haeger, John D. "A Time of Change: Green Bay, 1815-1834. *Wisconsin Magazine of History,* vol. 54, no. 1.

"Heritage Hill: Our Past Preserved." *Green Bay Press-Gazette*, Historical Edition, May 29, 1977.

History of the Fox River Valley, Lake Winnebago, and the Green Bay Region, vol. III. The S. J. Clarke Publishing Co., Chicago, 1930.

Holand, H. R. *Wisconsin's Belgian Community.* Door County Historical Society, 1933.

Holubetz, Sylvia Hall. *The Astor Historic District.* Published by the Astor Neighborhood Association, Green Bay, Wisconsin, 1981.

Holubetz, Sylvia Hall. *Farewell to the Homeland: European Immigration to Northeast Wisconsin 1840 - 1900.* Brown County (Wisconsin) Historical Society, 1984.

Ives, Gail. *Green Bay's West Side: The Fort Howard Neighborhood.* Arcadia Press, 2003.

"John Penn Arndt and the Durham Boat." *Green Bay Historical Bulletin*, vol. 6, no. 4.

Kay, Jeanne. " John Lawe - Green Bay Trader." *Wisconsin Magazine of History,* vol. 64, no.1.

Kellogg, Louise Phelps. "The Americanization of a French Settlement." *Green Bay Historical Bulletin,* vol. 5, no. 3.

_________________. "The Story of Wisconsin, 1634-1848." *Wisconsin Magazine of History,* vol. 2.

Kramer, James. *A History of Fort Howard.* Graduate thesis, MA history, University of Arizona, 1956.

"Lawe and Grignon Papers." *Wisconsin Historical Collection,* vol. 10.

Lord, Walter. *A Night to Remember.* Holt and Co., New York, New York, 1955.

Maes, Matthew J. *The History of Brown County and De Pere, Wisconsin.* 1914.

Martin, Deborah B. *History of Brown County.* The S. J. Clarke Publishing Co., Chicago, 1913.

________________ and Beaumont, Sophie. *Old Green Bay.* The Cheltenham Press, New York, 1899.

________________, Neville, Ella Hoes, and Martin, Sarah Green. *Historic Green Bay.* Published by the authors, Green Bay, 1893.

________________. "The Porlier-Tank Cottage: Its History and the People Who Lived In It." 1913.

Metzner, Lee W. "The Belgians in the North Country." *Wisconsin Magazine of History,* vol. 26.

Neville, A. C. "Early Ferries and Bridges Across Fox River." *Green Bay Historical Bulletin,* vol. 2.

The Oral History of Green Bay. WHA, University of Wisconsin Radio, Madison.

Porlier, Louis. "Narrative of Louis Porlier." *Wisconsin Historical Collections,* vol. 15.

Rudolph, Jack. *Green Bay: A Pictorial History.* The Donning Co. Publishers, Norfolk, Virginia, 1983.

___________. *Birthplace of a Commonwealth: A Short History of Brown County.* Brown County (Wisconsin) Historical Society, Green Bay, Wisconsin, 1976.

Smith, Alice E. *The History of Wisconsin.* State Historical Society of Wisconsin, 1973.

Smith, Alice E. *James Duane Doty: Frontier Promoter.* State Historical Society of Wisconsin, Madison, 1954.

Special Green Bay Edition, *The Wisconsin Magazine,* May 1929.

Thwaites, Reuben G. *The Story of Wisconsin.* D. Lathrop Co., Boston, 1890.

Titus, W. A. "Green Bay: The Plymouth Rock of Wisconsin." *Wisconsin Magazine of History,* vol. 11.

Voyageur Magazine. Brown County (Wisconsin) Historical Society, Green Bay.

Wells, Robert W. *Fire at Peshtigo.* Northword, Madison, Wisconsin, 1983.

Wisconsin Magazine: Special Green Bay Number. Madison Publishing Co., Appleton, 1951.

A Young Look at Old Green Bay. Green Bay Public Schools, 1977.

Index

A

B

C

D

E

F

G

H

N

O

P

T

U

V

Publications of the Brown County Historical Society

BIRTHPLACE OF A COMMONWEALTH: A Short History of Brown County, Wisconsin by Jack Rudolph. Published in 1976 for the U.S. Bicentennial; includes many historic photographs. Soft cover, 96 pages. $5.00

IN THAT PLACE, IN THAT TIME: REMEMBERING RUFUS B. KELLOGG by Betsy Foley. Published in 1999, this major addition to Green Bay history paints a detailed portrait of one of the community's most influential pioneers. The author also helps readers look into the past and see the threads that continue to run through the fabric of today's Green Bay and Brown County. Hard cover, 257 pages with some previously unpublished photos. $18.00 special

LA MYSTIQUE DU RENARD: The Fox River and the Passage to the West by George Nau Burridge. Recounts the Fox-Wisconsin waterway's development and the importance of keeping the Fox River lock system in operation. Soft cover, 39 pages, illus., c. 1997. $6.00

A YOUNG LOOK AT OLD GREEN BAY First published in 1977 by "The Summer Kids" of Fort Howard School in Green Bay. Written and illustrated by the students after interviewing 22 older area residents. A treasure house of memories. Re-published in 1997. Soft cover, 164 pages, illus. $12.00

ASTOR PARK HISTORIC DISTRICT: A Self Guided Walking Tour Published by the BCHS, this booklet has 31 pictures, descriptions and histories of homes in the Astor Historic District in Green Bay. Second printing with revisions and new map. $4.00

FAREWELL TO THE HOMELAND: European Immigration to Northeast Wisconsin, 1840-1890 Third edition, Sylvia Hall Linten, editor. Soft cover, 154 pages, illus., c. 1984. $12.00

THE GREEN BAY AREA IN HISTORY AND LEGEND: *Green Bay Press-Gazette* Articles by Jack Rudolph with Illustrations by Harold Elder. Betsy Foley, editor. A collection of 150 articles from more than 600 columns in a series featuring people, sites, and events from discovery through 1970. Hard cover, 345 pages including index. $29.95

For more information or to order, contact the
Brown County Historical Society
P. O. Box 1411
Green Bay, WI 54305-1411

telephone 920/437-1840, fax 920/455-4518, e-mail bchs@netnet.net, or visit our website
www.browncohistoricalsoc.org

BECOME A MEMBER

You are invited to join the Brown County Historical Society.
Your membership supports Society events, Voyageur Magazine,
and helps keep historic Hazelwood Museum open to the public.

CHECK ONE:

☐ Individual ($20) ☐ Family ($30) ☐ Supporter ($50)

☐ Centennial ($100) ☐ Provider ($250) ☐ Founder ($500)

NAME ____________________

ADDRESS ____________________

CITY____________________ STATE______ ZIP ____________

PHONE (__________) ____________________

CREDIT CARD NO.____________________
(Mastercard and Visa ONLY)

EXPIRATION (Mo/Yr)____________________

SIGNATURE____________________

Please clip and return with payment to:

BCHS
P.O. Box 1411
Green Bay, WI 54301-1411

Membership (excluding the first $20) is tax-deductible as allowed by law.